CULTURES
Diversity in Reading and Writing

Second Edition

Emily Thiroux

California State University
Bakersfield

PRENTICE HALL
Upper Saddle River, NJ 07458

Library of Congress Cataloging-in-Publication Data

Cultures : diversity in reading and writing / [compiled by] Emily
  Thiroux. — 2nd ed.
      p. cm.
    Includes indexes.
    ISBN 0–13–400128–1
    1. Readers—Social sciences.   2. Pluralism (Social sciences)-
-Problems, exercises, etc.   3. Culture—Problems, exercises, etc.
4. English language—Rhetoric.   5. College readers.   I. Thiroux,
Emily, 1949–   .
PE1127.S6C84   1997
808'.0427—dc20   95–53823
                                                                      CIP

Acquisitions editor: Maggie Barbieri
Editorial/production supervision: Patty Sawyer (Pine Tree Composition)
Cover designer: Bruce Kenselaar
Cover art: Circle on Square 1. 108″ × 108″ quilt by Lucy Wallis from the Ardis and Robert James
   Collection. Photo courtesy The Dairy Barn Art Center.
Buyer: Mary Ann Gloriande

This book was set in 10/12 Baskerville by Pine Tree Composition Inc.
and was printed and bound by Hamilton Printing Company.
The cover was printed by Pheonix, Inc.

 © 1997 by Prentice-Hall, Inc.
Simon & Schuster/A Viacom Company
Upper Saddle River, New Jersey 07458

Printed in the United States of America
10 9 8 7 6 5 4 3 2 1

ISBN: 0-13-400128-1

Prentice-Hall International (UK) Limited, *London*
Prentice-Hall of Australia Pty. Limited, *Sydney*
Prentice-Hall Canada, Inc., *Toronto*
Prentice-Hall Hispanoamericana, S.A., *Mexico*
Prentice-Hall of India Private Limited, *New Delhi*
Prentice-Hall of Japan, Inc., *Tokyo*
Simon & Schuster Asia Pte. Ltd., *Singapore*
Editora Prentice-Hall do Brasil, Ltda., *Rio de Janeiro*

for Mom

Contents

Part Two

ISSUES AND IDEAS   **139**

Part Three

CULTURE AND TRADITION   **269**

Topical Contents

War

Women's Issues

Rhetorical Contents

Definition—to explain what something is, what is included and excluded

Description—to explain in detail a scene or setting

Division and classification—how a single thing can be divided into parts or how single things can be grouped together

Exposition—to explain the nature of an object, a theme or an idea

Narration—to tell a story or recount an event, usually in chronological order

Process analysis—to explain how something works or how something is done explaining why

Preface to the Instructor

The second edition of *Cultures: Diversity in Reading and Writing* includes over fifty percent new articles to provide students with current, topical issues to think, read, and write about. This book was created for composition classes of our colleges and universities today, which are made up of an amazing variety of students. Rarely does a class come along with any one clear majority of a culture or lifestyle. The students all have different abilities, backgrounds, and interests. Finding reading material for such a group is difficult at best. *Cultures: Diversity in Reading and Writing* contains a mixture of articles all taken from an unusual collection of international magazines and newspapers. The articles are on topics covering a multitude of cultures, lifestyles, and issues. Students will be able to find material that they can personally relate to, as well as material that is totally different from their cultural and societal backgrounds.

Because the fluid process of thinking, reading, and writing is intricately interwoven, for students to improve their writing skills, they must also improve their ability to think and read. The apparatus for *Cultures: Diversity in Reading and Writing* allows the instructor great flexibility in planning the course and giving assignments and is set up in such a way that the entire writing process is emphasized. First, however, all students should be encouraged to read the Introduction and continue to use it as a reference section because it contains specific instructions on how to do the assignments throughout the book. Second, before each article there is a Prereading section, which gives the students an idea of what they will be reading about and gives them questions to help them to put the article into a familiar frame of reference. These sections make excellent journal writing assignments. Next, the

Defining section presents vocabulary words that may be unfamiliar to the students. Each word is accompanied by a brief definition that applies specifically to the context in which it is used because the variety of definitions available in the dictionary can be confusing.

Then come the articles. *Cultures: Diversity in Reading and Writing* is divided into three major sections: People and Careers, Issues and Ideas, and Culture and Tradition. Each section contains a wide variety of articles. The articles are further divided into more specific groups in the Topical Contents and Rhetorical Contents in the front of the book. These alternative groupings give the instructor flexibility in choosing assignments. The articles are controversial and stimulating in order to provide ample opportunity for interesting classroom discussion and writing. They are arranged in each section by length. The shorter articles come first to ease the students into the reading and writing process.

The articles in this book are suitable for the freshman writer and have been chosen to be challenging and sometimes difficult. As Anthony Petrosky, author of *Facts, Artifacts, and Counterfacts,* said in a speech for a NYMADE conference, "I think it is absolutely essential for students to begin working with difficult material. If students are put on dummied down reading materials, they know that." The readability levels for each article are included in the *Instructor's Manual.* The grade level, the Flesch-Kincaid formula, and the Gunning Fog index are all listed. Although the usefulness of such levels is often debated, they may help you take your class's reading proficiency into account as you make your reading assignments. The Flesch-Kincaid system attempts to present the grade level at which a student should be able to read the material. This formula is a standard required by the United States government and military. The Gunning Fog level, which was developed by Robert Gunning, attempts to indicate when the reading will become difficult for a student reading at a certain grade level.

The articles are followed by Reading questions that allow the students to review what they have read and check their comprehension. The Thinking section offers questions to allow the students to quietly contemplate and to apply what they have learned in the article to their lives. The questions can also be used to stimulate lively classroom discussion. The Prewriting section offers exercises to guide the students into the writing assignments. Each prewriting exercise is based on the skills learned from the Introduction of this book including freewriting, clustering, and brainstorming. In addition, these exercises make good journal assignments. Each article has two Writing assignments, each of which creates a situation and provides an audience for the student. These features are especially important for the inexperienced writer.

The Revision section follows the writing assignments. Each revision assignment refers back to the article that was read and provides a different revision strategy to apply to that assignment. As the students learn the revision strategies, they then can apply them to future writing assignments. The Editing section is like a mini-handbook. Each section teaches a new writing skill covering everything from sentence structure to punctuation and spelling. The revising and editing skills are listed in the index for easy reference.

New to the second edition is the Computers and the Writing Process section. Most students have access to word processors to write with either in the classroom, at home, or at work. This new section offers the students assistance in the best ways to utilize this technology while enhancing their writing skills.

An *Instructor's Manual* is available that provides sample course outlines, discussion questions, interview ideas, and collaborative learning assignments, and although there are more articles in the book than could usually be covered in a quarter or semester, the variety of articles provides many choices for the instructor so that different articles could be chosen for different semesters, classes, or levels. Separate indexes are included that allow course organization by topic, culture, revision strategies, or editing techniques. *Cultures: Diversity in Reading and Writing* may be used alone in the freshman composition class as a basic text or as a supplement. Its all-inclusive nature allows the instructor great flexibility while saving the student the price of a separate handbook.

ACKNOWLEDGMENTS

I am grateful for the help and support of many people with the second edition of *Cultures: Diversity in Reading and Writing*. First, thanks for the continued support of my mentor and consultant on the first edition of this book, Kim Flachmann of California State University, Bakersfield. The editorial support from Prentice Hall Publishing Company has been amazing, especially from Editor Maggie Barbieri and Joan Polk. I am grateful to my colleagues who offered useful advice: Saundra Sparling and Elizabeth Jackson of California State University, Bakersfield, and Patti Ross of Moorpark College. I am indebted to Joe Thornton who shared his expertise in developing the new Computers and the Writing Process section. I appreciate his support, respect, and encouragement. I also want to thank Ines and Ariel Auffant for their help in obtaining articles, and Charmen Goehring and Erin Hart for their support.

I offer very special thanks to my daughter Abby and to my husband Jacques for their patience, love, and assistance. Thanks are also due to the reviewers of this book: William Kulik, Community College of Philadelphia; Sara Dye, Elgin Community College; Lydia E. Hopkins, University of New Orleans.

Emily Thiroux

Introduction

According to the 1990 census, white Americans are rapidly becoming a minority group; on many college and university campuses in America, this is already the case. Students now voluntarily segregate themselves into social groups, which can be observed in any university dining room, where we are likely to see at least an Asian area, a black area, a white area, a Middle Eastern area, and a Hispanic area. But the groups are not only defined by cultural heritage. There may also be groups of older, reentry students, male students, female students, athletes, gays, lesbians, science majors, drama majors, computer majors, nursing majors, English majors, and more. We all tend to spend time in the company of people with whom we have something in common.

Higher education provides a place where students come for enrichment and an introduction to new ideas. Learning more about your classmates will only serve to enhance your overall education. One good way to discover the similarities and differences you have with your fellow students is to read about their different cultures and lifestyles. This book gives you the opportunity to explore many personalities, careers, issues, ideas, cultures, and traditions. You can think, read, and write about all these things while you improve your skills and enrich your mind.

READING

Reading Is Fundamental, a nonprofit organization that encourages young people to read, did a survey of eighty celebrities showing that they all loved to read during their childhood. Their reading stimulated their minds and their creativity. Their

1

success relates directly to the ability to communicate and express ideas that they developed from their early exposure to the written word. Not everybody has had the opportunity to grow up surrounded by stimulating reading material, but by reading more now you can learn better communication skills and also have the pleasure reading can bring. Reading in our society is becoming increasingly important to enable you to get a better paying job, become active in your community, and communicate with your family and friends. The better you read, the more pleasure and success you can get out of life.

Three steps will help you get the most out of what you read: prereading, reading, and responding. When following these steps, remember that when you are reading and studying a text you should write freely in your book if you own it. Underline and highlight important points, and write comments and questions about the material you are reading in the margins. Take notes in a separate notebook if you don't own your book.

Prereading: Closely examine what you are going to read by doing the following:

1. Look at the title. What does it tell you about what to expect?

2. Look for words in **bold print,** words underlined, and words in *italics.* These printing methods are used to catch the attention of the reader and are usually used for important information in the article.

3. Pay particular attention to the first and last sentence of each paragraph to get the main idea of what the paragraph is about.

4. Note maps in the appendix (pp. 381–385) for references to places in the article so that you can get a perspective on where in the world the action is taking place.

5. Do the Prereading exercise before each article to help you get in tune with the topic.

Defining: Before you read the article, read the words listed in the Defining section. The definitions for these words are written to correspond with how the word is used in the article. To get more complete definitions of the words, you may want to look them up in the dictionary. As you read, notice the context of the words in the sentence. Does the word seem to mean what you thought it did? Ask your instructor or tutor for clarification if you are still unsure.

Reading: After you have done your prereading, you are ready to read. You can get the most out of reading by doing the following:

1. Quickly read through the whole article for meaning.

2. Reread the article slowly to find answers for the following questions. What is the writer saying? Is his or her point clear? What is the writer's purpose in writing the article? To whom is he or she writing—people in general or a specific type or group of people? How do you know?

3. Examine the article to see the writing techniques used and look for ways you can apply these techniques to your own writing. Notice the organization of the information and look for variety in sentence structure. Is punctuation used that you are unfamiliar with? If so, use the index of this book to find out more about this punctuation form.

Responding: After you have read the article, examine how you feel about what you read.

1. Did you agree or disagree with the writer? Why or why not?

2. Is the article interesting? Why or why not?

3. Does the article apply to you and your life? Why and how, or why not?

4. Did you learn something new by reading the article? What did you learn?

5. What would you say to the writer of the article if you had the chance?

6. Answer the questions in the Reading section after each article to be sure that you understood what you read.

Get into the habit of using these steps whenever you read something of importance to you. Take your time to enjoy what you discover when you are reading. A college student recently confessed that she had gotten through high school and her first year of college without having read a book. She would merely skim through her textbooks and pay attention in class so she could earn passing grades, but she wasn't enjoying school. When illness forced her to stay home for a whole semester, a friend brought her a book to relieve her boredom. She read that book from cover to cover, and it changed her life. She discovered that she really enjoyed reading and realized how much she had missed by avoiding it as much as possible in the past. Since that time, her grades have improved tremendously, she is enjoying college, and she is looking forward to a good career.

Do not be discouraged if you have had problems reading in the past. Start reading now with a whole new outlook. If you need help with reading, talk to your instructor, see a tutor, or enroll in a literacy program. Take as much time as you need to get the most out of your reading, and, most of all, allow time to enjoy yourself.

WRITING

Just as we read every day, we write every day. Some days we may only sign our name on a check or take a phone message. Other days we may have to write a résumé to get a job or a letter to an insurance company to straighten out a bill. Our writing tells the reader a great deal about us. If an employer has to look through a stack of job applications, a neat, well-written application will catch his or her attention, while a sloppy one full of misspelled words and mechanical errors will probably be shuffled to the bottom of the pile. Although everything we write may not be as important as a job application, good writing is essential for communication to take place. Four steps can be applied in different ways to help you with different writing tasks: *prewriting, writing, revising,* and *editing.*

Prewriting: Prewriting is simply what you do before you write. You may like to write only while sitting in a certain chair, or you may have to use a certain pen or drink a certain soft drink while you are writing. We all have special routines we like to follow, so in order to do your best writing, your first step is to get comfortable. After you are comfortable, there are several ways to prewrite, or start generating ideas. The following is a list of prewriting techniques. Don't try to use them all at once, but experiment with them, and use those that work best for you. Remember that different prewriting techniques work for different writing tasks, so be flexible until you find the methods that you really like.

1. Thinking. Before your pen ever touches your paper, you should give yourself some time to consider what you want to say. Let your mind wander and tune into your ideas on your subject. To do this, don't try to compete with the television or the radio but think in silence so your mind is free to explore and create.

2. Talking. Find someone with whom you can share your ideas. Saying your thoughts aloud may give you a whole different outlook on your subject, and the person with whom you talk may prove to be an inspiration. Or find someone who has experienced what you are writing about to get this person's personal reaction to your topic. For instance, if you are writing about drunk driving penalties, talk to someone who has been arrested for drunk driving or someone who has been the victim of a drunk driver.

3. Freewriting. Set a time period of about fifteen minutes and write about your subject continually during that time. Don't stop to think or talk; don't worry about complete sentences, errors, or organization; just write, repeating words or thoughts if necessary to fill up the time. When you are finished, read what you have written, and find the ideas that you can best organize into your writing project.

4. Brainstorming. To brainstorm, you need to write down as many words and phrases as you can think of that relate to your topic. After you make this list, go through it and decide what is most important; then organize your ideas.

The student was asked to write about this topic for all of the following examples:

Out of all of the teachers you have ever had, which one had the biggest impact on your life? Why? What subject did this teacher teach? Did you learn more from the teacher than just the subject? Did this teacher have a positive or negative effect on your life?

Example: **Brainstorming**

Buck, my high school band director

music	inspiration
responsibility	Washington, D.C.
discipline, its effects on my later career	pride
opportunity	respect for self, others

small-town teenagers touring the country, the world

Pasadena Rose Parade

World's Fair

patriotism

Olympics

charity

love

band was more than music

the American flag

Buck's devotion to the band

"The Stars and Stripes Forever"

5. *Clustering.* To cluster, write your main idea on a paper, and draw a circle around it. Then write other ideas that relate to your main idea; draw circles around them, and connect them to related ideas with lines. As you write more ideas, draw circles around them and draw a line from each new circle to an existing circle already drawn to which it most closely relates. Clustering not only helps you generate ideas, but it also helps you organize your ideas by focusing your thinking on paper.

Example: **Clustering**

6. Topic Sentences. After you have generated some ideas by brainstorming or clustering, you need to decide on a specific topic. Write a topic sentence that clearly describes what your essay will be about. Then write another topic sentence, saying in a different way what you want to write about. Then write another topic sentence, and another, until you have from five to seven topic sentences. Generating several sentences will give you the opportunity to explore your topic and help you decide what you really want to write. Choose for your topic sentence the sentence you wrote that most completely states the concept you want to explore in your essay.

Example: **Topic Sentences**

1. Buck Shafer was the best teacher I ever had.

2. Buck Shafer was more than my high school band director; he was an inspiration for my life.

3. My high school band director, Buck Shafer, used music to teach responsibility for life.

4. Buck Shafer, my high school band director, is a great musician, a great teacher, and a great humanitarian.

5. Love of music and life made Buck Shafer, my high school band director, a wonderful teacher.

6. My high school band director, Buck Shafer, made our band a microcosm of society where we learned not only the joy of music but also discipline, patriotism, and responsibility.

7. Informal Outline. Formal outlines frighten many writers, but formality is not generally required. Informal outlines should basically include your main idea stated in the topic sentence you have chosen, the ideas with which you plan to support it, and the order in which you will write them. Keep outlines simple, but remember, the more information you include in them, the easier your writing will be.

Example: **Informal Outline**

My high school band director, Buck Shafer, made our band a microcosm of society where we learned not only the joy of music, but also discipline, patriotism, and responsibility.

1. Buck chose a wide variety of good music for us to play and expected us to do an excellent job.
   • guest professional soloists
   • music workshops
   • competitions

2. We learned many kinds of discipline by being in the band.
   • practicing diligently on our own

- behaving properly during rehearsals
- keeping our grades up so we could participate in band activities

3. We learned the importance of patriotism.
   - playing patriotic music
   - honoring the military during concerts
   - displaying the American flag during concerts

4. We learned responsibility not only for the band but also for our lives.
   - showing up on time
   - the importance of an individual to the whole group
   - the importance of doing the best job possible at anything we attempted

8. Sources. Sometimes, even with all these prewriting suggestions, finding what you want to write about can still be difficult. In this case, try looking at some good sources to discover ideas. Your ideas from your prereading and prewriting are an excellent place to start. Another source is the library. When you are stumped, browsing through magazines and good books may be just what you need to stimulate your own creativity. Another good way to always have writing topics and ideas is to keep a notebook handy where you can write down good ideas whenever they come to you. You can refer to your notebook later when you need a little stimulation. Modern technology also offers computers with CD ROMs, on-line services, and the Internet. These sources will provide endless ideas and support for your writing.

Writing: If you are prepared to write by using some prewriting techniques, your writing will be much easier to do and will probably be much more clear and complete. Be sure to organize your ideas before you start, then write the first draft of your essay. After you complete your first draft, try putting it aside overnight; then read it the next day to see if you've written what you really wanted to write.

Revising: Revising literally means "re-seeing" what you have written, so look at what you wrote and see what kind of improvements you can make. Ask yourself the following questions:

1. Can I omit anything to make my meaning more clear?

2. Can I add anything to make my meaning more clear?

3. Do I have enough variety in the kinds of sentences I have written? Can I combine any sentences?

4. Can I rearrange what I wrote to make the order more effective?

5. Do I have proper transitions and relationships between sentences and between paragraphs?

6. Do I like what I wrote, or could I say what I need to in a better way?

After you've answered these questions for yourself, ask a classmate, friend, or tutor to read over your paper with the same questions in mind. Discuss what you have discovered, and write another draft. Then ask the questions again. Depending on your essay, you may need only one or two drafts, but do as many as you need to make your essay say what you really want it to say.

Editing: When you are satisfied with the content of your essay, then it is time to edit. Be sure to check for

1. Complete sentences
2. Correct punctuation
3. Accurate spelling
4. Paragraphing
5. Proper tense and diction
6. Consistent point of view
7. Clear thesis statement
8. Legibility

If you need help with proofreading, ask your instructor or tutor. Having someone else look at what you have written is always a good idea. Sometimes it is difficult to catch your own errors. After you have made all the appropriate revisions and corrections, you are ready to do a final draft. Be sure to proofread your final draft carefully.

Good writing is a skill that must be practiced for improvement to be possible. Try to get as much practice as you can by writing in your journal, by freewriting, or by writing letters to friends and family. These are nonthreatening ways to help you practice expressing your thoughts and feelings. The more you do it, the more comfortable you will become with writing and the better you will write.

COMPUTERS AND THE WRITING PROCESS

Defining

back-up	to make a copy to a diskette of the material you write on a computer
boot	to start up a computer or program
cursor	the flashing mark on the screen that indicates where letters or numbers will appear when typed
cut	removing something you have written from your document. What has been cut may be moved to another area in the document or it may be discarded
E-mail	electronic mail sent by a number of different on-line systems

file   a document or part of a program stored on a hard drive or diskette

floppy   a diskette

format   how a document or diskette is set up

hard copy   a copy of what you have written that has been printed on paper

hard drive stationary hardware for storage of files and programs

hardware   computing equipment, such as the computer itself or its components

Internet   worldwide network of on-line services

laptop   a small, portable computer that can be used on a lap

modem   hardware used to connect one computer to another computer or on-line service via phone lines

network   connecting two or more computers so that they can work together or on a larger system

paste   inserting written material you have previously cut into a document

PC   personal computer

save   a method to insure that what you have written will be saved either to the hard drive or diskette

software   any program

Writing with a computer allows new freedom and creativity in your writing. Before people started using computers or word processors to write, the process of recopying or rewriting something that was already down on paper was so laborious that making changes, corrections, or revisions in writing was extremely limited. To revise writing, the writer would literally cut the paper he or she was writing on and paste the pieces in the desired order. Sometimes essays would resemble jigsaw puzzles before they were recopied into what would be a final form. Frequently, after the recopying was done, a writer would remember something that would have been brilliant to include, but it was too late.

Now, the whole writing process can be done with the assistance of a good word processor. Each step of the writing process can be aided by using available technology. The first step in the process is to decide what you are going to write about. When you are given a topic, start by thinking about what you already know about the topic. Talk to people about your topic. Listen to what they have to say. Browse through current magazines and newspapers to see what other people think. Go out onto the Internet and explore and chat about your topic. When you've gathered lots of ideas, go to your computer and create a document where you can record your ideas.

At this point in the writing process, you are using the right side of your brain, which is the creative side. Your right brain will view your whole essay idea at once, showing you the potential for what you are generating. Too many times people try to jump right into writing without taking the important step of thinking about what they want to express before they start. When you can clearly envision what you want to communicate before you start, the writing becomes much easier and is more specific and complete when you finish.

Use your word processing program to write down all of your ideas on your subject. At this point, don't write sentences; just put down all of the ideas you can quickly. Don't worry about making mistakes or judging or evaluating what you are writing down; just get all of your ideas out as quickly as possible. This is also using the right side of your brain. If you allow the left side of your brain to stop you on an idea to explore that idea, you may lose many more good ideas because you interrupted the creative process. When generating these ideas, there is no way to know in what order they will come out of your mind, so it may be that the last five items you write down are the best five for your paper. Do not stop writing down ideas until you just can't think of anymore. If you end up with a short list, you need to go back to the previous information-gathering step because proceeding without adequate information at this point will only lead to frustration.

After you have your ideas down, then you can allow the left side of your brain to start helping. Your left brain is the analytical, orderly side that will allow you to analyze all those items you wrote down and decide what the main idea of your writing will be. Develop that idea into a complete sentence that clearly states what you will prove or demonstrate in your essay. Create a new page and put that sentence at the top of the page. Now go through the ideas you have generated, and list them in the order you would like to discuss them in your paper after the title sentence. You can use the cut-and-paste feature of your program to do this task. With this you can arrange and rearrange your ideas as much as you desire until you are pleased with the order you have developed. Now is the time to analyze those ideas to be sure you include all of the good ones and discard the unnecessary ones. This process will give you a good, working informal outline.

Start writing your essay. A good way to start would be to make a copy of your informal outline, and use that to create your essay. Develop your first paragraph around the sentence you wrote to explain the main idea of the essay. Then develop the subsequent ideas on your list. At this point in your writing, just write your ideas down as specifically as possible without worrying about spelling or errors. Allow the right side of your brain to guide you through expressing yourself.

After you have written your essay, then allow the left side of your brain to go back and correct errors. At this point, use your spell checker. It will find the words you have spelled incorrectly, but it will not find words that you have spelled correctly but you wrote the wrong word, such as writing "their" when you meant to write "there." After you run the spell checker, go through your paper again to catch any errors of this kind. Now, leave your essay alone for at least a couple of hours, preferably a day or more. For the writing process to be truly effective, you need to give yourself time to forget about what you wrote so that you can look at your essay with a fresh perspective. If you ignore this step, your writing will not be as good as it could be because your brain will read what it thinks you wanted to say instead of what you actually put down on paper.

When you come back to your paper, read it through for content, ignoring errors. This is the time to make major revisions. Did you leave something out that needed to be included? New information is easy to insert using your word processing program. Did you spend too much time in one area? If so, cutting redundancy or wordiness is easy to do. Are your ideas in the most effective order they could be? If not, use the cut-and-paste mechanism of your program to reorder your thoughts. After you do all this, then you can proofread and edit your paper. Ideally, you should delay this step for another couple of hours or a day to be most effective.

The best way to start the proofreading and editing process is to keep a list of the writing problems you know that you have and evaluate your essay first for those problems. For example, if you know you have a tendency to write comma splices, check each sentence to be sure it is correctly punctuated. A good way to proofread is to read your paper backwards starting with the last sentence. Many times looking at the sentences individually out of context will help the writer to make significant improvement.

When you do the proofreading and editing process, you can use grammar or style checkers, depending on what is available with the software you use. Follow the directions that come with your program. While these programs can be of great assistance, sometimes they cause confusion. Ultimately, you are responsible for the writing you do, so when you make changes, be sure the changes work to improve your writing to make it more clearly express what you want to say. At this point you can also use the thesaurus which comes with your program if you really want to find another word for a specific meaning you are trying to express. Using a thesaurus any earlier than this is dangerous because it will interrupt your train of thought. This is also the time to add page numbers and adjust any formatting you need to with your computer program. Don't stop working on your writing until you are really satisfied. Always be proud of anything you turn in. If you are not proud of your writing, it is not yet ready to submit. When your writing truly says what you want it to say and looks like you want it to look, then you should submit it for grading.

Using computers opens a whole new world for the writer. What kind of computer you use doesn't really matter. You should choose the one that is most compatible with you and your lifestyle. For instance, if you know that only IBMs or their compatibles are used in the career you would choose, then that is what you should use. The Macintosh, however, is very easy to use and has wonderful graphics potential if you will be needing that. Laptop computers of either kind are wonderful for school and everywhere else. They are portable and small so they can be taken anywhere. Many libraries and hotel rooms now have special outlets for laptops. An item you need with any computer is a modem. With a modem a world of information is opened to you. You can go through library catalogs and do library research from the convenience of your computer. You can get on the Internet and discover information about just about anything imaginable.

When you get to use the computer in the classroom, many options are available to you. If the computers in your classroom are networked, you can exchange your writing with other students for comments and collaboration. You can create classroom notebooks where you all can exchange ideas and questions about your writing. You can get ideas from each other about topics you are thinking about developing. Be creative and get used to using the technology to the greatest extent you can imagine.

Knowing what problems may arise when using computers for writing can help you avoid falling into some problems. The most frequent problem writers have is that their writing looks so good on the computer that they don't easily see the errors, so proofreading even more carefully is vital. Also, because word processing becomes easy and fast as you become used to it, many writers have a tendency to get too wordy, emphasizing the ever present need to be concise. Saving your writing frequently is essential. Imagine going through the whole writing process and being very pleased with what you've done only to lose it all by a computer glitch when you go to print. This can only happen if you do not save your documents. To be safe, also always back up any important documents on another diskette that you store somewhere away from the original. Realize that taking diskettes from one computer to another sometimes creates problems. You may obtain a virus that can do great harm, or you may be going from one system to another that is not compatible, so be prepared for any contingency.

One further note: cumulative trauma disorders are receiving much attention. Some of the disorders that fall into this category have to do with using computers. To keep yourself healthy when using the computer, be sure to always use good posture, and keep your wrists loose and in a natural position. Be sure not to sit at the screen for too long at a time. Occasionally look away and close your eyes for a few minutes. Get up and stretch and move around a bit. The key to avoiding these disorders is to not stay in any one position doing the same repetitive task for long periods of time.

PART ONE
People and Careers

The People and Careers section contains articles about people from around the world and the ways they have chosen to live their lives. This picture is of a Native American who lives on a reservation. He has lived a long life and has much to look back on. When you reach his age, what would you like to be able to say you've accomplished with your life?

Photo by Gregory Day, used by permission of the photographer and Kenneth R. McDarment.

Meeting the King

Veronique Edwards

PREREADING

King Mswati II became president of Swaziland when he was only twenty-five years old. Before you read about the King, take a few moments to write about the kind of king or queen you think you would be. Do you think kings or queens should be of a certain age or above? Why or why not? Would you like to be the ruler of a country? What would be the first thing you would do if you became the King or Queen of the United States? Why did you choose to do this thing in particular?

DEFINING

Swaziland (¶1)   a tiny country in Africa on the northern east border of South Africa to the west of Mozambique

monarchy (¶1)   government by a monarch who reigns over a state or territory usually for life and by hereditary right

accession (¶8)   the attainment of a rank

consolidates (¶9)   combines, merges, brings together

equable (¶10)   not easily disturbed

Meeting the King
Veronique Edwards

1   I arrived in Swaziland two days after King Mswati III's 26th birthday. The flags and decorations put up for the celebrations were still floating, bouncing and glittering along the streets. His presence was felt everywhere. Visitors to the tiny kingdom, like me, might have been amused and surprised to find "Long Live The King" emblazoned on a banner hanging off a bridge over the road as you enter the capital, but not the people of this kingdom. "Everything starts and ends with the King," a young enthusiastic royal groupie told me. "We love the monarchy and that's why we have lived in peace all this time."

2   I told him I would be asking the powers that be for an interview with His Majesty. He laughed out loud, clapped his hands, and said "Don't you have any respect for your elders. The King has better things to do than speak to foreign women." We said our goodbyes.

3   Later that week I meet with the Minister of Information and Broadcasting, Prince Phinda, one of the senior sons of the late King. A softly spoken man, he promises to make the necessary arrangements. And during my last week in Swaziland he is as good as his word.

4   The King owns many residences but Lozitha is the official palace, situated on the slopes of the Ndzimba mountains in central Swaziland. The place is close to the birthplace of King Sobhuza II, the father of the present King Mswati. From my hotel in Mbabane, there is only one way of getting to the Lozitha palace, via the Valley of Heaven, known as the Ezulwine. You drive through this subtropical valley, skirting the Houses of Parliament and the national Stadium at Lobamba.

5   Suddenly, you see the road lights that lead to the palace, an oasis of royal luxury. Tall, huge iron gates are manned by three armed guards. They recognize my escorts and allow us in. We drive to another set of metal gates which lead to the entrance of the inner palace. Finally, we step out on to the manicured circular lawn and flower beds. Sitting on a high wall are soldiers and some of the palace hangers-on, playing a game of "Ematje," a board game using marble stones commonly seen around the country. They are so engrossed that our arrival means nothing to them.

6   We are led into the waiting room with an impressive interior decor. A large portrait of the King smiles down on us. The room is filled with children of the royal family glued to a large colour television.

7   We expect to be kept waiting for hours; in fact, we wait for just eight minutes before we are whisked in. I turn around and ask one of my escorts "How do I greet him?" but it is too late. My right foot is already in the open doorway and there is the King. I walk towards him. He rises from his seat smiling, standing tall and extending his hand. I curtsy and apologize for not wearing something traditional like his traditional Swazi dress, a "Mahiya" it is a two-piece colourful wrap, one piece tied across the shoulders hanging over a skirt. He also wears a white beaded neck-

Veronique Edwards, "Meeting the King," BBC Focus on Africa, July–September 1994, pp. 32–33. Reprinted by permission of BBC World Service.

Please note maps in appendix for references to places in this article.

lace and a pair of brown sandals. He sounds very young but his short trimmed moustache and beard give him the authority of a more mature man.

8　　For the next 45 minutes we talk about politics, the economy, his accession to the throne, his family. I remind him that he became King earlier than tradition normally would have allowed, and that he had been robbed of his youth. He laughs and says that the wishes of his people were more important than his.

9　　His views on democracy are not very precise: he is trying to follow a middle-of-the-road approach to avoid conflict between the traditionalists and the progressives who are calling for a new system of government. The traditionalists would like to maintain the 'Tinkhundla,' which consolidates traditional power but the progressives say this 'Tinkhundla' system of government may work at the local level but it is doomed to fail at the national level because it is simply too old-fashioned. One topic I am not brave enough to ask about is the subject of the King's many wives. By Swazi tradition the new King takes several wives from various areas of the community to consolidate his position. But I pluck up enough courage to ask him about the role of women in general in Swaziland. All women are supposed to be held in high esteem because of the status of the Queen Mother, but in practice women are discriminated against at work and through social customs that do not even allow women to sit with men or own property. Of late, women's organizations are challenging the attitudes of men towards Swazi women and want some of these outdated customs and traditions to be done away with. But the King refuses to be drawn on specifics. Whenever he is in a corner and risks offending one side or the other he tells me "that is up to the Swazi people to decide."

10　　The young King aims to please and has an equable disposition; nothing I say can disturb his equilibrium. As we leave the palace, the picture of the King was still smiling down at us. Hangers-on hang on. His children are still glued to the television. I wonder if they will be swept away by the democratic winds of change sweeping Swaziland's neighbours . . . or will they be glued to the past.

READING

1. What are the King's views on democracy?

2. Why does the King have many wives?

THINKING

1. Do you feel that America would do better if it had a king or a queen? What would be better? What would be worse? Why?

2. King Mswati III tries very hard to make all of his people happy by taking a middle-of-the-road attitude that won't offend or upset his people. Do you think it is possible for the ruler of a nation to make everyone happy? Why or why not? What kinds of things would the ruler need to do to be able to please most of the people?

PREWRITING

Now that you have read this article, write about being a king or queen. Are your feelings toward a monarchy the same as they were before you read about the King? Why? Do you think you would be like King Mswati III? Why? How would you be the same? How would you be different?

WRITING

1. You have just been nominated to be the president of the student body of your university. Write a well-organized article for the student newspaper convincing the students that you are the best candidate to govern the students of your school. Be sure to include what you would do if you were elected.

2. Your best friend is from a small country ruled by a king. Your friend has asked you to move to that country after you graduate to go into business together. Write a letter to your friend expressing your feelings about why you would or would not want to move to a country with a monarch. Explain your reasoning to your friend.

REVISING

Unity is essential when writing a paragraph or an essay. Check to see if "Meeting the King" has unity in content. To do this, decide what the main topic of the article is. After you decide, check the details and examples the writer uses to see if they all relate to the main idea of the article. If the article has unity in content, all of the ideas will relate.

Now check your writing assignment. What is your main idea? Do all of your details and examples relate your main idea? If they don't, then see if your details and examples need to be clarified, deleted, or replaced.

EDITING

The spacing of your writing on a page is very important. If you are using a typewriter, you should allow a one-inch margin on all four sides of your page. You should indent each paragraph five spaces. Be sure to center your title before you start; then skip a line before your first sentence. Be sure to skip one space after each comma and two spaces after each period. Never space before a comma or a period, and never start a line with a comma or a period.

If you are writing by hand, be sure to make your paper look like what is described above. Always be sure to leave margins, especially on the right-hand side and the bottom of the page. Also, be sure your handwriting is legible. If you write large letters, you may want to skip a line between your written lines so that your work will be easier to read.

Whether you type or write with a pen, take pride in your work. Your writing is a reflection of you, so you always should strive to make it be the best it can be, including how it looks.

Marley's Ghost in Babylon

Jerry Adler

PREREADING

Bob Marley, the famous reggae singer, was told that he was dying of cancer when he was 36 years old, but he refused to believe the diagnosis and ended up dying and leaving his legal and financial affairs in a terrible mess for his family and heirs to sort out. Write about what you would do if you were told today that you have a terminal illness. Who would you want to be with? What would you want to do?

DEFINING

Babylon   the capitol of the ancient kingdom of Babylonia

reggae (¶1)   a popular form of music with Jamaican origin

impedimenta (¶1)   things that get in the way

romanticism (¶1)   romantic tendency

Rastafarianism (¶1)   Jamaican religious cult that believes that Africa is the "promised land"

conducive (¶1)   helpful, contributing to

orthodox (¶1)   proper, correct

estate (¶1)   all of the assets and liabilities of a dead person

diverted (¶2)   turned in a different direction

compilation (¶2)   a bringing together of

discrepancies (¶2) disagreement

executors (¶2) people named to take care of a person's estate

relentlessness (¶3) the quality of not being affected by others' distress

disconcerted (¶3) confused, frustrated

pacemaker (¶3) an electronic device implanted in the body to stimulate the heart to beat

winnow (¶4) separate out, select, narrow down

indomitable (¶5) unyielding, not easily discouraged

Marley's Ghost in Babylon

Jerry Adler with Howard Manly

1   In life, the reggae singer Bob Marley disdained the impedimenta of what he called "Babylon"—modern Western civilization—such as lawyers, preachers, and barbers. His philosophy was a radical Caribbean romanticism, surcharged with the Biblical cult of Rastafarianism. His habits ran to regular indulgence in cigar-sized joints of powerful marijuana. Neither was conducive to an orthodox personal life. He did business with his band on the basis of a handshake, paying them when and what he chose; he fathered at least seven children by as many women, not counting four by his wife, Rita; and when he was dying of cancer in 1981 at 36, he refused to make out a will. Preferring to believe he would live forever, he ordered a new Mercedes Benz. A decade later, the car is one small piece of a monumental legal tangle over Marley's $30 million estate that just goes to show, as he might have put it, that "Babylon" always wins in the end.

2   At the center of the dispute are Rita, 46, a former dancer with Marley's band whom he married in 1966, and J. Louis Byles, the court-appointed administrator of the singer's estate. Under Jamaican law, Marley's widow would have been entitled to half his estate, with the remainder divided equally among his children. But Byles charges that for much of the 1980s money that should have gone to the estate was diverted to offshore corporations controlled by Rita and her lawyers. After the 1984 release of Marley's "Legend" album, a compilation of his greatest hits, Marley's royalties jumped from around $200,000 a year to $1 million, and eventually much more, but the estate never saw most of the money; a subsequent audit found discrepancies totaling around $16 million. Rita admitted in court forging her husband's signature on backdated documents transferring ownership of Marley's companies to her. She did this, she told NEWSWEEK, on the advice of her lawyers and in the belief that since she was the prime heir anyway, "how can I steal from myself?" The court dismissed her as one of Marley's original executors, but she was not charged with a crime; the estate has sued her lawyer to get the money back and, after more than four years, a federal court in New York is

Please note maps in appendix for references to places in this article.

expected to rule later this year. "I did nothing of my own thought," Rita added. "I was a lowly wife who went on stage and danced when Bob told me to dance."

3   Byles—a conservative 79-year-old Kingston banker who never cared for Marley when he was alive—has been hunting down the estate's assets with a relentlessness that has disconcerted even some of the heirs whose interests he is protecting. Since Marley never bothered to legally transfer to his mother the $400,000 house in Miami he bought for her in 1978, the estate's lawyers tried to evict her and put the house on the market. Chris Blackwell, the Island Records producer who gave Marley his start, eventually bought the property and gave it to her. "These people [the estate's lawyers] are so bright and so evil," Marley's mother says. "They are the devil's tools." The Mercedes Marley bought on his deathbed didn't arrive until after he died, and was paid for by the estate. When Byles discovered that Rita had been driving it since 1981, he began legal proceedings to reclaim the car, which by now has more than 90,000 miles on it. His efforts to make the strictest principles of English probate law fit the circumstances of a Jamaican folk hero and Rastafarian mystic have not endeared him to the Jamaican public, and he has been wounded by the bad publicity. "I can honestly say I have regretted the day I agreed to take this job," he says. "It has indirectly caused me three major operations and the addition of a pacemaker."

4   . . . Then there are the other heirs. Marley once said he wanted as many children as there were "shells in the sea," and appears to have made good on the boast. When the courts advertised for potential heirs, hundreds of would-be Marleys appeared from all over the world. Rita herself helped winnow the claimants down to seven. But the heirs, most of them poor, must have been quite disappointed to discover that their share of the great singer's estate at first came to approximately $210 every three months. The situation has improved somewhat since then. Five of the heirs have reached their majority and gotten cash settlements of around $70,000. They will receive more when the estate finally sells the rights to Marley's music, but the sale has been held up while the courts decide whether the price, $8.2 million, is fair.

5   Meanwhile, the estate gave about $100,000 to the heirs last year. This compares to roughly $2 million for "professional services" in the same year. The "stiff-necked baldheads," as Marley described Jamaica's ruling class of professionals and politicians, got it all, at the going rate of $300 an hour for the estate's lawyers. The one thing they couldn't take cuts of, though, was Marley's own indomitable spirit, which appears to have been passed down more or less intact to his and Rita's son Ziggy, 22. A reggae singer himself with several Grammys to his credit, Ziggy filed a statement in Florida's Dade County Court expressing his desire to be rid of the whole mess. "Let them have it," he said. "Me can go out and make me own money."

READING

1. How many children did Marley want? How many did he have? How many children is his estate being shared with?

2. How much money was Marley worth? How did he handle his money? What does his son, Ziggy, think about his father's money?

THINKING

1. How much money do you want to earn in your lifetime? How will you handle your money? Do you have a budget now? Do you think it would be hard for you to handle the large amount of money that Marley had?

2. After reading this article, how do you feel about having a will and planning for how your affairs will be handled when you die? Do you have a will now? Do you have life insurance? Do you think a will and insurance are important?

PREWRITING

Write about what you imagine your life will be like 30 years from now. What will your career be? How much money will you have? Will you be married? Will you have children? If so, how many? What will you have accomplished?

WRITING

1. Write a will. It can be for what you have now or for what you hope to have in 30 years. Be sure to include what you want done about all of your personal possessions, money, and investments. Also, name an executor for your estate, and name whom you want to have custody of your children or future children.

2. Write your own eulogy. A eulogy is a speech or a written essay that praises a person for his or her accomplishments in life. It is usually presented at a funeral or memorial service. Include in your eulogy what you most want to be remembered for in your life. This can be written either as if you died today or as if you will die 30 years from now.

REVISING

"Marley's Ghost in Babylon" was taken out of *Newsweek* magazine, which tends to use longer paragraphs than many magazines. Paragraph length is usually determined by the content you want to communicate. In journalism, paragraphs frequently are short, supposedly to keep the reader's attention. Longer paragraphs, of course, contain more information and details.

What kinds of paragraphs do you write? Look at your writing assignment. Are your paragraphs short, long, or medium length? Why did you choose to write the paragraphs in the length you did? A paragraph, as does a sentence, needs to contain a complete thought. Check each paragraph that you wrote to see if each one can stand by itself and make sense. Does it require more information? Paragraphs usually need to contain five or more sentences to be complete. How many sentences did you write in the paragraphs of your writing assignment? Try revising your assignment to improve the length and content of the paragraphs.

EDITING

A complex sentence is created when a **dependent clause and an independent clause** are used together in a sentence. Remember, a clause must have a subject and a verb. An independent clause can stand by itself as a sentence. A dependent clause cannot stand by itself as a sentence because it starts with a **subordinating conjunction**, such as:

> after, although, as, as far as, as if, as long as, as soon as, as though, because, before, even though, every time, everywhere, how, if, in order that, no matter, once, since, so that, than, that, though, unless, until, whatever, when, whenever, where, whereas, wherever, whether or not, while, why

Because a dependent clause starts with a subordinating conjunction, the sentence needs more information to be complete.

Examples:
When the courts advertised for potential heirs

This is a dependent clause. *The courts* is the subject and *advertised* is the verb, but because the clause starts with *when,* it can't stand by itself. This clause requires more information to be a complete thought.

> When the courts advertised for potential heirs, hundreds of would-be Marleys appeared from all over the world. (¶4)

In this sentence, *hundreds of would-be Marleys appeared from all over the world* is an independent clause, which when added to *when the courts advertised for potential heirs* makes sense and can stand alone. Notice that when a dependent clause starts a sentence, it is followed by a comma before the independent clause starts. If a sentence starts with an independent clause and ends with a dependent clause, then no comma is necessary.

> Hundreds of would-be Marleys appeared from all over the world when the courts advertised for potential heirs.

> Check through your writing assignment to be sure that you used commas correctly when you used dependent clauses with independent clauses.

Primo Action Dude

Jim Cubinar

PREREADING

Ernie Reyes, Jr. has relied heavily on the strength and support of his family throughout his career. Before you start reading this article, think about the role your family plays in supporting your educational and career choices. Are they actively involved or maybe not involved at all? How much of their involvement or lack of involvement do you think has to do with your culture or maybe the community where you were raised? Would you like their support to be different than it is?

DEFINING

debut (¶1)   first public appearance

tae kwon do (¶4)   a Korean art style of karate

heady (¶6)   an intoxicating feeling

unextravagant (¶8)   very modest, not lavish

Primo Action Dude

Jim Cubinar

1   People remember Ernie Reyes, Jr.—who had his acting debut in 1985 at age 13 in the movie *"The Last Dragon"*—as a tiny martial arts dynamo with big, devastating kicks and an even more devastating smile. His recent fame comes from the Ninja Turtles box-office hits. He performed as a stunt double for Donatello in *"Teenage Mutant Ninja Turtles"* and as a pizza delivery boy with a roundhouse special in the movie's sequel, *"Mutant Ninja Turtles 2: The Secret of the Ooze."*

2   Recently, Ernie became the first Filipino American filmmaker and lead star in a major American motion picture when he made the martial arts comedy, *"Surf Ninjas"* with Nicolas Cowan and Rob Schneider (who is half Filipino). He speaks of his accomplishment with a lot of pride: "I enjoyed the experience of being able to be on a project from day one and seeing it all come together. It's a very rewarding feeling."

3   Ernesto Enopre Reyes, Jr. was born on January 15, 1972 in San Jose, California to Ernie Reyes, Sr., a martial arts instructor, and Sue Asinas. Though his father did not force him into the martial arts, Ernie took to the field starting at age six. Two years later, he became the first top-rated child in a national karate adult division ranking. He then became a member of his father's West Coast Demonstration Team, an assembly of martial artists that performed exhibitions nationwide and in Asia and South America.

4   Reyes, Sr. remembers vividly the moments when his son would bring down the house with his performance. "He was so small and cute, but his technique was devastating," says the 1977 U.S. National tae kwon do champion. "Ernie's technique at that time was way ahead of everybody else's."

5   Ernie was "discovered" for the movies by Motown Records founder Berry Gordy, who also "discovered" Michael Jackson. Gordy's Motown Productions made *"The Last Dragon"* and after that, co-produced with Disney Productions *"Sidekicks,"* a series written specifically for Ernie. At age 13, he was on his way to movie success. Or so he thought.

6   Ernie, who is now 22 years old, 5'5", and 140 pounds, recalls those heady days after *"Sidekicks"* when he was caught up in the excitement and ego trips. "It was hard. I was growing up and growing up is tough enough. All of a sudden, you're making a lot of money, everybody notices you and saying how great you are. It has to affect you in some way. It took friends and family to bring you back to reality."

7   After *"Sidekicks,"* Ernie experienced the harshness of life in the entertainment industry. He couldn't find work. Having moved to Los Angeles, he and his father had to pay for a house in San Jose and an apartment in LA. His father had one martial arts school.

8   "We lived a very unextravagant life," Ernie recalls. "There were times when all we could afford to eat was rice and eggs for every meal. People think that just be-

Jim Cubinar, "Primo Action Dude," August 1994, vol. 3, no. 28, pp. 6–8. Reprinted by permission of Filipinos Publishing Inc.

Please note maps in appendix for references to places in this article.

cause you are a successful martial artist, you are rich. The martial arts don't bring financial stability."

9   Despite—or maybe because of—having gone through those hard times, Ernie is well-centered. "Even now, my dad says that some of the best times he remembers were in that small room [in LA] when we trained and lived together as a family. That's why I know that if everything is taken away from me, I'd still be a very happy person."

10   His early days of teaming with his father in martial arts competitions created a unique father-son relationship that remains strong to this day. "He's also my partner when it comes to the entertainment business," Ernie says. "Not very many people get to work with their folks. We are able to relate on many different levels. I think that's what keeps our relationship fresh and a lot of fun also."

11   Reyes, Sr., who has appeared in movies with his son, concurs: "We talk all the time. We're real good friends, too, not just father and son."

12   Ernie's mother and brothers are also involved in the martial arts. His mom, Sue, is an instructor in the chain of Ernie Reyes (Sr.) West Coast Tae Kwon Do Schools. Ernie's brother, Lee, 16, has a second degree black belt in tae kwon do and made his big screen debut in *"American Ninjas 5,"* while youngest brother Tino, 11, is halfway to his black belt.

13   Family has always been top priority for Ernie. Although he and his brothers do not speak Filipino and are no longer familiar with many Philippine traditions, he still invokes his heritage as an important part of his being.

14   "I think the kind of upbringing and family closeness is still the same," he says. "The main thing to me is the family unit and the spirituality that comes with the Filipino heritage. I think that's the most important thing that is kept and we'll continue to keep. That will never be lost."

15   Today, Ernie is focused on becoming a filmmaker. "I'm writing my own projects and developing myself because I feel that being a filmmaker, rather than just an actor, will help me and my fellow Filipinos break into the entertainment industry."

16   He plans to visit the Philippines eventually, when he is "more established" in his career. "By that time, maybe [I can] have an impact and be able to give back to the country a little bit."

17   Ernie is currently working on a screenplay that will not cater as much to kids' tastes as his past films did. "I definitely want to make more films for kids, but that's not my sole purpose as a filmmaker. This time, I'm going to go with something a little bit more for my age group."

18   Although some may see him as just "another Asian martial arts actor," Ernie believes that in time, more people will be aware of his ethnicity. "I've never not admitted that I am Filipino," he asserts.

19   Ernie appreciates his Filipino following in the U.S. and around the world. "Filipinos have been behind me 100 percent. I would like to thank them for that."

READING

1. What kind of a relationship does Ernie have with his father? With his mother?

2. What career is Ernie Reyes, Jr. focusing on? Why?

THINKING

1. Ernie Reyes, Jr. became famous at the age of thirteen, but then he couldn't get a job. How do you think it would feel to be famous at thirteen? If you couldn't continue to work as a movie star, what would you do? Many child stars have turned to drugs and alcohol, while others have returned to school. Some have gone on to eventually have other jobs in the movie industry. What do you think the best thing to do would be? Would you move to Hollywood with your child so that he or she could be in movies at thirteen?

2. Ernie Reyes, Jr. is obviously proud of his culture and wants to help fellow Filipinos get into the film industry. He says he'd like to give something back to his country. When you become successful, do you feel that you would like to help members of your culture to also become successful in your career? Why or why not? Would you like to give something to your country or your culture? Why or why not?

PREWRITING

Write about what special challenges you think a twenty-two-year-old would face in becoming a combination filmmaker/star. How would age affect that person's chances for success? Should he or she get family and friends involved in his or her project or should he or she rely only on professionals in the field? Would you like to be a filmmaker and/or movie star? Why or why not?

WRITING

1. You have the opportunity to get a contract with a major movie producing firm. To get the contract, you need to submit a written proposal that would describe in detail the movie you want to make, which would be about something you do very well, such as karate, cooking, studying, singing, or swimming. Or the movie could be about your family or your culture. Write a well-organized proposal with lots of details to convince the movie maker that you are the best person to hire.

2. Ernie Reyes, Jr. plans to eventually visit the Philippines. He said, ". . . maybe [I can] have an impact and be able to give back to the country a little bit." Write a one-page essay in which you explain what you'd like to "give back" to your country or culture and why.

REVISING

When you write, transitions create a smooth flow from one idea to the next. Read through "Primo Action Dude" again, and see how the writer ties his ideas together. What words does he use to provide a transition from one paragraph to the next?

Go through your writing assignment and be sure each separate idea is linked effectively to the other ideas. Using the following list of words is a good way to help you develop transitions in your writing.

after, also, and, because, before, behind, beside, but, consequently, during, finally, for example, for instance, gradually, however, in front of, inside, near, next, next to, nevertheless, outside, previously, since, so that, similarly, suddenly, then, therefore, when, with

EDITING

Sentence fragments occur when a sentence is not complete. Each sentence needs to have a **subject**, which is usually a noun that the sentence is about. A sentence must also have a **predicate**, which shows what happens to the subject of the sentence and contains a verb that shows the action of the subject or links the subject to the rest of the idea. Go through your writing assignment to make sure each sentence has a subject and a predicate and is complete.

Examples:

His father had one martial arts school.

His father is the subject, and *had one martial arts school* is the predicate, so this sentence is complete.

It was hard.

It is the subject, and *was hard* is the predicate, so this sentence is complete.

Ernie's technique at that time.

This is a subject with no predicate so it is a fragment.

Was way ahead of everybody else's.

This is a predicate with no subject so it is a fragment.

Though his father did not force him into the martial arts.

Although *his father* is a subject and *did not force him into the martial arts* is a predicate, the **subordinating conjunction** *though* makes the clause require more information, so it cannot stand alone in its present form.

Look through your writing assignments to be sure that you have not left any fragments.

Vice Girl's Suicide Troubles a Nation

Tony Allison

PREREADING

Liwjiew was a fifteen-year-old prostitute in Bangkok who took her own life. Have you ever run away from home or known someone who did? What happened? What would you do if you were fifteen, away from anyone you knew, had no money and no job, and you were hungry? Imagine what it would be like to turn to something like prostitution in order to keep alive while you were away from home.

DEFINING

brothel (¶1)   house of prostitution

ironic (¶4)   different than what was suspected

speculation (¶6)   an opinion based on guesswork

adamant (¶8)   stubborn, inflexible

inconceivable (¶13)   something so unlikely it would be thought to be impossible

baht (¶21)   a basic unit of currency in Thailand

Vice Girl's Suicide Troubles a Nation

Tony Allison

in Bangkok

1   In the tragic story of a young Thai prostitute's death there are a few certainties: her name was Liwjiew, she was also known as Anong Sae Fung, she was 15 years old, she came from Chiang Rai province, she worked in a brothel thinly disguised as a barber's shop, and she took her life by drinking cyanide in the presence of a police officer.

2   Beyond that, the facts of Liwjiew's death last month have become obscured under layers of accusations involving politicians, the press and police in Songkhla province, where the suicide occurred.

3   Liwjiew drank her lethal cocktail on the morning of July 16 in Hat Yai police station, just three days after cabinet approval of a new anti-prostitution bill which will, if legislated, make parents, brothel owners and, for the first time, clients punishable by steep fines and prison terms if convicted of subjecting girls below the age of 18 to prostitution.

4   By an ironic coincidence, the intention to introduce this legislation was announced almost exactly a year ago, one day before the highly publicized murder of a prostitute in the Songkhla City Hall.

5   Liwjiew fled to the police station from the brothel where she had been working for several months. She asked to be sent home to Chiang Rai, but the police said she could not go until that afternoon as relevant paperwork had not been completed.

6   Press reports claim the police then said she should take them to identify her brothel, at which stage, speculation goes, she drank the poison rather than return, perhaps fearing, as does happen, that the police would force her to start work again.

7   She died within minutes.

8   The police are adamant that they did their best to help the girl, and had every intention of sending her home, and that the suicide had nothing to do with pressure on their part.

9   The death is being investigated by the Department of the Interior, which has already transferred three senior policemen from separate stations in the south, while Lieutenant-Colonel Nophadol Phueaksopon, the inspector who witnessed the death, is also under investigation.

10   A key element in the investigation is the precise composition of the poison. Chemists at Songkhla University, who examined leftovers in the bottle from which she drank, have determined that it was cyanide, but a crucial question which will go a long way to determining the origin of the poison and possible guilt remains unanswered. Exactly what kind of cyanide did Liwjiew consume?

11   It is possible it came in powder form, extracted from tin, which is commonly

Tony Allison, "Vice Girl's Suicide Troubles a Nation," 13–14 August 1994, p. 8. Reprinted by permission of South China Morning Post.

Please note maps in appendix for references to places in this article.

mined in the south and used by fishermen to poison fish. If this is the case, it is more than likely that Liwjiew, or her minders, would have been able to obtain some themselves, mix it with water—it dissolves easily—and have it ready for when the fateful occasion demanded.

12   Conversely, if the mix was sodium cyanide, the source of supply becomes more problematic. Sodium cyanide was used as an agricultural poison until it was banned in 1989 because of its high toxicity. Its importation into Thailand is strictly controlled by the Agriculture, Industry and Public Health ministries.

13   It is highly inconceivable that a raw 15-year-old would have been able to lay her hands on some of this of her own accord, which would mean that it was given to her, either by her keepers or by persons with close connections to officials.

14   It is not accepted that Liwjiew drank rat poison or insecticide, which is freely available over the counter, as reported by the police in the early stages of the case. Chemists say these are not toxic enough to kill a human in a few minutes, if at all, especially in the small amount that Liwjiew drank, and it certainly would not have eaten a watch strap as the policeman who witnessed the suicide reported.

15   Naiyana Supapung, coordinator for the Friends of Thai Women Workers in Asia (FOWIA), a non-government organization closely involved with rehabilitating and educating prostitutes, said she first heard of cyanide being used by prostitutes several years ago.

16   "I learned of cases where young Burmese prostitutes, who tested HIV positive, were so fearful of being sent back to their country by the police, where they would face certain persecution, that they drank cyanide," she said.

17   Another worker at the FOWIA, who asked to remain anonymous, said it was a known practice for brothel owners to give the girls a bottle containing cyanide. They would not be told what was in the bottle, only that they should drink it if they ever had any problems with the police.

18   Liwjiew's death has prompted wide reaction, with the role of the police coming under strong attack. Sawai Na Phatthalung, president of the Songkhla Tourism Association, firmly believes the suicide should be blamed on lax officials.

19   A member of parliament for the ruling Democratic Party, Niphon Boonyamanee, agreed. The young girl arrived at the police station with hope, he said, but there the pressure mounted on her, with intense interrogation and attention from reporters who happened to be around covering another case, blurring her thoughts.

20   Lieutenant-Colonel Nophadol defended the role of the police, saying they did their best. He said he was the one who told Liwjiew she would have to wait before going home, at which point she became very anxious.

21   "I asked her how much money she had, and she said she had a hundred [baht] or so," he said. "So I asked for her purse, and she reached in and took out a bottle, which I knocked away. But she picked it up and swallowed from it. I really did not know it was poison, but I became suspicious when the liquid started to eat my watch strap. If I had known it was poison, I would not have tried to take it away because there was a big cut on my palm."

22   Investigations will continue, and are expected, like most in Thailand, to take some time. What will not change though, is the one certainty: a girl of 15, who sought police help to escape from the life she was leading, is dead.

READING

1. What kind of poison do they think Liwjiew took? Are they sure?

2. What does FOWIA stand for? What does this organization do?

THINKING

1. Why do you think Liwjiew drank the poison? Do you think that she knew it was poison when she drank it? Would you drink poison if you were in a similar situation? Why or why not?

2. The bill that passed Thailand's cabinet would make parents, owners of brothels, and clients punishable for subjecting girls under eighteen to prostitution. Who do you think should be punished for young girls being prostitutes? Why? Or do you think anyone besides the girl should be punished? Why?

PREWRITING

Write about how you feel about prostitution. What do you know about prostitution? Do you know someone who has ever worked as a prostitute? Do you think prostitutes are an inevitable part of our society? Why or why not?

WRITING

1. Your community has many young girls with serious problems at home. They try to escape by running away. Many times they end up on the streets because they have no place to go and they are too young to get jobs. Write a proposal for your city council suggesting a way to take care of these girls or to help the girls take care of themselves. Be sure to use details including at least who would do it, what would be done, where it would be, and who would pay.

2. The legislature in your state is considering whether to legalize prostitution. Write a letter to your representative arguing either for or against this legalization. Be sure to base your argument on facts rather than beliefs. The library can provide you with materials you can research on this topic. Be sure to fully develop your argument.

REVISING

To effectively illustrate people's opinions, Tony Allison effectively uses quotations.

Example:
> "I learned of cases where young Burmese prostitutes, who tested HIV positive, were so fearful of being sent back to their country by the police, where they would face certain prosecution, that they drank cyanide," she said.

Notice how the quote gives specific information about one person's point of view.

Look at your writing assignment, and see if you can add some quotations that would make your argument more powerful.

EDITING

When editing, a checklist can help you catch some common errors. Try using the following checklist with your writing assignment before you turn it in.

1. Does your paper stay on the given topic? If not, eliminate any sentence or section of your paper that strays from the topic.

2. Is every sentence complete? Check for run-ons and fragments.

3. Do you have enough details and examples?

4. Check to be sure that you have commas where you are supposed to and that you don't have commas where they don't belong.

5. Check to be sure that your subjects and verbs agree.

6. Check to see if all of your verbs are in the right tense.

7. Be sure that you have capitalized correctly.

8. Is each word spelled correctly?

9. Is your handwriting legible?

After you have gone over your paper and made the necessary revisions and corrections, have someone else—a tutor or a classmate—read through your paper and answer these questions. Then make any additional corrections or additions that are needed.

Breaking the Bonds of Hate

Virak Khiev

PREREADING

Virak Khiev writes that he has always wanted to find "perfect happiness." Before you read this article, think about what you think perfect happiness is. Is it different for different people? Does it have to do with what you own, where you live, who you know, what you know, or is it something else? Do you think it is possible for most people to be happy? Why or why not?

DEFINING

carrion (¶4) dead and decaying flesh

stereotype (¶5) when one member of a group is considered to be like all members of that group

unscrupulous (¶5) without having a conscience or principles

34

Breaking the Bonds of Hate

Virak Khiev

1   Ever since I can remember, I wanted the ideal life: a big house, lots of money, cars. I wanted to find the prefect happiness that so many people have longed for. I wanted more than life in the jungle of Cambodia. America was the place, the land of tall skyscrapers, televisions, cars and airplanes.

2   In the jungles of Cambodia I lived in a refugee camp. We didn't have good sanitation or modern conveniences. For example, there were no inside bathrooms—only outside ones made from palm-tree leaves, surrounded by millions of flies. When walking down the street, I could smell the aroma of the outhouse; in the afternoon, the 5- and 6-year-olds played with the dirt in front of it. It was the only thing they had to play with, and the "fragrance" never seemed to bother them. And it never bothered me. Because I smelled it every day, I was used to it.

3   The only thing that bothered me was the war. I have spent half of my life in war. The killing is still implanted in my mind. I hate Cambodia. When I came to America nine years ago at the age of 10, I thought I was being born into a new life. No more being hungry, no more fighting, no more killing. I thought I had escaped the war.

4   In America, there are more kinds of material things than Cambodians could ever want. And here we don't have to live in the jungle like monkeys, we don't have to hide from mortar bombing and we don't have to smell the rotten human carrion. But for the immigrant, America presents a different type of jungle, a different type of war and a smell as bad as the waste of Cambodia.

5   Most Americans believe the stereotype that immigrants work hard, get a good education, and have a very good life. Maybe it used to be like that, but not anymore. You have to be deceptive and unscrupulous in order to make it. If you are not, then you will end up like most immigrants I've known. Living in the ghetto in a cockroach-infested house. Working on the assembly line or in the chicken factory to support your family. Getting up at 3 o'clock in the morning to take the bus to work and not getting home until 5 p.m.

6   If you're a kid my age, you drop out of school to work because your parents don't have enough money to buy you clothes for school. You may end up selling drugs because you want cars, money, and parties, as all teenagers do. You have to depend on your peers for emotional support because your parents are too busy working in the factory trying to make money to pay the bills. You don't get along with your parents because they have a different mentality: you are an American and they are Cambodian. You hate them because they are never there for you, so you join a gang as I did.

7   You spend your time drinking, doing drugs, and fighting. You beat up people for pleasure. You don't care about anything except your drugs, your beers, and your revenge against adversaries. You shoot at people because they've insulted your

Virak Khiev, "Breaking the Bonds of Hate," Newsweek, 27 April 1992, p. 8.

Please note maps in appendix for references to places in this article.

pride. You shoot at the police because they are always bothering you. They shoot back and then you're dead like my best friend Sinerth.

8   Sinerth robbed a gas station. He was shot in the head by the police. I'd known him since the sixth grade from my first school in Minneapolis. I can still remember his voice calling me from California. "Virak, come down here, man," he said. "We need you. There are lots of pretty girls down here." I promised him that I would be there to see him. The following year he was dead. I felt sorry for him. But as I thought it over, maybe it is better for him to be dead than to continue with the cycle of violence, to live with hate. I thought, "It is better to die than live like an angry young fool, thinking that everybody is out to get you."

9   **Mad-dog mind-set:** When I was like Sinerth, I didn't care about dying. I thought that I was on top of the world, being immortalized by drugs. I could see that my future would be spent working on the assembly line like most of my friends, spending all my paycheck on the weekend and being broke again on Monday morning. I hated going to school because I couldn't see a way to get out of the endless cycle. My philosophy was "Live hard and die young."

10   I hated America because, to me, it was not the place of opportunities or the land of "the melting pot" as I had been told. All I had seen were broken beer bottles on the street and homeless people and drunks using the sky as their roof. I couldn't walk down the street without someone yelling out, "You f—ing gook" from his car. Once again I was caught in the web of hatred. I'd become a mad dog with the mind-set of the past: "When trapped in the corner, just bite." The war mentality of Cambodia came back: get what you can and leave. I thought I came to America to escape war, poverty, fighting, to escape the violence, but I wasn't escaping; I was being introduced to a newer version of war—the war of hatred.

11   I was lucky. In Minneapolis, I dropped out of school in the ninth grade to join a gang. Then I moved to Louisiana, where I continued my life of "immortality" as a member of another gang. It came to an abrupt halt when I crashed a car. I wasn't badly injured, but I was underage and the fine took all my money. I called a good friend of the Cambodian community in Minneapolis for advice (she'd tried to help me earlier). I didn't know where to go or whom to turn to. I saw friends landing in jail, and I didn't want that. She promised to help me get back in school. And she did.

12   Since then I've been given a lot of encouragement and caring by American friends and teachers who've helped me turn my life around. They opened my eyes to a kind of education that frees us all from ignorance and slavery. I could have failed so many times except for those people who believed in me and gave me another chance. Individuals who were willing to help me have taught me that I can help myself. I'm now a 12th grader and have been at my school for three years; I plan to attend college in the fall. I am struggling to believe I can reach the other side of the mountain.

READING

1. Who was Sinerth? What did he do?

2. What was Virak Khiev's philosophy?

THINKING

1. Do you think Khiev's experience was typical of the experience of immigrants to America? Do you know anyone who has immigrated to America or did you immigrate to America? How did expectations differ from the reality of being here for these people or for you? Did they or you find happiness here? Why or why not?

2. How would you describe where you live to someone of another country? In America there is an enormous variety in the kinds of places people can live from crowded inner cities to lonely rural farms, to warm Hawaiian beaches, to frigid cold Alaska. Do you think that Khiev was stereotyping America in his description? What would you do if you lived in a place you considered dangerous?

PREWRITING

Brainstorm a list of all of the good things about the country where you live. Include everything you can possibly think of. Then write a list containing important events in your life, things that happened that really changed something significant for you.

WRITING

1. You have been hired by your country to work on a task force encouraging immigrants to move to your country. Your job on the task force is to write an article for a brochure telling immigrants why they should move to your country. Be sure to include what your country has to offer for job opportunities, housing, and education. Remember, you are trying to make your country look appealing while being honest.

2. Virak Khiev is literally saving his own life by returning to school. His return to school was a major turning point for him. Write an essay to share with your classmates about a major turning point in your life. Be sure to include what your life was like before and after this event happened. Describe what the event that changed your life was using details, and explain why you think it made such a big difference to you.

REVISING

Reread "Breaking the Bonds of Hate" after waiting at least a day after your first reading. Does it say what you thought it did initially? Did you notice anything different than you remember from the first time you read it?

After you draft your writing assignment, put it away for at least a day. Then go back and read it to see if it really says what you intended. Have you thought of anything to add since you wrote the first draft? Rewrite your essay using your fresh perspective.

EDITING

When you work on the final draft of your essay, it is easy to make careless errors in punctuation and spelling. It is very important for you to correct these careless errors. This is especially easy if you write using a word processor or a computer because the changes are easy to make and you can just print a fresh copy instead of typing your paper over again. Always be sure to go over your writing assignment sentence by sentence to eliminate all errors before you turn it in.

The Dilemma of a "Mama Judge"

Hsieh Shu-fen

PREREADING

Judge Hsieh presides over a juvenile court in China. Before you read about the judge, take a few moments to write about the kind of judge you think you would be. Do you think you would be tough or compassionate? Would you be more tolerant of some crimes than of others? What kind of punishment would you give to first-time juvenile offenders? How would you treat the defendants who show up in your court time and time again?

DEFINING

dilemma (title)   a situation requiring a choice between undesirable alternatives
amiable (¶2)   friendly
defendants (¶2)   the ones who are accused
lenient (¶4)   merciful
branded (¶4)   permanently labeled
reconcile (¶5)   to settle
run afoul of (¶5)   get into trouble with

The Dilemma of a "Mama Judge"

Hsieh Shu-fen, tr. by Peter Eberly

1 At the mention of the Hsinchu juvenile reform facility, Judge Hsieh Chi-ta talks about "my children" in a tone of pity and affection, making one wonder, "Don't tell me she has sons of her own inside!"

2 Whenever she enters the facility, as soon as the watchman says, "Judge Hsieh is here!" a joyful chorus of voices greets her: "Hello Mama Hsieh!" "How are you, Mama Hsieh!" It turns out that all of the 50 or 60 young men and boys in the facility are her "sons." But as soon as kindly and amiable Mama Hsieh dons her black robes and takes her seat on the bench, she's strictly business, and defendants get a taste of her medicine.

3 "Every time I go to Mama Hsieh's court, I'm so scared my knees shake," a teenage delinquent says. He's been there three times, and each time she scolded him so badly "I got goose bumps, and my scalp went numb. And I'm one of the brave ones! Some guys burst out crying as soon as they enter the courtroom and see her expression."

4 Judge Hsieh chews out adults as well as children. She makes sure the parents are notified in juvenile cases because "when a child commits a crime, the parents have to bear part of the responsibility." When a junior high school student told her he gave up on himself and turned to drugs and stealing after his parents' divorce, she yelled at the father, "Now you see what kind of effect your divorce has had on your child!" Scolding aside, she is lenient in sentencing and tries to avoid sending youngsters to prison or reform school so they won't be branded with a criminal record when they're just starting out in life. A citizen who enjoys attending court and has seen more than a hundred criminal court cases wrote to Judge Hsieh praising her as "the judge with the strongest sense of justice and the most merciful heart."

5 With one third of the juvenile court cases in the Taoyuan, Hsinchu, and Maioli district handled by her, however, the question arises of just how appropriate it is that she build up such deep feelings for defendants. She herself is well aware that the roles of justice-dispensing "Judge Hsieh" and kind and loving "Mama Hsieh" are hard to reconcile, although the goal of each is to see that young people who have fallen into the toils of the law go straight. She wouldn't have to worry about the problem of role conflict if she were a lawyer specializing in juvenile cases, she says. But she's afraid that her leaving the court would remove a channel to assist young people who have run afoul of the law.

6 Her heart full of love and contradictions, Judge Hsieh continues to perform her dual roles with a mixture of difficult feelings. "Helping a child go straight is the same as winning one back," she says, looking out at a group of youths zipping past the court on motorcycles.

Hsieh Shu-fen, "The Dilemma of a 'Mama Judge,'" *Sinorama*, December 1990, pp. 40–41. Reprinted by permission of *Sinorama*.

Please note maps in appendix for references to places in this article.

READING

1. Why are defendants afraid of Mama Hsieh?

2. Why does Judge Hsieh find her job difficult? Why doesn't she leave her job?

THINKING

1. Judge Hsieh is generally lenient in her sentencing of youngsters. Do you think lenient sentences or harsh sentences are more effective when dealing with juvenile defendants? Why?

2. Judge Hsieh is harsh on parents because she feels they are responsible in part for the actions of their children. Do you feel that your parents or guardians are or were responsible for your actions? In what ways?

PREWRITING

Now that you have read this article, write about being a judge. Are your feelings toward juvenile offenders the same as they were before you read about Judge Hsieh? Why? Do you think you would be more strict or more lenient than Judge Hsieh? Why? How would you sentence the young junior high school student who "turned to drugs and stealing after his parents' divorce"?

WRITING

1. As a college student, you are exposed to the results of crime every day—crimes such as drunk driving, drug dealing, or shoplifting. Write a well-organized paragraph describing one crime and the effect of this crime on your life. Be sure to include what you think was the cause of the crime.

Homework (**2.**) Your best friend has been convicted of vehicular manslaughter because of a drunk driving accident. The judge is about to sentence your friend, and you have the opportunity to write to the judge expressing your feelings about the sentencing. You know that your friend has had a tough life because of his or her parents' divorce. Express to the judge whether you feel a lenient or strict sentence would be in your friend's best interest. Explain your reasoning to the judge.

REVISING

In "The Dilemma of a 'Mama Judge,'" whom do you think this article was written for? Do you think it was written for the parents of teenagers in the region of the juvenile facility? Was it for the teenagers? Was it for the general population of people who lived near the facility? Or was it for the population of China in general?

After you complete your writing assignment, reread what you have written, and identify who you feel you were writing to—your audience. Were you writing to other young adults in general, to people who commit crimes, to the authorities in general, or to a specific judge? Imagine rewriting the same assignment with a different audience in mind. How would this change the content of your writing? What would you include? In what order would you write your ideas? How would your word choice be affected? Before you start future writing assignments, be sure to identify who your audience will be so that you can direct your writing to a specific person or group.

EDITING

Remember that the subject of a sentence is always either singular or plural and that the **verb must agree with the subject**. When the subject is singular, the verb frequently has an *s* on the end. Look at this sentence:

> **Judge Hsieh** chews out adults as well as children.

The subject (in boldface) is singular, so the verb (underlined) has an *s* on the end. Now look at this sentence:

> **Some guys** burst out crying as soon as they enter.

The subject is plural, so the verb has no *s* on the end.

Now go back and look at your own writing. Identify the subject of each sentence you wrote, and note whether it is singular or plural. Then identify the verb in each sentence. Does it agree with the subject? If not, change it so that it does agree.

Grant Recipient Carol Swain

Nan McCoy

PREREADING

Before you read about the accomplishments of Carol Swain, write about your earliest memories of how you lived. When did you realize whether you were rich or poor or somewhere in between? What do you feel was the effect of your family's income on your childhood?

DEFINING

sharecropper (¶2)   a farmer who farms on someone else's land and shares his profits with the land's owner

crib death (¶2)   an infant's death from unknown causes

AAUW (¶3)   the American Association of University Women

doctoral dissertation (¶3)   a long, formal essay written to fulfill the requirements of an advanced graduate degree

meritorious (¶4)   deserving fame

impetus (¶5)   driving force

embark (¶5)   start out

fellowships (¶5)   money paid to support students in graduate study

tenure-track (¶5)   a job leading to a permanent position, usually in a college or university

Grant Recipient Carol Swain

Nan McCoy

1   "I always believed I was meant to have something better than what I had. I always felt that I didn't belong in my family, that there was some mistake. When I decided to go for my high school equivalency exam it was because I had come to believe in self-help, in positive thinking. For me it worked."

2   As the step-daughter of an impoverished Virginia sharecropper, Carol Swain grew up with 11 children in a four-room house without indoor plumbing. She dropped out of school in the ninth grade, left home at 13, married at 16, and—as the mother of two young sons—was divorced at 20. "Everything happened that year," Swain says. "I lost my third child, a daughter, from crib death. I was divorced. I passed the high school equivalency exam and entered junior college."

3   Today Carol Swain, Ph.D., teaches political science at Princeton University and, with the help of a special grant from the AAUW Educational Foundation, is writing a book about how black Americans are represented in the U.S. Congress, a subject she first researched for her doctoral dissertation. "I've found that, although blacks are discouraged by both black and white party leaders from running in areas with majority white populations, they can be elected," she says. "Democrat Alan Wheat, for one, of Kansas City, Missouri, won in a 1982 election in an 81 percent white district, and he's been reelected ever since. I've found too—although some blacks will never accept that whites can represent them—that a significant percentage of white Democrats represent black interests, that there's not much difference between the way they and black Democratic members of Congress vote on these matters, although there's a dramatic difference between Democrats and Republicans."

4   Dr. Swain's AAUW grant has not only given her the opportunity to travel to Washington for her research, but it has also enabled her to afford the assistance of a top-quality editor on the final draft of her book. The book will be published by Harvard University Press. In recommending her for funding, Fred Greenstein, chairman of the Department of Political Science at Princeton, referred to her as "an exceptionally meritorious person" with the potential for being "a real leader."

5   The self-help impetus that drove Carol Swain to embark on higher education sustained her through junior college, a master's degree, and a Ph.D., while she worked as a librarian and raised her sons. Her honors and awards include fellowships from the Ford Foundation and the National Science Foundation. She completed her Ph.D. in political science at the University of North Carolina at Chapel Hill in 1989 and spent the following year at Duke University, where she held a post-doctoral fellowship. In September 1990, she was appointed to a tenure-track position in the Department of Political Science at Princeton University. Her younger son is with her in Princeton; the older son graduated from high school and is in technical school in Virginia.

Nan McCoy, "Against All Odds: Grant Recipient Carol Swain," *AAUW Outlook,* Feb./March 1991, p. 25. Reprinted by permission of the AAUW publications office.

Please note maps in appendix for references to places in this article.

6   "This special [AAUW] grant provided an opportunity for a talented and competent faculty member to compete more strongly for a tenured faculty position at a major research institution," says Marion Kilson, chair of the American Fellowships Panel and dean of the College of Arts and Sciences at Salem State College in Massachusetts. Carol Swain's effort to achieve effective representation for all Americans has already gained national attention, and as a woman and as a scholar she exemplifies the highest aspirations of the Foundation's programs. AAUW salutes Carol Swain for her achievements and for beating all the odds.

READING

1. What were the circumstances of Swain's childhood and adolescence? Why did she go to school?

2. What does Swain teach? What are her special interests in her field?

THINKING

1. Swain seemed to have everything going against her, but she has been able to accomplish much. Why do you think a person in her circumstances could do so well? How do you think other people might respond to the circumstances she was in?

2. Swain is writing a book about black congressmen. Do you feel that a black congressman can fairly represent a largely nonblack population? Can a white congressman fairly represent a largely nonwhite population? Why or why not?

PREWRITING

Make a list of all of the reasons you came to college. Also, make a list of the people who are supporting you in any way to help you get through college. Then make a list of all the things you feel will be different in your life after you finish college.

WRITING

1. Your former high school counselor deals with many students who aren't planning on going to college. He has asked that you serve as a role model by writing an essay telling current high school students why you decided to go to college and what it's like there. Be sure to share about all the support you are getting while in school.

2. Write a one-page essay to yourself. In your essay talk about your career goal and your reasons for choosing it. Imagine what you will be doing with your career ten years from now and write about that. After you complete this assignment, seal the letter in an envelope, and on the envelope write the date it will be ten years from today. Store your letter in a safe place; then ten years from now open it to see how you have fulfilled your goals.

REVISING

Find the topic sentence in "Against All Odds." The topic sentence is the sentence that states what the article is about. Remember that the topic sentence is not always the first sentence of an article or an essay, and sometimes there is more than *one* topic sentence.

In your writing assignment, find the topic sentence. Experiment with the sentence structure or wording of the sentence to see how you can improve it. After you formulate the best possible topic sentence, go back and look at the rest of the essay to see what you need to do to change or improve it to better fit with your new topic sentence. Then revise your essay or letter.

EDITING

When you write contractions, be sure to always put the **apostrophe** in the right place. In a contraction the apostrophe always goes where the letter is missing.

Examples:

is not	isn't
should not	shouldn't
something is	something's
there is	there's

Be sure to only use an apostrophe with *it's* when you mean *it is*. *Its* is used only to show possession. For example:

Do you think it's going to rain? (contraction)

The book had its cover torn off. (possession)

Go back through your writing assignment to see if you have used any contractions. If you have, be sure they are written correctly.

Judy Baca's Art for Peace

Anne Estrada

PREREADING

Judy Baca is an artist who paints murals in public places. Write about how you feel about art. What kinds of art do you like? Why? Have you ever been to an art gallery? How many artist's names can you think of? Have you ever painted a picture?

DEFINING

muralist (¶1)   an artist who paints very large paintings, frequently on walls

empowerment (¶1)   giving power to

vehicle (¶2)   means, way of communication

philosophical (¶3)   thoughtful

nurtured (¶3)   educated, supported

condescending (¶3)   lowering oneself

oppressor (¶3)   person who uses power cruelly and unjustly

interdependence (¶4)   mutual relying on each other

adversity (¶5)   hardship, affliction

Judy Baca's Art for Peace
Anne Estrada

1   Now known as a muralist, activist, and spokesperson for the Hispanic community, as well as a professor at the University of California in Irvine, Judy Baca could not speak English when she entered public school in East Los Angeles in the '50s. But she could paint, and so began the power of her art to communicate what sometimes can't be said in words. Baca recalls her role in the beginning of the Chicano Mural Movement when she was searching for a way to express her own experience as a Hispanic American artist. Greatly influenced by the Mexican muralists, Baca discovered a means of community empowerment.

2   Her first mural projects began when she was working for the city of Los Angeles teaching art classes. During her lunch breaks, she spent time in the parks getting to know some of the kids who hung out there. As she observed the graffiti, the tattoos, and the decorated cars, she recognized a visual language used by these teenagers to express who they are and how they feel about their lives. Painting walls became a vehicle of communication as she brought them together to negotiate treaties in order to make it possible for the kids to cross rival gang territory and reach the mural site safely. This work led to the project she is best known for, the "Great Wall of Los Angeles," which she began in 1976. Located in the San Fernando Valley, the "Great Wall" is a half mile long and depicts scenes from the history of California. The muralists were young people from various ethnic communities in Los Angeles, some of whom were recruited when the court offered the choice of mural painting over reform school. The project proved to be an extraordinary educational experience for all those involved. In 1976 Baca founded her own nonprofit organization, Social and Public Art Resource Center (SPARC), as a means of supporting community art projects.

3   Where has Judy Baca found the will to overcome obstacles and accomplish her goals? She believes that her greatest source of strength comes from her early years, when she learned the meaning of human pride and dignity. She was raised by her grandmother because her single mother had to work long hours to support her family. "I was surrounded by extraordinary women," she remembers. Through her grandmother, Baca learned how to approach life in a philosophical manner. Baca remembers an experience she had with her grandmother. At the store, her grandmother realized that she had been given incorrect change and asked Judy to tell the cashier that he had made a mistake. Apparently, he had been trying to cheat them because they couldn't speak English well, and he became angry and threw the coins down. Although Baca couldn't understand why the man acted this way, she noticed a tattoo across his wrist that was given to prisoners in Nazi concentration camps. Her grandmother said, "You shouldn't be angry with him because people have hurt him. Every time you see that tattoo, you must remember what

Anne Estrada, "Judy Baca's Art for Peace," *Hispanic* magazine, May 1991. Reprinted with permission from *Hispanic* magazine.

Please note maps in appendix for references to places in this article.

happened to those people." These early lessons nurtured the genuine compassion that Baca now calls upon when she works with those who might otherwise be written off as hopeless. She is able to work with them in a way that is not condescending, but empowering. She also has the insight needed to find compassion for the oppressor, as well as the oppressed. "When people are treated badly, they treat other people badly," she says.

4   Baca has now moved from interracial to international relations with her current project, "World Wall: A Vision of a Future Without Fear." The "World Wall," when completed, will consist of seven portable panels with artwork on both sides, each measuring 10 by 30 feet, assembled into an octagon 80 to 100 feet in diameter. The images depict the material and spiritual transformations that must occur before world peace can be achieved. Baca traveled to Finland and the Soviet Union, where artists in those countries created their own murals to add to the series. Among the themes that emerge are the elimination of racism and sexism, the creation of positive interdependence between countries, and the need for people of all backgrounds to work together for world harmony. The "World Wall" now consists of six works and is expected to grow as Baca travels over the next few years. The completed panels were on view in Los Angeles at Plaza de la Raza on April 6 and 7 and will travel to the Smithsonian Institute in Washington, D.C. in July.

5   Judy Baca claims that adversity breeds a certain kind of strength. Nourished by this strength, her artistic vision has reached out to inspire those around her.

READING

1. Who raised Baca? What effect did her upbringing have on her life?

2. What was Baca doing for an occupation when she first started her mural project? Why did she start painting murals?

THINKING

1. Judy Baca believes: "When people are treated badly, they treat other people badly." What do you think about this philosophy? Do you think people should try to understand both sides of a problem, or do you think one side of a problem is usually superior?

2. Since Baca worked for the city of Los Angeles, she was able to have juvenile offenders sentenced to work on painting a mural rather than going to reform school. How would painting a mural be a substitute for reform school? What do you think the offenders learned from working on the painting?

PREWRITING

Make a list of the things that you like to do and the ways you feel you express yourself by doing these things.

WRITING

1. Write an essay with your city council as an audience. Explain why you feel graffiti is an acceptable means of expression or a blight on a neighborhood. Be sure to fully explain why you feel that it should be supported and encouraged or why it should be eliminated with harsh punishment going to the perpetrators.

2. Baca noticed that Los Angeles teenagers were expressing themselves through art when she saw their tattoos, decorated cars, and graffiti. We all express ourselves in different ways. Write an essay for your classmates explaining to them the way you like to express yourself the most, and why this is your favorite form of expression. Some examples of how people express themselves could be how they dress, what kind of music they listen to, the way they dance, or the kind of car they drive.

REVISING

Anne Estrada uses one long specific example taken from Judy Baca's childhood. She tells about how her grandmother taught her compassion by her actions toward a dishonest Jewish storekeeper who had been a victim of a Nazi concentration camp. Sometimes the story of one fully developed example can really enhance your writing.

Either of your writing assignments could be improved by a well-developed example. Look at your assignment to see if you have already used a good example. If you haven't, try adding a specific example that will make the meaning of what you wrote more clear.

EDITING

Try not to use too many **pronouns** in your writing. When you do use pronouns, make sure they agree with their antecedents. An antecedent is the noun before the pronoun that the pronoun is renaming. For example:

Judy Baca could not speak English when *she* entered public school.

In this case *Judy Baca* is the antecedent to the pronoun *she*.

Baca discovered a means of community empowerment. Her first mural projects began when she was working for the city of Los Angeles.

In this case *Baca* is the antecedent for *her* and *she*, even though it is in the next sentence because *Baca* is the closest logical antecedent.

She cites as an example . . .

In this case *she* is a pronoun without a clear antecedent because this is the first sentence in a paragraph. Always be sure that you have a clear antecedent for every pronoun that you use. Who is *she?*

Go through your writing assignment and identify all of your pronouns. After you identify all your pronouns, see if each one has a clear antecedent.

Also, be sure to avoid sexism in your writing. In the past you were probably taught to always use *he* or male pronouns when you weren't sure of gender. Now it is desirable to avoid the standard use of the male reference. A way that you can easily accomplish this is to use plural pronouns whenever it is logical to do so, but in order to use a plural pronoun, you must have a plural antecedent—that is, the word that the pronoun is referring to. For example:

A *person* should always strive to do *his or her* best.

or

People should always try to do *their* best.

Other ways to avoid sexism in language are to use *she or he* instead of always *he or she.* Some professional writers will use *she* and *her* in one chapter, then *he* and *him* in the next. Some writers even combine both words by using *s/he.* Whichever method you choose, be sure to use it consistently.

Go back through your assignment and find all of your pronouns. Be sure that they agree in number with their antecedents, and also be sure that, if they are singular, they aren't just male.

Hout Seng's Long March

Stanley W. Cloud

PREREADING

The communist rebels were at war in the streets outside of Hout Seng's apartment. Americans tend to think that war won't happen in America. Imagine that a war is taking place outside your front door. Write about what you think you would do. How would you feel? Why do you think you would feel this way?

DEFINING

Khmer Rouge (¶1)   Cambodian rebel and guerrilla forces

Phnom Penh (¶1)   a city in Cambodia

AK-47s (¶1)   automatic rifles

summarily (¶2)   promptly, quickly

cesspools (¶2)   filthy places

macadam (¶4)   broken stone used to create a roadway

Hout Seng's Long March

Stanley W. Cloud

1   The first time Hout Seng saw the Khmer Rouge up close, they were running past his ground-floor apartment on the southern outskirts of Phnom Penh. They

Stanley W. Cloud, "Hout Seng's Long March," *Time,* April 30, 1990. Copyright 1990 The Time Inc. Magazine Company. Reprinted by permission.

Please note maps in appendix for references to places in this article.

wore black pajamas and sandals made of tires, and had branches tied to their backs as camouflage. All carried AK-47s. It was the morning of April 17, 1975. After five years of war, the Communist rebels were on the brink of victory. As the government's remaining defenses collapsed, more and more guerrillas poured past Seng's residence into the capital. By midafternoon the war was over, and people were celebrating in the streets.

2　　For thousands, that celebration may have been the last happy moment of their lives. For millions, including Seng and his family, it marked the beginning of a nightmare of death and suffering. Before nightfall on that first day, the Khmer Rouge were rounding up "traitors" (those who had served in the previous government) and "collaborators" (professionals, people who spoke foreign languages, teachers, and the like). Most were summarily executed or tortured to death. By the next morning, the Communist government had begun the complete evacuation of the cities, which Cambodia's new rulers regarded as cesspools of bourgeois corruption. Nearly all Cambodians—men, women, and children—would be herded into slave-labor communes.

3　　Seng, a driver for the TIME correspondents who covered the Cambodian war, soon grasped the dimension of the crisis. The day before the final assault on the capital, with rockets landing less than a block from his apartment, Seng and his stroke-crippled wife asked a relative to take their two boys and two girls to a nearby hospital, thinking they might be safer there. The boys, Neang, 14, and Aun, 6, returned home later that afternoon as the rocket attacks subsided. But the two frightened daughters, Seng Ly, 9, and Theary, 12, stayed put. When their father went to pick them up two days later, they were gone, swept up in the first stage of the forced evacuation.

4　　Soon, he and the remainder of the family were part of the mass exodus. Carrying only a little rice and some blankets, they joined thousands of others on foot or bicycle heading south along the Basak River. No one knew where they were marching or why. The troops who rounded them up said only that they would not be gone long from Phnom Penh. At night they slept beside the road. After a few days, the flip-flops Seng and his family were wearing disintegrated, and they had no choice but to go barefoot on the road's blistering macadam. Frequently, Seng would ask if anyone had seen his missing daughters. No one had.

5　　About 35 miles south of Phnom Penh, the great throng ground to a temporary and unexplained halt, like a train whose engine had broken down. For several months, the Khmer Rouge did not seem to know what to do next. Some of the evacuees grew ill and died. Others wandered away to unknown fates. Most were assigned to villages where they worked in return for food rations.

6　　Eventually, Seng and his family were sent to a rice-producing commune in the Kampong Cham area of eastern Cambodia. There, father and sons labored twelve hours a day and more in the paddies, although Seng's wife was too weak to work. At that, they were lucky: in the same commune, perhaps a third of the 3,000 workers died of disease, starvation, and overwork, or were executed by their Khmer Rouge overlords.

7　　After the Vietnamese army ousted the Pol Pot regime in January 1979, Seng gathered up his family. He joined with the family of a recently widowed woman named Ol Sam, whom he would later marry, plus the orphaned daughter of a mutual friend, and set out to escape from Cambodia. Largely on foot, with occasional hitched rides on oxcarts and trucks, the group made its way to the northwest, a distance of some 250 miles. Along the way, Seng's wife died. Finally, in May—more than four years after he got his first close look at a Khmer Rouge guerrilla—Seng and his ragtag, nearly starved company of survivors crossed into Thailand. Today they live in the Washington, D.C. area, where Seng is a successful taxi driver.

8   His family's saga does not end there. Not long ago, Seng received news from Cambodia about his daughters: in 1975 they had been sent to a work camp in the western province of Battambang and assigned to dig irrigation ditches. Seng Ly died of malaria and malnutrition. She was ten years old. But Theary somehow survived. Married and the mother of three small children, she was reunited last month in Phnom Penh with her brother Neang. There were tears at the reunion—and many overdue smiles.

READING

1. Where did Hout Seng march from? Why was he marching?

2. Where did Hout Seng march to? What happened to his family?

THINKING

1. Hout Seng was separated from part of his family, and his wife died as they were marching. How do you think it would feel to have no choice but to have your family taken away? Many people were dying on this march. What do you think it would be like to have the people walking with you just die? What would you do?

2. Refugees frequently immigrate to America. What is your attitude toward these people? Have you ever become frustrated when someone has a hard time understanding you? Imagine going through what Hout Seng went through and then becoming a cab driver in a big city where everybody is in a hurry. How would you manage?

PREWRITING

Write a list of all the things that you think a family could possibly need if they suddenly arrived in America without anything but the clothes on their backs. Consider both material and emotional needs.

WRITING

1. You have been asked to sponsor a Vietnamese family when they arrive in America. You must write a response telling the placement officials why you will or will not be a sponsor for this family. Do you feel that you have something to offer this family to help them get a new start in life?

2. You are a member of a citizen's action committee working to be sure that the immigrants in your area have adequate food, clothing, shelter, and wages. Your responsibility is to write a persuasive news release, at least a page long, convincing the citizens in your community of the committee's need for assistance in helping these people. Be sure to include the kinds of help these people need.

REVISING

Stanley W. Cloud uses a variety of sentence structures when he is writing about Hout Seng. Each sentence has the necessary punctuation to make the sentence clear.

When you write a draft of an essay, it is often difficult to see punctuation and spelling errors if you read over the paper all at once. Write each sentence of your paper on a three-by-five-inch card. Draw a star on the card that contains your topic sentence. Now look at each card and see if there are any sentence errors you need to correct. Then look at each sentence and see if you have them placed in the most effective order; feel free to change the order of the cards. You may want to add cards with more information to make your ideas clearer. Check each sentence you have written to see that you have expressed your ideas clearly. To do this, read each sentence out loud to be sure it makes sense, or you might have a friend read each sentence to you. The key here is to look at each sentence individually to be sure that it says what you really want to convey.

After you finish experimenting with the cards, recopy your paper, being sure to include your improvements.

EDITING

You can add information to a sentence (or independent clause) by **adding a phrase** before your main clause starts. When you do this, you always have to include a comma after your introductory phrase.

Examples:
> *For thousands,* that celebration may have been the last happy moments of their lives.

For thousands is an introductory phrase. This phrase is followed by a comma, then the main clause.

> *Along the way,* Seng's wife died.

Along the way is an introductory phrase, also followed by a comma, then the main clause.

Now check through your writing assignment to be sure that you have included all necessary commas after introductory phrases.

A Good Fight

June Jordon

PREREADING

June Jordan writes about her summer experiences as a child at camp. How did you spend your summers as a child? Who did you spend them with? Do you think of things differently now than you did when you were a child? Has your attitude toward yourself and toward life in general changed since you've grown older?

DEFINING

> **notorious (¶3)**   known widely and regarded unfavorably
>
> **idyllic (¶4)**   having a natural charm
>
> **laconically (¶9)**   swiftly and silently
>
> **incendiary (¶30)**   capable of causing a fire
>
> **meridian (¶33)**   halfway point
>
> **misogyny (¶37)**   hatred of women
>
> **homophobia (¶37)**   hatred of homosexuals

A Good Fight
June Jordan

1   I was nine years old at Robin Hood Camp for Girls. Two and a half hours north of Brooklyn, by bus, and mountains and woods and lakes suddenly came together as a real-world situation for me.

2   I was short for my age, and very young.

3   It never seemed odd to me that our camp boasted the name of a rather notorious male hero.

4   I never wondered about the absolute difference between my regular concrete street life in Bedford Stuyvesant and the idyllic circumstance of our summertime cabins and dirt trails and huge, hearty, community meals on the outside deck of the rec hall.

5   I don't remember puzzling over my experience of seasonal integration, which meant that ten months of the year I lived and played in an entirely black universe, and then for eight weeks I became a member of a minority of three or four black girls in a white vacationland of seventy-five to eighty other kids coming from neighborhoods and schools quite different from my own.

6   I was nine years old and free! I was far away from home, and I was hellbent on having a great time. We played softball and we learned archery and we went on wilderness hikes, overnight, and we burned our tongues on hot chocolate in tin cups and we rode horses, English saddle, and we swam and we made things for our parents in arts & crafts.

7   I was nine years old and some of the counselors gave me *The Razor's Edge* and *Tender Is the Night* to read after lights out and some of them tried to take away what they called "that filthy rabbit's foot" that my best friend, Jodi, gave me to wear for good luck.

8   And we sat around campfires and sang under the stars. But best of all, we played softball and I supposed that when I grew up I'd probably become a professional shortstop for some terrific softball team, and then, maybe, after lights out, I'd write my own *Tender Is the Night,* or *Time Must Have a Stop,* or *Magic Mountain.*

9   Those were my plans. But, in fact, the most exciting thing that happened was that Jodi and I became Blood Brothers. Of course, it never occurred to us that maybe we should become Blood Sisters: We were thinking of David and Jonathan when we each cut the inside of our wrists with a penknife and mingled blood to seal our pact of eternal friendship. Not satisfied with that, we formed an elite club, The Dare Devils, and we hammered overlapping capital D's into our silver bracelets that we now could hardly wait to finish in arts & crafts where, formerly, we laconically wove lanyards or beaded belts or painted jewelry boxes for the "old folks" back home.

10   And, having mingled our blood, and, having hammered our bracelets into distinctive emblems of our bond, our tribe of Dare Devils leaped across big splits in the earth or we set loose the rowboats in the darkness or we swam across the lake,

June Jordan, "A Good Fight," The Progressive, December 1993, Vol. 37, No. 12, pp. 16–17.

Please note maps in appendix for references to places in this article.

secretly, by moonlight, or we raced each other, on horseback and on foot, and we looked for the highest trees to climb and we played out our days with utmost heart and utmost hilarity and we—nine- and ten-year-old little girls—thought we were young gods fully blessed by all of our lives full of energy and love and an insatiable appetite for danger. We were daredevils loose on a beautiful planet. We were nine- and ten-year-old little girls and we thought we were free.

11   Toward the end of that summer, we had a final campfire down by the boats, and the song we sang was, "For all we know—we may never meet again—before you go—make this moment sweet again." We were so young. We could tell that was supposed to be a sad song but we felt no sadness ourselves. We tried not to giggle. We tried to sit in sadness out of respect for the grownups sprinkled among us. And I remember wondering if I would sometimes feel sadness, too, when I got old enough to become a counselor.

12   But I wasn't sure. Back then I could not imagine the sadness reserved for girls, everywhere.

13   I would have been amazed by any societal surprise at our Dare Devil/Blood Brother activities.

14   I would have been dumbfounded to hear that every fifteen seconds a woman is battered in the United States.

15   I would never have believed that people kill babies if they're female.

16   Or that white people despise black people.

17   Or that half of all black mothers have no or inadequate prenatal care.

18   Or that one out of every eight women in the United States has breast cancer and that before this decade is out, 500,000 American women will die of breast cancer.

19   Or that only 5 per cent of the money spent for cancer research is spent on finding a cure for breast cancer.

20   Back then, my ideas of daredeviltry did not conjure up the taking of my black body into a roadside luncheonette for a forbidden cup of coffee.

21   I never would have imagined that my loving a white man or that my loving any woman or that my raising my son by my own wits would constitute high risk and certain jeopardy.

22   And I never would have supposed that the biblical story of Ruth and Naomi held as much heroism, or more, inside its humble womanly narrative as the story of David and Jonathan.

23   And I would have laughed at anybody who said that someday I'd have breast cancer and that, even after going through a mastectomy, I'd have only a 40 per cent chance of survival.

24   Then, last year, one early morning, there was my friend, Dr. Alan Steinbach, bending over me in the recovery room at Alta Bates Hospital, and Alan was saying, "There's bad news!"

25   I thought, immediately, that he must mean something godawful had happened to my son, or to one of my friends, but he meant there was bad news for me. They'd performed a biopsy and found an enormous amount of cancer in my right breast.

26   And so I became one of the millions of American women who must redefine courage and who must redefine the meaning of heroic friendship if we will survive.

27   And my son and my lover and my friends gathered around like Dare Devils daring themselves and their devotion and their walking of my dog and their changing of the dressing and their seamless and hilarious system of around-the-clock support to save my morale and to save my life.

28   And it was not easy. And it was not brief. And it is not over.

29   In between surgery number three and number four, I wrote this poem:

30   The breath continues but the breathing hurts
      Is this the way death wins its way
      against all longing
      and incendiary thrust from grief?
      Head falls
      Hands crawl
      and pain becomes the only keeper
      of my time

31   I am not held
      I do not hold
      And touch degenerates into new
      agony

32   I feel
      the healing of cut muscle/
      broken nerves
      as I return to hot and cold
      sensations
      of a body tortured by the flight
      of feeling/normal
      registrations of repulsion
      or delight

33   On this meridian of failure or recovery
      I move
      or stop respectful
      of each day
      but silent now
      and slow

34   I swear to you I never ever expected to write anything like that, my whole life, but I had to try to tell that truth.

35   The Women's Cancer Resource Center of Berkeley and the National Black Women's Health Network and Dr. Craig Henderson and Dr. Susan Love and Dr. Denise Rogers and Christopher and Angela and Adrienne and Dianne and Stephanie and Martha and Haruko and Amy and Sara and Pratibha and Lauren

and Roberta and Camille and my colleagues and students at school and the neighbors next door and Amigo, the Airedale who lives with me—they dared me to make this cancer thing into a fight: They dared me to practice trying to lift my arm three or four inches away from my side. They dared me to go ahead and scream and cry but not to die. And so I did not die. But I have faced death. And I know death now.

36   And in the mornings when I walk out into the garden and I see the ninety-seven-year-old willow tree and the jasmine blooming aromatic and the honeysuckle bulging into the air and Amigo gulping at a bumblebee and a stray bluebird lifting itself in flight above the roof of my little house, I am happy beyond belief.

37   And when I may join with men and women to end the disease of breast cancer and the disease of race hatred and the disease of misogyny and the disease of homophobia and the disease of not caring about the victims of ethnic cleansing and the victims of our malignant neglect, I am happy beyond belief.

38   Because this is a good fight. It feels good to me. And, yes, now I know about sadness but I do not live there, in sadness.

39   And I am happy beyond belief to be here and to join with you to make things better.

READING

1. How does June Jordon experience "seasonal integration"?

2. Only five percent of cancer research money is spent on what kind of cancer research?

THINKING

1. June Jordan didn't seem to recognize prejudice and discrimination when she was at camp, and she was shocked and dismayed to discover these things existed as she grew older. Do you feel that you are prejudiced against anyone? Why or why not? What do you feel influences you in your feelings about other races and cultured? Have your feelings changed as you matured?

2. Having a life threatening illness caused June Jordan to reexamine her life. If you discovered you have a terminal illness, what would you do? Who would you turn to? How would you spend the rest of your life?

PREWRITING

Do two clustering exercises. For the first one, put breast cancer in the middle circle and see how many ideas you can develop. For the second one, put either women's issues or racial issues in the middle, and see how many issues you can come up with and how many ideas you can discover about the issues. To write your essay, choose the topic you were able to generate the most ideas for.

WRITING

1. The number of women diagnosed with breast cancer has been rapidly increasing, while money for research to find cures or preventive measures for breast cancer in particular is low. You have the opportunity to work on a campaign to increase breast cancer awareness and to solicit funds for research. Write an article for your local newspaper that would educate people about breast cancer while encouraging them to support research. The library or your student health center should have materials to help you research the facts for this article.

2. June Jordan is dismayed at the harsh realities of the issues women face. Choose one of the issues that she mentions in the article or a woman's issue or racial issue that you are more familiar with, and write an essay to share with your classmates explaining this issue, what you know about it, and what you feel should be done about it. Be sure to base your argument on facts.

REVISING

"A Good Fight" is written in narration form, which is basically telling a story. Stories are usually told in chronological order—first this happened, then that happened, finally this happened. The more specific details and examples you use in a narration, the better it will be. When writing a narration, your story will be more vivid if you show rather than tell your ideas.

June Jordan started by telling about a significant childhood event. Then she told about how her perceptions changed as an adult. Next she told about the breast cancer she currently faces.

Try having someone you know who is familiar with the subject you are writing about read a draft of one of your writing assignments. Did this person agree with what you said? Why or why not? What details can you find out from this person that maybe you didn't think about while writing your first draft? Revise your writing assignment using the new information that you discovered.

EDITING

Hyphens (-) can be used to join two words to form a single adjective. Remember that an adjective is a word that is used to modify a noun or pronoun. The two words must work together to be correctly joined by a hyphen. For example, you could say **real-world situation,** but you probably wouldn't say **real situation** or **world situation** and mean the same thing. You could say **around-the-clock support,** but you probably wouldn't say **around support,** or **the support,** or **clock support.** Go through your writing assignment to see if you have used any two or more adjectives together to modify a noun. Do they need a hyphen? Try adding hyphenated adjectives to modify some nouns in your assignment.

The use of a hyphen (-) to indicate that a word will be continued on the next line cannot be avoided in some of the material you read. In a newspaper article, for instance, sometimes the columns are so narrow that a word on practically every line needs hyphenation, but you can make your own personal writing much easier to read if you avoid the use of the hyphen for this purpose. Go back through your paper and eliminate any hyphens you may have used. When you type or hand write your paper, you should always end each line with a whole word.

A Journey of Imagination

Lorenzo Chavez

PREREADING

As a young girl Nelida Pinon thought that when writers wrote books, they must have experienced everything that they wrote about before they could write. Take a few moments to explore your thoughts about this notion. Did you ever feel this way? How do you think that people can write about something they have never experienced?

DEFINING

precocious (¶1)   intellectually advanced

enthralled (¶1)   fascinated

parody (¶4)   an imitation of a serious literary or musical work done in a humorous manner

melancholic (¶4)   sad and depressing

outmaneuver (¶5)   outwit, to be more effective than

ideological (¶5)   ideal view or perception

ideologue (¶5)   one who studies ideas

idiosyncrasies (¶5)   personal peculiarities

subtly (¶6)   gently, lightly

ironic (¶6)   meaning the opposite of what is expressed

pessimistic (¶6)   looking at the bad side

insatiable (¶7)   unable to get enough of

induction (¶9)   introduction, initiation

A Journey of Imagination

Lorenzo Chavez

encantada

1   "*Conta mais* . . . Tell me more," implored a very precocious Nelida Pinon, a child enthralled by the adventurous tall tales told to her by the "old men" of Galicia during her family's trips to Spain. Those stories not only sparked a young girl's imagination but also helped lay the foundation for Pinon's writing career, says the Brazilian novelist.

2   "I was a very curious child. They told me more stories because I was an attentive listener. I learned of the Galician imagination, which is the imagination of the Celtic tall tales. That has been one of the major points in my creative vision of the world."

3   Pinon's curiosity and imagination have helped make her one of Brazil's best known women novelists and a highly sought out Latin American writer among universities, international literary congresses, and panels. A native of Rio de Janeiro, Pinon's roots lie in Galicia, the birthplace of both her Spanish parents. As the University of Miami's Henry King Stanford Distinguished Professor, she has joined UM's Department of Foreign Languages and Literatures to teach several classes every semester. The post was held previously by Isaac Bashevis Singer, winner of the 1978 Nobel Prize for literature.

4   Although her works have been translated into several languages, she is less well known in this country than other Latin American authors because, except for some short stories and *The Republic of Dreams* (Knopf, 1989), few have been translated into English. Pinon is excited about her eighth novel, *Caetana's Sweet Song,* a serial romance parody about a younger theatrical actress/singer in a small Brazilian town. *Caetana* will be published next spring by Knopf with a translation by Helen Lane. "It's a story about love and adventure as well as a story about the arts, theater, illusions, and the imagination," says Pinon. "It's profoundly melancholic."

5   *The Republic of Dreams* covers 20th century Brazilian politics through the eyes of a Spanish immigrant family. In describing the novel's complexity, Pinon noted that a writer must "outmaneuver reality" whenever telling a story from several points of view. "I treat my characters as if I didn't have any ideological view," she says. "I don't want to be an ideologue. Thus, I have to capture all of the characters' prejudices and idiosyncrasies. As writers, we have the responsibility of making a deep commitment to reflect all of the instances of reality or include all the layers

Lorenzo Chavez, "A Journey of Imagination," The Times of the Americas, June 12, 1991. Reprinted by permission of The Times of the Americas.

Please note maps in appendix for references to places in this article.

of reality in fiction. In one form or another, the characters in a novel become archetypes."

6   Her favorite U.S. authors are William Faulkner—for his narrative technique—and Mark Twain—"for his imagination, irony, and sense of adventure." Perhaps the greatest influences on her literary development were the subtly ironic and pessimistic works of Machado de Assis, considered Brazil's greatest writer. "He is among the best 19th century novelists in the world," she says. "I place him with (Gustave) Flaubert. He's a genius."

7   Among the factors that led to Pinon's writing career were her parents' free-rein in her pursuits and activities and an insatiable zest for reading at an early age. "When I was a little girl about eight years old, I adored books and always told people that I wanted to be a writer," she says. "I thought that it must be very fascinating because the writer must have lived all of these adventures he had written about. At that time I didn't know that all of it had been invented."

8   Latin American writers have a strong tradition of being intimately involved in the politics of their native countries, and, like Gabriel Garcia Marquez, of starting off as journalists. "In countries where people feel they have no voice," she says, "the people borrow the voice of writers, and the writer speaks for them."

9   Pinon has worked in Rio as a journalist and as vice chair of Brazil's Writers' Union in the late 1970s she fought for "redemocratization" of the country, then under military rule. Her teaching career began at the Faculdade de Letras da Universidade do Rio de Janeiro, and prior to her position at the University of Miami, she lectured at Columbia and Johns Hopkins universities. Among her greatest honors was induction into the exclusive Academia Brasileira de Letras in 1989.

10   Although she travels constantly throughout the year, Pinon lives in Rio, where the country's stricken economy has not left her unaffected. "No one can say what is going to happen," she says. "But I'm an optimist. You should always confront reality and try to improve it." She travels to Europe and Washington, D.C. this fall before returning to Miami in January.

11   "A writer does not have the luxury of deciding what is beautiful and what is not or what is suitable or unsuitable for literature," she says. "Everything is intertwined. One of my major attractions to literature is that it transports me and enables me to live everyone's life."

READING

    1. Where has Nelida Pinon worked? What honors has she received?

    2. What inspired Pinon to be a writer? What kind of writing does she do?

THINKING

    1. Pinon says, "Literature transports me and enables me to live everyone's life." What do you suppose she means by this comment? What does literature do for you? If you haven't read much literature, what form of entertainment affects you? How?

2. In many countries of the world, the political leadership is so powerful that the voice of the people cannot be heard. Pinon feels that in cases like these, the writers in those cultures can act as the voice of the people. Do you think that this is true? Can you think of such a situation where a writer could be the voice for your culture?

PREWRITING

Write about different events that you have witnessed along with other people. Think of things like weddings, accidents, trials, fights, or family dinners. List the different people who witnessed these events with you. How would the observation of these people differ from your observation?

WRITING

1. Nelida Pinon likes to write stories in which she tells about the same event from several different points of view. She could, for example, describe a crime from the point of view of the victim, the alleged criminal, and a witness. Write a story in which you describe the same event from three different points of view. You can use any event and have any three different witnesses that you can imagine.

In class **2.** When Pinon writes, she feels that "you should always confront reality and try to improve it." Think about one thing that is a reality about yourself that you would like to improve, and write a resolution for yourself with a plan on how you can make that change.

REVISING

Writing assignment 1 asks for you to write from different **points of view.** In "A Journey of Imagination," Lorenzo Chavez uses two different points of view: one voice for his own thoughts and another voice for Nelida Pinon. He speaks in third person when he is writing, using pronouns such as *he, she, it,* and *they.* When he is quoting Pinon, her pronouns are all first person, such as *I* or *we.* The point of view also reflects the time that the writing is set. This article is written in the present, using verbs like *are, says, has,* and *is.* He does refer to past events to give examples, using verbs like *thought, was, wanted,* and *had written.* The third item that is reflected in the point of view is the **tone.** The tone indicates the writer's attitude toward the subject, which may be formal or informal, or it may directly address the reader or remain distant. Chavez uses a somewhat casual, informative tone.

Read through your writing assignment and identify the point of view that you are writing from. See if you need to make any changes to make it consistent in pronoun reference, tense, and tone.

EDITING

When writing a series of words in a list or when joining two phrases, all items, whether they are words, phrases, or clauses, should be **parallel**, which means they should be in the same grammatical form.

Example:

"Pinon's curiosity and imagination have helped make her one of Brazil's best known women novelists and a highly sought out Latin American Writer among *universities, international literary congresses,* and *panels*." (¶3)

Notice that each element of this list describes a form of an organization and each element is plural.

Example:

"As writers, we have the responsibility of making a deep commitment to *reflect all of the instances of reality* or *include all the layers of reality* in fiction." (¶5)

In this sentence, you can see two phrases written in the same form.

Check your writing assignment to be sure that you have used parallel structure whenever needed.

Antonia Hernández

Liza Gross

PREREADING

Antonia Hernández is a lawyer who works for the Mexican American Legal Defense and Educational Fund. She finds it tiring and lonely to work with the leadership of her organization because they are mostly male. Do you think you would have problems working with people mostly of the opposite sex? Why or why not? Have you had the opportunity to work with people of other cultures, or have you mostly been around people from your own culture? Which do you prefer? Why?

DEFINING

kindle (¶1)   to ignite or excite

quest (¶1)   journey or search

precedent (¶2)   example

redistricting (¶2)   the rearrangement of areas on a map that determines voter representation

affirmative action (¶2)   a policy for the correction of past discrimination

helm (¶3)   lead or head

transcend (¶3)   rise above

litigious (¶4)   bringing of lawsuits

advocates (¶4)   strongly recommends

sanctions (¶5)   authorizations

coalition (¶6)   a group brought together for a specific purpose

Pollyanna (¶7)   a very optimistic person

coexistence (¶8)   getting along together

arduous (¶9)   difficult to do

 predominantly (¶10)   mostly

Antonia Hernández

Liza Gross

1   She didn't start the fire, but she keeps the flame well stoked and makes it her business to kindle sparks nationwide in her quest to advance the cause of Hispanics in the United States.

2   Antonia Hernández, 42, President and General Counsel of the Mexican American Legal Defense and Educational Fund since 1985, wants her community to be aware of these blazes of change. "We are the Hispanic community's law firm," she explains. And she has been keeping the law firm plenty busy, making MALDEF instrumental in precedent-setting cases, ranging from redistricting cases, such as the one against the County of Los Angeles, to affirmative action suits, such as the one against the HEB supermarket chain in Texas, or the Ralph supermarket chain in California.

3   "MALDEF has matured as an institution. Every person who heads [it] gives it his or her flavor. My flavor has been taking the helm of an organization and helping it into institutional maturity. My strong point is that, having lived in Washington, I am familiar with the powers that be. Living on the East Coast has helped me transcend the regional aspect of the organization by mixing with Puerto Ricans, Cubans, and other groups, and we have reached out to have a closer connection with community-based organizations."

4   Despite the litigious nature of MALDEF's work, Hernández advocates cooperation as a working approach. "I believe in strong cooperation with civil rights organizations to look for what we have in common. If we allow ourselves to be sucked into believing we should fight over crumbs, we will. We should not let the ones in power convince us of that. Our gains can't be at the expense of Blacks, and vice versa."

5   She cites as an example the flap with the Leadership Conference on Civil Rights. In May, the conference failed to support repeal of the immigration law's employers' sanctions because labor—a major component of the organization—did not support repeal. Several Hispanic organizations, including MALDEF, threat-

Liza Gross, "Antonia Hernández: MALDEF's Legal Eagle," *Hispanic,* December 1990, pp. 17–18. Reprinted with permission from *Hispanic* magazine.

Please note maps in appendix for references to places in this article.

ened to pull out of the coalition. A compromise at the eleventh hour prevented the pullout. Hernández does not believe the action meant lack of a willingness to cooperate on the part of Hispanic organizations. On the contrary.

6   "After painful soul searching we came back to the table and said, 'We must act as a coalition.' We can't have the coalition held hostage by one organization [the AFL-CIO]. We showed them our position." The Hispanic groups urged the NAACP to call for a repeal of the provisions, isolate labor, and show solidarity with Hispanics. The effort was effective. At its conference in July, the NAACP voted to support repeal.

7   Hernández insists there is no obstacle that a desire to work together can't overcome. Regarding Miami, the setting of tension and conflict between Hispanics and Blacks, Hernández suggests this is a case where "there has to be much more attention to the needs of the Black community. The Blacks see the growth of Hispanics at their expense. The Cuban community has done marvels resurrecting the city, but there is no dialogue. There is a need to come to a better understanding." Where does this "Pollyanna view of life," as Hernández herself describes it, come from? Perhaps from the closeness and understanding she experiences in her family and personal relations.

8   A native of Torreón, Coahuila, Mexico, Hernández came to the United States at the age of eight. Her father was a gardener and laborer, her mother a homemaker. As the oldest of seven children, she had a hand in the rearing of her siblings. That close-knit style has continued into adulthood. "I have extended family, and I firmly believe in it. My house is across the street from my parents'. I have six siblings. We all live close together and help each other." Her marriage also seems an extraordinary example of harmonious coexistence of diverse elements. Her husband of thirteen years, Michael Stern, is also a lawyer and of Jewish origin. They have three children ("my greatest accomplishment," says Hernández) and successfully juggle a busy schedule. Still, all is not always wine and roses.

9   "I do have a very demanding job. Can a woman have it all? There are a lot of sacrifices I make. I try to balance my life and it has worked. But I have little time to myself. I have very few good friends and I'm away from home a lot." It was an arduous climb all the way through. Hernández earned her bachelor's degree at the University of California at Los Angeles, a teaching credential at the University School of Education, and her J.D. at the UCLA School of Law in 1974. She began her career as a staff attorney with the Los Angeles Center for Law and Justice in 1974. Three years later, she became the Directing Attorney for the Lincoln Heights office of the Legal Aid Foundation of Los Angeles. She worked with the U.S. Senate Committee on the Judiciary in 1979 and 1980. Hernández joined MALDEF in 1981 as Associate Counsel of the Washington, D.C. office and was later appointed Director of the Employment Litigation Program and Executive Vice President and Deputy General Counsel of the organization before assuming absolute leadership.

10   "When I got started, a Hispanic and a woman, I was one of the very few coming into the legal profession. Also, it gets very lonely and very tiring working with

our leadership, which is predominantly male. I tried to always keep my view on the issues and substance." It will be a different world for her children—Ben, 9, Marisa, 7, and Miguel, 5. "[It will be] much better for my children. They will have the opportunities I had to fight for. As a consequence, they'll have a bigger responsibility to give to the community." In fact, Hernández is convinced the future will be better for the entire Hispanic community, provided the willingness to struggle is there. "The '80s was not the Decade of the Hispanic. Madison Avenue put up the expectation and said we failed. The '90s is a threshold decade. We need to move. Otherwise, we'll develop into a community with a small middle class and a large poverty class. We need to grab control of our destiny."

11   In addition to negative images created by outsiders, Hernández also sees the need to overcome hangups within the community. "We have our own inhibitions to get over. This business of who is more Hispanic than who, I call it passing the Hispanic test. It's ridiculous."

12   True to herself, she focuses again on the positive. "I see a lot of young people in their 30s and 40s who've taken advantage of the educational opportunities. We have lots of leaders. Now," she adds, "it is incumbent upon us to demand our share of power. We need either money or participation in the political process. We need to register and vote, participate from the lowest level to the highest level. Our success will be determined by our willingness to be a part of the solution." Under Hernández's leadership, MALDEF is more than ready to be a part of the solution. The organization's plan calls for action on six main fronts: redistricting, immigrant rights, repeal of the employer sanction laws, equitable allocation of funds for education, a language rights program to confront the English Only movement, and the leadership development program, which has already trained 1,300 graduates to move onto decision-making positions.

13   For Hernández, this is no battle of half-measures. Nobody is to be left behind. The fire will rage on while the current perceptions are applied to so much as one Hispanic individual because "until we have all of our community out of the negative stereotype, we'll all be painted with the same brush."

READING

1. What kind of law is Ms. Hernández interested in? Who does she think her firm should cooperate with? What battles is she fighting?

2. What kind of home life does she have? How does this affect her career?

THINKING

1. Antonia Hernández shows that she feels that people can gain power by participating in the political process. How do you feel about this? Do you feel that your vote is important? Do you know who represents you in local, state, and national government? Have you ever thought of running for an office? Why or why not?

2. Hernández demonstrates that different groups need to work together to have an impact. How do you think your culture can work together with the Hispanics or another culture to make needed changes in society? What are the most important issues our society needs to work on right now? Why are these the most important?

PREWRITING

Hernández works as a professional in an environment dominated by men, which is a break from tradition for most women. She married a man of another culture and religion, so she also lives at home in a nontraditional environment. In your life you play many different roles, such as student, worker, daughter or son, and friend. In which of those roles do you feel that you live in a traditional environment? Which roles are in a nontraditional environment? Describe what you feel the effects of these environments are on your life-style.

WRITING

1. You have been asked to give a talk before a group of students at your college who are considering going into a profession dominated by the opposite sex. You are to inspire them with how it can be enjoyable and rewarding to challenge past traditions and become successful. Write this speech, based on Antonia Hernández's experiences.

2. You have the opportunity to apply for a job at the political office of the party of your choice for the summer. The person who will be chosen for the job will be hired on the basis of an essay in which that person writes what he or she can do to help the party grow by putting more emphasis on either getting votes or getting minorities more involved in the party. Write an essay explaining why you would be the best person for the job.

REVISING

Read through the article about Antonia Hernández and see how many specific examples you can find. Notice the details used in the examples. Then read through your writing assignment and count how many specific examples you have used. Examples are used to illustrate and clarify your argument. Think of two additional examples, and try adding them to your assignment.

Now look at your writing assignment, and see if you have carefully organized your ideas. Do you clearly state your subject? Do you end your paper with a conclusion that wraps up your ideas? Ask one of your fellow class members to read your assignment to see if it is better. See what kind of information that person feels you need. Take those suggestions into consideration as you revise your assignment.

EDITING

Misplaced modifiers create confusion because they are too far away from the words they modify or because they could modify the words closest to them. Misplaced modifiers can be words, phrases, or clauses.

Example:
> The guide showed the waterfall to the tourists splashing down the mountainside.

Chances are that the tourists would not be splashing down the mountainside. A better way to write this sentence would be:

> The guide showed the tourists the waterfall splashing down the mountainside.

Example:
> Running down the street, the apartment building appeared right in front of us.

This obviously doesn't make sense because apartment buildings don't run. A better way to write this sentence would be:

> As we were running down the street, the apartment building appeared right in front of us.

Go through your rough draft to be sure that all of your modifiers are placed correctly.

Dangling modifiers in a sentence can be words, phrases, or clauses that don't modify anything.

Examples:
Incorrect: Unhappily, Jane was having a great time with her friends.

How could Jane be having a great time unhappily? Who was unhappy is left out of the sentence.

Correct: As Sue watched unhappily, Jane was having a great time with her friends.

Incorrect: Waving his arms, she walked by.

Was she waving his arms? How confusing this is.

Correct: Even though Bob was waving his arms, she walked by.

Incorrect: While jogging in the park, Mary did aerobics.

Either Mary is very energetic, or someone else is jogging. The meaning here is not clear.

Correct: While her husband was jogging in the park, Mary did aerobics.

Now go through your writing assignment to be sure that you have not included any dangling modifiers.

What a Man!

Kevin Powell

What do you think it would be like to be a famous movie star? How would your life be different? How would you spend your money and your time? Where would you live? Would you have a family? Why or why not? What kinds of roles would you play? Would you accept parts that portrayed people in negative roles? Would you accept parts in movies that contained violence or sex? Why or why not? Would you like to be a movie star?

DEFINING

NAACP (¶1)   National Association for the Advancement of Colored People

caucus (¶4)   a group within a decision-making body seeking to represent a specific interest

flaunt (¶5)   to show off

aloofness (¶5)   to stand apart from others, or to consider oneself higher than others

self-aggrandizement (¶5)   exaggerating one's own importance

oppressive (¶7)   difficult to bear, weighing heavily

apartheid (¶7)   an official policy of racial segregation once practiced in South Africa

asylum (¶11) a place offering protection and immunity from extradition for political refugees

ingratiating (¶13) bringing oneself into the good graces of others

dyslexia (¶19) a learning disorder marked by difficulty in recognizing written words

PC (¶25) Politically Correct, avoiding language that could be considered offensive

Everyman (¶28) representative of the human race; from the play *Everyman,* a medieval drama

substantiated (¶32) supported with proof or evidence

What a Man!

Kevin Powell

1   Danny Glover just couldn't say no to an appeal for help that was left on his answering machine a little more than a year ago. The call was from Richard Burr, a former attorney with the NAACP Legal Defense and Educational Fund. Burr was rallying support for his client Gary Graham, a 29-year-old Black man scheduled to be executed within 24 hours for a murder he said he didn't commit, but who had been barred by a bizarre Texas law from presenting evidence that just might prove his innocence.

2   The very next day the actor was on a plane bound for Texas, unsure he'd even make it to the state prison in Huntsville in time. As it turned out, Texas governor Ann Richards had granted Gary Graham an eleventh-hour temporary stay of execution. That gave Glover a chance to meet with the condemned young brother while the ticking of the death clock was still vivid in his mind.

3   "Meeting him that first time was painful," Glover recalls. His voice is raspy. At times his words are almost whispered. "That kind of pain forces you to respond in some way, to do something. I made a choice to become involved in this brother's case because I could not stand the pain of *not* making that choice. When I went down there that first time, the only way I could relieve the pain was to do something."

4   The next thing you know, Glover is pulled neck-deep into the condemned man's struggle. He has been to Houston about eight times to appeal Graham's case before the Texas House of Representatives and other state officials. He has also spoken on his behalf before the Congressional Black Caucus and the news media. Thanks to Glover and the groundswell of support from Amnesty International, scores of church officials and human-rights activists, Gary Graham is still alive,

Kevin Powell, "What a Man," *Essence,* July 1994, vol. 25, no. 3, p. 524. Reprinted by permission.

Please note maps in appendix for references to places in this article.

going from one day to the next on an indefinite stay of execution while his legal counsel presses for a new trial.

5   In an industry where success and fame seem also to confer the right to flaunt one's aloofness and inaccessibility like the Nobel Peace Prize, Danny Glover's social activism is legend. It is also for real. "Most people in Hollywood have a token thing they do," says actor Mel Gibson. Glover's costar and pal since 1987 when they made their *Lethal Weapon* debut. "But it's mostly about self-aggrandizement and ego. That's not the case with Danny. He's up to his eyeballs in devoting time to community activities and just causes. He keeps going whether or not the public knows about it. He's one of the most socially aware persons around."

6   The truth is, Danny Glover could probably retire from acting tomorrow and live off the proceeds from the millions he made playing police officer Roger Murtaugh in the Gibson and Glover moneymaking *Lethal Weapon* series. Instead the busier-than-ever actor flexes his bankable leading-man clout to reject roles that portray Black men as fools, pimps and drug dealers. His characters don't have the automatic sex appeal of Denzel Washington's or the super cool under fire of Wesley Snipes's. Glover's screen power comes from his soul-baring portrayals of the "Everyman," seemingly ordinary characters who are always far more complex than they appear.

7   In this month's *Angels in the Outfield,* a Disney family feature, Glover stars as George Knox, the hot-tempered manager who eventually manages with compassion his losing baseball team of major-league misfits, the Angels. In last year's *Bopha!* he played a troubled South African father torn between his love for his revolutionary son and his do-or-die duties as a police officer in the oppressive apartheid system.

8   In this latter role Danny got the chance to bridge the gap between the actor and the activist. Glover calls his role in *Bopha!* "part of the journey." The trip started in the 1970's with his leading roles in a series of stage dramas by the White South African playwright Athol Fugard: *Sizwe Banzi Is Dead, The Blood Knot, The Island,* and *Master Harold . . . and the Boys.* These plays helped educate and rally public opinion against apartheid and were also basic texts in Danny Glover's education about its horrors.

9   "A lot of research and reading goes into playing those roles," he explains. "You can't do a work of that magnitude without understanding the issues."

10   This year Glover visited the country for the first time as part of a group of actors—among them Alfre Woodard—who spent eight days there lending support through their presence to the movement toward democratic elections. As cochair of the Fund for Democratic Elections in South Africa, he has also helped raise money to finance the country's massive voter-registration drive. In April he returned to South Africa to serve as an election observer.

11   More recently Glover has been speaking out publicly on Haiti. In April he teamed up with Randall Robinson, executive director of TransAfrica, and Harry Belafonte for a guest slot for the Phil Donahue show in which they challenged U.S. policy toward the country and its people. Along with film director Jonathan

Demme and others, he also helped raise thousands of dollars in bail-bond money to help free five Haitian refugees incarcerated in Louisiana for a year while awaiting asylum hearings.

12   "These people of African descent are denied the rights of others who are trying to escape oppression," he says with a mixture of quiet outrage and disbelief. "It's easy to holler racism, but the fact is we aren't giving them the rights normally accorded to people who try to escape brutality. Yet we provide minimal support to their struggle within that country."

13   There are also his less public acts of service, of grace, if you will, on the artistic front. He was critical to the making of *To Sleep With Anger,* director Charles Burnett's cult masterpiece, which no Hollywood distributor wanted to touch. A definite underground classic, it's arguably among the best African-American feature films ever made. Danny played Harry, the ingratiating and manipulative houseguest from hell, and his name helped add credibility to the project.

14   Burnett recalls that when South Central Los Angeles residents complained about the film crew's turning their neighborhood inside out, Danny Glover made the rounds, shooting the breeze with local folks and diffusing tension. The last day on the set he whipped up a huge batch of seafood gumbo, enough to feed folks from the cast, crew and part of the 'hood. "He made the movie happen," Burnett insists.

15   Glover's social consciousness and life choices are inseparable from the man. "There's a history to all this," he explains. "It's not like I just jumped up and decided that this was my calling."

16   It began in 1947 when Danny was born in the Bay Area, the first of Carrie and James Glover's five children. (Glover still resides there with his wife, Asake Bomani, owner of the Bomani Gallery, and his 18-year-old daughter, Mandisa.) His mother was killed in a tragic 1983 car accident; from her side of the family, he inherited his physical stature. At six feet four inches tall, he weighs in at about 215 pounds—provided, he says, he does his daily hour-long morning workouts on the stationary bicycle and goes easy on the fried chicken.

17   He seems to have inherited his super-easygoing nature from his father, whom Glover calls "his best friend" and "one of the kindest people I've ever met." He explains, "My dad harbors no anger toward anyone. He's not threatened by your space."

18   Although the solidly working-class Glover family was close-knit and loving, Danny admits he grew up shy, quiet, and "uncomfortable with myself." He recalls, "Kids made fun of me because I was dark-skinned, had a wide nose and was tall and skinny."

19   As if that weren't enough, he had mild dyslexia. As a student he was strong at math but found reading a chore. "Even as an actor it took me a long time to realize why words and letters got jumbled up in my mind and came out differently," he concedes.

20   During those early years his sensibilities were also being shaped by the political and social upheaval of the fifties and sixties. Those images of the sit-ins, demonstrations, marches, the bulldogs, and bullhorns he witnessed on the nightly TV

news left a lasting impression. His moment of action, however, came in the mid-sixties, when the movement had broadened from challenging blatant race discrimination to embracing an artistic and social revolution. Few places were more charged with the spirit than the Bay Area, home to the Black Panthers, the flower children and the free-speech movement—not to mention Sly Stone, Santana, and young Danny Glover.

21   Nineteen and a college dropout, he began teaching kids in a tutorial program sponsored by San Francisco State University. "What I saw that year was amazing," he reminisces. Sonia Sanchez was reading her poetry. Huey Newton was reading his. And as he puts it, "All these bad motherf—ers were there *talking*!" Suddenly, reading became worth the effort. He read Frantz Fanon's *Wretched of the Earth* five times and studied James Baldwin's *Notes of a Native Son* and Nelson Mandela's *No Easy Walk to Freedom.*

22   That was also when Danny Glover discovered his life's calling. Poet and playwright Amiri Baraka visited San Francisco State and urged the young would-be revolutionaries in the Bay Area to perform revolutionary plays. Glover took up the challenge and snagged a part in *Papa's Daughter,* "the play that the fewest people were auditioning for."

23   Over the years Danny Glover's commitment to his craft has made him one of the most respected men in Hollywood. Casting director and producer Reuben Cannon remembers the way the young actor took charge of his fledgling career. In the mid-seventies Glover and actor Carl Lumbly showed up in Los Angeles, where they staged and starred in their own production of Athol Fugard's two-character drama *The Island.* "Actors usually wait to be employed," Cannon recalls. "But they created an opportunity to employ themselves."

24   Glover remained principled about his acting, even when it wasn't always practical. He and his wife and daughter were living in New York on a meager salary from the Broadway play *Blood Knot* when Glover's agent called him back to L.A. to do a *Hill Street Blues* pilot. He did the unthinkable; he said no. He had no understudy, and if he had quit the play, he would have forced it to close. Glover later learned that Fugard was so impressed by his performance in the play that he deliberately sought him out to take the leading role in *Master Harold . . . and the Boys,* which ran on Broadway in 1982 for close to 350 performances.

25   Ironically, this artistically "PC" actor finally graduated into the big league with *The Color Purple,* which some critics have denounced for being so politically *incorrect.* "I'm glad it happened," he says of the controversy surrounding the movie.

26   "You can't keep child molestation, incest, and spousal abuse in the closet. These issues are just as critical for us and just as apparent in our relationships as they are for anyone else."

27   What is less debatable is Glover's talent. There's a common thread that connects the sinister Mister in *The Color Purple* with the demonic Harry in *To Sleep With Anger* and with Simon, the tow-truck driver with the heart of gold in the masterfully scripted *Grand Canyon.* All three are refreshingly multidimensional Black men whose character runs deeper than the costumes they wear and the lines they read.

28   Glover makes his Everyman roles intriguing. The tragedy is that his Everyman

never gets the girl. His sweet but innocent flirtation with Jane (played by Alfre Woodard) in *Grand Canyon* is, amazingly, the closest he has come to showing his sensuality on-screen. He has played the loving family man, but hot and heavy on-screen romances continue to elude him. The question many of his female fans want to know is: When will Danny Glover get some? Maybe it's because his looks are not just a blacker shade of pale that Danny Glover might be more than Hollywood is ready to handle.

29   It's clear he wouldn't mind seeing himself with the leading role in a Black love story. "We see Black men who have families and who express love," he observes, "but what we don't see is the fantasy of falling in love, of romance. So many of our references to those things are simply what we see Whites do in the movies, and so it's a way of denying our humanity."

30   The way he acknowledges that long-denied humanity is by providing Black characters with as many different realities as possible. In August he makes his directorial debut with a made-for-TV 30-minute short entitled *Override,* slated to air on Showtime. It's a tale set in the future about a Black mother on "workfare," struggling to support her family while driving a truck. Meanwhile his film-production company is turning its attention to projects that focus on women.

31   And, of course, he'll continue with his social activism. "I'd be lying if I didn't worry sometimes that my politics might hurt my career," Glover concedes. If he backed off a bit, cut down on the college tours and high-school visits, said no to his work with the literacy campaign and to the numerous fund-raisers, declined invitations to speak at this group's dinner or that group's luncheon, certainly if he left his old Haight Ashbury neighborhood and moved someplace more private and remote, more befitting his celebrity, his fans would understand. But that wouldn't be Danny Glover.

32   What's important, he says, is making choices. "I want to feel that I made choices that empowered me and substantiated me as a human being," he says. "My career is going to be here and gone. But I'm always going to be a human being. And I want to look myself in the mirror and say that I was the human being I wanted to be."

READING

1. Why did Glover say he became involved in Gary Graham's case? What did he do for Graham?

2. What kinds of movie roles does Glover refuse to play? Why won't he play these roles?

THINKING

1. Danny Glover considers himself to be socially responsible. From what you read about him in this article, do you believe that is true? Why or why not? He says he wants to "look myself in the mirror and say that I was the human being I wanted to be." Do you feel you could look in the mirror and say that? Why or why not? What would you like to change about you?

2. Glover has been tremendously successful even though he was a shy child and is afflicted with mild dyslexia. Many people allow their problems to dominate or destroy their lives while other people succeed in spite of enormous challenges. What kind of person do you consider yourself to be? Think about people you know who fit into either of the two categories described. How are they the same? How are they different?

PREWRITING

Write a list of all of the things you feel you should do in your life to be a socially responsible citizen. See how long you can make your list. Think of personal responsibility as well as responsibility to your family, community, country, and the world in general.

WRITING

1. Write a letter to yourself that you will open twenty years from today. In this letter write what you feel would indicate that you have had a successful life. Be sure to include the most important things you would like to accomplish in the next twenty years. Explain to yourself why you have chosen your goals.

Homework **2.** Write an essay to share with your classmates on about what you feel it means to be socially responsible. Write it from a personal point of view indicating what you do to be a socially responsible person. Be sure to include details and specific examples.

REVISING

Who is the audience for "What a Man!"? Why do you suppose Powell used the audience and tone he chose? How do you think this article would be different if Powell's audience was another culture?

Try rewriting either writing assignment from the opposite perspective of the one you took the first time. See if you are able to clearly see both sides of the argument.

EDITING

Check your assignment very carefully for spelling errors. Go through the assignment word by word checking any words that you aren't positive you spelled correctly. Don't look for any other errors when you are checking for spelling. After you check your paper yourself, have a classmate or friend go through the assignment word-by-word to pick out any words he or she is unsure about. Then look up those words, too.

The Songs of the Forest

Julia Preston

PREREADING

Before you read about the music of Brazil's Milton Nascimento, take a few moments to consider what you know about the Amazon rain forest. What does it have to do with people in America? Do you think Americans have a responsibility to try to protect the rain forest? Why or why not? If you don't know about the rain forest, you can find out about it at the library.

DEFINING

radiating (¶1)   sending out

awash (¶1)   full of water

serendipity (¶2)   apparently accidental fortunate discovery

abated (¶2)   ended

finale (¶2)   the last musical piece in the concert

aura (¶2)   an invisible atmosphere surrounding someone

odyssey (¶4)   a long journey

encroachment (¶4)   the trespassing or intruding of

browbeater (¶5)   someone who is abusive, trying to force something on people

terse (¶5)   brief and to the point

evoking (¶5)   calling forth

undulating (¶5)   moving in waves

celestial (¶6)   heavenly

collaboration (¶6)   working together

transcultural (¶6)   crossing over cultural limits

limelight (¶6)   center of attention

epoch (¶7)   a period of time in history

vying (¶7)   trying to get to

conciliation (¶8)   soothing the anger caused by something

affinity (¶10)   close relationship

timbre (¶11)   quality of sound

retaliated (¶11)   paid back for

snippets (¶13)   short pieces

atonal (¶13)   with a singular tone

veritable (¶14)   true

The Songs of the Forest

Julia Preston

1   These days Milton Nascimento is radiating so much moral energy, he even seems to be affecting the weather. In March, four days before the Brazilian musician was scheduled to give an open-air concert on a beach in Rio de Janeiro at which he would present a new crop of songs inspired by the Amazon rain forest—and at a moment when the city's streets were awash with the year's most relentless tropical drenching—Nascimento made a public prediction that the rain would stop in time for his show. "There will be too much power in one place for it to rain," he said.

2   Sure enough, in an almost mystical serendipity, the week-old downpour abated a few hours before Nascimento's appearance. To the even greater satisfaction of the 20,000 fans by the bay, it resumed in a drizzle just as he hit the last notes of his finale. Another artist might look silly in 1991, making such '60s-era claims about his harmony with the universe. But in a nearly 25-year career that has produced at least 25 albums, Nascimento has earned his aura of "being right with life," as he puts it in one of his new songs. He has managed to combine a sophisticated and varied musical sound with an unshakably direct and optimistic spirit.

3   In an interview, Nascimento said that in the late '60s, when he moved away from his hometown in the state of Minas Gerais, "I wanted to leave for a place with no borders. I didn't want to be just a man from Minas, or just a Brazilian. I wanted

Please note maps in appendix for references to places in this article.

to be a person of the world." Today he believes he has achieved that. "I have my inner freedom to say anything I want," he said. "Since I have that freedom, I know that at least some people are going to listen to what I have to say."

. . .

4   Nascimento's new work is the fruit of an 18-day odyssey he made through the Amazon two years ago. Traveling with him . . . are several Indians from Amazon tribes whose survival is threatened by the encroachment of loggers and gold prospectors. Also joining him is a representative of a rubber tappers' union whose past president was the activist Chico Mendes, who was assassinated in 1988.

5   For Nascimento the rain forest is only the latest in a series of social causes. Through the years he has sung songs for Brazilian democracy and human rights and against racism. He says he seeks to mobilize with his music. But he is not a browbeater. Even at home in Brazil, his talk onstage is terse. He just sings his melodies, evoking, in the case of his recent work, the undulating water, the hush and darkness of the rain forest. On his foreign tours he still sings and speaks almost entirely in Portuguese.

6   Some Americans may have heard Nascimento for the first time as the celestial voice singing in Portuguese on the "Spirit Voices" track of Paul Simon's "Rhythm of the Saints." On "Rhythm" Nascimento was returning a favor to Simon, who sang a duet in Portuguese with Nascimento on the latter's 1987 "Yauarete" album. But, Simon's collaboration with Nascimento is quite different from Simon's transcultural "Graceland" album, which rocketed a number of South African musicians into the American limelight. Nothing Simon could do could boost Nascimento's already giant stature in Brazil. And Nascimento's work with American musicians began as long ago as 1967, shortly after he won three prizes at an international music festival in Rio with some of the first songs he ever wrote. Wayne Shorter, Herbie Hancock, Hubert Laws, and Pat Metheny are among the Americans who have played with Nascimento.

7   He resents the American practice of categorizing musicians by jazz, pop, or rock. His own music was born of the diversity of Minas Gerais, which during Brazil's colonial epoch was a prosperous mining region with a considerable slave population. Nascimento, born in 1942, grew up with black work songs, Afro-Brazilian percussion, gyrating sambas, and the somber chant of the Catholic Mass all vying for his ear.

8   Brazil is a society in which racism lies just beneath a smooth surface of tolerance. But Nascimento, who is black, says he was brought up keenly aware of the existence of bias but at the same time protected from its pain. He explains that he was adopted as a 2-year-old by a white family (he doesn't offer details about his natural parents) and raised with three white siblings. "There was never any distinction in my house because of color. So my attitude toward the issue of race has always been one of conciliation," he said.

9   Nascimento's father sponsored a radio club in their town. Nascimento and his friends spent hours with their ears pressed to the radio, trying to pick up the hit parade over the hills from Rio. So when Nascimento emerged onto the interna-

tional scene in the late '60s, he brought a generation of Minas Gerais musicians with him. Wagner Tiso, Beto Guedes, and Lo Borges are some of those still making the lilting, jazzy Minas sound here and adding to the jazz mix in the United States. In 1967 Nascimento's lyricist, Fernando Brant, who still lives in the Minas capital of Belo Horizonte, wrote the words for "Travessia" ("Crossing"), Nascimento's first big hit. To this day, Brant said in an interview, he remains a kind of anchor for Nascimento, who is on the road overseas for months each year.

10   "He gets the glory. But I lead a calmer existence. I stay in my own place. It's important for me to live day-to-day life. I can still go anywhere and observe things as they are," Brant said. Wherever he is, Nascimento writes tunes and sends the tapes to Brant. Brant faxes back the words. "Our affinity is so great, he very rarely says anything to me about the music. It just takes us in the same direction," Brant said.

11   During the early '70s a military dictatorship censored many of Brant's lyrics. Nascimento, whose voice retains its bell-like timbre through a multi-octave range, retaliated by singing the songs without words in discordant mumbles and howls.

12   Nascimento has not always had the confidence he displays today. He is naturally reserved and uses words with caution, as if he considers them mainly to be a source of trouble. For some years only an excess of vodka could get him up on a stage. He has spoken with fear of flying in airplanes, and of the attentive silences of American theaters, in contrast to Brazil, where the audience expects to be part of the show.

13   His ecological concerns began to show up in "Yauarete" ("Jaguar"), on which he contemplated the similarities between himself and a jungle cat. On his Amazon trip Nascimento "discovered that Brazil is a very big country," according to Carlos Alberto Ricardo, an anthropologist who accompanied him. "He was almost anonymous in many places. The people knew him only as 'the singer.'" The "Txai" album includes snippets of music recorded in Amazon Indian villages. To generate funds for the Amazon cause, Nascimento registered the author's rights for those tracks to the Indian tribes that performed them, so some record royalties will go to them. The windy, atonal sound haunts some of Nascimento's new tunes. But "Txai" also has much vintage Nascimento-Brant, aching melody and blunt declaration:

> *Man is not just an animal*
> *His history is more than*
> *physical*
> *He opens his eyes to be free . . .*
> *The city's ease does not need*
> *to kill the trees . . .*

14   On tour Nascimento and his acoustic guitar will be accompanied by, among others, drummer Robertinho Silva, a veritable patriarch of percussion. Silva's sons Vanderlei and Ronaldo back him up with chimes, cymbals, and congas from a rack that takes up 25 feet of stage. Nascimento's abiding conviction that something can

still be done for the human race is particularly striking in modern Brazil, which is sunk in a gray depression after its push toward development in the '70s failed amid corruption and disorder.

15   "I make music for people," he said. "If my music was for me, I would stay at home in my room and play. But when I go out to the street I carry a message, that in spite of everything, we have to have confidence in human beings. Otherwise, nothing we do makes any sense."

READING

1. What social causes is Nascimento concerned with? Why does he worry about these issues?

2. How long has Nascimento's career lasted? What famous Americans has he sung with? Who does he make music for?

THINKING

1. Nascimento tries to make people think and act about ideas that are important to him and to the people of the world. If you could have the people of the world listen to what you have to say, what would be the most important issue you would deal with? Why would you choose this issue?

2. As a black child raised by a white family, Nascimento feels differently than many people about issues related to race. What do you think would be different about your life if you had been raised by a family of another culture than your own? What would be the same?

PREWRITING

Make a list of all of the important world issues that you can think of. Then go through this list to prioritize which issues you think are the most important. Write your reasons for thinking the top three are the most important.

WRITING

1. You have been chosen as a representative of the United States to make a very brief statement in front of the United Nations telling what you think the most important world issue is today and what you think the United Nations, or the people of the world, should do about this problem. Your presentation should be about 200 words long.

2. The lyrics written by Fernando Brant for Nascimento's songs were censored during a military dictatorship. America recently had a controversial court case over the censorship of the lyrics of 2 Live Crew. Write a letter to one of the justices of the Supreme Court stating your feelings about censorship. Should it be allowed? Why or why not?

REVISING

"The Songs of the Forest" could be considered a cause-and-effect essay. Look back through the article to see what you would consider the cause Nascimento is fighting for. What is the effect of his fight?

Think of your writing assignment as a cause-and-effect topic. Go through the first draft of your paper and decide first what the problem is that you are writing about. Next, see if you have clearly identified the cause of this problem. Then examine the paper again and see if you have included what the effect of your proposal should be. Do you feel that using this approach improved this draft of your paper? Why or why not?

EDITING

Homonyms are words that sound alike but are spelled differently and have different meanings. The most commonly confused homonyms are listed here.

to toward
too also, excessive
two the number

affect to influence
effect result

accept receive
except leave out

whether if
weather climate

are form of *to be*
our belonging to us

its possessive form of *it*
it's contraction of *it is*

there in that location
they're contraction of *they are*
their possessive form of *they*

you're contraction of *you are*
your possessive form of you

wear to put on
where in what place
were past tense of *to be*

then at that time
than as compared with

Check your paper to see if you have used any of these words and if you have used them correctly.

The Rebirth of Sichan Siv

Sheldon Kelly

PREREADING

Sichan Siv was a target for being killed by the communist guerrillas in Cambodia because he was well educated and had associated with the United States. Write about why you think the guerrillas would want to kill well-educated people. Why would they see people who have been educated in the United States as a threat?

DEFINING

Khmer Rouge (¶2)   Cambodian rebel and guerrilla forces

capitalist (¶3)   a holder of great wealth

counterrevolutionary (¶3)   a person going against the revolution

leech (¶8)   a bloodsucking worm

cadre (¶15)   a military unit

floundered (¶21)   became confused or hesitant

squalidly (¶34)   in filth, extremely dirty

The Rebirth of Sichan Siv

Sheldon Kelly

1   Shortly after Communist guerrillas overran Phnom Penh, Cambodia's capital, in 1975, they began killing all those who were educated or had associated with foreigners. Sichan Siv, an English-speaking college graduate and a U.S. relief-agency employee, was a certain target. Earlier American co-workers had arranged for him to be evacuated. But Sichan had promised a food delivery to thousands of refugees. As he worked feverishly, the last flight from Phnom Penh soared overhead. He had been left behind.

2   Now, as the Khmer Rouge consolidated their power, black-clad troops issued a warning to the city's terrified civilians:

3   "Angka (Khmer for the Organization) will take care of you! But do not displease Angka!" A man accused of being a "capitalist counterrevolutionary" was led away. His crime, serious enough to warrant execution, was that he wore glasses.

4   Soon gunfire could be heard everywhere. "Angka wants you out of the city!" voices began shouting fiercely. "Now!"

5   Sichan and his family—mother Chea Aun, sister Sarin, brother Sichhun, plus his sister-in-law, nieces and nephews—pushed their way through streets crammed with tens of thousands of refugees. Fly-covered corpses, blindfolded, lay on the roadside; pregnant women collapsed in labor; many of the frail and elderly simply lay down to die.

6   "Remember, children," Chea Aun told them that night, "hate does not end with more hate but with love. And from that we take hope. Without love and hope, our lives will be empty."

7   **"Good-By, Brave Brother."** The family reached Tonle Bati, their ancestral village, ten miles from the capital. Quickly, they learned the new rules for survival. Either family members worked hard and obeyed Angka, or they were sent to Angka Leu—the Organization on High—code words for torture and execution. Material possessions, loose talk, or other "imperialistic tendencies" would also lead to Angka Leu. "This is your new life," a solider announced. "Live or die. It doesn't matter."

8   Chea Aun, Sarin, and Sichhun's wife worked in leech-infested rice fields; Sichan and his brother labored at a dam construction project. Evenings were spent listening to political lectures, learning how not to displease Angka. Friends and acquaintances were disappearing.

9   "To survive you must adapt," Chea Aun told her family. Snails and boiled insects added nutrients to their meager rice rations; lizards and rats provided protein.

10   Under the Organization's "purification" program, anyone believed to be even vaguely unsympathetic would be eliminated. The family soon learned to con-

Please note maps in appendix for references to places in this article.

vey messages by staring directly into one another's eyes: *I love you; be strong; do not give up hope!*

11   As the Tonle Bati villagers knew the elder Siv children were college graduates, it seemed only a matter of time before they would be discovered. One day, the horrifying news arrived: Sichhun, his wife, and daughter were instructed to attend a festival in the jungle. Everyone knew the "festival" would be a killing-field massacre. For the moment, Sichan and Sarin had been spared.

12   Sichhun was resigned to his fate. There was now little chance for the family's escape—only Sichan, the youngest, could make the dangerous 500-mile trek to Thailand and freedom. The family agreed he was to leave immediately.

13   Before he did so, he went to say good-by to his brother, who was awaiting his execution. Neither man said a word but their eyes spoke: *Good-by, brave brother; I love you.*

14   Sichan pedaled slowly out of Tonle Bati. The roads were packed with refugees barely moving in 100-degree heat. He held back his tears, reciting childhood prayer lessons: "Cultivate a heart of love that knows no anger, no ill will. . . ."

15   **"I Died in Cambodia."** By announcing he was "on a mission for Angka," Sichan, skeletally thin, slipped through 200 miles of checkpoints. Then, in Staung, a Khmer Rouge cadre stopped him, shouting, "Angka wants you!"

16   Sichan and 300 others were ordered into a clearing to be executed. Sichan had inched his way to the rear as women cried, searching for their children. Finally, as the group milled in confusion, Sichan fled into the dense jungle. Minutes later, he heard machine-gun fire.

17   Captured again within 40 miles of Thailand, he was assigned to a manual-labor unit. He worked dawn to dusk, seven days a week. Disease was rampant; exhaustion and hunger were the rule.

18   One day, while riding a truckload of logs as it bounced down a frontier road just 25 miles from the Thai border, Sichan felt the moment to escape had arrived. When the road curved sharply, he jumped from the truck and began running west toward the setting sun.

19   Still wandering in the jungle two days later, he suddenly plunged into a deep, carefully camouflaged Khmer Rouge trap lined with sharpened bamboo stakes. At first he lay there, too weak to move. Finally, he dug his fingers into the earthen wall and began climbing. At daybreak, he freed himself. Then he saw his blood-caked trousers. One of the stakes had ripped deep into his leg. He rose unsteadily; infections in the jungle were swift and deadly as a bullet.

20   Hours later, Sichan was surprised by a farmer wearing brightly colored clothes. "Welcome to Thailand," he said. "You are safe." The farmer, also a refugee, held a cup of water to Sichan's lips. *I died in Cambodia,* Sichan thought. *And now I shall be reborn.*

21   **Luckiest Man on Earth.** Sichan was taken to the Wat Koh refugee camp, packed with thousands of Cambodians who had fled Khmer Rouge tyranny. Soon he was teaching English to 200 students. He also was ordained a Buddhist monk. His head shaven, clad only in a saffron robe and sandals, he meditated each morn-

ing before classes. "Never give up hope," he told his students when they floundered. "It is all we have."

22   On June 4, 1976, Sichan was granted refugee status and flown to the United States. When he arrived, sickly and frightened, at the home of his sponsors, Bob and Nancy Charles, in Wallingford, Connecticut, he had $2 in his pocket.

23   After picking apples for months at a nearby orchard, Sichan slowly regained his health and began searching for a better job. Loans from his American sponsors were refused graciously. "Once you've been a slave, then find yourself free, you want very much to earn your own living," he explained.

24   Sichan, then 28, had been an English teacher and a relief-agency supervisor, yet few firms seemed interested. Finally, he was hired by a Friendly Ice Cream restaurant.

25   He rented a room near the restaurant and walked to his new job. He mopped floors, washed dishes, and hauled garbage. Gradually, he was given more responsibilities: cooking, scooping ice cream, and working as cashier. Often, walking home after a 16-hour workday, he would look around his American neighborhood, convinced he was the luckiest man on earth. *Hey, I'm free! Nobody's trying to kill me!*

26   The opportunities in Sichan's adopted country seemed endless. He had sent letters to colleges, asking for assistance—and in January 1980 he won a full scholarship to Columbia University's School of International Relations and Public Affairs. He tacked a note he'd written above his desk: "The road to success in America is paved with hard work."

27   Indeed, after moving to New York City three years earlier, he had worked 70 hours a week as a taxi driver. His fellow drivers found him a cheerful and sympathetic immigrant with a surprising talent for solving tough emotional or financial problems for them. None of them knew that he had witnessed unsurpassed human horror.

28   Then an American friend wrote him about a young woman who had worked for the U.N. in Thailand and had transferred recently to New York: Martha Pattillo, a native of Pampa, Texas. Sichan telephoned, and they had tea together.

29   Within weeks they began dating. Martha, a high-school valedictorian who went on to get degrees in French and library science, became Sichan's sounding board. He told her how desperately he wanted to become an American citizen and how he wanted to help make the world a better place. Martha listened, enthralled by his optimism.

30   One day Martha found him waiting in a restaurant, pale and solemn. A letter had reached him. His family had been executed. Initially, his mother had been spared, but when she "insulted" her captors, she, too, was killed. "Her faith is the reason I am alive," he said, his voice breaking.

31   **White House Calling.** After earning his Master's degree, Sichan, by now a U.S. citizen, took a job as a Wall Street analyst. But then, taking a sharp pay cut, he quit to become an administration and finance officer working with refugees for the Episcopal Church Center in New York City. Martha understood perfectly. Unless he could "do good deeds" for others, he said, his escape would mean nothing.

32   A year later, Sichan accepted a position assisting the non-communist Cambodian delegation to the United Nations. Soon he was working 18-hour days, pleading the cause of democracy and human rights before U.N. committees—some of which, he believed, were hostile to his mission.

33   Sichan and Martha married in Pampa on Christmas Eve, 1983. The Texas Panhandle was buried in 12 inches of snow, and Sichan's flight from New York had nearly been canceled. "I guess you're serious," Martha had said, grinning.

34   Sichan's stint at the U.N. became increasingly frustrating: he felt the world watched as more than a million of his countrymen were murdered by the Khmer Rouge and hundreds of thousands of refugees lived squalidly on the dangerous Thai border.

35   Finally, in 1987, Sichan resigned his diplomatic post and joined the nonprofit Institute of International Education. As director of its Asia and Pacific programs, he was able to bring bright, aspiring educators, scientists, doctors, and engineers, many of them refugees, to the United States for training. And when George Bush's Presidential campaign kicked off, he volunteered.

36   For a moment Sichan thought is was a practical joke. "Would you repeat that, please?" The caller explained once more that President-elect Bush wanted Sichan to come to work for him, as a liaison to public-interest groups. After agreeing, Sichan collapsed in his chair, dazed.

37   On February 13, 1989, two months after his call from Washington, the handsome 41-year-old Sichan was sworn in as a deputy assistant to the President. It was the 13th anniversary of his escape—and he had just become the first Asian refugee in history to be appointed a ranking Presidential aide.

38   Now, whenever Sichan pleads the case of the world's refugees, this proud new American is able to paint an unusual and starkly clear picture of their suffering. For he can truly say of those whom he would help, "I was one of them."

READING

1. What was Angka? What did it do? Why were people afraid of it?
2. How big was Sichan Siv's family? What happened to them? How did Siv escape?

THINKING

1. Angka rounded up large quantities of people and executed them just as other regimes have in many parts of the world for centuries, such as the regimes led by Adolph Hitler, Idi Amin, and Papa Doc Duvalier. Americans aren't usually directly exposed to such atrocities, but they have participated in similar actions in the past, such as the persecution of American Indians, Mormons, and blacks. Imagine your campus being invaded by terrorists who have decided to murder all college stu-

dents. Could something like this ever happen? Why do you think it could or could not happen? What would you do if it did?

2. Sichan Siv has gone through many career changes, from being a U.S. relief-agency employee, to a Buddhist monk, to a Wall Street analyst, to the first Asian refugee in history to be named a U.S. Presidential aide, to several other jobs. What do you see as the similarities in his jobs? What do you see as the differences?

PREWRITING

Make a list of major issues facing our world today that you feel must be corrected in order for society to survive. List also some ideas you have on how these problems could be corrected.

WRITING

1. Sichan Siv became frustrated with his position at the United Nations because he felt that the people of the world really didn't care that so many from his country were being killed. With all of the death, poverty, and starvation existing in the world today, sometimes it is hard to believe that there is hope for the survival of society. Write an essay arguing why or why not you feel that there is hope for the future of our society.

2. Siv has worked for an organization that brought brilliant Asians to America to study. In America today there are thousands of refugees who held professional positions in their countries, such as doctors, teachers, and engineers who cannot work because the United States does not accept their credentials or training as valid. Write an essay offering a solution to this dilemma.

REVISING

Sheldon Kelly effectively uses quotations from Siv's mother and Siv. He also quotes voices from Angka. His quotations are brief but well chosen for the impact that they create. Angka says, "Angka . . . will take care of you! But do not displease Angka!" (¶3) Then they say, "Angka wants you out of the city! Now!" (¶4) One soldier said, "This is your new life. Live or die. It doesn't matter." (¶7) Compare these quotes to the quotes of Chea Aun, Siv's mother: "Remember, children, hate does not end with more hate but with love. And from that we take hope. Without love and hope, our lives will be empty." (¶6) She also said, "To survive you must adapt." (¶9) When Siv escaped, he said, "Never give up hope. It is all we have." (¶21) Then, when his mother died, he said, "Her faith is the reason I am alive." (¶30) These few brief quotes provide a powerful impact, indicating the meaning of the article.

Look back through your writing assignment to see if you can find places where quotes would make your writing more effective. Try adding at least two quotes that will help add to the meaning of your writing.

EDITING

The use of the **dash** is an effective way to draw attention to important information. When typing, a dash is indicated by two typed hyphens with no space on either side of them.

Examples:

> Either family members worked hard and obeyed Angka Leu—the Organization on High—code words for torture and execution.

> It was the 13th anniversary of his escape—and he had just become the first Asian refugee in history to be appointed a ranking Presidential aide.

Check through your writing to see if dashes are necessary, and if they are, be sure they are used correctly.

When writing the numbers one through ten spell them out. For numbers higher than ten, either use the numeral or use a combination of the numeral and the spelled-out number.

Examples:

> I live in a community of about *30* families.

> South Africa is not an integrated country of *37 million,* it's a country with *eight* to *ten* different peoples, all of whom should rule themselves.

Look through your writing assignment to be sure that you have written numbers correctly.

Against All Odds

Elinor L. Horwitz

Imagine what you think it would be like to be the Chief of the Cherokee Nation. What kinds of stories have you heard about Native Americans? What do you think it would be like to live on a reservation? Do you think that Native Americans are being treated fairly? How do you think they fit into American society today?

DEFINING

acculturated (¶3)   the change in a culture caused by contact with a different culture

feminism (¶4)   belief in the social, political, and economic equality of the sexes

innovative (¶7)   given to doing something new

tremulous (¶7)   trembling, shaking

belies (¶7)   hides, contradicts

torrent (¶11)   heavy, uncontrolled outpouring

consensus (¶15)   an opinion or position reached by a group

daunting (¶19)   discouraging

injunction (¶19)   command, directive

unilateral (¶20)   one-sided

emphatically (¶24)   forcefully, with strong emphasis

allocation (¶26)   setting apart, designation

Against All Odds
Elinor L. Horwitz

1   She grew up right where she lives today—at Rocky Mountain, near the town of Stilwell, Oklahoma—not far from Tahlequah, the historic capital of the Cherokee Nation. Her family—she was one of 11 children—lived in a house with no electricity or running water in an area abandoned by all but the poorest of poor rural people. When she was 12, a drought ruined their modest strawberry and peanut crops and, under a federal government program to urbanize rural Indians, the Mankiller family was moved to a high-crime area of San Francisco.

2   "San Francisco was total culture shock," Wilma Mankiller recalls. "I had never used a telephone, been in an elevator, seen a television program. I absolutely hated school. I was teased about my name, my accent, about being poor, and dressing differently. You know how cruel kids can be at this age to classmates who are different. They laughed at the fact that I didn't know how to ride a bike, and there I was, not even accustomed to plumbing."

3   She denies having had any role models as a teenager, but she picked up a few heroes from the history books. "I read about and admired Chief Joseph of the Nez-Percé tribe," she recalls. "He stuck with his principles. I had his picture on my wall. Later I was fascinated to learn about a Navajo social worker, Dr. Jennie Jo, who worked for her people. But I had no sense of self, no personal ambition. I was very much a product of my time, focused only on traditional female roles. Women of my age—I'm not just talking about Indian women but about American women in general—were not acculturated to think of themselves as potential leaders."

4   After completing high school, she married an Ecuadorean businessman, had two daughters, and settled into the life of a middle-class housewife. But change was in the air. "Remember," she says, "this was the '60s and I was in San Francisco. The women's movement was taking hold and I started going to some meetings. I came to understand that feminism means having choices. I realized there were things I wanted to do—things that other people were not doing—and although I was used to hanging back, I took a deep breath and spoke up. When Native Americans occupied the prison at Alcatraz in protest against their treatment by the federal government, I was there. I went to college and got a B.A. in sociology. I was changing, but this wasn't acceptable to my husband. When I became interested in activities outside the home, my marriage broke up."

5   As an adult, she had found another hero. "I became fascinated with the art and life of Georgia O'Keeffe," she says. "Here she was—a woman—and she did exactly as she liked!" She points with pleasure to the O'Keeffe posters on the wall of her comfortable office at Cherokee Nation headquarters.

6   Don Greenfeather, who works down the hall, in the tribal employment rights division, remembers when Wilma Mankiller returned to Oklahoma after her divorce

Elinor Horwitz, "Against All Odds," *American Association of University Women Outlook,* Spring 1993, vol. 87, no. 1. Reprinted by permission.

Please note maps in appendix for references to places in this article.

and took a low-level job with the Nation. "That was 15 years ago. You wouldn't have picked her to be anyone exceptional when she came to work here," he says, smiling. "She was just a little Indian girl trying to make it for herself and her children."

7   No one else ever refers to the chief as "little." At 47, Mankiller is imposing in stature, in intellect, in the intense dedication she brings to her work. Members of her staff speak with awe of her innovative ideas and approaches, the revenue she has brought to the tribe, the success of her community development projects, the multimillion-dollar community health clinics she's brought to this area of northeastern Oklahoma where most of the Oklahoma Cherokees live, the new Talking Leaves Job Corps Center, the Headstart Program, the range of educational facilities she's promoted. Their voices become tremulous with devotion and anxiety when they talk about the long work days she puts in, her exhausting travels around the country to promote the needs of her tribe, her frequent visits to Washington to lobby Congress on issues affecting Native Americans. The chief's vigorous appearance, they remind you, belies grave health problems.

8   "I think her tragedies had a lot to do with the kind of person she is," says Greenfeather. "She's got her values and priorities in line."

9   Soon after her return to Oklahoma, as Mankiller was driving home from graduate school classes at the University of Arkansas, her car was hit head-on by a vehicle driven by her best friend. Her friend died instantly. Mankiller suffered multiple severe injuries including broken facial bones and shattered legs, faced the possibility of amputation, and would eventually endure 17 operations. As her long convalescence was coming to an end, she developed myasthenia gravis, a totally debilitating neuromuscular disease that eventually responded to chemotherapy and surgical removal of her thymus gland. Later, a severe kidney infection threatened her life. She underwent a kidney transplant in 1991.

10   Despite these dramatic setbacks, Mankiller worked her way through the ranks. "When I came back home I realized I had learned something about community development and organizing in California," she says. "I started new programs and obtained grants. At that time there were no women executives here. I simply began at low level management and worked up. I certainly didn't aspire to be chief. My leadership position came through evolution; it was built on actual deeds, on things I had accomplished."

11   In 1983 Ross Swimmer, an attorney and banker from Tulsa, ran for election to the post of principal chief of the Cherokee Nation and asked Mankiller—then the tribe's director of community development—to run as his deputy chief. His announcement brought on a torrent of opposition from tribal members.

12   "It really astonished me," she says. "The man didn't oppose my being department director. They didn't object to the fact that I was doing some traditionally male jobs like laying pipeline and supervising carpenters. But all of a sudden when it came to high office there was this line that, as a women, I wasn't supposed to walk over."

13   Her second husband, a full-blooded Cherokee named Charlie Soap, who speaks fluent Cherokee, campaigned with tribal elders, reminding them of her ac-

complishments and the fact that historically Cherokee women played a strong political role. The election was won, and two years later, when Swimmer was appointed head of the Bureau of Indian Affairs in Washington, DC Mankiller moved into the position of principal chief. In 1987 she ran for election on her own and won. In 1991 she ran for a second full term and was elected by a landslide 85 percent of the vote.

14   "When I was sworn in as deputy chief, I was actually very unhappy," she says. "I realized I would be away from the area more, that I would be removed from the hands-on grassroots work I was so totally committed to. It took me time to recognize the significance of being a leader, the fact that you can have an even broader effect because you're in a policy-setting role."

15   Pamela Iron, chief of staff, describes Mankiller's method as consensus management. "She establishes work groups, or commissions, pulling in community members and people in industry to get ideas. We go around the circle talking, and everyone's opinion is considered worthy. When we do reach consensus on an action it works because everyone has bought into it."

16   Iron adds that, "In older times the Cherokee women elected the men to the council. The men then made the decisions, but if there was a struggle in coming to agreement they consulted a wise woman who was designated 'the beloved women.' Wilma is our modern 'beloved women.'"

17   "Often there's a big distance between leaders and the people, but not with Wilma," Greenfeather says. "She belong to the Salem Indian Baptist Church, but she also goes to the traditional Cherokee ceremonies. She comes to the stomp grounds and joins in the dances. She gets all these awards and honorary degrees and she can go out for dinner with the president of Harvard, or she can go over to a falling-down cabin back in the mountains with no sanitation at all and sit down in the kitchen and talk to folks.

18   "She's never been for giving anyone a free handout. She organized communities in self-help projects where they use government money and their own labor to lay water lines and rehab houses, and people really trusted her. I've seen 70-year-old women working laying water lines. Wilma and Charlie live in a simple house, and she drives an old car with a cracked windshield. When the Finance Committee voted to increase her salary, she turned it down. When a rich Cherokee from Texas who had a car dealership wanted to give her a new car she turned *him* down and asked him to give the money to the Indian Children's Home—and he did!"

19   "In public service, you must be motivated by hope, by a feeling that you can make a change," Mankiller says. "We've had daunting problems in health care, education, housing, law enforcement, and other critical areas. I believe in the old Cherokee injunction to 'be of a good mind.' Today it's called positive thinking. When I was younger I was full of anger, but you can't dwell on problems if you want to bring change; you have to be forward thinking, dwelling on the positives, not the negatives."

20   Women, she says, have a very different style of leadership from that of men. "Women in leadership are more collaborative. We build teams. We are more consultative, less ready to make unilateral decisions. I think women see things in an in-

terconnected way. We understand, for instance, that preparation for higher education begins with prenatal care."

21 "When Wilma became chief it started a wave of confidence and awareness among women here," says Director of Community Development Gwendolyn Grayson. "She taught us that we have an obligation to use our talents, to run for public office. She encouraged me to run for school board and I won, and then I became the first woman president of the Board of Education. Now we have a woman mayor and a woman superintendent of schools."

22 Mankiller is intensely gratified by the fact that her leadership has made her a role model. "My feeling is that women have to take more personal responsibility for turning the country around. Suddenly you hear young Cherokee girls talking about becoming leaders," she says. "And in Cherokee families there is more encouragement of girls. Cherokee girls have the usual self-esteem problems of all American girls, plus the added problems caused by society's goofy misconceptions about them. So many Americans still think Indian women are down by the creek washing clothes. An accomplishment I'm proud of is helping people feel better about themselves and their tribal government. There's no contradiction in celebrating being Cherokee and being an American."

23 It's impossible to find anyone in Tahlequah who isn't eager to talk about the chief. The manager of a fast-food restaurant proudly announces that the chief and her husband both often stop in for lunch ("We try to please her—just like we do all our customers"). The woman who minds the gift shop in the museum at the Cherokee Heritage Center lifts her eyes from her reading—the Gospel of St. John in Cherokee. She says the most important work Mankiller has done is starting a youth alcohol rehabilitation program. And as a full-blood brought up in a Cherokee-speaking home, she is pleased about the recently developed classes that help others learn to read and speak the tribal language. A new program will permit Oklahoma high school students to fulfill their foreign language requirement by studying Cherokee.

24 Down at the Tahlequah Chamber of Commerce, in the old Cherokee capitol building at the corner of Muskogee Avenue and Keetoowah Street, a man heading upstairs to the tribal district court wants to make the point—emphatically—that "All those guys who opposed her back then now say they were wrong. They'll come right out and tell you. Every single one of them."

25 "People have stopped judging me simply on the basis of gender," says Mankiller. "I always felt that if I failed, people would say it was because I was a woman. Now people agree or disagree with me based on the issues."

26 Under Mankiller's leadership, the tribe has signed a self-governance agreement with the Department of Interior that gives them a say in the allocation of resources. Her guiding philosophy is that "Indians should be problem-solvers for Indian problems." Cherokee people, she says, should not think of themselves as victims. They have the ability, interest, and wish to solve their own problems. All projects the tribe undertakes now have elements of self-help and mutual help.

27 Her plans for the future tumble out: A major residential vocational education center is being built; more adult literacy programs are in the offing; she wants to

start programs for older women going back to school; expand summer youth programs; bring in more industry. Some light industry has come to the area—most recently a chicken-deboning plant—but the chief wants to attract businesses that require high skill levels and pay high wages. She hopes to settle the Arkansas River land claim against the federal government, a territorial dispute that has been in litigation for 25 years. The job still has challenges galore, and some of the problems are shocking. There are still Cherokees living nearby who drink from the creek and haul water because wells are dry or contaminated.

28   Chief Mankiller's vision extends far beyond the problems of 130,000 tribal members who live in a 7,000-square-mile 14-country jurisdiction (the Oklahoma Cherokees are a non-reservation tribe). She marched in Birmingham with Coretta Scott King on Martin Luther King's birthday ("I felt I should go to give a sense of solidarity, a sense that we must fight together against racial hatred"). She was appointed an advisor on tribal affairs to President Clinton's transition team soon after his election, and she views this administration as a time for a renewal of hope.

29   Don Greenfeather wraps up his discussion of the chief's accomplishments. "Wilma," he says, "is my idea of a great stateswoman. She's done everything for us, and she's restored dignity and self-esteem to our people—but you'll never hear her brag on it. Other tribes now wait and see how the Cherokees act, what decisions we make. She's put us out front."

READING

1. How did Wilma Mankiller become chief of the Cherokee Nation? Was she accepted and supported by her people? Is she now?

2. What has Mankiller accomplished for her tribe since she became Chief?

THINKING

1. Mankiller has had tremendous physical problems, but she has still gone on to work for the Tribe and accomplish many things. How do you think your life would change if you had the serious injuries and illnesses that she has endured?

2. Mankiller's first husband couldn't tolerate her breaking away from the role of only staying home to be a wife and mother. He did not want her to become educated. She has come from that relationship to be a significant political leader. What do you feel woman's role in society is? Is it different than man's? How? Should it be? Why or why not?

PREWRITING

Read the two writing assignments below and decide which one you would like to do. Freewrite for ten minutes without stopping including all the ideas you can think of that you would like to include in the writing assignment you chose. Remember when you are freewriting to not stop for any reason. Do not stop to think.

Do your thinking on the paper. Remember that when you are freewriting errors don't matter. Just write down all of your ideas as they come into your mind. When you finish, go back through what you have written and decide what you would like to actually include in your writing assignment. Be sure to write down any new ideas that come to mind while you are reviewing your freewriting.

WRITING

1. Your friend has recently gotten married, and she just wrote to tell you that now that she is married, her new husband has demanded that she drop out of college and start taking care of the house and having babies. He had not told her he felt this way before the wedding. She is asking for your advice. Write her a well developed letter expressing how you feel about her situation using details and specific examples.

2. You are running for a political office that would make you a leader (chief, mayor, governor, associated students president, you choose). Write a well developed essay saying why you are the most qualified person for this position and describing in detail at least three things that you would accomplish in this leadership position. Be convincing so that you can win the election.

REVISING

Horwitz uses a chronological strategy in this article to organize her ideas. She covers a long period of time, from when Mankiller was a child to the present day. In an article of this length, she obviously could not spend a great deal of time on all of the details of Mankiller's life, so she choose the examples of her lifetime that most clearly related to her thesis and then wrote about them in order. Another organizational strategy is spatial. With this strategy, your organization would be done by starting at one space or area and moving toward another with your writing. A third strategy would be logical, with each element of your argument or thesis building in the element that came right before in your writing.

Examine the rough draft of your writing assignment to determine if you have used one of these organization strategies. If you have not, how have you organized your writing? Would it be better if you organized this assignment with one of these strategies? Revise your assignment accordingly.

EDITING

When a pronoun is used in a pair with another pronoun or a noun, treat each pronoun as if it were being used by itself to determine which pronoun to use.

Examples:
   She and **I** went shopping.

You can tell that this is correct because you would say "**she** went shopping" or "**I** went shopping," so when they are used together, they must be **She** and **I.**

Mother loved to go shopping with **them** and **us.**

While this may sound strange, you can tell that it is correct because you would say "Mother loved to go shopping with **them**," or "Mother loved to go shopping with **us.**"

Check your writing to be sure that you have used the proper pronouns.

Putting on the Ritz

Stanley H. Murray

PREREADING

Terry Holmes had the good fortune to get a job as a teenager because of a comment Terry's father's employer made when Terry's father died. Write about what kind of job you would have today if you went to work for the employer that your parent or guardian had when you were sixteen. Do you think that you could have developed that job into a successful career? Why or why not?

DEFINING

hall porter (¶1)   a manager for guests in a hotel

disarmingly (¶2)   taking away all threat or fear

contradictory (¶2)   in a position that totally opposes another position

page (¶3)   a person who runs errands for someone else

latent (¶4)   hidden or undeveloped

larder (¶4)   a room where meat and food are kept

swank (¶5)   stylish

ecstatic (¶5)   filled with joy and delight, extremely happy

comptroller (¶6)   an official in charge of spending money

commis **(¶6)**   clerk

1950 *Lafite-Rothschild* (¶6)   rare wine

chef de rang (¶6)   chief cook of order

chef de brigade (¶6)   chief cook in charge of other cooks

sommelier (¶6)   wine butler

bidet (¶7)   a bathroom fixture designed to wash the crotch

mentor (¶7)   a wise counselor

condescension (¶8)   the act of lowering oneself to speak to someone seeming inferior

Freeman (¶8)   a person who has all civil and political rights in a state

shortlisted (¶9)   chosen out of a larger number

prestigious (¶11)   with a reputation of excellence

exuberance (¶11)   a condition of overflowing with good health and spirit

eccentricity (¶11)   being different from what is considered normal

Putting on the Ritz

Stanley H. Murray

1   When Terry Holmes, Vice-President and Managing Director of Cunard Hotels Limited, was nine years old, his father took him to visit the Dorchester Hotel in London where the elder Holmes worked as a hall porter. On the way, sitting on top of the Number Nine London bus, they passed the Ritz Hotel, which captured the youngster's imagination. "One day," he said to his father, "I'd like to sleep there."

2   Today, 44-year-old Terry Holmes, a man who is both disarmingly charming and contradictory, recalls that at the time he had two ambitions—to go to the moon and sleep at the Ritz. Nothing else mattered. He never got to the moon, and the road to sleeping at the Ritz was to be almost as difficult.

3   Terry Holmes's entry into the hotel business was not planned, though its origins can be traced to his father who had started his career as a page at the Dorchester Hotel when it opened in 1931. His father died from wounds sustained during the Second World War when Terry was just 11, and it was a chance remark at the funeral by the Dorchester's General Manager which led him, five years later at the age of 16, to apply there for a job. "It was the sort of thing people say on such occasions," Terry Holmes recalls, but the General manager interviewed him personally. "I was completely without qualifications. I had never passed an examination. How well I remember that day. I had absolutely no problems with the questions, only the answers."

4   According to Holmes, what followed were six years of the best training that anyone who wanted to succeed in the hotel industry could have. Unfortunately, he

Stanley H. Murray, "Putting on the Ritz," *British Heritage,* April/May 1991, pp. 30–35. Reprinted by permission of the author.

Please note maps in appendix for references to places in this article.

did not display any latent talent as he moved from department to department, and the spark of ambition was not to glow for some time. "I started in the kitchen, in the larder," recalls Mr. Holmes. "I don't think they expected me to stay. I was absolutely terrified. Everything was new to me. It was the first time I'd seen a lobster. When I had to fetch one, it moved and I dropped it. The next day I sent an Israeli melon on up to the Sheikh of Dubai who was an hotel guest. He was furious, but I didn't know at the time that melons had religions."

5   After two-and-a-half years, the kitchen staff had enough of young Terry. He was booted upstairs, not as an advancement, but to get him out of the way. He landed in the hotel's swank Terrace Room, which in those days had a 20-piece orchestra. It was 1966, the year England won the World Cup. "When I heard the news, I was ecstatic," says Terry Holmes. I picked up a silver serving bowl and ran round the restaurant with it on my head shouting, "We won the cup, we won the cup!" Hearing the commotion, the General Manager dismissed him on the spot. As had happened in the past, he was reinstalled a few hours later.

6   Despite such incidents he began to assume greater responsibilities. Having started as a *commis,* he first progressed to *chef de rang,* then to *chef de brigade.* But the road to the top was filled with obstacles. Terry Holmes's next position was back downstairs in the wine cellars, as a wine *commis.* He was sent to collect a bottle of 1950 Lafite-Rothschild, which he found covered with dust. Innocently, he washed it, for which the *sommelier* threw him down a flight of stairs. Terry Holmes had become somewhat of a celebrity within the hotel because of his inability to avoid trouble. Repeatedly dismissing him did no good, since the General Manager, out of his memory of the boy's father, always rehired him. Out of desperation, he was moved to the comptroller's office, where, still without ambition, he found that he was better at arithmetic than he had seemed at school when, in his words: "I was bad in everything, but worst at maths."

7   He lasted in the comptroller's office for eight months, and then moved to reception, where his duties included escorting guests to their rooms, and he finally became excited about the hotel business. "Can you imagine that after 5½ years, it was the first time I'd been above the ground floor? I couldn't believe it when I saw the enormous suites, with two bathrooms and something called a bidet," he said. After working in reception for more than two years, Terry Holmes went to his mentor, the General Manager, to see what was in store for the future. This single encounter was perhaps the major turning point in Holmes's career, since quite unexpectedly, it gave him the long-needed push to advance himself.

8   The General Manager told him: "You've done well, but I actually think you should get out of the hotel business. You come from a poor family, have little or no education, and you talk funny." Such condescension angered Terry Holmes. He didn't care that he came from the Old Kent Road district of South London. It was the only home he'd ever known. He was proud of his strong cockney accent. And above all, he had great pride in his family, especially in his father, who had been his best friend and role model. He vowed that he would not only say in the hotel business, but be one of the world's most successful and respected hoteliers. Little did he know then that he would eventually be honored as England's Hotelier of

the Year, elected a Master Innkeeper, and be named a Freeman of the City of London.

9   He immediately began to write letters answering advertisements for hotel jobs in the United Kingdom and the United States. After six months, he was still waiting for a positive response. The aspiring hotelier realized that he was probably not ready for a better position and spent the next six months preparing himself. When he thought he was at last ready he applied for another 30 jobs, but once again, came up without an interview. While none of his enquiries drew a response, he did receive an interview from an hotel he'd never written to. His wife, Lynda, had seen an advertisement for the position of assistant manager of the Stafford Hotel and applied on his behalf, forging his name on the letter. Fifty people had answered the advertisement, and only two were shortlisted. For his third interview at the Stafford, he was asked to bring his wife. "Several days later, I got a phone call offering me the job."

10   The year was 1969, and it can be described as the time when either the takeover of Terry Holmes by the Stafford took place, or when Terry Holmes's takeover of the Stafford began. Terry Holmes's success still was not certain. The longtime barman at the hotel at that time said that he'd give Holmes two weeks in the job. Fortunately, Mr. Holmes's personality and ability, together with some luck, once again brought him through. He was named General Manager in 1973. The Stafford prospered like never before. Still, there was always a lingering doubt about Terry Holmes's lack of education and his further advancement.

11   In 1977, the Managing Director of the Stafford left to oversee the catering at Oxford University. Terry Holmes was determined to reach the top spot. He went to the owners and said he would like to formally apply for the position of Managing Director of the hotel. When told that one couldn't apply, but rather had to be approached for the job, Mr. Holmes's answer was simply: "Then approach me." And approach him they did. When his appointment came through, he was the youngest Managing Director of any hotel in London's prestigious West End. "I'd never been so lonely since by Mum and Dad died. Yet, because my parents passed away when I was very young, it probably moulded me to cope with the loneliness of being at the top." This statement provides deep-rooted insight about Terry Holmes the hotelier, and the survival of Terry Holmes, the man. It explains why, even to this day, the snobbery and rejection he has encountered from time to time, which might have hampered others, have not suppressed the gaiety and exuberance, or the natural eccentricity, which is never far from the surface of his personality.

12   Terry Holmes's honesty, fairness, and sense of fun has made him totally irrepressible. For instance, when he was made a Freeman of the City of London, following his appointment as a master hotelier, guests and staff held a surprise party for him at the hotel. Learning that as a freeman he was entitled to drive sheep across London Bridge, his hosts arranged for a shepherdess, leading a live sheep, to be brought into the party. Upon seeing the sheep, Terry Holmes with his characteristic spontaneity, proceeded to lead it into the next room where there was a private party in progress for eight guests whom he knew well. Upon entering, Mr. Holmes asked with a straight face: "Would you like your lamb on or off the bone?"

13   Terry Holmes's success is based on his ability to get along with people, a talent reflected in the tenure of his staff at the Stafford, many of whom have been there for more than 30 years. He claims: "They just won't quit. After all, besides their other duties, they have to look after me." When Holmes had been at the Stafford for about three years, he began to think of leaving to manage a private club. The barman asked Mr. Holmes to meet him after work at a nearby pub. At the meeting, the barman said: "In here we're just two men, friends, and not boss and staff. I'm telling you that if you leave the hotel for the club, you'll be out of work in about two months when it folds." He was persuaded to stay at the Stafford, and four months later, the club folded. Cunard Hotels have since made him their top hotelier, in charge not only of the Stafford, but of the Ritz and Dukes Hotel as well.

14   That and numerous other informal meetings with his staff have made Terry Holmes a firm believer that the staff kept him over the years, rather than the other way around. Often, by his own admission, the staff would correct him or give him ideas and have him think that they were his own. This has led to a management philosophy which Terry Holmes described as being a two-way street: he tries to be as good to his help as they are to him.

15   As to Terry Holmes's values, they're always out in the open. On most days, you'll find an expensive Rolex watch on his wrist. But on those occasions when he really wants to impress people, he wears a very special watch, with an inscription on the back, for 21 years of dedicated service to the Dorchester Hotel. It was the one given to his father as a retirement present from the management.

READING

1. Why did Holmes start working in the hotel business? Who helped Holmes get started? Why did that person help Holmes?

2. What was Holmes' childhood dream? How did it come true? How does Holmes treat his employees? Does that help him to be successful?

THINKING

1. Holmes had worked for the hotel for five and a half years before he went above the ground floor. What was the significance of going upstairs? Why do you suppose he didn't just go up there before?

2. Have you ever stayed in luxurious accommodations? Imagine what the rooms in the Ritz would look like. How big would they be? What kind of furnishings would they have? What colors would you see? What kinds of services would be available? How would you feel about staying there?

PREWRITING

Write about jobs for teenagers. Think of all of the different jobs you and your class-mates have had. What kind of work did you do for these jobs? Was it manual labor, clerical work, domestic help, or other types of work? What kind of money could be earned? What were the chances for advancement?

WRITING

1. Write an essay for your classmates telling them about your first job. Be sure to include what your responsibilities were and what you learned by having this job. Also, predict what the influence of this job will be on the rest of your life. Share this assignment with the rest of the class to compare your ideas.

2. Your high school alumni organization is putting together a career handbook for students to help them plan their future careers. You have volunteered to write a section telling about the jobs that are available in your community to 16-year-olds who have not finished high school. Be sure to include what the potential for advancement in the future is for these jobs.

REVISING

In "Putting on the Ritz," Stanley Murray used **chronological organization.** This means that he arranged the information in the article according to when Mr. Holmes held his different jobs. For instance, he started when he was 16 and had six years of training. The first two and a half years he spent in the larder. Then he started working in the Terrace Room, and so on. Chronological organization is useful to show the progression of events. It can show if things get better or worse over time.

Check your writing assignment to see if you used chronological organization. Either writing assignment here could use this form of organization, mentioning first the past, then the present, and then looking forward to the future. If you haven't organized this assignment in this fashion, how would your essay be different if you used chronological organization?

EDITING

"Putting on the Ritz" is enhanced by the use of quotes by Terry Holmes because the article is about him. **Quotes** can be an effective way to enhance your writing, but there are some rules that must be followed to use them correctly. **Quotation marks** come immediately before the quote begins. The quote is followed by end punctuation, then final quotation marks.

Example:
"Several days later, I got a phone call offering me the job." (¶9)

If there is a pause in the middle of a quote, the comma goes before the quotation marks.

Example:
"One day," he said to his father, "I'd like to sleep there." (¶1)

If the quote is followed by who said it or by more information in the sentence, then the comma comes inside the quotation marks.

Example:

"When I heard the news, I was ecstatic," says Terry Holmes. (¶5)

Using capital letters correctly is a skill that is necessary for a good writer. Mistakes in **capitalization** are frequently made when quotations are used. Check over your writing assignment to be sure that you have capitalized according to the following rules.

1. Always capitalize the first word in a sentence, the first word in a quoted sentence, and the first word in a title. Also capitalize most words in titles. Don't capitalize articles (a, and, the), prepositions, or conjunctions in titles unless they are the first or last words of the title, and don't put quotation marks around your own title.

Examples:

He immediately began to write letters. . . .

I picked up a silver serving bowl and ran around the restaurant shouting, "*We* won the cup, *we* won the cup!"

Stanley *H.* Murray wrote the article, "*P*utting on the *R*itz."

2. Always use a capital to indicate the proper names of people, places, or things.

Examples:

*U*sually, *I* sit them down and just explain the story.

*T*oday, 44-year-old *T*erry *H*olmes, a man who is both disarmingly charming and contradictory, recalls that at the time he had two ambitions—to go to the moon and sleep at the *R*itz.

Go back through your writing assignment to be sure that you have used quotation marks and capital letters correctly. If you haven't used any quotes, try adding some.

Her Main Squeeze

Alicia Stephens Guffey

PREREADING

Sheila Cardenas became a multimillionaire because she had the courage to say "I can!" when a good idea came long. Write about courage. Do you think that you are brave enough to take on a risky challenge if it has the possibility of bringing you great wealth and a sense of achievement?

DEFINING

sprawling (¶1)   spread out

egocentric (¶3)   self-centered

impetus (¶7)   something that stimulates activity

meticulously (¶14)   very carefully

adhering (¶14)   sticking to

punctuality (¶14)   being on time

perfectionist (¶14)   person who want everything to be perfect

Alicia Stephens Guffey, "Her Main Squeeze," *Entrepreneurial Woman,* June 1991, pp. 46–49. Reprinted with permission of Entrepreneur Inc.

Please note maps in appendix for references to places in this article.

Her Main Squeeze

Alicia Stephens Guffey

1   Drive through the gates of Sheila Cardenas' four-acre estate and you see a number of impressive sights: a sprawling home, a brick office building, tennis courts, a swimming pool, and a big blue camping tent, which serves as the children's playhouse. A slender gray cat rubs against you as you step into the offices. Inside, the office is buzzing. The telephone is ringing. Cardenas' husband, Enrique, sits at the front desk talking on the phone; the secretary is home sick. Their daughters Sheila, 8, and Jalene, 6, run in chattering.

2   An attractive woman rushes from her office wearing a pair of black stretch pants and an oversized sweater. Her long brown hair is pulled back into a ponytail, and she is wearing little makeup. She is Sheila Cardenas, and you have just entered her world. Cardenas, 31, is founder and president of Cardenas International Inc., a multimillion-dollar McAllen, Texas-based company that imports frozen orange, apple, and grape juice concentrate from Mexico. Cardenas, a fiery ball of energy, is like a 33 rpm record played at 45 rpm. She quickly greets her children and ushers you into her office. Her nervous energy bounces off the walls of the room, affecting everyone around. One employee describes her as "very hyper, but when you get her away from the office and she relaxes, she becomes a totally different person." Cardenas has channeled that fantastic energy into her 4-year-old company, which sells juice concentrate not only to the United States, but to Canada, Europe, and Asia as well.

• • •

3   Cardenas likes living well and readily admits that her motive for starting Cardenas International was egocentric. "I wanted to buy a Mercedes-Benz," she says, smiling. Her opportunity to make that a reality came in 1986. A family friend, who was a grocery store chain representative, knew that Enrique was a Mexican national and involved in the agriculture business, so he asked Cardenas if she knew someone who could supply the chain with orange juice concentrate from Mexico. Cardenas unhesitatingly answered, "I can!"

4   Enrique helped her get started by establishing initial contacts with a few suppliers he knew in Mexico who were interested in selling orange juice concentrate to the United States. Combine that with $50,000 of the Cardenases' own savings, and the full-time mother and homemaker was ready for business. Cardenas more than kept her promise to deliver. Last year, sales of her orange, apple, and grape juice concentrates surpassed $30 million. Needless to say, Cardenas bought her dream car. She has sold enough juice concentrate to buy an entire fleet of cars. Cardenas International exports one-third of Mexico's orange-juice production.

5   Suppliers from Mexico send Cardenas 600-pound drums of frozen orange juice by refrigerated truck. Once the juice reaches the United States, it is shipped to the buyers, who package it into 6- and 12-ounce containers and sell it to grocery store chains. For the first two years of her business, Cardenas did everything except load the huge drums of juice. "I coordinated the sale, purchased the product, [met

the shipment] at the U.S. border, supervised inspection with the USDA, and shipped it to the buyers," she says. Clad in jeans and sneakers, Cardenas would open the huge doors of the trailers and rail cars and climb inside to check the juice for any signs of heat exposure.

6   Remembering those long, hard days, she says, "I wanted to hire someone else to climb into the trailers and rail cars. When I mentioned it to Enrique, he said I really needed to know how to do it myself before I could tell someone else how to do it." That rang a bell with Cardenas. Growing up, her father had always told her the same thing. So she became an expert at climbing into rail cars. "Now, I can climb up into the trailers and rail cars in a dress and heels," Cardenas says, proudly. "I'd probably shock a lot of people if they knew everything that I do."

7   Cardenas found that knowing every detail of her business was essential to the success of the company. The impetus for that philosophy came during her first year in business. A chemist checked Cardenas' juice concentrate and said it was not 100 percent pure. "That was not true," she exclaims, still upset five years later. Cardenas immediately set out to learn every aspect of the juice concentrates she was importing. Helping her with her mission was Alan Brouse, a chemist who analyzed the samples she sent him, and patiently taught a naive Cardenas the chemistry of orange juice.

8   Cardenas vigorously studied every detail of the juice concentrate business, often working 12 hours a day. She also made it a point to research every company in the business that was big enough to buy juice concentrate, as well as the companies that could potentially be the biggest buyers. "I am not shy or easily intimidated, so perhaps that helps," she says. "I sent letters and samples, and then I'd call to follow up on those letters and samples." She also spent hours on the phone tracking her competition. Cardenas did her homework well, and, as a result, she secured more contracts with suppliers and buyers. By the end of her first year, gross sales reached $3 million.

9   By her second year in business, everyone in the juice industry knew of Cardenas. It was then that she became the first woman in history to give a speech at the National Juice Products Association in Denver. As word spread about Cardenas in Mexico as well, she began receiving requests from suppliers who knew of her reputation and wanted to contract with her.

10   Cardenas believes her college education helped prepare her for the challenge of international business. She has degrees in political science with a focus on international politics and history. She also minored in economics and speaks French and Spanish fluently. Cardenas International had more than doubled by the end of its second year, and Cardenas knew she needed help. So she hired a secretary to answer the telephone and keep the books.

11   She also enlisted the help of Enrique, an agricultural engineer. Although he was busy with his own cattle ranch, an orange and corn growing business, and his hotel in Mexico, he reorganized his workload so he could work with his wife part time. "I needed someone intelligent handling every contact," Cardenas explains, "and I couldn't handle the volume of contacts we were making and receiving."

12   She and Enrique agree completely that two heads are better than one. "Sometimes things become a real challenge, and Enrique always has a different point of view, which helps," Cardenas says. It also helps that Enrique is a Mexican citizen and an expert on the customs and culture of Mexico. Enrique doesn't feel that being married to the president of the company is an obstacle. "When we're together for business, I don't think of our [personal] relationship," he says. "I respect her because she is my wife, but business is business." And, he adds, "Whatever Sheila wants in business, she goes after." Which is exactly what Cardenas did in 1988, when she decided to expand her business to include apply and grape juice concentrates so the company would be busy year-round.

13   For the first two years, Cardenas ran the company out of her home, but as the business grew and the family needed more living space, they bought their present home and office property. Now, a converted guest house serves as the business office. When asked why she thinks Cardenas International has been so successful, Cardenas hesitates, then replies, "Well, it has been a lot of hard work and long hours, but mostly, I guess it is because of our dedication to service, quality, reliability, and price. Also, as the company grew, I was never afraid that I couldn't handle it."

14   Cardenas is meticulously devoted to quality, researching, and adhering to all of the latest pesticide regulations. She is also a firm believer in punctuality and keeping her word. "I love what I do," she says. "As long as there is a need for juices, I'll be [involved] in the industry." Her employees say she expects a lot, and Cardenas agrees. "I'm a perfectionist. But when you have high expectations, it is hard to lower them." For Cardenas, the hardest aspect of business is finding good employees. "My suppliers expect top performance, and I in turn expect that from my employees," she says. "I don't always get it; finding responsible people is hard." Her solution to this problem is very simple: She only has four office employees, and maintains a loading crew of just 13.

15   Cardenas' high expectations have paid off admirably. She is content with the size of her company, and plans for the future will focus on minimizing risks. Few problems occurred in the business's first three years, but the honeymoon ended when Cardenas got her first taste of the uncertainty of the juice business. "In October 1980, a hurricane hit Mexico, destroying half of an apple crop we had contracted," remembers Cardenas. "I now realize that in a business like this, nothing is ever really certain."

16   How does she plan to minimize risks? "You do that with weekly attorney bills," Cardenas laughingly replies. Other plans include maintaining the company's high quality and dependable service. "I never dreamed this would be a multimillion-dollar company, and I don't plan on it becoming a billion-dollar company either," she says. "My plans are to be happy with what I have."

17   Despite her busy schedule, Cardenas always makes time for her two children, whether supervising their homework at the conference table in her office, or car pooling with other mothers in the neighborhood. And when the children are at home with the housekeeper, she still keeps up with their activities. It is not unusual for her to receive telephone calls from her children when she's in the office. Some-

times it's Sheila asking Mom how to make frozen strawberry pops; other times it's Jalene calling to ask if she can go over to a friend's house.

18   Now that her client base is well-established and she has Enrique to help out, Cardenas' 12-hour days are behind her. She tries to maintain an 8-to-5 work schedule, so she has time to spend time with her family. However, business is never completely out of mind—Cardenas' customers can always reach her at home. Soon, Cardenas will take on yet one more responsibility. Her third child is due in July, and like everything else in her life, she is facing this new addition with energetic optimism. Anticipating few changes as a result of the new infant, she details her latest strategy: "I plan to bring a little crib to the office. [The timing is even right]; the baby will be born in the off-season for citrus. The grape season will be just beginning, but I will have my plans under control by then."

19   Cardenas believes being a woman has made it harder for her to be taken seriously in this business. "If there has been any obstacle, it's the fact that I am a woman," she contends. "I have had to work twice as hard, especially in this business, which is dominated by men." Even so, Cardenas is making inroads into this industry. In fact, she is the only women in the United States who owns a juice concentrate business.

20   Her advice for other entrepreneurial women: "Make sure you know what you're doing because you will get challenged in every way—challenged more than if you were a man. It's important to maintain feminine qualities, yet behind all that you must have a sense of assertiveness."

21   Suddenly, remembering a business appointment, Cardenas springs from her chair. As she rushes out the door, she stops long enough to feed the cat. By the time she flies past the double gates in her gold Mercedes, she is already talking on her car phone. You smile as the car disappears around the corner, for somehow you sense the juice business is just the beginning for this superwoman.

READING

1. Why did Sheila Cardenas go into the orange juice business? Who helped her? Where did she get the idea?

2. Why is she so successful at what she is doing? What is her main advice to other women who would like to go into business?

THINKING

1. Cardenas is the only woman in the United States who owns a juice concentrate business. She feels this means she has had to work twice as hard. Why or how would being a woman make a difference in business?

2. Cardenas feels her education really helped her to be successful. What did she study in college? How do you think those fields of study helped her in the business that she is in? How do you think that your education will help you with your future plans?

PREWRITING

Write a list of the things you feel you do the best. Look at this list and determine the things you enjoy the most. Write why you enjoy these things.

WRITING

1. Cardenas found that she had to learn everything possible about her business in order to be successful. Think of what you feel you do best, and write an essay for your classmates telling them how to do it. It can be something like grocery shopping, studying, sewing, changing the oil in your car, writing poetry, or mowing the lawn. Be sure to include every detail that you can think of.

2. Cardenas expects and receives top performance from everyone she works with. You are the boss for a company that you have created. Write an instructional essay for your supervisors telling them how to get top performance from their employees. Use some of Cardenas' ideas as inspiration.

REVISING

In "Her Main Squeeze," much of the process of running a frozen juice importation company is described. Notice how the process of operating the company is woven into the essay. The most frequently used organizational style for writing a process paper is to arrange your description in chronological order. Writing assignment number one asks for the process of some activity. To do this assignment in chronological order, you need to arrange the steps that should be taken in the order in which they should be done. For example, to describe how to load the dishwasher, you could make a list to help you remember the steps so that you wouldn't leave out any important details.

Example:
1. bring the dirty plates to the sink from the table
2. scrape any large pieces of food or bone into the garbage
3. quickly rinse the dishes with running water
4. load the top rack first with glasses, cups, and small items
5. be sure anything plastic goes on the top rack
6. place the silverware in the silverware basket
7. place any large items on the bottom rack
8. be sure not to overload the dishwasher
9. be sure not to block where the water enters
10. place the detergent in the dispenser

11. close and lock the door

12. set the controls for the desired cycle

13. turn on the dishwasher

14. be sure to let it run until the cycle is complete

15. let the dishes dry and cool off inside the dishwasher

16. put the dishes away

There are many steps to doing what seems to be a simple task. Each one of these steps can be described more fully.

Look at the draft you have written, and see if you have included all of the necessary steps and details that you need.

EDITING

Commas are used in a sentence to set off words, phrases, or clauses that are not necessary to the meaning of the sentence. These are called **nonrestricive elements.**

Example:

Cardenas' husband, *Enrique,* sits at the front desk talking on the phone. (**¶1**)

Cardenas only has one husband, so when it says "Cardenas' husband," his name, *Enrique,* is just added information.

Example:

Cardenas, a fiery ball of energy, is like a 33 rpm record played at 45 rpm. (**¶2**)

A *fiery ball of energy* adds to the description of Cardenas, but it is not necessary for the sentence to be complete and make sense. The sentence could just as easily be, "Cardenas is like a 33 rpm record played at 45 rpm."

Check your paper to see if you have any sentences using nonrestrictive elements. If you do, be sure that they have commas on both sides.

Heir Roselló

Philipe Schoene Roura

PREREADING

Puerto Rico has been experiencing many problems with its government, but their new governor has great plans for changing things. Do you think the change of a governor can make a significant difference? Why or why not? How do you think that the way the public views what a public official does affects the official's ability to be effective? How do you find out about what your governor is doing? Are you happy with your governor? Why or why not?

DEFINING

antidotes (¶1)   remedies

fervor (¶1)   intensity of emotion

implicit (¶1)   understood but not directly stated

analogy (¶1)   comparison based on similarities

entrepreneurial (¶1)   personally responsible for new and different business concepts

La Fortaleza (¶2)   the governor's mansion

opulent (¶3)   showing great wealth

hallowed (¶3)   greatly honored

blanched (¶3)   turned pale

queried (¶4)   questioned

bistec encebollado **(¶4)**   beefsteak with onions

gastronomic (¶4)   the art or science of good eating

frugality (¶6)   being economic

disenchanted (¶8)   being freed from illusion

unorthodox (¶9)   not traditional

technocrats (¶9)   being in favor of a society run by scientists and/or technical experts

grueling (¶10)   physically or mentally exhausting

ensuing (¶12)   resulting

punto **(¶14)**   to the point, accomplished

reiterates (¶16)   says or does repeatedly

consummate (¶17)   complete, perfect

emasculation (¶17)   deprived of strength, weakened

umpteenth (¶19)   large, unspecified number

NPP (¶22)   a political party

qualms (¶25)   uneasy feelings about the rightness of an action

spawned (¶38)   produced in large numbers

ancillary (¶38)   something not as important as the main thing

conciliatory (¶38)   an attempt to overcome distrust

altruists (¶40)   people with unselfish concern for other people

autonomy (¶42)   independence

voluted (¶44)   spiral, scroll-like ornamentation used in architecture

infrastructure (¶47)   foundation

de facto (¶47)   actual

divergence (¶48)   departure from the norm

Heir Rosselló

Philipe Schoene Roura

1   In only his first year of getting acquainted with big league politics, Governor Pedro Rosselló has made his transition from pediatric surgeon to the prescriber of antidotes for the ills of all Puerto Rico by following with religious fervor the philosophy implicit in that analogy. And, while the application of concepts—entrepreneurial and mission-driven government—has made him

Philipe Schoene Roura, "Heir Rosselló," *San Juan City Magazine,* vol. III, no. II, 1994, pp. 44–53. Reprinted by permission.

Please note maps in appendix for references to places in this article.

aware of some hard realities, empowerment of the people remains at the core of his quest for change.

2   From the very moment he pressed his black Dexters to the worn marble of La Fortaleza's front steps, Rosselló has faced the "reinventing" workshop of his life: an island marred by social problems so rooted in a deteriorating moral fabric it will take decades for even the most sweeping reforms to make inroads.

3   His first look at the excesses of opulent government was not in the hallowed halls of some government agency, but right at home in La Fortaleza. The way one aide tells the story, the governor and the first lady had just finished a formal lunch in the state dining room. The long rectangular table, embossed leather-backed chairs, and Oller paintings that had served as decor for John F. Kennedy, Richard Nixon, and the King of Spain were the backdrop for one of the governor's first official visitors, a special envoy from George Bush. The luncheon ended a two-day inaugural madhouse, and as soon as the stately good-byes were said, the first lady was approached by the executive mansion's chef to approve the next day's usual five-course menus. The chef blanched at the first lady's surprise.

4   "What is this, are we expecting dignitaries?" she queried. "No? This is standard fare? Okay, then we'll have coffee and toast for breakfast, *bistec encebollado* and rice and beans for lunch, one light dish for supper. And you had better buy a ton of hot dogs and hamburgers for the kids." A week later the chef quit.

5   That gastronomic change order sliced La Fortaleza's food expenditures by over 67 percent, from $242,182.64 to $77,756.17 in the first six months of 1993, compared with the same period in the previous year.

6   The shift toward frugality is the bottom line in every area of the executive mansion. A comparison with the first six months of 1992 shows a marked decrease in spending in payroll (12%), representational expenses and travel (67%), and professional and consulting services (91%). In fact, all operational costs associated with the first family were reduced by 40 percent. The parallels between lean cuisine and lean government are evident.

7   The process that placed the governor in the executive mansion began in earnest more than five years ago, says a close acquaintance. Dr. Rosselló was sitting in the overstuffed Lazy Boy that had always given him solace while drinking his coffee, the latest bold headline staring at him from the morning newspaper. Suddenly it was obvious to him that someone had to do something about Puerto Rico's disturbing downward spiral. He decided he was that someone.

8   The decision certainly has changed the style of governing as Puerto Rico has known it. Alberto Goachet, director of communications for La Fortaleza, recalls Rosselló's coming out with particular enthusiasm. "I was disenchanted at the time, because I realized that new leadership was needed," he recalls. "Suddenly this guy appears, so fresh, so nice, so full of ideas, so goddamn smart. And I said, 'My God, this can't be possible!' So we began working together and it was a hell of a lot of fun, because we were able to explore ideas, to go a little beyond regular politics—you know, don't do this because it's politically incorrect. We tested new ground and it worked."

9   In an unorthodox political assent, Rosselló went from the relatively obscure

position of director of San Juan's Health Department to become a leading candidate for the Commonwealth's resident commissioner. At breakfast the morning of November 4, 1988, after Rosselló lost his bid for the resident commissioner's post, his "team of technocrats and professionals" would not let go. "Okay, Pedro, now we go for the governorship." The grueling campaign only just behind them, Maga said, "No way!" and everyone at the table laughed. "But we weren't joking," stresses Goachet, shaking his head. "The party had recognized something new was coming, something different."

10   The governor remembers it as a much more gradual process. "After we lost that election in 1988, I went on a cruise with Maga," says Rosselló. "She resisted my getting back into public life, especially after my campaign for resident commissioner. That had been a very intense and difficult campaign. Little by little, when we were already well into the process, when I was elected president of the party, Maga made a radical conversion. So that rather than having to convince her, she convinced herself. Then she was very supportive."

11   Nearly 400 days after he swore to defend the common good of all Puerto Ricans on the steps of the Capitol Building, Rosselló has needed every ounce of that support. Rosselló's first year, a self-inflicted baptism by fire, has been an ambitious crusade to turn around crime, healthcare, and education, along with "little" extracurricular projects like the appellate court battle, balancing the budget, and defending what was left of Section 936 (of the U.S. tax code) thrown in for good measure.

12   His cabinet nominees set the battleground. "The whole selection of nominees for cabinet positions I took very seriously, and from the day after the election—we started very early—I chose Baltasar, Marimer, Alvaro," the governor says, raising his eyebrows in recollection of the ensuing furor.

13   "We started a very intense period. I took over a huge space from Maga and put a lot of papers on the floor. I spend my days there, and I interviewed people. It was a process that was very important for me, because it would be the key to whether or not we would be successful. A lot of time and effort went into getting good people. I submitted the names for nomination, believing that these were good people, and that they would have the support of the Senate."

14   In making good on his promise to headhunt for the best talent—*punto,* Rosselló challenged the very essence of politics as we know it in Puerto Rico. His is a vision fashioned by a new order of politics—one that he calls black and white, one that for the most part has filled his cabinet with people "who have talent and commitment" with little reference to political affiliations.

15   That's been a difficult pill to swallow for some of the party faithful, but that was only part of the problem with his nomination for secretary of justice, Enid Martínez Moya.

16   "In the governor's mind she had all of the qualifications . . . competence and . . . integrity," reiterates Chief of Staff Alvaro Cifuentes. "He gave me instructions to work out the details with Martínez Moya, so I met with her and filled her in on what was expected of her for the position, what the governor was looking for. Then I reported back to him." After a successful interview with the governor, she was on her way to slaughter in the Senate.

17   Senators operating business-as-usual cringed at the nomination. Unlike Secretary of Education nominee Anabel Padilla, rejected by the Senate on questions of competence, Martínez Moya was considered truly talented by many people outside the Legislature. But she was not a statehooder and, worse, the similarities between her and the consummate crusader against corruption, Comptroller Ileana Colón Carlo, left images of political emasculation dancing in senatorial heads. Hiding behind old labels—inexperienced, unqualified—the suits from the Capitol Building rejected her, too. It was the first time during his administration that the moral dimension of Roselló's governorship was challenged by his own party.

18   Staffers, cabinet members and the governor were saddened by the incident. "I remember, after the rejection I invited her here, and Maga and I talked with her and her husband," says Roselló. "I felt very sad for her, because I had put her and her family through a very difficult time."

19   Two days after the rejection, I watched him as he stood against a wall observing the makeshift TV studio that cramped the airy Spanish Caoba Room at La Fortaleza. Waiting in the wings were Channel 4 anchors Guillermo José Torres and Luz Nereida Vélez who would ask the governor his umpteenth question that day. They didn't know he had been up since dawn, being asked softball questions about what he had had for breakfast and, at least five times, "What happened to Martínez Moya?"

20   When he finally crossed the patio to the tropical Salón Rattan, where Teleonce anchors Margarita Aponte and José Enrique Torres had set up their crew, he would be asked the question again: "Okay, Mr. Governor, we're going to go to a break, and when we come back we're going to discuss the Martínez Moya rejection." The governor's eyes rolled up and the lines on his face finally betrayed his exasperation. He motioned to one of his aides, and tiredly muttered, "You know . . . I think I've talked more today than I have in my entire adult life."

21   The comment is typical of his openness, and the controversial nomination typical of his style, attitudes that critics within his party contend have brought problems to the administration. Rosselló's unorthodox talent search may have given his reforms a chance to work, but it touched off the party faithful's accusations of political infidelity. Some of the old guard demanded that Rosselló name some of "their own" to positions of confidence, not some "Popular" who happens to be extremely talented. That he won't play the game is one of the milder of the criticisms leveled at him.

22   Impressions gathered over a cup of coffee with NPP Senator Kenneth McClintock, chairman of the Senate's Federal and Economic Affairs Committee, offer further insight into conflicts between the party machinery and the Island's chief executive.

23   "I feel the governor is doing a great job, and that he will be our candidate for the 1996 election," McClintock said recently. "My only misgiving with the governor is that he needs to do more recruiting of politicians to carry out his efforts. For instance, I'm totally in agreement with the Rosselló economic plan. I filed legislation to virtually eliminate capital gains taxes, which I know the governor supports. I've also come out for a number of other economically related bills that are very pro-

business. But nobody has recruited me. I have to be an active supporter and enforcer of the Rosselló agenda in the Legislature . . . and in the Senate I'm the chairman of the Federal and Economic Affairs Committee. I'm serving as a supporter of the agenda, because I believe in it; I don't have to be recruited. But, I think in a sense La Fortaleza could be more pro-active in recruiting members of the Legislature to look after the governor's interests there."

24   A taskmaster with an agenda that is booked solid, Rosselló isn't inclined to spend much time on issues that are not directly related to the mission at hand. He tends to focus on platform objectives with task-oriented singlemindedness. The same is true of Chief of Staff Alvaro Cifuentes, who is accused of stonewalling the party's mayors and top brass. The complaints during the first months of the new administration: "Alvaro doesn't take my calls," or "Alvaro's pulling the wool over the governor's eyes," don't seem to have been in tune with the Fortaleza insider dynamics.

25   "I don't think that Alvaro has done anything that has not had the backing of the governor," says McClintock. "So, if anybody has any qualms about Alvaro, they have those qualms about the governor."

26   That isn't the way many people within the party see it, casting Cifuentes as the villain at La Fortaleza. "Many people blame Alvaro, and I think that happens because they didn't read the party platform," says McClintock. "I mean, we ran on a platform to reinvent government. What these people should be thinking is that Alvaro Cifuentes is following the governor's orders. And the governor is following to the letter what he promised to do during the campaign."

27   While they are often viewed as a perfect good guy–bad guy routine, Rosselló and Cifuentes consider their ideology a "shared vision." The governor and his chief of staff have been on the same page of the Osborne and Gaebler bestseller from the outset. Their mission-driven agenda isn't easily sidetracked.

28   "Some government and elected officials have to understand that in the first four months we had to do things in one-shot deals. We took over an administration and had to start from scratch: with a $260 million deficit, almost all paperwork shredded, lack of communication, lack of access to jobs done, no one willing to give out information. In terms of priorities, that took its toll. It meant you didn't have time to take care of other situations," explains Cifuentes about conditions at La Fortaleza in the earliest days of the administration.

29   In following that agenda, Cifuentes cemented his reputation as the administration's resident zealot. As one senator put it then, "In five months I haven't had any trouble with Alvaro returning my calls . . . because I haven't called him in five months."

30   That was mostly during the first year of the administration. These days, says McClintock, Cifuentes is far more accessible. "I have to admit that the last time I called him he returned my call within 24 hours," he says. The chief of staff explains the improved access to La Fortaleza: "Now that all of that is out of the way, and we have certain things in place, I have more time to take care of logistics in terms of being available for mayors, senators and members of the house," says Cifuentes.

31   Nonetheless, the rumblings of discontent are still heard throughout the

party. Ex-governor Luis A. Ferré's comments in *El Nuevo Dia*'s February 17 edition point to the governor's faulty communication with the party's political base, saying "there hasn't been a satisfactory solution to that problem yet."

32   Political analyst Luis Davila Colón expresses those concerns more vividly, adding that "the administration is operating in a vacuum and that can be very harmful for the party and for the governor's chances for re-election in 1996."

33   Can Rosselló improve his relationship with the party base?

34   Davila Colón doesn't think so. "You can't ask for pears from an elm tree," says the political pundit. "It isn't part of his being to be a politician."

35   While his non-political image had a lot to do with why people voted for Rosselló, party members outside La Fortaleza aren't buying into the singlemindedness the governor believes is necessary to implement profoundly radical reforms. Cifuentes and his boss, nevertherless, have kept their focus. Persistence remains as their primary shared virtue.

36   "We know that the only way to get this across is to keep hammering, because there is always going to be a lot of resistance," says Cifuentes, speaking for both. "And that is precisely what has happened. . . . We've had resistance from the powers that be, from people that are used to the same old style. We realize that sometimes there is no room for talking about it too extensively or things just don't get done."

37   While Davila Colón agrees that it is a good thing that they are rocking the boat, he adds that "sometimes, they may be rocking the boat the wrong way."

38   In the more than one year after taking charge, getting "other" factions of Puerto Rico's political system to buy into the "reinventing" philosophy is still a pretty hard sell. Consider the battle to reform education. The debate over the constitutionality of Law 18 to decentralize the Island's education system has spawned its share of ancillary distractions. Topping the list is the personal battle between the heads of the various teachers' organizations and Secretary of Education José Arsenio Torres, another controversial Rosselló appointee, over the community school concept. The conflict led to a strike paralyzing the public school system islandwide for a day, and teachers' negotiating representatives sent the conflict to arbitration under Secretary of Labor César Almodovar. The final meeting is documented in a Jan. 25 letter from José Arsenio Torres to Governor Rosselló: *"Dear Mr. Governor: In conformity with your instructions to the Government Negotiation Committee, I . . . inform you of the balance of conversations . . . with the leaders of the teachers' organizations beginning Dec. 1, 1993 and ending yesterday, Jan. 24, 1994. As a result of those conversations, both parts agreed on Dec. 1, 1993 that the agreements reached on Nov. 3, 1993 would be put into effect by the negotiating parties as recommendations to Puerto Rico's Legislative Assembly as amendments to Law 18 of June 1, 1993. I am including a copy of that document. I am also including the latest document approved by the Government Negotiating Committee, submitted to and rejected by the organizations' negotiators. In that document submitted yesterday, our committee adopted a conciliatory proposal by Secretary of Labor Almodovar that is self-explanatory. That proposal contains plausible solutions to concerns expressed by the heads of the teachers' organizations that we wanted to clarify, although they had no basis in reality or in the realities surrounding Law 18.*

39   *In refusing to answer the Government Negotiation Committee's proposal or offering a new proposal for discussion on their part, the Organizations' Negotiating Committee left the mediator without an agenda that would warrant continuing the negotiations. Based on that, the Government Negotiating Committee unanimously decided to conclude negotiations. [Signed] José Arsenio Torres, Secretary of Education.*

40   Now passing to the Senate, the conflict is labeled by administration supporters as a power struggle between true reform of an admittedly ineffective public school system and teachers' organization heads. The "magisterio brothers," say pro-reformers, masquerade as altruists by portraying the issue as one of teachers' rights against a bully administration. Proreform observers in and around the proceedings say, "The teachers' union wants to get rid of the community schools because they know that the more teachers there are that are happy the less need there is for a union."

41   Pedro Barez Rosario of the Labor Department will give minutes of the meetings to anyone who asks, and, at least on paper, events show good faith on the part of the government. "I believe the leaders of the teachers' organizations have had ample opportunity to present their point of view," says Barez.

42   The governor uses Kant's categorical imperative—does the solution, that is, community schools, result in the greatest amount of good for all? "I think the problem disappears if you can agree on what you major goal is, and we've stated many times that our motivating goal is the child—the best education for the child," explains Rosselló. "We will not respond to special interests as groups, as organizations that you might have in the current system. When we're saying that there will be autonomy in the schools, maybe there is a negative effect on the teachers' associations, but not the teacher. We've already said that we're willing to ensure that the rights of the teachers be protected, and we're willing to do that. But we're not willing to simply allow interests outside the main goal—providing the best possible education for children—to interfere with that goal."

43   The record shows that only one out of every two children entering a public school graduates from high school, and three out of four ninth-graders have inadequate language and math skills. Those grim statistics and the ballooning bureaucracy that is the highly centralized Department of Education add substance to Rosselló's push for drastic reforms.

44   While the governor admits that education reform has been tough because it requires "radical and mind-shattering change," he says that the toughest fight is that against crime. He told me this just after returning from visits to two housing projects, sitting in an elegant chair in his elegant oval office flanked by columns topped with gold and white voluted capitals. His housing project tour underscores the contrasting realities of different social strata.

45   "The fight against crime and drugs has been more difficult because it has so many factors to deal with," says Rosselló. "And, while some of the measures [we are taking] will have a long-term effect, we're struggling to see if we can bring about some short-term changes immediately to see if we can establish some safety and security for our people. So, in terms of immediate gratification, that fight is a tough one."

46   No one knows that better than Rosselló's closest advisor on crime, Police Superintendent Pedro Toledo, who sits outside with Robert Opfer, special agent in charge of the FBI in Puerto Rico, and Ted Jackson and Anthony Riggio, FBI inspectors from Washington. In their scheduled conversation with the governor, they will certainly discuss the various stages of "take-overs" at 34 public housing projects.

47   In the administration's Operation Restore, 24 housing project interventions are in their second stage, following the armed sweeps for drugs and weapons. Sixteen agencies form the Quality of Life Congress, including the departments of Social Services, Parks and Recreation, Health and Education, overseen by Housing Secretary Carlos Vivoni. In what the administration calls "a mission to restore hope," the Congress identifies community and infrastructure problems, working with de facto community leaders to find and implement solutions. One such leader is Letti Marín, whom I met on a visit to a veritable badland known as López Sicardo. She testifies that life after "El Congreso" is "much improved and full of hope for further progress," a good indication that there's more to the governor's intervention scheme than a show of force.

48   It is still too early to tell whether enough kids will trade their Uzis for basketballs, whether the universal healthcare pilot project in Fajardo will recruit a proper administrator, or how exactly the administration plans to diversify the economy or refurbish the island infrastructure, all questions fueling Rosselló's detractors from the opposition. And he also continues to deal with what he calls the "leal divergencia," or loyal divergence within his own party.

49   So what about it?

50   "I think [the divergence] is part of the process," says Rosselló. "The only way I know how to get a point across is to refer it to the people. The people have told us that we need to reinvent government; it is something the people want. So politicians are going to have to respond to that. If they don't, they're going to be accountable to the people."

51   How, I ask him, do you deal with a system that hasn't learned to accept a new style of governing?

52   He smiles: "With great difficulty."

READING

1. What are two of the main problems Rosselló is trying to solve? How is he trying to solve them?

2. What was the first thing the First Lady did to cut expenses? Was what she did effective? Why or why not?

THINKING

1. Rosselló spent a great deal of time choosing his cabinet after he was elected. How important do you think the choice of cabinet officers and/or advisors is to a politician? How do you think he handled his first attempt at appointment for the secretary of justice? How do you think he may have handled things differently? What would you have done? Why?

2. Rosselló made his efforts to turn around crime, healthcare, and education his main priorities as he took office. Do you think that these three items were too much to tackle at once? Why or why not? Which item do you think is the most important? Why? Are these problems you see affecting your own local or state government? How? What do you think should be done about the problems?

PREWRITING

Make a list of all the important issues that you can think about that you would like your governor to fix. After you make your list, pick three of the items on the list and make an individual list about each of the items stating ways you think these issues could be addressed.

WRITING

1. Write a letter to your governor. In the letter, explain why you are happy with the job he or she is doing, or why you are unhappy. Give specific praise or specific suggestions for improvement. In order to write this letter, you will need to know what your governor is doing, so check at the library to see how you can find out what is going on in your state.

2. Write a well organized essay to share with your classmates stating whether you think crime, healthcare, or education is the most important issue the government should be dealing with. State your reasoning being sure to base your argument on facts, but also use examples from your personal experience or good examples that you know of.

REVISING

"Heir Rosselló" could be considered a division and classification essay because it divides what the governor does into several different categories, then classifies these categories by explaining them. Read through the article again to see how many categories the article is divided into.

Either of your writing assignments for this section could be written using the division and classification rhetorical mode. Go through your rough draft and identify the divisions that you have included. Do you think that you have enough divisions? Does each division have an adequate explanation? Revise your draft as necessary to improve your emphasis on this mode.

EDITING

The word **that** is frequently used incorrectly when a writer is referring to a person. In this case, the writer should use the word **who.**

Examples:

A real man is one **who** displays efficiency in all walks of life. (¶ 15)

An incompetent man, one **who** is stingy, weak, or impotent, is scorned as effeminate. (¶ 15)

Notice that the word **that** could be used in either case, and you probably see it written and hear it spoken that way frequently, but to put **that** in place of **who** in either of these sentences would be incorrect.

Check through your writing assignment to be sure that you have used **who** in place of **that** when you are referring to a person.

Double Play

Radhika Radhakrishnan and Arthur Pais

PREREADING

David Hwang is famous for writing plays about his culture as well as other cultures. Write about any plays you know of that are about different cultures or your own culture. If you can't think of any plays, what stories from other cultures or your own culture do you think would make good plays?

DEFINING

hi-rise (¶1)   multistory building

penthouse (¶1)   an apartment that sits on the roof of a tall building

reminiscent (¶2)   suggestive of

devoid (¶2)   empty

flanking (¶2)   standing on either side

inconspicuous (¶3)   not obvious

heady (¶4)   strong

sublimely (¶4)   proudly

ego-exorcising (¶4)   freeing from conceit

Tony (¶5)   an award given by the American Theatre Wing, which is a professional school for the performing arts

Obie (¶5)   an award given for achievement in off-Broadway theatre

inoculated (¶6) protected

Joseph Papp (¶6) highly respected New York theatre producer

pit orchestras (¶8) live accompaniment for musical plays

ruthless (¶11) cruel, pitiless

feign (¶11) pretend

foreclosed (¶ 11) excluded

assimilationist (¶12) one who tries to blend in or merge with cultures

atrocious (¶17) horrible

coolie (¶17) unskilled Oriental laborer

subservient (¶17) of service in a lower capacity

brothel (¶21) house of prostitution

Samuri (¶22) Japanese military officer

espionage (¶26) spying

escalate (¶26) speed up

explicable (¶28) explainable

deconstruct (¶29) take apart

antithesis (¶30) opposite

duped (¶30) deceived, fooled

exploited (¶30) taken advantage of

clandestine (¶31) secret, private

Actor's Equity (¶36) professional actor's union

debacle (¶38) a great disaster

platitudes (¶38) dull remarks

equanimity (¶39) composure

blurb (¶41) an exaggerated advertisement

book jackets (¶41) protective paper cover on a hardcover book

chauvinism (¶43) unreasoning devotion to one's race

hypocrisy (¶43) deception

Double Play
Radhika Radhakrishnan and Arthur Pais

1   When he's in town, David Hwang inhabits an apartment in an elegant hi-rise on the Upper West Side. Within a block are ethnic restaurants, a small movie house, and a bookstore. With its smiling doorman who announces you, calling the residents by their first names, the apartment looks, as you enter, like a thousand

Radhika Radhakrishnan and Arthur Pais, "Double Play," *Transpacific,* May/June 1991, pp. 30–37. Reprinted by permission of Transpacific Media Inc., Malibu, California.

Please note maps in appendix for references to places in this article.

others in Manhattan. Past the doorman is a seemingly unending corridor accented by mirrored alcoves with partially hidden couches. All the way at the end is a set of elevators, one of which whisks us up to Hwang's penthouse apartment.

2   A pastel foyer opens directly onto a dining/living area that contains an almost hidden stairway. Reminiscent of the settings of Ishiok, the living room walls are bare, devoid of hangings commemorating Hwang's triumphs. The visual focus is toward the French doors that open out onto a narrow balcony. A pair of streamed leather sofas are turned away from the seldom used kitchenette whose vertical surfaces are covered floor to ceiling with cabinets. Hwang apparently doesn't believe in displaying his books either. There is an antique clock awaiting mounting an a pair of gigantic speakers flanking the windows. Beyond the windows glow the amber lights of the Upper West Side.

3   "I haven't had much time to fix up the place," Hwang says as we sip drinks. In a small alcove above the dining table, placed quite high on the wall, is a rather inconspicuous photo of a smiling Hwang with a happy blond. I presume she is Katheryn Layng whom Hwang is seeing regularly. Layng, an actress with a regular role on *Doogie Howser, MD,* is committed to life in L.A. where Hwang has a home. Contrary to a statement made by Hwang's banker father in his own Transpacific profile, David Hwang is not engaged to Layng. In fact, he denies having marriage plans. For the time being Hwang is happy with his bicoastal existence, alternating between his Los Angeles home and Manhattan apartment. He will also spend several weeks in San Francisco when he begins shooting *Golden Gate,* his directorial debut, in June.

4   While *M. Butterfly* continues to enjoy a record-breaking international run three years after it opened on Broadway, Hwang has moved on to movies. Currently he is responsible for scripting and/or directing movies whose combined budgets may exceed $150 million. Few writers have been associated with so many interesting films at one time. Last year *Time* described Hwang as having "the potential to become the first important dramatist of American public life since Arthur Miller, and maybe the best of them all." *The New York Times* called him "a true original." That must have been heady praise, but, slight and full of boyish charm, Hwang wears the praise as lightly as he does his years. He discusses it all in a tone so sublimely matter-of-fact that one wonders if he possesses some ego-exorcising magic.

5   You watch him discuss Asian American experiences with a group of fledgling filmmakers and writers. You listen to him reminisce about *F.O.B.,* his first play, which he wrote and produced in 1979 when he was a 22-year-old student at Stanford University. You hear him talk about how *M. Butterfly,* his most famous play, is still setting records on its national tour, and how it will soon become a big-budget Warner Brothers movie. You can't help wondering how this 34-year-old, whose plays have won a Tony and an Obie and who is now collaborating with Oscar-winning directors like Martin Scorsese, can be so spontaneously friendly and relaxed.

6   "I guess I have been inoculated by the early success I have had," he says, fingering the strings on his navy T-shirt. Relaxing on a jade leather sofa, Hwang recalls the scars left by his early successes, the lessons he has learned. "I was eaten up

by my early success," he says. "After all, how many people win an Obie when they're just about 23? And how many writers in their twenties have their first play produced under the New York Shakespeare Festival Public Theater through Joseph Papp?" After the success of *F.O.B.*, Hwang admits to having "developed a certain amount of contempt for the Establishment." It took him a few years to realize where he was going wrong.

7   "It started to bug me to feel that I could write anything and it would be okay. Since I had success at a much earlier age than most other people, and since I also made many mistakes in my career and in my personal life, I guess I have learned a lot from them." Between 1980, the year *F.O.B.* was first staged, and 1988, the year *M. Butterfly* began making Broadway history, Hwang's life underwent many changes and his health suffered. He also began the hard process of looking within and subjecting himself to more intense self-criticism and discipline. He hopes that those lessons will stay with him and instruct him as he tries new thing[s].

8   Hwang is the eldest child of Henry David Hwang, a prominent member of LA's Chinese American community who founded and chairs the board of Far East National Bank. His mother is a nationally recognized master piano teacher. Younger sister Dorothy is a renowned cellist. Hwang got his introduction to theater playing violin in pit orchestras for amateur musicals in and around his home town of San Gabriel, California.

9   Drawn to literature form his early teens, Hwang still wasn't sure that he wanted to be a writer. Journalism and law were two of the options he considered. Another was becoming a violinist. "[My parents] hoped I would become a business-man, a lawyer, a doctor," Hwang says, studying his well-manicured hands. "But medicine was certainly out because I'm so clumsy with my hands."

10   During his first year at Stanford he hardly paid any attention to the subject that was to become so close to his heart: Asian identity and the fight against stereo-types. "I read Pearl S. Buck's *The Good Earth* and didn't find anything wrong in it," he says, referring to what many Asians feel to be a condescending portrayal of the Chinese, and by extension, all Asians. As one magazine article observed, "as a youth he certainly felt integrated into the surrounding sun-kissed culture."

11   College debate was an experience that left Hwang with mixed feelings. He found it to be an exciting, ruthless activity. "I had to feign enthusiasm for positions I did not believe in, and when our coach bribed the judges with beer, victory became more important than verbal engagements." Ultimately, it disillusioned him and may have foreclosed any interest in pursuing a career in law. At the same time it may have propeled him toward playwriting by awakening his interest in the Asian's place in America.

12   "I discovered in college that the assimilationist model was dangerous and self-defeating," he wrote a few years ago. The various Black empowerment movements also stimulated Hwang's newfound interest in learning more about his own roots.

13   School plays proved a welcome tonic and an outlet for the new insights about identity with which Hwang had begun grappling. "Seeing a lot of plays on the campus, I thought I could probably do them too," Hwang says. During one summer break he enrolled in a playwriting workshop given by Sam Shepard in Claremont,

California. It took Hwang nearly two years to conceive, write, revise, and produce his first play. *F.O.B.,* which stands for fresh-off-the-boat, focuses on the clash between newly arrived Chinese immigrants and their Chinese American cousins. It contains autobiographical elements. Hwang had finally begun to rebel against the not uncommon urge among many Asians to out-White the Whites. The play's American-born Chinese character Dale despises the newly arrived Chinese immigrant Steve because the latter embodies everything from which Dale had been trying to distance himself.

14   Hwang first produced the play in his dorm. "When I told my parents, they thought the idea was crazy," he recalls. But they turned out for the premier when he was ready to present it on the Stanford stage. They liked what they saw and encouraged him to write more plays. *F.O.B.* turned out to be a huge campus hit. It impressed Hwang's professors so much that they urged him to take it to New York. Now completely supportive, his proud parents financed the trip.

15   Hwang met with Joseph Papp, a highly respected producer and one of the most influential figures in New York theater. Papp suggested that Hwang make some changes to the play. Hwang did and was rewarded with the job of directing it. *F.O.B.* wasn't a big success though it won Hwang an Obie. Papp saw in the play the promise of a brilliant career for its author. Encouraged, Hwang moved to Greenwich Village in 1981 and lived there for the next four years. It was a bad time for the displaced Californian.

16   Papp showed his faith in the young playwright by producing his next three works, *The Dance and the Railroad, Family Devotions,* both in 1981 when Hwang was only 24, and *The House of Sleeping Beauties* in 1983. For the themes of his plays Hwang mined Chinese American history and studied the works of other writers. In an introduction to *F.O.B. and Other Plays* (New American Library), Hwang wrote that Fa Man Lan, the girl who takes her father's place in battle in *F.O.B.,* is from *The Woman Warrior,* Maxine Hong Kingston's highly praised first novel. *The House of Sleeping Beauties* was inspired by a novella of the same name by the Nobel-prize-winning Japanese novelist Yasunari Kawabata.

17   *The Dance and the Railroad* is a two-character play set during the 1867 strike by Chinese railway workers to protest their atrocious working conditions. The laborers endure the boredom of a strike by producing a Chinese opera that illuminates their struggle. One part was played by John Lone, the star of Bernardo Bertolucci's *The Last Emperor.* "So often coolie laborers have been characterized in America as passive and subservient," Hwang wrote, "two stereotypes often attached to Asians. The strike is important because it reminds us that in historical fact these were assertive men who stood up for their rights in the face of great adversity."

18   Like *F.O.B., Dance* was written in a spirit of examining his own roots, but he never lost sight of the greater truth. He characterizes his plays as "my attempts to explore human issues without denying the color of my skin," as he put it in one of his interviews.

19   *Dance* was followed by *Family Devotions,* another autobiographical work. Three generations of Chinese Americans living in an affluent suburb of Los Angeles struggle to integrate their two conflicting cultures. The playwright describes it as a

work "about the myths that grow up around a family history and how legends of past family members affect the lives of the living."

20   "I was raised as a born-again Christian, and the rejection of this Western mythology is, among other things, a casting off of the brainwashing white missionaries have consistently attempted to impose on 'heathen' Asian cultures," Hwang notes. The father in *Family Devotions* is a bank president, like Hwang's own. The son plays the violin, and various relatives are twice-born Christians. There is an uncle just arrived from China whose life is turned upside down by the spectacle of capitalist success.

21   After these three plays on Chinese Americans, Hwang looked beyond the history of his own people for his next two projects. "As an artist, I now desired to work within different areas," he notes, "while remaining committed to working within the Asian community." The result: two plays set in Japan. A bizarre brothel is the setting of *The House of Sleeping Beauties.* "My play is a fantasy about how the story may have come to be written, with Kawabata himself as a major character," Hwang says. "Subsequent to the play's composition several people who knew the author during his lifetime confided in me that the bizarre brothel described in [Kawabata's] novella does actually exist, so perhaps my speculations are not so fantastic."

22   *The Sound of Voices* was inspired by Japanese ghost stories. It tells of an extraordinary chance encounter between a medieval wandering Samurai and a seductive woman living in solitude. But Hwang feels that the play could have been set anywhere, in a mysterious forest on any continent.

23   A three-year lull followed *Sound.* Hwang was gripped by a severe case of writer's block. He broke out if it in 1985 with *Rich Relations,* the only one of his plays in which all the characters are White. Reasoning that Whites were free to write about any topic they chose, Hwang wrote it to show that ethnic writers didn't have to be restricted to ethnic material. By this time he had drifted from Papp, and the play was produced by The Second Stage. It was a resounding dud, Hwang's first real failure. Yet he remains proud of it.

24   "I don't feel that I really became a writer until the failure of *Rich Relations,*" Hwang says. "Until then I had a fair amount of success, and when *Rich Relations* failed, it was important to me that I still found myself feeling glad I wrote it." The work remains important to him as the piece "which reestablished my commitment to writing. A play about the possibility of resurrection," he says "indeed resurrected my own love for work and pointed the way toward non-Asian characters that were to follow in such works as *M. Butterfly.*" That was Hwang's gloss on it years later, but the immediate aftermath of a failure is seldom so neat.

25   Hwang began to lose faith in his work even as critics and admirers expected him to come out with something bigger and more significant to make up for the disappointment of *Rich Relations.* "Emotionally it was a hard time for me. I felt terribly lonely," he says with a mild shrug. In a semi-humorous tone he adds, "I hoped to solve the dating question. I got married and decided to settle down." He had met Ophelia, a Chinese Canadian, in 1984 while he was in Toronto to stage a production of *F.O.B.* Less than a year later, the two were married. In an earlier inter-

view Hwang told Transpacific: "Ophelia's opinion is important to me and the relationship allows a certain amount of work to be done which would not have otherwise been done. The existence of the relationship gives a certain stability to one's life—a certain anchor—which liberates the mind to be more creative." One product of the marriage was *M. Butterfly,* far and away Hwang's biggest critical and commercial success.

26   The play was suggested to him by a bizarre story he first heard at a dinner party. After a two-day trial a former French diplomat and a Chinese male opera singer had been sentenced to six years in prison for espionage. Their relationship had begun during the turbulent 1960s as the Vietnam War was beginning to escalate. A little later Hwang read about it in *The New York Times.* The story was so bizarre it could only be true; it began haunting him.

27   "When first researching this story," he writes in his author's note, "I found a quote from the real-life French diplomat, Bernard Bouriscot. Attempting to account for the fact that he had never seen his Chinese 'girlfriend' naked, he said, 'I thought she was very modest. I thought it was a Chinese custom.'" Hwang knew there was no such Chinese custom, that an Asian woman is no more shy with her lover than is a western woman. "I was also aware that Bouriscot's assumption was consistent with a certain stereotyped view of Asians as bowing, passive flowers." He concluded that the diplomat must have indeed fallen in love, not with a person, but with a fantasy stereotype. "I also inferred that the Chinese spy must have encouraged these misconceptions of oriental women as shy and submissive.

28   "From my point of view the 'impossible' story of a Frenchman duped by a Chinese man masquerading as a woman always seemed perfectly explicable. Given the degree of misunderstanding between men and women and also between East and West, it seemed inevitable that a mistake of this magnitude would one day take place.

29   "I was driving down to Santa Monica Boulevard one afternoon and asked myself, 'What did Bouriscot think he was getting in this Chinese actress?' The answer came to me clearly: 'He probably thought he had found Madame Butterfly.'" This is how Hwang decided to deconstruct Puccini's celebrated 1904 opera *Madame Butterfly.* "This despite the fact that I didn't even know the plot of the opera. I knew Butterfly only as a cultural stereotype: speaking of an Asian woman, we would sometime say, 'She's pulling a butterfly,' which meant playing that submissive Oriental number."

30   He decided that his play would be the antithesis of *Madame Butterfly* to the extent that it would go against the stereotyped Asian image presented by Puccini in which Pinkerton, an American naval officer, has an affair with a Japanese teahouse hostess. In the end he leaves her. Within a few weeks Hwang had extracted from Puccini's opera the basic arc of his own play. The French diplomat fantasizes that he is Pinkerton and that his lover is the Butterfly. "By the end of the piece, he realizes that it is he who has been the Butterfly in that the Frenchman had been duped by his love. The Chinese spy, who exploited that love, is therefore the real Pinkerton."

31   As production of *M. Butterfly* began in 1987, Hwang started spending more and more time in New York while Ophelia stayed behind in Los Angeles. At about the time the play was premiering on Broadway, the marriage ended. During the preview runs before its Broadway premier *M. Butterfly* won rave reviews and standing ovations. Its success was surprising for many reasons. Not only did the public accept a story of clandestine love and international intrigue between a French diplomat and a star of the Peking Opera who turned out to be a man, it also accepted the psychological rationale for this bizarre affair that lasted nearly 20 years. Not everyone was happy with the message they read into the play. Some even complained that it was anti-American.

32   "Quite to the contrary, I consider it a plea to all sides to cut through our respective layers of cultural and sexual misconceptions, to deal with one another truthfully for our mutual good, from the common and equal ground we share as human beings," reads Hwang's author's note. "From the myths of the East, and the myths of the West, the myths of men and the myths of women. These have so saturated our consciousness that truthful contact between nations and lovers can only be the result of heroic efforts. Those who prefer to bypass the work involved will remain in a world of surfaces. This is to me, the convenient world in which the French diplomat and the Chinese spy lived. This is why after 20 years, he had learned nothing at all about his lover, not even the truth of his sex."

33   *M. Butterfly* was directed by John Dexter, one of the greatest directors on both sides of the Atlantic. It went on to break *Amadeus's* record as the longest running drama on Broadway with 777 regular performances before it closed on January 27, 1990. Last September it opened its tour in Boston and garnered brilliant reviews. It also broke box-office records, taking $2 million in just five weeks. It enjoyed similar successes in Toronto, Tampa, Baltimore and a number of other cities around the world.

34   While *M. Butterfly* was still winning thunderous applause from Broadway audiences, Hwang joined with composer Philip Glass to write a science fiction opera, *1000 Airplanes on the Roof*. It evolves around a character named M who claims to have been abducted by creatures from outer space. Conceived by Glass, it uses Hwang's narrative for poetic monologues spoken in alternating performances by a man and a woman. The work received mixed reviews, but became a small off-Broadway success. Hwang told *Contemporanea* that *1000 Airplanes on the Roof* also relates to themes that are present in all his work: "a search for identity and acknowledgment of our past." Apparently happy with their collaboration, the duo is working together on another production, *The Voyage,* inspired by Andre Malraux's *Man's Fate,* scheduled to open late this year at the Metropolitan Opera.

35   Since 1989 Hwang has slowed the pace at which he is writing new plays. For the time being, at least, he is shifting his focus to the big screen. "I thought that since *M. Butterfly* was such an outstanding success, anything I would do soon will be weighed by extraordinary standards. So I said, 'Let me try my hand at the movies.' Even if I have average success there, I won't be hurt." He spend the better part of 1989 and 1990 working on two movie scripts, including the screen version of *M. Butterfly* for Warner Brothers. . . . Not until early this year did he resume serious

work on a new dramatic play inspired by the recent outbreaks of racist incidents in united Germany and across the United States.

36   Outside of his writing Hwang has found time to voice concern over issues affecting Asians. He was one of the most visible participants in a protest against ethnically biased casting on Broadway where Whites often land parts calling for non-Whites. The protest was prompted from the casting of a White actor in the role of a Eurasian in the multimillion-dollar musical, *Miss Saigon*. The protesters raised enough of a furor to panic Actor's Equity into ruling that the role had to go to an Asian. The incensed British producer threatened to cancel the show altogether, which would have meant lost work for dozens of actors, Asian as well as White. A chastened Actor's Equity reversed itself, leaving visible protesters like Hwang to pick up the pieces.

37   "The way the controversy developed, it appeared as if I was the only person behind it, as if I started the whole controversy," Hwang says. "I did not start it but when one of the organizers asked me to lend my name, I readily did so and wrote a letter to Actor's Equity. But I never expected the debate to become so shrill. I was not encouraging confrontation but was pleading for more understanding, an open and healthy debate." Hwang isn't against a White actor playing a Eurasian. "But this has to be done after a certain amount of justice has been met, after the non-Europeans have played, in significant numbers, the roles that are non-European."

38   All in all the protest was a debacle that generated millions of dollars of free publicity for a play that many Asian Americans would have preferred to see die a quiet death. Hwang tries to put a good face on it, though, saying, not convincingly, that he felt "pretty good" about the outcome, meaning the producer's platitudes about a commitment for increased efforts to cast minority actors. "The net effect is that it has encouraged me to speak out," Hwang told the *Boston Globe*. "I may have had some reluctance to take on an unpopular position in the past. But now having done it, I think a lot of good has come out of it in terms of stimulating debate."

39   At the peak of his career now, Hwang is full of equanimity about the past. Whatever shadows may have fallen on him in his early years in New York are being washed away by the warm glow of youthful success. One might say that Hwang has now been stripped of the right to complain. One real luxury that his success has afforded him is travel. Trips to London and across the continent are almost routine. Two years ago he visited India for the first time to explore locations for a film based on a celebrated novel by an Austrian who spent seven years in Tibet. Hwang's eyes twinkle with pleasure as he talks about that trip. He loved the complex fiber of daily life in India, and its spicy food; food is one of the great adventures for Hwang the traveler.

40   What does he do when he isn't writing? The question seems to catch Hwang by surprise. "I guess I do what anybody will do in his spare time," he says. "I take long walks, jog, experiment with food. This afternoon I felt like seeing a movie, and I walked into the theater downstairs and saw *Red October*." He doesn't like to talk about his personal life but adds that he also spends a lot of time with young Asian American writers on both coasts.

41   "There are a number of Asian American writers who are breaking ground," he says. "From time to time I read their work, encourage them to improve, and if I

like something strongly, I write a blurb or two for their book jackets." Hwang has become an embraceable figure.

42   "David Hwang's plays are not just about what is familiar," writes Maxine Hong Kingston. "They take us far imaginatively . . . Chinese American theater, which started out with a bang—firecrackers, drums—keeps dying out. David Henry Hwang gives it life once again."

43   Hwang knows precisely what he wants to do with his talent. In a forward to an anthology of his plays he observes, "As the eighties draw to a close, my preoccupation with identity continues to evolve. I now believe that racial and ethnic distinctions in this country are useful only to a point. "It is important not to stray across a fine line and lapse into chauvinism that would render one culture superior over any other." He also observes that actual American history has more often been one of hypocrisy and prejudice.

44   "Though Misters Bush and Reagan may preach otherwise, the greatness of America lies not in a return to the past. We will try to evolve a truly progressive nation, one in which different ethnic, political and social groups co-exist in a state of equality. In both my life and my work I will continue to grapple with an American dream for the future."

READING

1. How old was David Hwang when he had his first success? How did this affect his writing career?

2. What does Hwang see as the stereotype of the Chinese woman? What did this have to do with *M. Butterfly*?

THINKING

1. David Hwang had a severe problem with writer's block, which means that he went through a period of time where he couldn't think of anything to write. Has this ever happened to you? How did you or how would you solve this problem? Why do you suppose people get writer's block?

2. Hwang feels that ethnic writers don't have to be restricted to ethnic materials. He has had successes writing about his own culture and other cultures, but his first real failure came when he wrote a play with all white characters. He said, however, that he didn't feel that he had become a real writer until he had failed. He even felt that his early successes worked against him. How would failure make you appreciate success? Do you think you have to fail before you can really appreciate your successes?

PREWRITING

Freewrite about important decisions that you have made in your life. Which of those important decisions have you changed your mind about? Why did you change your mind?

WRITING

1. David Hwang was considering becoming a lawyer until he got involved in college debate. There he saw how dishonesty and bribes were what persuaded the judges. He decided that he didn't want to spend his life in a career that would always seem so corrupt to him. Write an essay with your teacher as your audience. Describe an incident that happened to you that made you change your mind about something very important in your life. Be as specific as possible.

2. David Hwang became involved in the fight with Actor's Equity, the actor's union, over the casting of a white actor to play the part of a Eurasian in the play *Miss Saigon*. Write an essay stating your views on whether characters in plays should have to be played only by people of the same race as the character.

REVISING

The paragraphs that you write need to be fully developed. If they are too short, then chances are you need to add more information to develop your ideas so your reader can understand what you are trying to convey.

Look at the draft of your essay and count how many sentences are in each paragraph. Then count the sentences in the paragraphs of "Double Play" and see if your paragraphs are as long as the paragraphs in the article. See if you can add more information to your paragraphs to make them more interesting.

EDITING

Adverbs modify verbs, adjectives, and other adverbs. They are easy to spot in your writing because they answer the questions when, where, how, and to what extent. Adverbs often end with "ly." Not the following examples:

> *Encouraged,* Hwang moved to Greenwich Village.
>
> I *readily* did so.
>
> He protested against *ethnically* biased casting.
>
> . . . and if I like something *strongly,* I write a blurb for their book jackets.

Read through the rough draft of your writing assignment and pick out the adverbs that you have used. See if you can add more adverbs to your essay to help make it more clear and lively.

Adjectives make your writing much more vivid by adding descriptive details. They modify nouns or pronouns only, and they answer the questions how many, which, or what kind. Radhika Radhakrishnan and Arthur Pais effectively use adjectives in the following examples:

> *ethnic* restaurants
>
> *smiling* doorman

pastel foyer

French doors

narrow balcony

antique clock

gigantic speakers

happy blond

interesting films

boyish charm

national tour

many mistakes

Read through your writing assignment to pick out the adjectives you have already used. Are they the most effective choices? See if you can add some adjectives to enhance your writing.

PART TWO
Issues and Ideas

The Issues and Ideas Section has a wide variety of articles exploring controversial subjects. This picture shows a mother and the biracial son she adopted as an infant. Now as he prepares to enter kindergarten, his family worries about the challenges he will face. What are the issues or challenges that concern you most now in your community, nation and world?

Photo by Gregory Day used by permission of the photographer, Drane Emerson, and Seth Emerson

Cuba: Freedom vs. Equality

Mario Vargas Llosa

PREREADING

This article about Cuba talks about the difference between freedom and equality. How would you define freedom? How would you define equality? What do you think the difference is between freedom and equality, or do you think that there is a difference between these two terms?

DEFINING

asylum (¶1)   a place of protection or sanctuary

egalitarian (¶2)   believing that all people should have equal political and social rights

eradicating (¶2)   eliminating, getting rid of

disparities (¶3)   differences

onerous (¶3)   laborious, burdensome

reactionaries (¶5)   people who seek to undo or reverse political progress

entity (¶8)   an individual existence

ignominies (¶8)   shames, dishonors

regimentation (¶9)   something that makes people think and act alike

Cuba: Freedom vs. Equality

Mario Vargas Llosa

1   In April 1980, the Cuban government decided to withdraw its police guard from the Peruvian embassy in Havana. Within three days the place was overrun by 10,000 people wanting asylum. Even when political persecution was at its worst in Anastasio Somoza's Nicaragua, Augusto Pinochet's Chile, and Jorge Videla's Argentina, nothing like this occurred.

2   As Cuba celebrates the 30th anniversary of its revolution, it is worth trying to understand why that crowd was milling about the embassy. Nobody can deny that Cuba is the most egalitarian society in Latin America. No other Latin American country has achieved what Cuba has in eradicating illiteracy and in putting medicine, books, the arts, and sports within everyone's reach.

3   Despite this, thousands, hundreds of thousands, or perhaps millions of Cubans would prefer to live in a society different from their own. Why would so many rather go to Latin American countries with terrible unemployment and poverty, where economic disparities are enormous and the poor—the great majority—lead onerous lives?

4   It is because the ideal of equality is incompatible with the ideal of freedom. We can have a society of free men or of equal men, but not one that combines both equally. This reality is hard to accept. Above all, it faces mankind with the dilemma of having to choose between two aspirations, of identical moral force, that appear to be inseparable. But they are not.

5   Cuba has opted for the egalitarian ideal. At the same time, however, it has also been distancing itself from the other ideal. The personal, family, professional, and cultural lives of the people are held captive by an almost impersonal mechanism that concentrates all power. Left-wing intellectuals explain that "real" freedom consists of education, employment, social protection, and so forth. They question whether the "abstract" freedom of the reactionaries means anything to the poor.

6   The answer is apparent in the 10,000 Cubans who massed at the embassy in Havana. Unlike social equality, freedom is not measurable in quantitative terms alone. Freedom means the opportunity to choose between different options, not just those decreed "positive." In a society like Cuba's this opportunity has been reduced to a minimum. In an egalitarian society a person is not allowed to choose unhappiness.

7   Does this mean that in other societies people can choose what they want to be and do? Obviously not: Choice is influenced by each person's social, economic, and cultural potential, as well as by natural ability. But the fact is that within these limits there are many more options to choose—thinking differently from others, changing one's job or home, having opinions about the system. These options

Mario Vargas Llosa, "Cuba: Freedom vs. Equality," *World Press Review*, March 1989, p. 45. Reprinted by permission.

Please note maps in appendix for references to places in this article.

make this type of society, latently at least, closer to that paradise where we could lead the lives we want.

8   Freedom in inegalitarian societies—even when in political terms they are dictatorships—is always greater than it is in egalitarian societies because in the former, power is not concentrated within a single structure but divided among several. Although the distribution of power is a continuous source of inequality at all levels, it also guarantees a substantial degree of autonomy. Even if the president of the U.S. were to propose abolishing freedom of the press, he would fail, since this freedom depends not on him but on freedom of enterprise. In Cuba, since all organs of information belong to the state, they cannot publish anything that is in conflict with this all-embracing entity that ideologically regiments Cubans and plans their lives but has also spared them many ignominies that still burden most Latin Americans.

9   We are not doomed to suffer either extreme inequalities or extreme regimentation, but we must renounce extremes of both equality and freedom. This middle-of-the-road course has been taken by those countries that have achieved the most civilized ways of life.

10   The trick is to tolerate enough freedom to keep citizens from doing what the 10,000 Cubans did at the Peruvian embassy, but not so much as to cause the degree of socioeconomic inequality that makes people willing to revolt. Such revolutions produce egalitarian societies, from which their children will go to any extreme to flee.

READING

1. What is the status of illiteracy in Cuba? Who has access to medicine, sports, and the arts in Cuba?

2. How does Mario Vargas Llosa define "freedom" in this article?

THINKING

1. Why did 10,000 Cubans seek asylum in Peru? In Cuba citizens have equality, and in Peru there is terrible poverty and unemployment. Why do you think the Cubans want to leave their country?

2. In American society, all people are supposedly considered free and equal. Why don't we have the same problems that the Cubans do? Do you think that all people in America are really free and equal? Why or why not? Think of some specific examples to support your point of view.

PREWRITING

Freewrite on freedom and equality. Do you personally feel that you are free in our society? Why or why not? Do you feel that you are equal? Why or why not? Whom do you feel that you are equal to?

WRITING

1. You have the opportunity to enter an essay contest sponsored by the NAACP for which the grand prize is a scholarship. The essay subject that you must write about is "Freedom vs. Equality." First decide whether to be in favor of freedom or equality. Develop a thesis statement to help you clarify your topic. The contest suggests that you use examples from American history to prove your argument. Be convincing so that you can win!

2. Suppose that you have the opportunity to choose whether you would like to raise your children in American society or Cuban society. Write an essay explaining your choice, being sure to use specific examples.

REVISING

Mario Vargas Llosa uses several difficult vocabulary words more than once in this article. Go through the article to discover how many times he has repeated the words in the defining section. Did you discover any other words that were repeated noticeably? Repetition of key words can be effective when they link ideas and alert readers to the importance of certain concepts. Repetition can also be annoying when used unnecessarily or too frequently.

Look at your own writing assignment. Have you repeated key words or phrases? Can you find a place where the repetition of a key idea or word would help to link your ideas together or help to identify key terms? Make any changes that you think would improve your writing.

EDITING

When three or more items are mentioned together in a list that is joined by **and** or **or,** you must place a comma between each element of the list and before **and** or **or.** You should not put a comma before **and** or **or** if you are only joining two items.

Examples:

The *personal, family, professional, and cultural* lives of the people are held captive by an almost impersonal mechanism that concentrates all power.

We are not doomed to suffer either *extreme inequalities or extreme regimentation.*

No other Latin American country has achieved what Cuba has *in eradicating illiteracy and in putting medicine, books, the arts, and sports within everyone's reach.*

Look through your writing assignment and identify each time that you have used **and** or **or.** Have you used a comma when necessary? Have you eliminated any unnecessary commas?

When Fantasy Life Turns into Murder . . . What Is Really to Blame?

Justin Webster

PREREADING

How many hours a week do you spend watching television? Playing video games? If you don't spend much time with these activities, do you know people who do? Based on your experiences or by observing people you know, how much do you think these activities affect their behaviors? Have you ever played a role playing game? If so, how did you feel about the actions you took while playing the game? Do you think spending too much time playing violent video games is potentially harmful? Why or why not?

DEFINING

mesmerised (¶1)   enthralled, hypnotized

Polytechnic (¶3)   a school specializing in industrial arts and applied sciences

neo-Nazi (¶4)   an extrememist group inspired by Adolf Hitler's Nazis.

hierarchy (¶4)   categorization by status

psychopathic (¶4)   antisocial personality disorder characterized by agressive, perverted, criminal, and/or amoral behavior

intricate (¶5)   complex, detailed

derangement (¶7)   state of being mentally disturbed or insane

paraphernalia (¶9)   articles used for a specific activity

When Fantasy Life Turns into Murder . . .
What Is Really to Blame?
Justin Webster

1   Just as a Spanish parliamentary commission is halfway through a year-long study of ethical standards in broadcasting, a chilling case of adolescent violence has mesmerised the country and brought the role of the media firmly back into the spotlight.

2   Javier R, 20, and Felix M, 17, stand accused of killing a man for fun. The game they were playing involved finding "an old fat man with a stupid face" and mercilessly knifing him to death as he waited for a bus home after his afternoon shift as a cleaner. For the killers this was to be the first step to taking their role-playing game, which had developed into the obsession of a small group of friends, "live."

3   Role-playing has caught on fast in Spain, particularly among university students studying subjects such as computer science and engineering. Introduced eight years ago, it is typically played around a table with each participant acting as a defined character, according to rules laid down by "the master" and the cast of a 20-sided die. The game's appeal lies in its endless variability, a heavy dose of fantasy—one standard text is *Lord of the Rings*—and the chance to act out a role. "It's not so much about winning or losing as living an imaginary adventure," said Samuel Alvarez, a student of computer science at Madrid Polytechnic.

4   Javier, the master of his group, and Felix used to play for up to five hours a day. Their version of the game had heavy neo-Nazi overtones and divided the world into a hierarchy of 360 races. To outsiders they showed no signs of being psychopathic. Javier is a middle-class son of a businessman and a nurse, who, before his arrest this month, lived in a comfortable district of the capital and diligently studied chemistry at a Madrid University. Felix had just failed his university entrance and had recently decided to be a writer.

5   One of the most disturbing aspects of the case is that none of their classmates or teachers noticed anything unusual about their behavior after the murder at the end of April. After they were arrested, police found an extensive collection of violent horror videos in Javier's flat and, most shocking of all, an intricate account of the murder written by Javier. This was published in the press alongside an extract of *American Psycho* by Brett Easton Ellis. The detached, sadistic tone is the same in both. At one point Javier also mentions the film *Hellraiser* as the inspiration for a particular technique used during the murder.

6   As the background to the case emerged, groups of role-players banded together to demonstrate that the game itself is not harmful. They have also opened a bank account to collect money for the victim's widow and two children.

7   Experts have launched instead into more general criticisms about the repre-

Justin Webster, "When Fantasy Life turns to Murder . . . What Is Really to Blame?" *The European,* 24–30, June 1994, no. 215, p. 5. Reprinted by permission.

Please note maps in appendix for references to places in this article.

sentation of violence in Spanish society. "Children are constantly exposed to violence from television, the cinema, comics, and computer games," said Josep Tomas Vilatella, president of the Spanish Society of Infant and Juvenile Psychiatry. "There's an absolute epidemic." For several years the society has been campaigning for a better way of detecting cases of mental derangement, from which, he says, the two students are clearly suffering.

8   Eduardo Garcia-Camba, a psychiatric doctor, echoes his concern: "Have we developed a psychopathic society which is the perfect breeding ground for this type of terrifying event?" He laid some blame at the door of the entertainment industry: "Undoubtedly violence is very much present in the lives of some young people and it is systematically encouraged by themes offered by television, cinema, comics, and video games."

9   A twist to the episode is that while the debate over the evils of television violence still rages just weeks after news of the horrific murder, sales of role-playing paraphernalia have shot up.

READING

1. What book was the role-playing game Javier and Felix played based on? How was the game played?

2. What does the president of the Spanish Society of Infant and Juvenile Psychiatry say there is an epidemic of in Spain? What is this society campaigning for?

THINKING

1. When teenagers and young adults commit crimes, who do you think is responsible? At what age do you think a person becomes responsible for his or her own actions? Until that age, who do you think is responsible? Do you think watching television and playing games or video games can affect a person's behavior? Why or why not?

2. What do you think the punishment should be for the boys who murdered "an old fat man with a stupid face" because the game told them to? Why do you think this would be an appropriate punishment?

PREWRITING

Make two lists about television. On the first list, write all of the good things you can think of about television. On the second list, write all of the bad things you can think of about television. Make two more lists, this time answering the same questions about video games.

WRITING

1. You have a seven-year-old niece whom your brother and sister-in-law allow to watch all the television she wants and whatever shows she wants. You have a close

relationship with your brother and sister-in-law, but they live out of town, so you decide to write a letter to them to tell them what you feel about their decision to allow your niece this privilege. Be specific and use examples.

2. A company has requested permission to put a large video game arcade across the street from your local junior high school. Your city council has asked the public in your community to let them know whether this permission should be granted. Write a letter to your city council stating specifically why you think the arcade should or should not be built. Find facts from the library that will help your argument.

REVISING

The majority of writing that you do in your lifetime is likely to be letters. Since letter writing is not considered academic writing, little emphasis has been placed on this form of composition in higher education. Now, however, a more realistic approach is taken that realizes the value of teaching this skill that you will be practicing for most of your life. Writing is used for communication, and letter writing is simply another form of communication. When you write a letter, always consider the following points:

1. What is the purpose of my letter? What am I trying to convey or argue?

2. Who is my audience? What level of vocabulary are they most likely to respond to? For instance, if you are writing to the president of a corporation, you would use more sophisticated language than you would if you were writing your newspaper carrier.

3. Are my sentences easy to understand? Am I expressing my thoughts clearly? (If you express your thought clearly, you will make a better impression.)

4. Have I been as specific as possible? (Instead of saying, "Your service is awful," explain how the installation crew destroyed the new floor they were trying to install in your kitchen.)

5. Have I alienated my audience? (If you are writing a letter of complaint or a letter suggesting change, your reader is likely to not pay attention to your point or not even read the letter if he or she feels personally attacked.)

Look through your writing assignment and answer all of these questions. Make any changes you feel make a more effective letter.

EDITING

Running the ideas of two separate sentences together into one sentence is a common error that must be avoided for good writing. When two independent clauses, each containing a subject and a verb and the ability to stand by itself, are written together with no punctuation between them, then a **run-on or run-together sentence** results. When the same two clauses are written with only a comma between them, then a **comma splice** results. Look at the following examples.

Examples:

Their version of the game had heavy neo-Nazi overtones and divided the world into a hierarchy of 360 races. (¶4)

To outsiders they showed no signs of being psychopathic. (¶4)

These examples are simple sentences.

Example:

Their version of the game had heavy neo-Nazi overtones and divided the world into a hierarchy of 360 races to outsiders they showed no signs of being psychopathic.

The above sentence is an example of a run-on or run-together sentence consisting of two complete sentences with no punctuation between them.

Example:

Their version of the game had heavy neo-Nazi overtones and divided the world into a hierarchy of 360 races, to outsiders they showed no signs of being psychopathic.

The above sentence is an example of a comma splice consisting of two complete sentences with a comma in between.

Check through the draft of your writing assignment to be sure that you have not included any run-together sentences or comma splices.

Asian Americans Anonymous

Emil Guillermo

PREREADING

When you watch television news, do you see your culture represented in the news anchors? When you watch television shows, how is your culture represented there? In movies, do you see your culture? Why do you suppose you do or do not see your culture represented? Which culture do you see the most of? Which do you see the least of? Why do you think this is? In movies and on television, is your culture portrayed positively or negatively or a mixture of both? What effect do you think this portrayal has?

DEFINING

indictment (¶9) the bringing of criminal changes against a party by a grand jury
credibility (¶10) believability
disdain (¶11) to consider beneath oneself
specter (¶14) ghostly appearance, or haunting, disturbing image

Asian Americans Anonymous

Emil Guillermo

1   I am an Asian American anchorman, a Filipino American who works for NewsChannel 8, the regional all-news channel in Washington, DC. I say that with a special gusto because the simple matter is there are far more Asian American anchorwomen than there are Asian American males in TV Land.

2   Go ahead. Try counting. How many Asian American anchormen have you seen? In history. In your lifetime. There are more American bald eagles, more Elvis sightings, and even more honest Congressmen.

3   *The Wall Street Journal* reported last year that Asian American men "are almost invisible in the anchor chair." We must not fit the throne. According to the Radio TV News Directors Association, Asian Americans, 3% of the nation's population, make up just 2% of broadcast newsroom jobs in the country. Of that number, 33% of the women did some news anchoring. Only 3% of the males did.

4   The statistics are so bad, David Louie, a San Francisco TV reporter and a former president of the Asian American Journalist Association (AAJA) was quoted as saying, "There is not a single male Asian American news anchor that I know of. With none in the pipeline, there aren't going to be any equaling Connie Chung soon."

5   Well, now there's me. Asian American Anchorman. The three A's. I could start an organization. News and Emergency Road Service. That way I could help all the Asian guys whose careers have stalled on the side of the road. Or maybe I'll start a version of AA-A, Asian Americans Anonymous. That's our situation in TV news.

6   For me, joining the Anchorhood happened after years as a television reporter in San Francisco and Dallas, covering murders and prison riots and breathing deadly ammonia fumes. It happened after two and a half years of hosting National Public Radio's *"All Things Considered,"* covering sundry events from Tiananmen Square to the Gulf War. Finally, someone gave me a break. A door opened. And now I sit in the anchor chair.

7   Up there, in front of the lights, I am being given the opportunity to develop my anchor chops. I am learning to do all the anchor things. Just like Connie. Just like Dan, Peter, and Tom.

8   I wear make-up, pay attention to my "look." I am involved in the mechanics of "anchoring." I toss to the weather gal. I turn to Camera 1. You learn to use your face. I am developing muscles in my eyebrows and "transitional banter." I can go from O.J. Simpson to a plane crash story. I can tease ("Coming up . . .") and plead endearingly: "Stay with us."

9   But primarily I deliver the news. Better than Domino's, and in thirty minutes

Emil Guillermo, "Asian Americans Anonymous," *Filipinos,* August 1994, vol. 3, no. 28, p. 33. Reprinted by permission.

Please note maps in appendix for references to places in this article.

or less (28:55). I've developed the judgment to read in a tone that fits the weight of the news. For instance, Dan Rostenkowski's indictment was a tad harder than the lead to the scuba diving dog.

10   Being an anchor is about creating trust. I'm a messenger of the good and the bad. The news program is a mixture of my good will, charm, and credibility— things I can help. The news, you can't help. Sure, you can present the news with varying degrees of "oomph." But you can't control news. That's why anchors like to play with their hair. That, they can control.

11   I used to disdain Anchordom. I used to say, "I don't care about anchoring or making $5 million dollars. I just want to be out in the streets—as a reporter." I have come to my senses.

12   So why has it taken so long? Not just in my case, but in general? Why don't we see more Asian American anchormen?

13   When Emperor Akihito visited the U.S., some American POWs demanded he apologize for this father, Hirohito, and his actions before and during World War II. This is the root of the "Villainous Asian male" image that remains. But it is mixed up with the other images. Busboy. Service guy. All smiling, just like Mickey Rooney in "Breakfast at Tiffany's." No wonder we're not anchorman material. Anchors are General Patton. Not the Filipino cook. But when Patton needs a comfortable co-anchor? Enter Suzy Wong.

14   The situation is getting a little better. There's hope in the new wave of managers with fresh contemporary perspectives. World War II memories are being replaced by a different mindset, of Asians being bright, talented, and better than them in math class. The new guys have respect. As managers go through generational changes, perhaps then we'll see the changes reflected on our TV screens, and Asian males will be given more opportunities to anchor . . . though the specter of a karate-kicking weatherman still looms large.

READING

1. Who is Guillermo referring to in ¶7 when he mentions Connie, Dan, Peter, and Tom? Why are these people significant?

2. What does AAJA stand for? What do they say about Asian American news anchors?

THINKING

1. Does the culture of the news anchor you are listening to affect your perception of the news he or she delivers? How important do you think it is that news anchors reflect different cultures?

2. Guillermo writes in a light, entertaining style. How does this affect your perception of his message? Do you take him seriously, or does this just seem humorous to you? Do you think this article would have been more effective if the tone had been serious?

PREWRITING

Do two clustering exercises. For the first one, put in the center "Why I should be anchor," and for the second one, put "Who should be national anchor?" See how fully you can develop each cluster being sure to draw relationships within the cluster. Complete the writing assignment that you have been able to generate the most ideas for.

WRITING

1. You have the opportunity to audition to be a news anchor on your local news station. In order to become a finalist for the job, you must write an essay stating why you would be the best person in your community to be a news anchor. Be sure to include what about you makes you special and different, as well as what would make you appealing to your community. Be specific.

2. The national news network you watch has only one culture represented. They are asking for input on how they could improve their news show. Write them a well developed letter explaining how you feel about their anchor situation. Be sure to base your argument on facts and examples.

REVISING

"Asian Americans Anonymous" quotes percentages as examples telling how many Asian Americans are news anchors. Look through the article and see how many different statistics you can find.

What kinds of statistics could you use to improve your writing assignment? You could find studies with surveys and percentages of specific incidents if you check at your campus library. Go to the library and look through the listing that shows all of the magazines available and see how many you can find dealing with the culture you are writing about. Try using the *Reader's Guide,* which comes in either book form or on the computer, to look up articles specifically about your topic. Are these articles in magazines of the culture that you are writing about? Look through a few copies of the magazines you find to see what is already available. Go over the draft of your assignment and see what statistics you need to include. Then find the appropriate figures and insert them. Be sure to accurately document any quotes, summaries, or paraphrases that you take from the articles. Remember a quote must be written exactly as it is in your source and be enclosed in quotation marks. A summary condenses the material that you read into a much shorter form, and a paraphrase restates the material in your own words. Both summaries and paraphrases must have credit given to their sources.

EDITING

Prepositional phrases are used to add information to your sentences. A prepositional phrase cannot stand by itself, but it can be added to an independent clause to clarify your sentence or provide more information. A prepositional phrase is a group of words that starts with a preposition. The following is a list of commonly used prepositions.

> **about, above, across, after, against, along, among, around, as, at, before, behind, below, beneath, beside, besides, between, beyond, by, despite, down, during, except, for, from, in, inside, into, like, near, of, off, on, onto, out, outside, over, past, regarding, since, through, to, toward, under, until, up, with, without**

See how prepositional phrases are used in the following example:

> **For me,** joining the Anchorhood happened **after years as a television reporter in San Francisco and Dallas,** covering murders and prison riots and breathing deadly ammonia fumes.

This sentence alone has four prepositional phrases. Look at the sentences in "Asian Americans Anonymous" to see how many prepositional phrases you can find. Check your own writing assignment and see how many prepositional phrases you have used. Try adding some more detail and description to your writing. Note that prepositional phrases do **not** have commas before or after them just because they are prepositional phrases. A comma may be used after a prepositional phrase if it acts as an introductory element in a sentence as in the example above.

Another important thing to remember about prepositional phrases is that a verb in a sentence will never refer to a prepositional phrase when you are making the subject agree with the verb. Singular subjects need a singular verb to go with them, usually a verb with an s on the end, while plural subjects require verbs that agree with a plural subject, usually a verb without an s on the end. See the example:

> One **of the residents** was afraid.

In this sentence **one** is the subject that agrees with the verb **was. Residents** is plural and is closest to the verb, but since it is part of a prepositional phrase, the verb can't agree with it. Check your writing assignment to be sure that prepositional phrases have not gotten in the way of your subject/verb agreement.

Life Behind the Veil

Lisa Beyer

PREREADING

Before reading about the attitudes toward women in Muslim countries, think about the attitudes toward women in America today. Do men have control over the actions or behavior of women? What is the attitude of men toward women who work? What is the woman's role in the family? Are rights and attitudes toward women in America improving? What role does religion play in the treatment of women in America? How do you feel about how women are treated? Why do you think you feel that way?

DEFINING

concubine (¶1)   a woman who lives with a man without being married to him

imam (¶1)   a Muslim priest

doused (¶2)   soaked, covered with liquid

zealots (¶3)   fanatics, extremely enthusiastic people

shahs (¶3)   the rulers of several Eastern countries

puritanical (¶5)   extremely strict in morals and religion

sects (¶5)   small groups of people believing in the same religion, usually broken off from a larger religious group

adherents (¶5)   followers, believers

perverting (¶6)   misusing, turning away from

expansionism (¶8)   extending a nation's territory or influence, often at the expense of others

erosion (¶8)   wearing away, deterioration

stifling (¶9)   holding back, quieting

profound (¶9)   deep, intense

Life Behind the Veil

Lisa Beyer

1   The wives of the Prophet Muhammad were vibrant, outspoken women. His first, Khadija, ran a prosperous trading business and at one point was Muhammad's employer. A'isha, the Prophet's favorite, was at various times a judge, a political activist, and a warrior. Among Muhammad's 11 other wives and concubines were a leatherworker, an imam, and an advocate of the downtrodden, revered in her day as the "Mother of the Poor."

2   Some women hold relatively high positions in Muslim countries today. But if the wives of Muhammad lived in parts of the contemporary Islamic world, they might be paying a high price for their independence. Consider events in the refugee centers of Peshawar, Pakistan, where more than a dozen Afghan women have been "disappeared" by radical Islamic groups for the crime of working in women's centers or with foreign aid organizations; or an episode in the Algerian town of Mascara, where a Muslim nurse was doused with alcohol and set on fire by her brother, who was furious with her for treating male patients.

3   While such violence represents an extreme, women are under fire wherever Muslim zealots are on the march. Following the Iranian revolution of 1979, which swept away progressive legislation passed under the shahs, extremists in many Islamic countries have whittled away at the legal rights of women. In Egypt, for instance, the Supreme Court in 1985 struck down a 1979 law that gave a woman the right to divorce her husband should he take a second wife. Sudan's military regime, which seized power in 1989, refuses to allow women who are not accompanied by a father, husband, or brother to leave the country without permission from one of the three.

4   The Family Code adopted by Algeria in 1984 gave a husband the right to divorce his wife for almost any reason and eject her from the family home. During debate over the code, one legislator actually proposed specifying the length of the stick that a husband may use to beat his wife. Algeria's Islamic Salvation Front,

Please note maps in appendix for references to places in this article.

which swept local elections last June, is pushing to forbid women to work outside the home.

5   Pressures to curtail the rights of women come from various puritanical sects within Islam. "They want to impose a new social order by force," says Khalida Messaoudi, president of an Algerian women's organization. "They start by attacking women because women are the weakest link in these societies." Particularly strict is the Wahhabiyah, a movement founded in the 18th century that counts among its adherents many Afghans and the Saudi ruling family. Wahhabi women live behind the veil, are forbidden to drive, and may travel only if accompanied by a husband or a male blood relative. The demands of the gulf crisis prompted the Saudis to loosen some constraints on women, but it is not clear that such liberalizations will endure.

6   Some Muslim women argue that the zealots are perverting the very religion they claim to hold so dear. "This terrifying image of unhappy women covered in veils is not Islam," says Leila Aslaoui, an Algerian magistrate. Certainly, Muhammad was a liberal man for his time. He helped out around his various households, mended his own clothes, and believed sexual satisfaction was a woman's right. The religion he founded outlawed female infanticide, made the education of girls a sacred duty, and established a woman's right to own and inherit property.

7   But Islam also enshrined certain discriminatory practices. As decreed by the Koran, the value of a woman's testimony in court is worth half that of a man's, and men are entitled to four spouses, whereas women can have only one. Males are superior, some argue, because the Koran says they have "more strength."

8   The current appeal of such male chauvinist beliefs can be traced to Islam's response to Western expansionism in the 18th and 19th centuries. Fearing the erosion of their culture, the Wahhabis and others chose to assert values that set them apart, including the negative aspects of Islam's treatment of women. Modern Islamic fundamentalism is essentially a revival of this earlier reaction against the West.

9   Despite such stifling interpretations of Islam, many women have found their liberation in their faith. The veil may be a symbol of oppression to the Western eye, but, to many who wear it, it is freedom—not just from the tyranny of Western culture but also from unwanted sexual advances. In Cairo veils have become so popular that fashion shows are occasionally staged to show off new styles. Says Leila Takla, a Christian member of the Egyptian parliament: "As long as women are covering their heads and not their minds, it is an individual expression." Unfortunately, however, as laws are revised and rights withdrawn, the cloaking of Islamic women grows ever more profound.

READING

1. What is the law in Egypt regarding women and divorce? What is the policy in Sudan about women traveling outside of the country?

2. What does the Koran say about the value of a woman's testimony in court?

THINKING

1. In Pakistan, women have been "disappeared" for "working in women's centers or with foreign aid organizations." What do you think about this? What do you suppose "disappeared" means? Who works in women's centers in America? What would happen to women's centers if women couldn't work there?

2. Men have almost total control of women in Islamic countries. Men can have four wives while women can only have one husband, men can divorce women for almost any reason, and men are passing laws forbidding women to work outside the home. How do you think actions like these would be accepted in the United States? How do you think they are accepted in Islamic countries? Why do you think attitudes can vary so much from one society to another?

PREWRITING

Freewrite on how you feel about the Muslim attitudes toward women. Do you support their beliefs, or do you believe in women's rights? Do you think that you would like to live in Muslim society? Why or why not?

WRITING

1. Many spouse batterers feel that they have the right to abuse their mates, claiming that this is a private matter within a family relationship. Write an essay to share with your classmates indicating to what extent you feel the privacy of a family relationship should take precedence over interference from society.

2. Imagine that the Muslim sector in America is trying to get legislation passed that would allow Muslim men to have four wives while Muslim women could have only one husband because of their religious beliefs. Write a letter to your congressperson telling why you support or oppose this bill.

REVISING

The thesis statement for "Life Behind the Veil" is clearly stated in the final sentence of the article:

> Unfortunately, however, as laws are revised and rights withdrawn, the cloaking of Islamic women grows ever more profound.

Look back through the article. Do you feel that this clearly states its argument or intent? Stating or restating the thesis of an article or essay at the very end is an effective way to conclude your writing because it leaves your readers with a clear idea of what you really wanted them to get from reading what you wrote.

Look at your writing assignment. Identify your thesis statement. Try stating it or restating it at the end of your letter if you haven't already done this. How do you like the effect of having the thesis statement at the end of your writing?

EDITING

The word **of** is never a verb, but some people try to use it as one following the words *should* or *might* in place of the word *have.*

Examples:
>He *should have* written you. (not *should of*)
>
>He *should've* written you. (not *should of*)
>
>She *might have* been late. (not *might of*)
>
>She *might've* been late. (not *might of*)

Notice how much *should've* sounds like should of. People make this mistake because the words do sound very similar, but use of the word *of* in these cases is always wrong.

Check your writing to be sure that you haven't used **of** when you should've used **have.**

Zarbadoh's Children

Olivia Ward

PREREADING

Imagine what your community would be like if there were no men. All the men have either gone off to war or have been killed. What would that mean to you? You may be off at war, or dead, or caring for orphans. Imagine what it would be like to have lived a peaceful life, then suddenly armed men come into your community with guns and torches and murder many people and burn many buildings. How would this be different than the way some communities live with gangs in America today?

DEFINING

prosperous (¶3)   having success, doing well

militants (¶3)   aggressive warring party

resettlement (¶4)   government assistance in reestablishing a home after war

stealthy (¶5)   secret, quiet

Tajikistan (¶6)   a country in the Commonwealth of Independent States just north of Afghanistan

fundamentalist (¶6)   a movement characterized by rigid adherence to basic principles

turbulence (¶6)   chaotic disturbance

coalition (¶6)   a temporary bringing together of a group for a specific purpose

marauding (¶7)   raiding to rob by force, especially in times of war

papooses (¶9)   very young children

awash (¶13)   overflowing

anguish (¶14)   agonizing physical or mental pain

Zarbadoh's Children

Olivia Ward

1   Men mean trouble in this village of children that is no longer a village but a collection of rearranged rubbish. Men fire guns, leave family members lying in pools of blood, and send children scurrying into the fields or burrowing under flimsy mattresses.

2   The children remember and are afraid.

3   One summer day two years ago gangs of armed men from the neighboring countryside invaded their quiet, prosperous farm community and stripped it of cars, machinery, food, and household goods. The children didn't understand why. Their parents had no time to explain. When the militants came back the next day with guns and torches the children saw only blood and ricocheting bullets and sheets of flame that devoured everything in their small, limited world.

4   Now about 500 babies and young people have returned from refugee camps and villages near the Afghan border. Fifty women are with them. The only men here are four grey-haired elders who braved a trail of violence to accept the Government's offer of resettlement.

5   But the war—the stealthy, confusing, terrifying war—has never really ended. Night and day gunfire echoes through the muddy plain on which the settlers cannot afford to sow more than a handful of vegetable seeds.

6   Tajikistan's civil war is one of the most complex in the former Soviet Union. During its course it has displaced 500,000 of the country's 5.5 million people and acquired an unmatched reputation for brutality. Strife began when the Soviet Union collapsed in 1991 and Communist Party boss Rakhmon Nabiev seized power. The Pamiri minority from the east of the country and fundamentalist Muslims from the Garm Valley formed an alliance and clashed violently with government forces. As turbulence spread, the storm center shifted to the area around Zarbadoh, 25 kilometers north of Afghanistan. By the time Nabiev was driven out of the capital at gunpoint and a hastily installed Islamic-Democratic coalition collapsed, the southern villages were awash in blood. The battles died down when

Olivia Ward, "Zarbadoh's Children," *New Internationalist,* July 1994, no. 25, 255, p. 27. Reprinted by permission.

Please note maps in appendix for references to places in this article.

neighboring Uzbekistan sent troops, and a new communist leader, Imomali Rakhmonov, was elected.

7   The six-month war had a shattering effect on families who were forced to flee. The devastated villages are now settlements of children—lively, dark-eyed children who are strangely quiet and seldom leave their mothers' sides. Marauding men turn up suddenly, searching for the children's fathers. One of them was the father of 15-year-old Gueraftor Hajieva, a slender, serious teenager who has only a mother and sister left of her family of seven brothers and sisters.

8   "I think about them all the time. I can't get through the day without crying," she says, hiding her face in embarrassment.

9   Gueraftor's days are bleak and cheerless. Fear, boredom, and endless, repetitive chores are her daily fare, predictable as toothache. Day by day the women and older children work together, rebuilding shelter for themselves by hand. During the worst days of winter most of the villagers huddled in the damp-smelling basement of a destroyed schoolhouse where classes were no longer held. Now, as spring turns the frosty soil to a sea of mud, darkness puts an end to bone-wearying days. While the younger children are wrapped up in donated blankets and laid out for sleep like tiny papooses, older ones can only listen in the dimness for what they fear most—the vehicles of armed men.

10   "I'm afraid to go very far from here," Gueraftor says. "Men might come and . . . insult me."

11   They have come in the past, swooping down and demanding "a girl" to take back with them. So far groups of angry shouting women have driven them away. But no one is safe and fear is like a sour coating on a life that has already lost its savor.

12   The youngsters, confined to their shelters or carried around by their mothers because they lack proper shoes, cannot live as normal children do. The sound of cars or gunfire fills them with panic as violent memories surface and some have fits of nervous trembling.

13   The capital, Dushanbe, is now an armed camp awash in terrorism, crime, and poverty. Young men in their teens carry guns openly and the violence they have witnessed has taken root and grown.

14   "Many children in this country are suffering from the war," says psychiatrist Minhoj Gulyamov. "It isn't just physical diseases, it's mental anguish."

15   "I have spells when I feel as though I'm going to die," says Nigora Vohidova, a tall, gentle girl of 15 with a face of exotic beauty. "It's terrifying and I don't know what to do."

16   Nigora's anxiety attacks began after the street battles ended in Dushanbe. They were sudden, unexpected, and completely terrifying.

17   "She would stand up and scream 'I don't want to die!'," says her mother, Maya Vohidova. "We did everything to comfort her, but it didn't have any effect."

18   At the Internat children's home across the city, Nadezhda Tsayova cares for 130 parentless children under harsh conditions that have improved little since the war.

19   "God will help us," recites a tiny five-year-old with sandy hair and a pixyish face.

20   The children gather round excitedly to talk to the first foreigners they have ever seen. They are quick to smile and hug each other playfully. Most of them, Tsayova says, eat uncontrollably when food is put in front of them. "It's as though they remember the days of the war when they were hungry. They eat even when they really don't need the food . . . After everything they've been through I think they will grow up determined to prevent more violence."

21   The children giggle and clasp each other's hands. But one little boy gets up and sings:

22   "My brother patrols the border, that's why I sleep so well . . . because he is carrying a gun."

READING

1. Where does the civil war described in this article take place? What are the people fighting about?

2. How do the children of the orphanage react to foreign visitors? How do they react to food when it is served? Why do they react that way?

THINKING

1. Have you lived where there was a war going on? Has anyone you know fought in a war? What was it like to be involved in a war? If you weren't, talk to someone who has been.

2. What do you think of the way the young girls deal with the stress of being in a war-torn community? How do you think you would react in similar circumstances?

PREWRITING

Write freely about everything you know about war. Set a timer for ten minutes and write without stopping everything that enters your mind about war, how it affects people, the devastation it leaves behind, the orphans, and anything else you can think of to do with war.

WRITING

1. There are many orphans in Zarbadoh. Suppose that these children would be freed for adoption. Write a letter applying to adopt one of these children stating why and how you could provide a good home. Or, write an essay stating why you think children should or should not be adopted internationally. Be sure to include specific reasons for your argument, including facts.

2. The civil war in Tajikistan is one that the United States has not been involved in, while it has been involved in others, such as Vietnam. Write a well developed argument stating why you think the United States should or should not be involved in the civil wars of other countries. Be sure to do research to find facts to back up your argument.

REVISING

"Zarbadoh's Children" is a description of a war-torn community. The article describes how the people in the community react to the devastation they have suffered. Paragraph one offers a vivid description of what the village looks like. Paragraph three describes what happened when the militants came. The sense of **touch** is felt with the heat of the sheets of flame. The sense of **sound** is heard with "ricocheting bullets." The sense of **sight** shows the countryside stripped of all belongings and the blood, bullets, and flames. The sense of **smell** is invoked with imaging the smoke from the flames. The sense of taste is not included in this paragraph, but can be part of an effective description.

Look through your rough draft and see how many times that you have used your senses in your writing assignment. See if you can add details by using the senses that you haven't used in this draft so far.

EDITING

In writing, the **tenses of verbs** in sentences frequently shift to make the sentence logical, but sometimes a shift can be made between tenses that makes your sentence meaning unclear.

Example of the correct sentence is:

> The children **giggle** and **clasp** each other's hands. **(¶21)**

The verbs in this sentence are all in present tense. See how illogical the sentence would be if the verbs shifted needlessly between past and present:

> The children **giggle** and **clasped** each other's hands.

The use of the past tense **clasped** with the present tense **giggle** is not logical here. Go through your writing assignment and circle the verbs. Then check to see that they express time or tense in a logical fashion.

Race on Campus: Failing the Test?

Tom Morganthau

PREREADING

What do you know about racism? Do you feel that it exists on your campus today? Have there been any racial problems or conflicts that you know of on your campus since you've been there? How do you feel about racism?

DEFINING

separatism (¶1)   the act of separating, choosing to be separated

archaic (¶1)   old-fashioned, that which is no longer used

fascistic (¶1)   having to do with fascism: rigid, one-party dictatorship

brouhaha (¶2)   commotion, noisy uproar

impasse (¶2)   a situation that has no solution

opéra-bouffe **(¶3)**   comic opera

neocon (¶3)   newly conservative

tweak (¶3)   a sharp pinch

buffeting (¶4)   striking

bureaucratic (¶4)   inflexible, government system

euphemisms (¶4)   the use of less expressive or less offensive words

ethos **(¶4)**   the distinguishing attitudes of a group

balkanization (¶4)   the process of breaking up into small, hostile political units

recrimination (¶5)   meeting one accusation with another

recanted (¶5)   took back a statement

roiled (¶6)   made angry or irritable

amity (¶7)   harmony

elusive (¶7)   evading, escaping by deception

Race on Campus: Failing the Test?

Tom Morganthau with Marcus Mabry, Laura Genao, and Frank Washington

1   The real truth about race relations on college campuses today is that they have never been better—and that they are, as Ohio State University student Sheron Smith puts it, "Terrible. Horrid. Stinky!" Got it? This is the best of times, the worst of times, and, without doubt, the noisiest of times in America's long march toward equal opportunity in higher education. Almost everyone, it seems, is mad about something: racial slurs, affirmative action, separatism, multiculturalism or the tyranny of manners that is known as the PC ("politically correct") movement. The lofty notion of college campuses as havens of tolerance, free inquiry, and reasoned discourse seems as archaic as panty raids. "I lament the loss of civility and accommodation," sighs Marjorie Garber, associate dean for affirmative action at Harvard. "It's not 'fascistic' or 'politically correct' to be aware of others' sensitivities. Think, with imagination, of others. Think of how what you're saying will be heard."

2   But good advice is rarely heeded, even at Harvard. . . . The nation's oldest university has been transfixed by one of the more perverse and complex controversies of a contentious academic year—a brouhaha over symbolic speech in the form of a Confederate flag. It began when Brigit Kerrigan, a senior from Great Falls, Va., displayed the Stars and Bars from the window of her dormitory room. Kerrigan, insisting that the flag was merely a statement of regional pride, steadfastly resisted pressure from fellow students and university officials to take it down. The university, recognizing the legal and political pitfalls of cracking down on a student's First Amendment rights, declined to compel her. And this impasse led Jacinda Townsend, 19, a junior from Bowling Green, Ky., to hang a bedsheet spray-painted with a swastika from *her* dormitory window. "I wanted people to know what the Confederate flag really means," she said. "I don't see it so much as a part of free speech, but as a threat of violence."

3   The battle of the symbols continued until Townsend, succumbing to protests from Jewish students and criticism from the Harvard Black Students Association, finally removed the swastika bedsheet. Kerrigan's Confederate flag, on the other hand, remains defiantly in view, and it is worth considering her motives in touch-

Tom Morganthau et al., "Race on Campus: Failing the Test?" *Newsweek,* May 6, 1991, pp. 26–27. From *Newsweek,* May 6, 1991. © 1991, Newsweek, Inc. All rights reserved. Reprinted by permission.

Please note maps in appendix for references to places in this article.

ing off this *opéra-bouffe* dispute. Kerrigan is a conservative activist, and she seems to want to give Harvard's liberal sensibilities a vigorous neocon tweak. "If they talk about 'diversity,' they're gonna get it," she told *The Boston Globe.* "If they talk about tolerance, they'd better be ready to have it."

4   You could make the case that the race-relations debate now buffeting many U.S. colleges and universities is like the flag war at Harvard—a shadow play, for the most part harmless, of larger social conflicts. But the analogy is probably wrong. There are real stakes, real losses, and real victims as schools all over the country struggle to negotiate the kind of social accommodations that most Americans avoid. The catchword for all this—Kerrigan is exactly right—is "diversity," and like all bureaucratic euphemisms, it covers a multitude of sins. . . . Diversity is achieved, in the bare statistical sense, by including minority students and teachers in the university community. But the *ethos* of diversity, which is tolerance and mutual respect, is much harder to come by—and there is ample evidence that the grand experiment in race relations may be failing. It is like a college mixer where no one mixes—and it is leading, in the view of Troy Duster, a Berkeley sociologist, to the "balkanization" of campus life.

5   Tension between the races is, of course, nothing new on campus. What *is* new, and surpassingly ugly, is the apparent rise in racial incidents of all sorts—name-calling, scapegoating, accusations, and recriminations. There are no truly comprehensive statistics. But Adele Terrell, program director of the National Institute Against Prejudice and Violence at the University of Maryland's Baltimore campus, says one in five black students reports some form of racial harassment and that racist episodes have been reported at more than 300 colleges and universities over the past five years. An incident at Ohio State . . . is a depressing example. A woman graduate student claimed she had been raped by a black student. She later recanted her story, but the case led to altercations between campus police and black students and a series of student confrontations along racial lines. "There is some very serious tension," an OSU official concedes. "It seems to be a national trend."

6   He may be right. The list of name schools that have been rocked by race-related controversies in recent years includes Yale, Brown, Penn State, Georgetown, the University of Texas, the University of Michigan, and many others. At Yale, 10 black law students received anonymous "nigger" notes in their dormitory mailboxes after a reported rape last fall; not long afterward, eight black undergraduates got into a dispute at a local pizza parlor that further roiled the waters. A Georgetown University law student, Timothy Maguire, recently prompted an uproar over affirmative action with an article charging that the LSAT scores and grade-point averages of many black law-school students are significantly lower than whites'. (Maguire has apologized.) Racially offensive fraternity pranks have led to disciplinary action at the University of Texas and George Mason University in Virginia. An official at the University of Georgia, where fraternity rushes are still segregated by race, says flatly that the school is twenty years behind the times.

7   There's no disputing that big issues are in play here: affirmative action, free speech, the competition between liberty and justice. There is also no disputing, as many university administrators maintain, that the social and economic tensions of

society at large will inevitably be played out on campus. Blacks (not to mention Hispanics and Asian-Americans) are becoming more assertive of their separate ethnic identities, of their right to protest even the most casual snub or slight, and of their need for firmer support from college authorities. Whites, wary of increasing competition for jobs and mindful of conservative attacks on liberal social policies, increasingly object to affirmative action and to the accusation that they are racists, too. Both sides—all sides—seem to harbor a sense of grievance and victimization. The great battles of the '60s and '70s are only history to the twentysomething generation, and blacks and other minorities are now questioning the very idea of integration. That does not mean the progress of the past two decades is actually in jeopardy. But the dream of racial amity—of blacks and whites learning and playing together—still seems sadly elusive.

READING

1. What are the big issues on campus having to do with racism?

2. Which big name schools have been having problems with race relationships? What kinds of problems are they having?

THINKING

1. The article mentions that the Civil Rights Movement is history to most students in their twenties today. What do you know about the Civil Rights Movement? What do you think that it accomplished? Do you remember who any of the leaders of the movement were? Where are they now?

2. The last sentence of the article says, "But the dream of racial amity—of blacks and whites learning and playing together—still seems sadly elusive." Is this the case on your campus? In your community? Tom Morganthau argues that blacks are being more assertive now, which brings their problems more into the public eye. Do you think that this is true? Are other minorities as assertive for their rights?

PREWRITING

Freewrite about how you think your campus is affected by racism. Have there been specific incidents? Are certain organizations or groups of students involved? Do you feel that there is no discrimination on your campus? Do you feel that only black students are affected by racism, or do you see other groups of students affected as well?

WRITING

1. You are in charge of planning a "mixer" for the students on your campus to get to know each other. You need to submit a written plan to the student activities office to show how you will attempt to reach out to and include all students on your campus and how you will ensure that there will be no discriminatory activities. Write that plan.

2. Morganthau argues that American campuses are facing "the best of times and the worst of times" on racism issues. Write a comparison/contrast essay with your classmates as audience that expresses what you see as "the best of times and the worst of times" on issues regarding racism on your campus today.

REVISING

Writing assignment number two asks you specifically to write a comparison/contrast essay, but comparison/contrast techniques can be used in much of your writing, including writing assignment number one. Comparing ideas points out their similarities, and contrasting ideas shows their differences. There are two main ways that you can organize a compare/contrast essay. The first is to list and explain the main similarities in the idea you are writing about, and then list and explain the differences in the same ideas. The other way that you could organize a comparison/contrast paper is to discuss the similarities and differences in your first idea, then go to the next idea, and so on until you have discussed all of the ideas you want to compare and contrast.

Go through the draft of your writing assignment and see how you have actually compared and contrasted your ideas. Just comparing ideas or just contrasting ideas in this kind of an assignment is an easy error to fall into. Be sure that you have adequately covered both sides.

EDITING

Apostrophes are used to show possession as well as to indicate contractions. The use of contractions is covered in the Editing section of "Against All Odds." To see if a word needs an apostrophe to show possession or ownership, convert the phrase that you are writing into a *belonging to* or *of* phrase.

Examples:

the man's tie, which could be converted to *the tie belonging to the man*

James's car, which could be converted to *the car belonging to James*

one week's pay, or the pay of *one week*

Notice that the apostrophe follows the word that shows ownership. If the word is already plural, the apostrophe will still come at the end of the word.

Examples:

the children's toys, or the *toys belonging to the children*

several ladies' lunches, or the *lunches belonging to several ladies*

two weeks' pay, or the *pay of two weeks*

Personal possessive pronouns never require apostrophes to show possession because they already show possession: yours, his, hers, its, ours, theirs, and whose.

The only time that it's requires an apostrophe is when it serves as the contraction for it is.

Examples:

It's not "fascistic" or "politically correct" to be aware of *others'* sensitivities. (the *sensitivities of others*)

Kerrigan is a conservative activist, and she seems to want to give *Harvard's* liberal sensitivities a vigorous neocon tweak. (the *liberal sensitivities of Harvard*)

Check through your writing assignment to be sure that you have used apostrophes correctly when needed.

Bad for the First, Good for the Third World

Syed Neaz Ahmad

PREREADING

What do you think about smoking? Do you smoke? Do your friends or family smoke? Do you think smoking is harmful? Why or why not? If you don't smoke now, do you think advertising could convince you to start smoking? Why or why not? There is a tremendous rise in the number of American teenagers who smoke. Why do you think this is happening?

DEFINING

multinationals (¶2) companies operating in more than two countries

coveted (¶4) wished for

shrewd (¶6) characterized by awareness, intelligence, and practicality

metaphors (¶7) figures of speech where words that usually stand for one thing are used to stand for something else

attributable (¶8) caused by, given credit for; "smoking-attributable mortality" means deaths related to smoking

imperialist (¶9) the policy of extending a nation's power over other nations

colonialism (¶9) the policy by which a nation maintains control

agrarian (¶9) concerning the land and its ownership and cultivation

commodity (¶9) something useful that can be sold for a profit

momentous (¶10) of extreme importance

vested interests (¶10) groups that seek to control something they receive a private benefit from

aubergine (¶13) eggplant

Bad for the First, Good for the Third World

Syed Neaz Ahmad

1   The Marlboro Man and his horse have found greener pastures in Asia. The tough weather-beaten character in rugged jacket, leather gloves, his lasso carelessly thrown over his shoulder and half of his face hidden under the ten-gallon hat will soon have to find a new profile. Out of the backcovers of magazines, the man is now bound for exotic destinations in Asia: Seoul, Bangkok, Tokyo, Shanghai, Hong Kong, and Phnom Penh. His smoke signal: "Come to where the flavor is. Come to Marlboro Country," however, remains unchanged.

2   Tobacco industry projects the Asian market to grow by more than a third during the 90s with much of the revenue going to the multinationals. Some 60 per cent of the world population lives in Asia and Marlboro sells more on the continent than anywhere else.

3   Triggered by a ban on smoking in public places, cigarette sales are expected to decline by about 15 per cent in the West, but the unlimited earning possibilities in Asia and throughout the Third World make the Western markets insignificant.

4   Beyond Asia, smoking is a catching habit in Africa, Latin America, Eastern Europe, and the Commonwealth of Independent States. China, with 1.2 billion inhabitants, is another coveted market. There are some 300 million smokers in China who buy 1.6 trillion cigarettes a year. Philip Morris, the company behind Marlboro, has signed an agreement with a Chinese corporation to produce Marlboro and other brands in China. While profits in the American market fell by half in 1993 the company's foreign market profits grew by 17%.

5   For a trade wholly built on smoke, cigarette brands, since the early 1950s have been introduced in bewildering numbers, each aiming at a particular class and type of consumers. Marlboro was first a luxury then a women's cigarette. In the wake of the cancer scare in the 50s, it underwent a transformation, a filter was added, packaged in a flip-top box, and was taken away from women and given to men with the help of the cowboy image. Its advertising campaign has been one of the most successful. "The Marlboro image represents escape, not from the responsibilities of civilization, but from its frustrations."

6   The growth and expansion of Asian market is a result of aggressive and

Syed Neaz Ahmad, "Bad for the First, Good for the Third World," *Impact International*, Vol. 24, No. 6, June 1994, p. 42. Reprinted by permission.

Please note maps in appendix for references to places in this article.

shrewd marketing by Western companies, economic prosperity of large Asian nations, and a shift in local customs. Foreign brands, once scarce and expensive, are
now affordable by millions in Asia. Cigarette smoking, once a social taboo for
women, is now seen as a sign of their liberation.

7   Power, status, success, and confidence appeared to be the appeal of other
brands. The culture of cigarette consumption, however, is not simply that of the
advertisement: rather it is a blend of the advertised images and metaphors together with prevailing social customs. As a result, the U.S. cigarette advertising expenditure increased from $47 million in 1947 to $1.9 billion in 1983. Some multinationals, like BAT, sold cigarettes worth $8.3 billion, employing 280,000 and
Rothmans International, "the best tobacco money can buy," sold $4.3 billion worth
of cigarettes in 1980.

8   Notwithstanding the power it exercises on the economy, "smoking-attributable mortality" constitutes a serious threat. Death caused by tobacco world-wide
was estimated by WHO at 3 million in 1991, roughly two-thirds in the developed,
and one-third in the developing world. Influenced by the anti-tobacco lobby in the
West those who think that the multinationals are heading for extinction need to
take a closer look at the Asian market.

9   Like other trades, tobacco too has served as a tool in the hands of the imperialist masters. It was the first of the range of non-European exotica to establish itself
permanently as a European commodity, well before chocolate, coffee, and tea. A
close study of the tobacco industry unfolds its function in different stages of economic culture, showing its key role in colonialism and slavery, the formation of
multinational corporations, and the huge expenditure on advertising and marketing. Tobacco's history cuts across many larger themes, such as colonialism, consumerism, medical discourse, agrarian culture, and power of people and institutions who have created the complex network of relationships surrounding this
controversial commodity.

10   The medical evidence of tobacco has been debated since its first introduction
into Europe in the 16th century. But what happened in the 1960s was momentous.
For the first time there was solid evidence that tobacco was a dangerous substance
and that cigarette smoke caused fatal diseases. This had considerable impact. First,
tobacco was put on the political agenda and it became increasingly clear that there
were powerful vested interests involved. Almost immediately an intense war broke
out between the pro-tobacco forces, including tobacco companies, some government agencies, tobacco producers, and some consumers, and the anti-tobacco
forces. Large breweries have joined the fray to keep the pressure on the tobacco industry and attention away from their own doors.

11   The contradictory role of government came under close scrutiny, especially
since, on the one hand, it had a duty to protect consumers from potentially dangerous substances, while, on the other, it acted to protect its own interests. In the
US, where tobacco growing is big business, the scale of the problem is enormous.
In 1980 the British treasury received around £3 billion in taxes and duty from tobacco; tobacco sales from 350,000 retail outlets amounted to $4,300 million; ciga-
rettes valued at £464 million were exported to 150 countries; overseas aid to Zam-

bia, Malawi, and Belize to develop and support tobacco growing amounted to £3.5 million since 1974.

12   Whatever goes up in smoke is unlikely to bring benefit, but tobacco is a vice which is a rare exception. "This vice brings in one hundred million francs in taxes every year. I will certainly forbid it at once—as soon as you can name a virtue that brings in as much income." What was good at the time of Napoleon III also holds true for many governments today. Tobacco is big business. There are thousands who live by smoke and millions who die by smoke every year, generating billions of pounds in income for the manufacturers and taxes to various governments.

13   Some recent researches reveal that potato and aubergine are rich in nicotine. Bad news for the multinationals.

READING

1. Where is the best market for cigarettes? Why is this the best?

2. How has advertising for Marlboro cigarettes changed over the years? Why were these changes made?

THINKING

1. In America we have proved the damaging effects of smoking and we try to educate the public why they should not smoke and that smoking is harmful. Knowing this, how do you feel about the American tobacco industry expanding in Asia and the rest of the world? What do you think this means to the world? What does it say about our nation?

2. Do you think the government has the right to control where you smoke? Why or why not? Some states have laws that do not allow smoking in public places, while other states just regulate that smoking and nonsmoking areas be provided. Which of these alternatives do you feel is correct? Why? Or do you think another alternative would be better? If so, what would that be? Why?

PREWRITING

Write two lists, seeing how long you can make each list. For the first list, write all of the benefits of smoking you can think of. For the second list, write all the reasons someone should not smoke. Then write two more lists. For the first list, write all of the reasons tobacco should be marketed out of America. For the second list, write all of the reasons it should not be marketed outside of America.

WRITING

1. You have been offered the opportunity to invest in a multinational that has the potential for great profit by marketing tobacco in third-world countries. You have the money to invest, but you need to consider whether you believe in what you are investing in. Write a letter to the president of the company who offered you this opportunity, and tell her why you will or will not be investing. Be specific.

2. In your state there are no laws regulating smoking in private residences such as apartments and dorm rooms. Your university is debating whether it should adopt the policy of smoke-free dorms. Write a paper to be presented before the governing body of the university making the final decision that states how you feel about this proposed rule. Include all of these reasons why you think it should or should not be adopted.

REVISING

Each article in this book is preceded by a Defining section where words that you may not be familiar with are identified to help you understand the article more easily. Frequently the writer has chosen to use these words instead of simpler alternatives because these words may have a meaning that is clearer or more specific. Using some of these words in your writing may help you be more specific, too. Reread "Bad for the First, Good for the Third" and note how the words in the Defining section are used in the article.

Review the draft of your writing assignment. Are there places where you could insert more specific terminology? Try using a thesaurus to look up different words if you are having difficulty thinking of them on your own.

EDITING

Remembering when to change a final **y** to **i** when adding a suffix (ending) to a word can be confusing, but three simple rules can help.

1. Change the **y** to **i** when adding a suffix to a word that ends in **y** preceded by a consonant.

Examples:
> busy–business
>
> dry–driest
>
> easy–easily
>
> lonely–loneliness

2. Never change the final **y** of a word when adding the suffix **ing.**

Examples:
> deny–denying
>
> fly–flying
>
> try–trying
>
> study–studying

3. Do **not** change the **y** to **i** when adding a suffix to a word that ends preceded by a vowel.

Examples:
    alley–alleys

    attorney–attorneys

    holiday–holidays

    annoy–annoys

Exceptions to the rules:
    day–daily

    gay–gaily

    pay–paid

    say–said

    lay–laid

Check your writing assignments to be sure you have used this rule correctly.

One of the most frequent spelling errors people make is when **i** should come before **e.** Most of us remember the rule "**i** before **e** except after **c**," but we need to remember the rest of that rule. The whole rule is "place **i** before **e** except after **c** when pronounced as **ee,** but place **e** before **i** when not pronounced as **ee.**" The exceptions to this rule can be best remembered by learning this sentence: **"Neither friend of either species seized weird leisure."** Go through your writing assignment and pick out all of the words with the **ie** or **ei** combination and determine if you have spelled them correctly.

Why I Fear Other Black Males More Than the KKK

Essex Hemphill

PREREADING

Essex Hemphill wrote this article out of frustration after he was mugged. What do you think you would do if you were mugged? Would you be willing to give up your belongings to a stranger? What if your attacker threatened your life? What would you do if you witnessed a mugging?

DEFINING

apartheid (¶3)   racial segregation and discrimination once practiced in South Africa

AIDS (¶3)   acquired immunodeficiency syndrome, a fatal illness

taunting (¶4)   insulting, teasing, mocking

slurs (¶4)   harmful statements

Essex Hemphill, Pacific News Service, "Why I Fear Black Males More Than the KKK," *Utne Reader,* Jan/Feb 1991, pp. 115–116. Reprinted by permission of *Utne Reader* and PNS.

Please note maps in appendix for references to places in this article.

Why I Fear Other Black Males More Than the KKK

Essex Hemphill

1   Last summer, I was robbed six blocks from my home in Washington, D.C. I had $13 in my pocket. As I strolled to the market in the breezy summer evening, I debated buying a pint of vanilla ice cream to accompany a night of television. Near 16th and Irving Streets, a cocked gun was placed to my head. I had enough presence of mind to remain calm and passive. I didn't want to die for $13. The smallest robber kept singing, "Shoot him! Shoot him! Shoot him!"

2   The robbers were in their late teens or early twenties. A difference of at least 10 to 12 years separated us. The one pressing me against a parked van with his arm against my throat cussed in my face and slammed me again and again against the van. When he released me, I slumped to the ground. They did not run from the scene; they casually walked away and never looked back. If a gun at that moment had suddenly materialized in my hand, I would have used it without mercy. I would have put bullets in their backs. Then I would have stood over their bodies and put bullets in each of their heads.

3   Need I point out that we were all black males? Need I also say that the Ku Klux Klan is less threatening to me than other black males? Apartheid is less threatening to me than other black males. AIDS is less threatening to me than other black males. Why is it so hard for so many black Americans to acknowledge publicly the crimes blacks commit against other blacks? Why do we excuse black misbehavior by hiding behind charges of racism?

4   Black protestors march around a store in West Philadelphia, where I now live, taunting the shopkeeper, Yong Chang, with racial slurs and verbal intimidation. The protestors are angry because the shopkeeper's son, 27-year-old Yung Su Chang, killed a black male. The black male, Gregory Dorn, also 27, had reached for a knife during a robbery attempt. Police determined that the shooting was a justifiable homicide and charges against Chang were dropped. To the protestors, this was just another example of injustice against a black male. But I, too, would have shot the robber. He was, after all, committing a robbery. And he was going to use a weapon. Tell me why it is racist to defend your property and your life.

5   The protestors in Philadelphia complain about the shooting of a black male by a white police officer, but I doubt that they would protest the shooting of a black male by another black over drugs, radios, or sneakers. I doubt the protestors dare go to the sites where drug killings occur and demand that the violence stop.

READING

1. Who is less threatening to Hemphill than other black males? Why are they less threatening?

2. Why were the black protestors marching around the store in West Philadelphia?

THINKING

1. Essex Hemphill could easily have died for the $13 in his pocket. Other people have died because someone wanted to steal their sneakers. Do incidents like this make you fear for your safety, or do you think that things like this only happen to someone else? Have you changed anything you do in your life because of fear? Are there places that you avoid because you don't feel that they are safe?

2. The attitude of the assailants really bothered Hemphill. The smallest robber "kept singing, 'Shoot him! Shoot him! Shoot him.'" After they attacked him, "they casually walked away and never looked back." Do you sympathize with the victim's feeling that he desired to shoot the robbers? Why or why not? This article seems to lack a conclusion. What do you think should be included in a final paragraph for this article?

PREWRITING

Make a list of the main problems with crime that exist in your neighborhood. Explore through clustering your ideas about one of the major criminal problems. What are its causes? How could it be prevented?

WRITING

1. You are fed up with the crime in your community, so you have joined a coalition made up of your neighbors who have decided to work toward making your area a safer place to live. Each member of your group is supposed to come up with one idea to combat the high crime rate. Clearly express your idea for a solution to this problem in a short essay that you can share with the coalition.

2. Hemphill asks two rhetorical questions in his essay: "Why is it so hard for so many black Americans to acknowledge publicly the crimes blacks commit against other blacks? Why do we excuse black misbehavior by hiding behind charges of racism?" Write an essay expressing your answers to these questions. Feel free to substitute a culture that you are more familiar with if that would help your argument.

REVISING

Writing assignment number two mentions rhetorical questions. A rhetorical question is one that is asked in a speech or piece of writing when an answer is not expected. The writer simply asks the question to get the audience to think about what the answer may be. Generally, the most effective way to communicate a specific message to an audience is to make a direct statement, but when your goal is to actually have your audience think and come to their own conclusions, rhetorical questions can be effective. Hemphill asks several effective rhetorical questions. In addition to the two that are used in writing assignment two, he also says, "Need I point out that we were all black males?" He goes beyond a question to almost a command when he says, "Tell me why it is racist to defend your property and your life." Rhetorical questions can also be used effectively to begin or end a piece of writing.

Look at your writing assignment and see if you can insert one rhetorical question. Remember, rhetorical questions work best when they are used sparingly.

EDITING

Exclamation points are used to add extra emphasis to writing. They can be very effective when they aren't overused. Writing tends to look juvenile or unsophisticated when there are too many exclamation points. When you do choose to use exclamation points, they come at the end of the sentence immediately following the last word.

Example:
"Shoot him!"

Notice that this example quote from the essay has the exclamation point inside the quotation marks, because what is being said in the quotation marks is what is being emphasized. If there is a quotation in a sentence where the sentence is emphatic, but the quotation isn't, then the exclamation point comes outside the quotation marks.

Example:
We were shocked when he casually said, "I'll shoot him"!

Check through your writing to be sure that you haven't overused exclamation points.

Living With AIDS

Ruth Evans

PREREADING

Margaret is HIV-positive, but she is not sure how she contracted it. It could have been either from her former husband or from a blood transfusion. Do you know how AIDS is transmitted and how to prevent getting it? Do you think AIDS could affect you? Do you know anyone who has AIDS or is HIV-positive? Do you think practicing safe sex is important? Why or why not?

DEFINING

testament (¶1)   proof or evidence

solace (¶2)   comfort in sorrow

chattels (¶16)   slaves, personal property

banger (¶18)   a noisy old car (British)

whilst (¶21)   while (British)

Living with AIDS
Ruth Evans

Margaret's Story

A large pile of red bricks outside Margaret Nalumasi's house is testament to the plans she has to extend and improve her home. She has even built a garage for the old car she hopes to buy one day.

Some people might find her plans for the future surprising given that 33-year-old Margaret was diagnosed HIV-positive in 1984. "I had heard of AIDS," she says, "but I thought it only affected girls who have three boyfriends at a time."

2   A small vibrant woman with a warm wide smile, Margaret lives twenty miles south of Kampala with her 11-year-old son Patrick and 8-year-old daughter Winnie, the two surviving children from five pregnancies. Margaret separated from their father some time ago.

3   She believes her children are free of the virus, but she says she hasn't got the guts to have them tested.

4   One of Margaret's younger sisters, eighteen-year-old Justine, lives with them. Margaret is paying for Justine's education, and Justine will be responsible for looking after the children when Margaret dies.

5   Margaret has had a hard life. In 1979, she was doing a typing course in Kampala. Then Museveni's guerrilla war broke out and she found herself stranded in the city with no money or support coming from the village.

6   "I was green," she says, and a man staying in the house where she was renting a cheap room forced himself on her. She found herself pregnant, and when an attempted abortion failed, she had to accept this man as her husband although he "wasn't a man of my choice."

7   The baby did not survive, but other pregnancies followed. Patrick was born soon afterwards. A third baby died at the age of two from burns after falling in a pot of boiling beans. Then Winnie was born, and a fifth baby died at birth.

8   With the third pregnancy, Margaret needed a blood transfusion so, she says "I can't say it was the husband, and I can't say it was the blood that infected me. I will never know." Her husband became very ill in 1980 and she herself fell sick in 1984.

9   Astonishingly, Margaret told me: "Discovering HIV has been a way to improve the quality of my life. Before I was diagnosed, I wasn't as happy as I am now." It's hard not to believe her.

10   She says she was very worried at first, but now her main concern is building the house as a way of "putting something inside you into a physical thing to touch." She's making the most of what she has left of her own life and is working on ways to secure the future for her two children.

Please note maps in appendix for references to places in this article.

11   As a way of generating some income, she keeps 170 chickens and sells their eggs at market. She also gets milk from her two cows and keeps a couple of pigs.

12   In addition, she has become a born-again Christian and finds great solace in her faith. "Sometimes I used to cry," she told me, "But I know Jesus is looking into my well-being now. I know I can work for myself and I know that whatever I do, with God's help, will be of value and importance for my children."

13   Occasionally she is tortured by fevers and fatigue, especially when she has been overworking. But she says people with AIDS are "doctors to themselves. You can do a lot to help yourself, because you know your own body."

14   People like Margaret Nalumasi give the tragedy of AIDS a very human face. By going public about her illness, and through her work with TASO, a Ugandan non-governmental organization which cares for and counsels people with AIDS and HIV, she hopes to help others like herself and, more importantly, make people not yet infected aware of the ways they can protect themselves.

15   Each day she travels the twenty miles to Kampala's Mulago hospital, where she works as a typist for TASO's counselling services, helps prepare food for patients who come for twice-weekly clinics, and coordinates the Women's Support Network.

16   With the money she earns at TASO, Margaret has bought her own plot of land and built her own house on it. This is unusual in a country where women are still regarded as chattels. She also helps feed, clothe, and educate other members of her family.

17   Her main concern now is that when her children are orphaned, like thousands of other children in Uganda, there will at least be enough money to provide for them. Her children know that she will die.

18   Margaret's determination and love of life are, for the moment, a match for the deadly virus within her body. She is sure her pile of bricks will be put to good use and is calculating how long it will take her to save for an old banger that will help her transport her eggs to market.

19   She lives without sex, and when I asked whether she missed it, she simply laughed and said: "No, I have too much to do. I have no time to think of a man!"

Justine's Story

20   Justine Nalumasi sits under the shade of the mango tree behind Margaret's house waiting for the school exam results that will determine her future. She would like to be a doctor, but doesn't think she will get the grades, so has set her sights on becoming a social worker instead.

21   Whilst she waits, she weaves papyrus grass into the baskets she makes to earn a little pocket money. One basket takes two days and will earn her at most two dollars. But if she isn't very careful, the dry grass cuts her fingers.

22   Justine is a bright, vivacious and very pretty eighteen year-old. Margaret is more like a mother to her than an older sister, and Justine lives in Margaret's house rather than in the overcrowded family home. She is not HIV-positive, but in many ways the virus has affected her life as fundamentally as Margaret's.

23   She has known for a long time that Margaret has AIDS. When she first found out, she couldn't sleep and used to cry all the time. "I was afraid," she says, "I could not stand it." At first, she did not tell any of her friends about Margaret because of the stigma attached to the virus, but with time that has changed as more and more people have been affected.

24   The future worries Justine very much. Margaret pays for her school fees and encourages her to study hard because the responsibility for Patrick and Winnie will fall on her when Margaret dies, although they rarely talk of this.

25   Without Margaret's financial support, Justine will not be able to continue her education, so she is doing the best she can whilst she can. She wants to get a well paid job. "Nothing can fail when you have money," she told me.

26   It's hard for young people like Justine growing up under the threat of AIDS. She has joined the AIDS Challenge Youth Club that TASO runs, and says she has learned a lot there about how to protect herself from infection. She wishes everyone could join the club.

27   Justine is no prude, but when she sees her friends behaving in an irresponsible way she talks to them about the risks they are taking and tries to persuade them to change their behavior. She even tried to tell a much older cousin that she was taking unnecessary risks by having unprotected sex, but found her advice dismissed as "mere schoolgirl talk."

28   What has happened to Margaret will always be in Justine's mind. It has curtailed her freedom as much as Margaret's. For the time being, Justine says she is too frightened to start a sexual relationship with anyone. "I have never played sex before," she says, "I can't afford to make a mistake."

READING

1. Since Margaret is HIV-positive, what is she doing for her children? How many children does she have?

2. Who is Justine? What is she doing for Margaret?

THINKING

1. When AIDS was first isolated in the United States, most of the population chose to ignore the situation or felt that it was just a "gay" disease or God's retribution on homosexuals. What do you think about how the United States has handled the AIDS crisis? Even though the United States has seen how damaging it has been that we didn't pay attention to the problem when it was first discovered in our country, Asia is making the same mistake today, choosing to deny that AIDS is a problem in its countries. What measures do you think these countries should be taking at this point to prevent further spread of the problem?

2. AIDS education is vital to help stop the spread of this dread disease. Do you think that people will pay attention to education about this disease if they don't feel that they will be affected by it? Do you know who can be affected by AIDS?

PREWRITING

Freewrite about how you would feel if one of your friends got AIDS. What would you do? How do you think you could help your friend the most? Would you visit your friend? How can you prevent yourself from exposure to HIV?

WRITING

1. Because of the diagnosis of several cases of AIDS on your campus, the students have become very frightened, the rate of dating is down, and everyone seems to be afraid of casual contact with each other. You know that the HIV is NOT transmitted through casual contact such as hugging, sneezing, touching, and even kissing. Write an article for your campus newspaper encouraging people to become more educated about AIDS so that they can get on with their lives and not miss out on human contact.

2. A good friend of yours has recently died of AIDS. When you asked him what you could do to help him before he died, he said his one request was for you to help educate people so that they would not have to suffer the same fate that he did. Write a proposal for the implementation of AIDS education on your campus or in your community. Be sure to include who would be involved, where you would get necessary financial support, and what would be done.

REVISING

A checklist can be helpful when you work on a revision to be sure that you have considered all the points that will make your writing strong. Reread "Living with AIDS" and answer the questions asked in the following checklist as if you were the writer of the article. Do you see ways that this article could be improved? If so, what are they?

1. What is your thesis sentence? Does it clearly express what you want to say about your topic?

2. How many paragraphs do you have? An essay must always have at least three but usually more paragraphs.

3. Does each paragraph have a topic sentence?

4. Does each sentence in each paragraph relate directly to the topic sentence of that paragraph?

5. Does each sentence clearly express your thoughts? Is it complete?

6. Have you organized your paragraphs in the most effective order to express your ideas clearly? Can they be rearranged to make your writing more effective?

7. Do you have a strong introduction and conclusion to your writing assignment?

8. Have you proofread carefully?

Now use this checklist with your writing assignment. Do you see ways that you can improve your writing? If so, revise your assignment accordingly.

EDITING

Generally abbreviations should not be used when writing essays. They lead to confusion by the reader since many abbreviations can stand for more than one thing, such as WPA stands for the Work Projects Administration as well as for the Writing Programs Administrators. How your reader interprets what you write depends on that reader's personal background. Also avoid using the abbreviation "etc." When you use etc., it looks like you have run out of things to say or you don't know anything else.

The use of abbreviations is acceptable, though, in some cases. If the abbreviation is widely known and readily acceptable as meaning only one thing, then it may be less cumbersome in your essay to use the abbreviation than to write the whole meaning out. AIDS, which stands for acquired immune deficiency syndrome, a deadly disease, and HIV, which stands for human immunodeficiency virus, thought to cause AIDS, are two good examples of acceptable abbreviations.

"We're Staying: We Won't Bow to Terror"

Askold Krushelnycky

PREREADING

Have you ever been the victim of violence or known someone else who has been? Most people have the feeling that things like that won't happen to them. How do you think you would feel if a violent crime occurred in a place where you frequently are at a time when you were not there? If the victim of the crime was a friend of yours, how would you feel? Would you want to go back to that place? Why or why not? Would you want to get back at the person who committed the crime? Why or why not?

DEFINING

physique (¶1) the muscular proportions of the body

oppression (¶6) cruel exercise of power

squalid (¶6) dirty and miserable from lack of care

notoriously (¶7) known widely and unfavorably

befallen (¶7) happen to

picturesque (¶7) attractive, vivid, suitable for a picture

desolation (¶10) state of loneliness and misery

eloquent (¶10) powerfully moving way

paramilitary (¶11) civilians organized in a military fashion

joinery (¶13)   cabinetmaking

rudimentary (¶14)   related to basic facts, elementary

empathy (¶16)   understanding of someone else's situation

retaliation (¶23)   to pay back an injury in the same way

communal (¶23)   relating to a community

riven (¶23)   to tear apart

We're Staying: We Won't Bow to Terror

Askold Krushelnycky

1   Paul Rogan is a kindly, tough-looking young man with the powerful physique of someone used to hard manual labor. Watching his face work with emotion, and then lose the fight to stop tears flowing, is a shocking and humbling experience.

2   As he studied for the first time a photograph of the wrecked and bloodstained Heights Bar, which was attacked by terrorists in his home town of Loughinisland in Northern Ireland last weekend, his voice trembled and he gasped: "Oh, Jesus . . ."

3   The color picture showed the aftermath of the attack, in which six customers at the bar were killed and five injured as gunmen sprayed the confined space with machinegun bullets. It was a grim scene of destruction: the carpet soaked with blood, broken glass everywhere, overturned stools—and bullet holes in the wooden panels of the bar.

4   Rogan passed the picture to his companions. Some wept, too; others just stared in horror. He and the other eight men are regular customers at the pub, and the dead and injured are their friends and, in some cases, their relatives—like Adrian Rogan, shot down while attempting to flee from the murderers.

5   All nine had been drinking there last Saturday morning before setting off on a ten-day mission to restore an orphanage and old people's home in Romania. They knew that it could easily have been their own blood staining the floor of the bar.

6   The group had been preparing for months for their trip to the Romanian town of Galati, 250 km northeast of Bucharest, and were pleased to be able to help some of the neediest in Romanian society: people who had been condemned by decades of political oppression to live in squalid misery.

7   It was only on the morning after the murderous attack, when the wife of one of them managed to get through on the notoriously bad Romanian telephone system, that they learned of the tragedy that had befallen their own tiny community, which lies in a fertile and picturesque landscape 30 km south of Belfast.

Askold Krusyhelnycky, "We're Staying: We Won't Bow to Terror," *The European,* 24–30 June 1994, no. 215, p. 3. Reprinted by permission.

Please note maps in appendix for references to places in this article.

8   The pub's owner, Hugh O'Toole, whose son Aidan was badly wounded in the attack, returned to Northern Ireland, as did another man, but the others have decided to respond to the cruelty of the gunmen by staying on to complete the work in Romania as a tribute to their dead friends.

9   Hugh Murdock, a 26-year-old plumber, said: "When we heard about it we were devastated—we couldn't believe something like that could happen in our community. The troubles in Northern Ireland have not touched us before, and we are proud of being a tight-knit community where Protestants and Catholics live together as friends. The people who go to the pub are from both religions, although nobody asks what anyone else's religion is in Loughinisland."

10   He explained that, at first, people had tried to come to terms with their grief on their own: some praying, some crying, some going for walks. But as the day went on, the initial numbed feelings of desolation and the instinct to return home to attend the funerals and share in the grief were replaced by a desire to fight back against the killers in a touchingly eloquent way.

11   At a meeting that evening, Murdock said, "the atmosphere was very emotional, and I think all of us were quietly crying. There was very little said, but what we did say was that we had come here to do a job, and no paramilitary was going to stop us.

12   "All the people who died had contributed cash or in other ways for us to come here. They were all decent people who wanted to help others, and they would have wanted us to carry on."

13   All the group's members have practical skills—electrical, plumbing, joinery, or bricklaying—to help with the reconstruction of the two institutions they have adopted at Galati, on Romania's border with Ukraine.

14   The buildings, both of which also house mentally handicapped inmates, are grim by western standards: their floors are uneven and crumbling, the sanitation is rudimentary and the white-wash on the walls is flaking after decades of neglect.

15   However, James Goodlett, a former Roman Catholic priest who formed the charity Romanian Helpline Appeal four years ago, said that conditions had improved enormously since the volunteers—including the group from Loughinisland—first came in 1992. This year, by the time they leave, the two buildings will have water storage tanks to avoid the frequent shortages that have been common until now, new electrical wiring and lighting, and individual shower and bathroom facilities.

16   Goodlett said: "With the help of these people, we will be able to get the standards here up to such a level that we can start to work on real improvements in the way that the children and the elderly are treated. The charity has always had tremendous support from all sections of the community in Northern Ireland—perhaps it's easier for them to have empathy with people in places like Romania."

17   The Romanian staff at the orphanage—which houses around 150 children—and at the old people's home were shocked when they heard about the tragedy. Some of the elderly people and a mentally handicapped young woman seem to

sense the tragedy enveloping the men, despite their smiles, as they work their 12-hour days.

18   The young woman trails after some of the workers, reaching out an arm to comfort them. The men respond with cheery jokes which she cannot understand, but they make her feel better—they do not want to add their own grief to the misery they are working to relieve.

19   The orphanage administrator, Liliana Salmanis, said: "They came here to help us, and a horrific tragedy has taken away their friends and relatives. We see their courage: They work all day and don't say anything about what has happened. They want the people here to be happy. But at night we see what they are thinking about, and we can feel their tears."

20   Murdock said: "How can you not help the people here? They are so badly off, and live in such sad conditions. Maybe if the murderers came here and looked at the mentally handicapped children, the elderly with no hope, the abandoned, orphaned kids, they might change their minds. Perhaps they would lay down their arms then?"

21   But he added: "The vast majority of people in Northern Ireland, both Catholics and Protestants, are good people, and have no time for these men with guns who talk about religion but have none themselves. If we had gone home, it would have been like surrendering to the terrorists—and we were determined not to do that. We will not bow to them."

22   Rogan agreed, and told how Protestants among the aid group had expressed shame for their religion. "We told them: 'You can't blame all Protestants for what those boys did.' I was in a real bad state that Sunday evening, and one of the Protestant men stayed up talking to me all night. He isn't even from Loughinisland, but he was crying more than me."

23   The people of Loughinisland will not be calling for retaliation killings, and are confident that the outrage will not destroy the spirit of goodwill that has sheltered their community from the communal violence which has riven Northern Ireland since 1968.

24   But Gerald Ralph—who missed the initial flight his friends were taking to Romania and would have returned to be in the Heights Bar that fateful evening if he had not managed to get on to another plane to Bucharest—admitted that he and his companions would have to confront their grief again when they returned to Loughinisland. He said: "Our friends are being buried as we work over here, and the full force of that will only hit us when we get home."

25   Murdock, for one, says he is haunted by the fact that on the evening they had arrived in Galati they found a late-night restaurant where the owner allowed them to watch on television the same football match their doomed friends were watching in the pub in Loughinisland.

26   He said: "Little did we know that, as were watching, our friends were being slaughtered. I can imagine where each of them was standing—we all have our own special places—and it is sad to know that we will not be drinking together again. We also knew that if we hadn't been here, some of us would most probably have been among the dead."

READING

1. Where were the people in this article from? Where were they at the time of the crime? Why were they there?

2. What does the orphanage in Romania look like?

THINKING

1. What do you know about the ongoing war between the Protestants and Catholics in Northern Ireland? Are you religious? Do you think you would commit violent crimes against people who had a different religion than you may have? Do you think that there can only be one religion or that one religion is better than another? Why or why not?

2. This group of men went from Ireland to Romania to help refurbish an orphanage and an old folks' home. Why do you suppose these men would leave their native village to help people out in another country when their own country is involved in a war? Would you do what they did? Why or why not?

PREWRITING

Read each of the suggested writing topics below. Write freely for five minutes about each of the topics, including any ideas you can think of having to do with everything included in the assignment. Remember while you are freewriting to not worry about making errors. Just be creative and think on paper.

WRITING

1. There is an extreme shortage of foster homes in your community. Many children do not have a place to go when they need to have care outside of their homes or when they become orphaned. Write a proposal to present to your city council making a recommendation for what should be done about this problem. Be creative. There are many possible solutions. Be sure to include details like where the money and people would come from for your project.

2. Your two best friends practice different religions. Lately they have been arguing to the point that they won't speak to each other any more because each believes his or her religion is the only right one. You love both your friends and have a hard time dealing with their anger. Write a letter that you will send to both of your friends explaining how you feel and suggesting a way to alleviate the bad feelings between them.

REVISING

Askold Krushelnycky uses visual imagery in his writing. He paints a very vivid picture of what he wants you to think about.

Example:

> The color picture showed the aftermath of the attack, in which six customers at the bar were killed and five injured as gunman sprayed the confined space with machinegun bullets. It was a grim scene of destruction: the carpet soaked with blood, broken glass everywhere, overturned stools—and bullet holes in the wooden panels of the bar. (¶3)

This is a great attention getter for the beginning of a writing assignment. After you have written the first draft of your essay, try adding a visual image at the beginning to draw your reader into your writing. Be sure to use as many details as possible so that the reader will visualize an image close to what you are imagining.

EDITING

When writing the numbers **one through ten** you should spell them out. In numbers higher than ten, you should use the numeral.

Examples:

> ". . . to help with the reconstruction of the **two** institutions they have adopted at Galati, on Romania's border with the Ukraine." (¶13)

> "The Romanian staff at the orphanage—which houses around **150** children . . ." (¶17)

Look through your writing assignment to be sure that you have written numbers correctly.

Free At Last?

Roger Wilkins

PREREADING

How do you feel that your cultural heritage affects your social standing? Why do you feel that way? What do you feel your social standing is? How do you feel the heritage of other people you know affects their social standing? Think of famous people you admire. What is their cultural heritage? Do you think it affects their social standing?

DEFINING

peril (¶1)   danger
besieged (¶2)   harassed
hideous (¶4)   repulsive, revoltingly ugly
recoils (¶5)   pulls back away from
precipitous (¶5)   extremely steep
contemplated (¶6)   considered carefully and at length
trajectory (¶6)   a chosen course
inkling (¶6)   a slight hint
recapitulation (¶7)   a summary
irreparably (¶8)   beyond repair
deindustrialization (¶9)   loss of industrial capability

globalization (¶9)   worldwide in scope

expendable (¶10)   unnecessary

grassroots (¶15)   people working together at a local level

array (¶16)   impressively large number

shackles (¶16)   restraints to progress

marginalize (¶17)   to confine to a lower level of social standing

Free At Last?

Roger Wilkins

1   It is both odd and sad that 40 years after the Supreme Court of the United States ruled in Brown v. Board of Education, African-Americans are facing what historian John Hope Franklin describes as their greatest peril since slavery: a socioeconomic devastation that affects 40 percent of them and contributes to the continuing distintegration of the black family.

2   During the next 40 years we must make a sustained effort to rebuild the black family—especially in that besieged part of society. But before I sketch out my prescription, let me give a brief overview of the problem and a glimpse at how we arrived at this catastrophe.

3   A third of America's black population lives below the official poverty line, as opposed to 11 percent of whites. More than 60 percent of all black births are to single women, and almost 50 percent of black children are being raised in poverty. According to William Spriggs, Ph.D., of the National Commission for Employment Policy, the unemployment rate for black males (*excluding* those who've become so discouraged they've given up looking for work) has been above 10 percent since the late 1970s. During the 1980s it averaged almost 12 percent. Those are figures white Americans absolutely would not tolerate for themselves.

4   This economic devastation has resulted in hideous social disintegration. Murder is now the leading cause of death among black males ages 15 through 24. Our inner cities and the schools in them are so dangerous that the majority of law-abiding people who live there and the children who want to learn lead lives of sheer terror.

5   The rest of the nation sees the crime and the family disintegration and recoils. The political manifestation of this revulsion is a precipitous drop in federal support for cities from 11.5 percent in 1980 to 3.8 percent in 1990, according to the Census Bureau. Our national leaders respond with loud cries about getting people off welfare and being tougher on crime. They give precious little emphasis to jobs and community-development programs in the devastated ghettos.

6   The idealists—both black and white—who fashioned the legal strategy that cracked segregation did not foresee the economic and social disasters that have be-

Roger Wilkins, "Free at Last?" *Modern Maturity,* April–May 1994, pp. 27–33. Reprinted by permission.

Please note maps in appendix for references to places in this article.

fallen the most vulnerable blacks in our society. Had they contemplated the trajectory of blacks coming out of slavery, they might have had some inkling of the problems that face the country today.

7   The masses of blacks who were at the bottom of society when the Brown case was evolving (and whom Richard Kluger described so well in *Simple Justice,* his masterful recapitulation of Brown) were trapped in the post-Civil War semislavery of the South. They had never been integrated into the mainstream of the economy. Kluger described conditions among the rural blacks of Clarendon County, South Carolina, in the late 1940s this way:

8   "It was nothing short of economic slavery, an unbreakable cycle of poverty and ignorance breeding more poverty and a bit less ignorance, generation upon generation. 'We had to take what was given us,' says a Clarendon farmer, 'or leave.' And a lot of them did leave, for urban ghettos. . . . But wherever they went and whatever they tried to do with their lives, they were badly disabled, irreparably so for the most part, by the malnourishment, the poverty, and meanness their Clarendon birthright had inflicted upon [their childhood years]."

9   The boom economy of the 1960s and the attitudes fostered by the Civil Rights Movement permitted some poor blacks to break out of that vicious cycle. But in 1973 the boom ended. Income growth began to decline and the subsequent deindustrialization and globalization of the economy meant that those who had not escaped the pull of their slave history had nothing to offer America but unskilled labor.

10   The problem of integrating those African-Americans most damaged by history into the rest of society has troubled some of the best minds this country has ever produced. Jefferson, Madison, Monroe, and Lincoln all thought former slaves should be deported. Ralph Bunche, the first black winner of the Nobel Peace Prize, thought that only a coalition of black and white workers could save the poorest blacks from being excess labor. W. E. B. Du Bois, who struggled for equality for three-quarters of a century, concluded that poor blacks would always be condemned to the expendable fringe of the labor pool.

11   So the problem of the undigested black masses still confronts us. Not only is it destroying black lives, it is also destroying our cities, dividing our country, and warping our political priorities.

12   The only adequate response is to develop and nurture healthier black families. Families are transmitters of values, discipline, a sense of connection to the economy, and, ultimately, hope and self-respect.

13   But it is almost impossible for families to function effectively or even exist when people live in ghetto conditions with no jobs. Just as lack of work is the most destructive force in the inner city, jobs are the central organizing principles of families. They provide a positive connection to the outside world; they offer self-respect; they force the household to develop discipline, and they give children a reason to believe study and hard work will give them a future. Government and industry should form councils that would place as many unemployed people as possible in private employment. Then government—at the federal, state, and local levels—should develop coordinated plans to offer employment as a last resort to those who cannot find work in the private sector.

14   But, important as it is, work alone cannot undo the damage. The children who live in these devastated communities need better parents than they now have, better schools than they now attend. Inner city schools should be physically connected to multipurpose service centers that meet the welfare, child- and health-care needs of parents and children. Most important, these centers should provide parenting classes for immature young people so they can support their children's education, and job-counseling services for those seeking work.

15   The final arm of this strategy is to support the many effective grassroots organizations that exist in our communities. These groups know the problems intimately and could provide superb assistance if they only had the resources.

16   Many white Americans believe that contemporary racial problems stem from a lack of black leadership. Nothing could be further from the truth. There is a broader, richer, abler array of black leadership in this country than at any time in our history. What is missing is white leadership. The black leaders of the '60s could not have changed the country by themselves. Whites in Congress, in city halls and statehouses, in pulpits, and ultimately in the White House provided leadership to white Americans that made it possible to destroy some of the shackles history had placed on us all.

17   Now, many white political leaders and opinionmakers push to marginalize the strongest black voices and condemn the behavior of those blacks most damaged by history and our current economic conditions.

18   Condemnation misses the point. People and families of all backgrounds fall apart under severe economic stress. Black America has been in a depression for 20 years, but white America rushes past obvious economic answers to settle on an ugly and persistent fretting about the wretched behavior patterns of the black poor. In fact, vast numbers of poor black people desperately want to work. Last November, when there was a strong hint of a new enterprise in Detroit, 10,000 people, mostly black, lined up in the cold to apply.

19   Neither, however, should white leaders embrace the fantasy that all poor blacks are saintly victims. They are not. Poverty and isolation have produced some very bad and some very reckless people. But many more people want law, order, and opportunity.

20   In any event, the black poor are part of us; a part of America that will have an enormous impact on our common future.

21   White politicians will not respond to this need until white opinion leaders join black leaders in demanding that we begin the final push to repair the deep and ugly racial damage our history has done to us all. But this will take time. Blacks arrived on the North American continent in 1619. For almost 250 of the ensuing 375 years we had slavery or something very close to it. And for a century after that we had Constitutionally sanctioned racial subordination. We have had something other than slavery or legal racial subordination for only 29 years.

22   The question for white leaders is simple: Would you rather spend our treasure on police and prisons or on programs that promote families and put people to work? Both are very expensive. It's just that the family program works a whole lot better for the people who are targeted—and for America's future as well.

READING

1. Where does the article say that white Americans believe social problems stem from?

2. What does John Hope Franklin describe as the greatest peril since slavery that African-Americans are now facing?

THINKING

1. What is the argument in this article? Do you agree with the author's assessment of the current situation? Why or why not? Do you think other cultures face similar challenges as the author says that African-Americans face? Which cultures do or don't? Why do you feel this way?

2. The article says that it is almost impossible for families to function when they live in ghettos. Do you agree with this? Why or why not? How much do you think where a family lives affects its ability to function as a family, or do you think the personalities of the members of the family have more affect on their ability to function? Why do you think the way you do on this issue?

PREWRITING

In class ⅔ for this chapter.

Write freely about what your family was like when you were growing up. Was your family typical or would you consider it different? How was it typical? How was it different? How do you think an ideal family should be?

WRITING

1. Write a two-page essay to share with your classmates that describes how it was to be brought up in your family. Be sure to include all the members of your family and the roles they played. Use specific examples of things that happened in your life that could show an outsider what your family was really like.

2. Write an essay in which you either agree or disagree with what Roger Wilkins says in "Free at Last?" Develop a strong thesis statement that indicates how you feel, then use specific examples to show why your argument should be believed.

REVISING

Many of the problems that occur in families are caused by poor communication. As you were doing your writing assignment, you probably noticed examples of this. Your instructor is a person who can really help you if you develop a good line of communication. Try getting a draft of your paper to your instructor. Then make an appointment to see him or her to discuss your paper after your instructor has had a chance to read it. Frequently talking about ideas and problems is the best way to help you improve your writing skills.

EDITING

An **ellipsis** can be used for two different purposes in your writing. An ellipsis is three spaced periods (...) that indicate that something is missing or that something is implied.

When you quote material from a source, you may omit some of the text by inserting an ellipsis where the text is deleted.

Example:

"And a lot of them did leave, for urban ghettos. ... But wherever they went and whatever they tried to do with their lives, they were badly disabled ... by the malnourishment, the poverty, and meanness their Clarendon birthright had inflicted upon [their childhood years]." (¶8)

In this sentence, text is deleted from the sentence and replaced by the ellipses to indicate missing text. If an ellipsis is used at the end of a sentence, then the ellipsis is followed by a period, which is then followed by two spaces before the start of the next sentence. In this example, text is deleted at the start of the second sentence, so there is a period at the end of the first sentence, an ellipsis, and a new sentence.

Some writers use the ellipsis to imply ideas without directly stating them, or to imply a lapse of time or pause.

Examples:

Let nobody fool him- or herself that adult life is beyond children's understanding—more often than not our kids understand surprisingly much ... to switch off or not to switch off—that is the question.

... Suddenly I forget all my gnawing fears.

The ellipsis is a matter of style. It's not something everyone would use, but it can be effective if used sparingly. Look through your writing assignment to see if there is a place where you can insert an ellipsis for effect.

No Pablo, No Story

Sarah Stewart

PREREADING

What kinds of stories do you think should be covered on the news? What makes news interesting? Why? Who do you think chooses what information actually makes it to the newspaper or the television news? Do you watch television news or read the newspaper? Why or why not?

DEFINING

guerrilla (¶2)   local military operating in small groups to harass, surprise, and undermine their enemy

permeates (¶3)   spreads through, penetrates

activists (¶3)   active supporters of

lorries (¶5)   trucks (British)

thwart (¶12)   defeat efforts or plans

enviable (¶13)   desirable

disingenuous (¶14)   not completely honest

ascribed (¶14)   attributed to, related to a particular cause

culprits (¶15)   ones charged with or guilty of a crime

indisputable (¶16)   beyond doubt, undeniable

repression (¶16)   the act of putting down by force

humanitarian (¶17)   one who is devoted to the promotion of human welfare

extortion (¶17)   the act of obtaining something through intimidation

ostensibly (¶18)   appearing to be

impunity (¶19)   without punishment or penalty

ineffectual (¶20)   useless, worthless

abandonment (¶22)   surrendering, giving up

magnate (¶23)   powerful or influential person

genocide (¶24)   planned, systematic, extermination of a race or political group

oblivious (¶28)   unaware of

No Pablo, No Story

Sarah Stewart

1 In 1990 the death lists appeared on the main roads of the university town. "My name was there, too," says Jorge, sitting with Amelia, his young, heavily-pregnant wife and two-year-old son in the windswept Bogotá shantytown of Ciudad Bolívar.

2 "Then the threats began—telephone calls all the time. We left the city but they put a bounty on my head. I was accused of being a guerrilla. They arrested my eight-year-old nephew. Finally Amelia, my wife, was put in prison for 'rebellion'."

3 Fear permeates the life of this young couple, as it does the lives of most political and human-rights activists. Colombia's political death toll is now reaching 11 a day, reflecting a human-rights crisis which ranks as the most grave in Latin America and one of the worst in the world. Each year more people die for political reasons than in the entire 17-year reign of General Pinochet in Chile.

4 Jorge fears he is still being pursued despite the lack of any evidence of wrongdoing. He and his wife have told no-one of their past—not even the other family with whom they live. And they never get involved in politics.

5 They are so alone here, I think. If they were to be tracked down and killed no-one would even realize why. Their bodies, like so many others, would just turn up in the ravines on the mountainous outskirts of Ciudad Bolívar. If they were never identified, their bodies would be picked up, loaded onto lorries and trucked to the cemetery for the NNs—*ningun nombre,* or "no name"—for the anonymous dead.

6 There, three times a week, the lorries drive up, bearing their grisly loads: the street children, the rubbish collectors who recycle paper and glass, the drug addicts, and other unknowns. Holding his handkerchief to his face to block the

Sarah Stewart, "No Pablo, No Story," *New Internationalist,* June 1994, no. 256, pp. 20–22. Reprinted by permission.

Please note maps in appendix for references to places in this article.

stench, the graveyard worker says hundreds are buried in the vast, open pits of un-
marked mass graves.

7   I think of Amelia and Jorge's story two days later when I am sitting in a lovely
restaurant on the outskirts of Bogotá chatting with some journalists. "There's no
story here any more," one of them says, fidgeting with his steak. The others nod in
agreement over their lunches. "No Pablo, no story."

8   For years the mythical figure of drug baron Pablo Escobar has defined
Colombia. His death last December, gunned down as he ran barefoot over the
rooftops in a middle-class Medellín suburb, has changed the focus somewhat. But
Colombia is still the original single-issue country: drugs and the drug barons.

9   There are good reasons for international concern about the drug trade.
From inner-city London to Detroit or Cali, lives around the world are being destroyed by it. But within Colombia there's another war, far more pressing than the
war on drugs. No matter where you turn, there are stories of pain and bloodshed:
from the telephone call saying that the peasant leader you met the day before has
just been gunned down in a restaurant by unknown assassins, to the Medellín ar-
chitect who says calmly that he and his wife discuss with their young children what
to do in the event that they are kidnapped.

10   But somehow these are not "stories."

11   What does it take to make human rights a story, I wonder? I go to visit the
Colombian Government's office of the Presidential Adviser on Human Rights. But
again I find myself talking about drugs.

12   "No other country in the world has had to fight the *narcos,* or drug traffickers," says Mauricio Hernandez, adviser to the Presidential Human Rights Counsel-
lor. "I'm sure this would thwart the best police force in the world."

13   No question, the Government's position is not enviable. The murder rate is
28,000 a year—more than in the US, whose population is eight times the size. An
estimated five million arms are circulating illegally.

14   But the insistence on drugs as the key is disingenuous at best and dishonest at
worst. Despite Mr Hernandez's words, drugs have almost nothing to do with
human-rights violations. In 1992, fewer than two percent of all political deaths
were committed by *narcos.* In the first nine months of 1993, none was ascribed to
drugs.

15   Far more to the point is the fact that the major culprits in human-rights violations are Government forces. According to the respected Andean Commission of
Jurists, 56 per cent of the political killings (excluding combat) where the killer
could be identified in the first nine months of 1993 were carried out by Government forces. Paramilitary groups, which are closely linked to the armed forces,
were responsible for 18 per cent; guerrilla groups—involved in a 40-year war in
which neither side is prepared to negotiate—for 25 per cent.

16   "It is indisputable that the state is involved in human-rights violations—and
this is frequent," says a senior member of the Catholic Church's human-rights
group. "They are carried out by both state civilian and military personnel, and documented by the Attorney General's office and in the courts. Disappearances, extra-
judicial executions, torture—these are the main forms of repression," he adds.

17   For their part, the guerrillas also routinely violate the Geneva Convention and humanitarian accords on war. They assassinate civilians and politicians, execute captured soldiers, and plant landmines which cause mostly civilians to suffer—the 11-year-old boy whose photo was featured on the front page of the newspapers during my visit, for instance. To fund their operations some guerrilla groups resort to kidnapping, extortion, and levying taxes on drug exports—a form of corruption which effectively erases their legitimacy.

18   The war against the guerrillas, like the drug war, justifies most of the repression: peasants are run off their land, trade unionists imprisoned for "terrorism" when they go on strike. Recent economic policies have caused poverty levels to rise sharply. But protesters are now faced with new public-order laws—ostensibly aimed at the guerrillas and *narcos.*

19   And yet Colombia is not a dictatorship. It is inconceivable that in this formal democracy deaths and disappearances would be planned by central government. Nonetheless, government forces routinely carry out crimes with impunity. Soldiers, officers, and the police are tried by their peers. The results are predictable: almost no convictions. These crimes may not be ordered by the center of government, but the Government is nonetheless guilty in the sense that it is not bringing people to trial. It is guilt by omission.

20   In a new report, Amnesty International condemns the "largely ineffectual measures ostensibly designed to safeguard human rights, but which in reality have mainly served to protect the Government's national and international image." Pierre Sané, Amnesty's Secretary General, is more blunt: the Government is marked, he says, by "hypocrisy and lies."

21   In March and April 1988 paramilitary groups backed by military officers murdered 20 banana workers in the northern region of Uraba. Three officers involved were investigated—but instead of being disciplined they were promoted. One of them, Lieutenant Colonel Felipe Becerra, was sent to the US for training. Four years later he resurfaced. Late one night in October 1993, men under his command broke into the home of the Ladino family in Riofrio, tortured and murdered seven family members from 15 to 75 years old, then executed another five people. Apparently to back up the later accusation that all 13 were guerrillas, they forced several women into camouflage uniforms before executing them. Bercerra has not been charged or convicted of any crime.

22   I make a trip to the hamlet of Mesetas. It seems like the end of the world. The town plaza is empty, with weeds growing in the main square and the trees covered in dust. The sense of abandonment is overwhelming.

23   In this region a war is being waged between the FARC guerrilla group and the army and paramilitary groups in league with both the army and emerald magnate Victor Carranza. The political targets: anyone thought to be on the other side.

24   The guerrillas engage in selective assassination, gunning down alleged informants or individuals said to belong to paramilitary groups. For the army and the paramilitary groups, the targets are alleged guerrilla supporters: communities—

such as Mesetas—which have voted for the legal left-wing Patriotic Union (UP) party. Nationwide, 1,500 leaders and members of the UP have been killed since it was founded in 1985—a record which constitutes genocide.

25   José Julian Velez, a simple farmer and mayor of Mesetas, sits at his desk, his hat by his side. Five of his family, including a six-year-old son, lie in the cemetery off the dirt road leading into town.

26   He doesn't really want to talk about the killings. "For me it's too painful to re-member the past," he says. He's agreed to stay on as mayor because of what he calls the commitment to the people, but it is evident that he does not expect to survive either. Of the dozen or so towns in the area which once boasted UP governments, there are now only three.

27   One by one I meet people who are not likely to live out the year. One young man, involved in youth theatre, never leaves his house at night. "You can be gunned down at any point," he says.

28   Meanwhile, the language of drugs and drug wars continues to provide the smokescreen for political murder. And the outside world carries on, oblivious.

READING

1. Where does the action of the article take place? What is this place known for?

2. Who is Pablo and why was he so newsworthy? Why do the reporters feel that there is no longer anything to report without Pablo?

THINKING

1. What do you think about the living conditions in Bogatá? Do you know anyone who has lived there or has lived in similar conditions? There is much repression in Colombia. Why do you think this is so? Do you think anyone who lives in America now lives in similar conditions? How?

2. What is meant by human rights? Who is affected by human rights issues? Who in the world fights for human rights? Why do they fight for these rights? Who violates human rights? Why do they do this?

PREWRITING

Do two clusters, one for each of the writing assignments below. Pick the writing as-signment that seems most interesting to you after you have completed the cluster-ing exercises.

WRITING

1. A friend of yours is murdered in front of his own house in a drive-by shooting. Your local newspaper chooses to only do a small article about the murder in the back of the local section of the paper. Write a letter to the editor of the paper explaining how you feel about this news coverage.

2. Go to the library and look up "human rights," "Amnesty International," and "the Geneva Convention." Write a paper to share with your classmates explaining what you have learned, being careful not to plagiarize.

REVISING

"No Pablo, No Story" is a long article with material that would provide good examples and quotes for your writing assignments. In order to quote from the article, you need to use **parenthetical documentation.**

The Modern Language Association (MLA) has set up specific rules for how this is to be done. If you use a short quote of three or fewer typed lines, you start the quote with quotation marks, type the quote, put the end quotation marks, insert the page number that you acquired the quote from in parentheses, then place the period. For instance, Sarah Stewart says, "Jorge fears he is still being pursued despite the lack of any evidence of wrong doing" (**¶4**). Notice in the sentence that precedes the quotes, the name of the author is mentioned. If the author's name is not mentioned, then it must be included in the parentheses, for example (Stewart 60). Notice that there is not a comma between the name and the page number and that *page, p,* or *pp* is not included in the parentheses. If the author's name is not known, then a shortened form of the title must be included, for example ("No Pablo" 20). Notice that even though the whole title is not included, quotation marks must still be used. If you have included more than one article by this author on your Works Cited sheet, then you must identify the article as well as the author, for example (Stewart "No Pablo" 21). When quoting more than three typed lines from your source, the same information is included in the parentheses, but the whole quote is indented ten spaces, quotation marks are not used, and the period comes immediately following the sentence instead of after the parentheses. For example:

> No question, the Government's position is not enviable. The murder rate is 28,000 a year—more than in the US whose population is eight times the size. An estimated five million arms are circulating illegally. (Stewart 21)

For each article you quote, you must include an entry on a Works Cited sheet at the end of your writing. The documentation for this article would be:

Stewart, Sarah. "No Pablo, No Story." <u>The New Internationalist</u> June 1994, 20–22.

Stewart, Sarah. name of author

"No Pablo, No Story." name of article

<u>The New Internationalist</u> name of magazine

June 1994, date

20–22. page numbers

Notice also the placement of the periods and commas. These are necessary. Go through your writing assignments and see where you can effectively add quotes from the article to illustrate your argument. Writing assignment two would be an excellent place to use quotes from the information you found at the library.

EDITING

Use the pronouns **we, I, he, she,** or **they** when they are used as the subject of the sentence. Use the pronouns **us, me, him, her,** or **them** when they are used in the objective part of the sentence.

Examples:

We left the city but they put a bounty on my head.

The rate of unemployment, crime, and high-school dropouts in the city is lead by *us.*

Check your writing assignment to be sure that you have used pronouns correctly.

Fatal Fires of Protest

Edward W. Desmond

PREREADING

"Fatal Fires of Protest" tells of young men in India who set themselves on fire to protest actions of their government. Can you imagine feeling so strongly about something that you could actually set yourself on fire? What do you think about these young Indian men who have done this?

DEFINING

doting (¶1)   excessively fond

mediocre (¶1)   fair, medium level

martyrs (¶3)   people who choose to suffer or die for their beliefs

incensed (¶3)   provoked to violent anger

momentous (¶3)   of great importance

cynical (¶4)   sarcastic, distrusting of virtue

constituency (¶4)   a group of voters

animating (¶5)   bringing to life

inexorable (¶8)   unchanging, inflexible

Fatal Fires of Protest

Edward W. Desmond

1   Rajiv Goswami, 20, does not have the obvious makings of a hero. His father is a postmaster, and he grew up with six doting sisters in a typically middle-class family belonging to the Brahmin caste, the highest in the Hindu social order. At Deshbandhu College in New Delhi, he was a mediocre student, and he hoped to start work as a refrigeration engineer after graduation.

2   Ramakant Chaturvedi, 26, showed no more tendency toward dramatic self-sacrifice. The son of a political-science teacher, he also came from a middle-class Brahmin family. After finishing college in Bhind, he tried in vain to get a government job but found it hopeless because of quotas that limit positions for upper castes.

3   What has made these two men so remarkable is that they, along with scores of others across northern India, have become martyrs over the past three weeks, in most cases by setting themselves on fire. Chaturvedi and 38 others died, while Goswami and at least 126 others were hospitalized. All the young men and women were upper-caste Hindus and all were incensed by Prime Minister V.P. Singh's announcement that as part of an affirmative-action effort, he would more than double, to 50%, the job quota for the lower castes and other disadvantaged groups. Singh called his move on behalf of what amounts to 52% of the population a "momentous decision for social justice."

4   Students like Goswami and Chaturvedi, however, saw the tactic as a cynical stunt aimed at winning Singh a new constituency among the lower-caste voters. At stake are an estimated 50,000 government jobs that until now were open to upper-caste students. The competitive university system produces far more graduates than the job market can absorb, and young upper-caste Indians are extremely eager to find jobs that will pay well enough to meet their middle-class expectations. Now they face a situation where no matter how well they do in school, it will be considerably harder to get those posts. "Politicians are playing vote-catching gimmicks at our cost," says Abhishek Saket, 22, a history student at Delhi University. "I will end up a beggar or something." Says Madan Lai Goswami, the father of the hospitalized Rajiv: "My son has done the right thing. Some good will flow out of his sacrifice."

5   Another key factor animating the students' rage is a sense of betrayal. There is a widespread belief that Singh, who enjoyed a large following among students because he stressed honest, "value-based politics," compromised those principles by setting aside the jobs for lower castes. Though Singh does have a history of commitment to social reform, it is also undeniable that he needed a stronger mandate to prop up his minority government. The affirmative-action decision not only gave Singh fresh support from a huge part of the electorate; it also undermined several

Please note maps in appendix for references to places in this article.

of his political enemies who rely on the allegiance of lower-caste members. Arun Shourie, editor of the *Indian Express,* a New Delhi–based daily, called Singh's move "crass casteism disguised as progressive reform."

6   To Singh's supporters, the students are simply opposed to reforms that will help the disadvantaged. "All this hysteria is because the ruling elite sees a challenge to its hold on power," says Bhabani Sen Gupta, a leading political analyst. There is a long-standing consensus in Indian politics that the government must intervene to improve the status of Indians demeaned and impoverished by the traditional Hindu caste system, which still stratifies a large sector of society, condemning as much as 75% of the population to lives of drudgery and discrimination.

7   In 1950 the government set aside 22.5% of slots in schools and jobs for members of "scheduled castes," predominantly untouchables, who are at the bottom of Hindu society, and "scheduled tribes," native peoples who live in primitive conditions. In 1978 a commission headed by B.P. Mandal, a prominent political leader of lower-caste Indians, recommended that additional jobs be set aside for more than 3,000 groups designated "other backward classes" that suffer from a lack of status. Singh used that recommendation as the basis for his decision to reserve 27.5% of government jobs for the "other backward classes."

8   While there is significant support among intellectuals and lower-caste politicians for Singh's action, there are also doubts that his efforts will reach those most in need. For one thing, Singh has done nothing to increase educational opportunities for the most deprived, which is perhaps the most important key to improving their lives. For another, politicians representing some large lower-caste groups, like the Yadavs (cow herders) of the northern states of Bihar and Uttar Pradesh, already dominate state politics. They are bound to use the new quotas as a means to spread their own patronage, a practice as inexorable as caste itself in Indian politics.

READING

1. What caused Rajiv Goswami and Ramakant Chaturvedi to set themselves on fire?

2. What is the "caste system" in India? Who belongs to it?

THINKING

1. In India the university system produces many more graduates than there are jobs for, and the politicians are making it harder on the graduates by making more jobs available only to those who do not have an education. What do you think of this system? Do you think America will be having more graduates than the market can absorb?

2. The father of one of the victims feels that his son did the right thing because it would be better to die in honor than to be a beggar because there were no jobs available. What do you think about this system? Do you see any similarities in American society? If so, what are they?

PREWRITING

In India, the caste system is based on heredity. There is no way to move from one caste to another. In America we sometimes have a sort of invisible caste system based on wealth, birth, education, race, occupation, or social status. Freewrite about the "caste" systems that you can identify in our society. Who belongs? Do they exclude people? What purpose do they serve? Are they a positive asset to society or are they a problem?

WRITING

1. In India the government believes that it is doing the right thing by making more jobs available to the masses of people in the low caste of their system even though this means that the upper castes who are more educated literally have no jobs available to them so they become destitute. Write an essay expressing your feelings about job opportunities in America today. Express what you think the chances are of you and your fellow classmates being able to find jobs in the careers of your choices after you complete your educations.

2. In many classrooms throughout America today, an artificial caste system is used that categorizes students into different levels based on what the school thinks the students are capable of achieving. This is sometimes referred to as "tracking." Write an essay examining the pros and cons of such a situation.

REVISING

The organization of "Fatal Fires of Protest" makes the article easy to read and easy to understand. Look at the opening sentence of each paragraph. When these sentences are listed in order without the rest of the paragraphs attached, they make a good outline for the article. Edward W. Desmond has chosen to use the first sentence of each paragraph as a topic sentence. Then the rest of each paragraph develops the ideas written in the first sentence.

1. Rajiv Goswami, 20, does not have the obvious makings of a hero.

2. Ramakant Chaturvedi, 26, showed no more tendency toward dramatic self-sacrifice.

3. What has made these two men so remarkable is that they, along with scores of others across northern India, have become martyrs over the past three weeks, in most cases by setting themselves on fire.

4. Students like Goswami and Chaturvedi, however, saw the tactic as a cynical stunt aimed at winning Singh a new constituency among the lower-caste voters.

5. Another key factor animating the students' rage is a sense of betrayal.

6. To Singh's supporters, the students are simply opposed to reforms that will help the disadvantaged.

7. In 1950 the government set aside 22.5% of slots in schools and jobs for members of "scheduled castes," predominantly untouchables, who are at the bottom of Hindu society, and "scheduled tribes," native peoples who live in primitive conditions.

8. While there is a significant support among intellectuals and lower-caste politicians for Singh's action, there are also doubts that his efforts will reach those most in need.

The only main bit of information that is left out of these opening sentences is what is meant by "the tactic" in sentence four, but that is clearly explained in the previous paragraph.

On a separate piece of paper, list the first sentences of all of the paragraphs in your writing assignment. When you look at them separately, do they act as an outline for your assignment? Which sentences need to be clarified to help the meaning of your paragraphs? Do you need to add any more paragraphs to help you fully develop your ideas? Revise your assignment as necessary based on the changes you make to these sentences.

EDITING

The revision exercise in this section asks you to make the first sentence of each paragraph very specific. Lack of clarity in sentences occurs when a sentence is started with "It is" or "There are." These words can lead to confusion, especially at the beginning of a paragraph where there is nothing to look back to for a reference of what "it" is or what "there" are.

Look at the sentences that you wrote for the revision exercise. Have you started any sentences with "It is" or "There are"? If you have, be sure to change them to make them more specific.

China's Antidrug Tradition and Current Struggle

Ling Qing

PREREADING

Ling Qing tells about the way drugs have been handled in Chinese society over the years. Think about how drugs have been handled in American society in the past. Does it seem like drug use and drug availability is on the rise? Why or why not? What are the effects of drugs in society on your life?

DEFINING

opium (¶1)   a narcotic drug derived from the opium poppy

imperils (¶1)   puts in danger

eradicate (¶1)   put an end to

concerted (¶1)   concentrated, strong

pernicious (¶2)   destructive, evil

memorial (¶2)   a written summary or presentation of facts

kilogram (¶2)   2.2046 pounds (1.18 million kilograms=2.6 million pounds)

faction (¶3)   a number of persons within the government working together to-ward a different goal

capitulate (¶3)   give in, surrender

slanders (¶3)   lies that cause harm to someone

retaliation (¶3)   an act done for revenge

spawns (¶5)   creates

cliques (¶5)   small exclusive groups of people

hectare (¶8)   10,000 square meters

drug details (¶9)   groups assigned to investigate illegal drug affairs

colluded (¶9)   shared in secret

Yunnan (¶10)   a province of southwest China

malady (¶11)   illness

capitalism (¶11)   the free enterprise system

munitions (¶11)   military supplies

collusion (¶12)   secret agreement

scourge (¶12)   severe punishment

brooks no delay (¶13)   demands quick action

stipulate (¶13)   indicate, make clear

bilateral (¶15)   two-sided

multilateral (¶15)   several-sided

China's Antidrug Tradition and Current Struggle
Ling Qing

1   China's 1839 banning of opium smoking and the opium trade, led by the Qing court official Lin Zexu . . . , moved her onto the world stage in the struggle against drugs. Today, 150 years later, worldwide efforts have brought home the fact that drug abuse seriously imperils human life. To eradicate its harm, it is necessary for people all over the world to make a concerted effort.

2   Using the opium trade, Britain drained China of her silver. In less than a year—July 1837 to June 1838—Britain dumped opium worth 3.4 million pounds into China, seriously harming the Chinese people. Lin was keenly aware that opium meant no end of trouble for China. In his youth he had begun to investigate its pernicious influence. Later, as an official in Jiangsu Province, he had been outspoken against opium and had submitted a memorial to the throne on its harm. On March 10, 1839, he was sent as imperial commissioner to Guangzhou, on the southern coast, to deal with the problem. On June 3 he ordered the public burning of opium, and on that day 170 chests were burned. The burning continued for 24 days, ending on May 15 and disposing of a total of 1.18 million kilograms of opium, all that had been confiscated or surrendered so far except for eight chests kept for display. This first mighty act against drugs sparked a great patriotic movement of the Chinese people.

Ling Qing, "China's Antidrug Tradition and Current Struggle," *China Today,* Dec. 1990, pp. 22–24. Reprinted by permission of *China Today.*

Please note maps in appendix for references to places in this article.

3   When Britain replied with cannon, Lin mobilized the people to fight back. Because a faction in the Qing Dynasty government blamed him for the trouble and wanted to capitulate, Lin suffered all kinds of slanders and retaliation. Even after he was dismissed from office, he kept pointing out to the court the harm being done. He fully deserves to be honored as a hero in China's antiopium movement and a pioneer in the international antidrug movement.

4   Today, unfortunately, narcotics are still polluting the world. The situation is grim. First, there has been a sharp growth in the drug output in recent years. The 1987 production of cocaine in the region from the Andes Mountains to the Amazon River Valley, one of the three major producing areas, is estimated at 162,000 to 204,000 tons, and this amount increased in 1988 and 1989.

5   Second, traffic in narcotics spawns illegal international organizations and cliques that will stop at nothing, even murder. More and more innocent people are dying under the guns of drug-traffic cliques.

6   Third, the number of drug addicts has increased sharply. United Nations data reveal hundreds of millions in the West scrambling for marijuana, morphine, heroin, and other drugs. A recent United States Department of Justice investigation found that 72 million people, or 37 percent of people in the US over age 12, had used drugs at least once. Drug addiction is also growing rapidly in some developing countries.

7   Fourth, the number of drug-related deaths is increasing. In the US it rose from 604 in 1984 to 1,696 in 1988.

8   Opium first came to China from Arabia and Turkey in the late seventh and early eighth centuries, its use confined to medicinal purposes. Starting from the 1620s it was taken orally; by the end of the 18th century, smoking of opium was practiced in all parts of the country. In 1949, on the eve of liberation, 20 million Chinese were opium users and opium poppies grew on a million hectares. In 1949, soon after the founding of the People's Republic, the government embarked on a resolute antidrug campaign, and by the end of 1950 drug abuse was wiped out. In the 30 years that followed, China could proudly claim to be one of the world's few drug-free countries.

9   In recent years, however, along with the open policies, drugs have come back. Some international cliques have colluded with Chinese lawbreakers to transport narcotics across China's borders. At the same time, drug abuse has increased in these provinces and spread farther inland. In 1987 Chinese police and drug details cracked 56 narcotics-traffic cases and seized 137 kg of opium and 43 kg of heroin. In 1989 these numbers rose to 269 kg of opium and 488 kg of heroin. A total of 749 traffickers were arrested, involving 547 cases. These figures show that the menace is growing.

10   In the four months up through last March, in the biggest case of international drug smuggling in the history of new China, 51 persons, 221 kg of heroin and 1.6 million yuan RMB as well as guns and vehicles were seized. Opium was burned at the June 26 meeting held in Yunnan to observe the 130th anniversary of the Opium War and the third annual International Drug Prohibition Day. This was an act of real significance, for China is again faced with an arduous and complicated struggle against drug abuse.

11   China's own history and the present international antidrug struggle show
that the spread of drug trafficking for enormous profits is a chronic malady of capitalism. The 19th-century opium trade with China was one of the sources for primitive accumulation of capital in the United Kingdom. Today the US and Western
Europe are the main markets for narcotics. With a value of over US $500 billion
yearly, narcotics rank second only to the munitions industry in value of traffic, according to a survey issued last February by the U.N. In Western Europe drug use
and smuggling work hand in hand with prostitution and violence to produce a
hotbed of crime. Now this virus has infected many third-world countries.

12   Why doesn't drug prohibition work? I believe the main reason is collusion between officials and traffickers. Money smoothes the way for the passage of narcotics,
whether in the producing, trafficking, or consuming countries, thus poisoning the
whole world. The next 10 years will see decisive efforts on the part of the United Nations concerning the drug problem. Many countries, including China, have already
joined the urgent call for joint efforts to fight and rid the world of this scourge.

13   Reviewing the past helps one understand the present. Today's struggle can
draw inspiration from Lin Zexu's opium ban. For instance, after he reached
Guangzhou and saw the extent of the smuggling, his plan quickly turned from prohibiting opium addiction to cutting off opium at the source. Today's narcotics ban
is a struggle that brooks no delay. Since 1983 a series of laws have been passed in
China that stipulate the standards for conviction and sentencing of drug producers, traffickers, and transporters, and also penalties for drug abusers, small producers of the opium poppy and users of narcotics.

14   In March 1983 the Chinese government established a committee, consisting
of representatives of the public health, foreign affairs, and public security ministries and the customs office, to coordinate drug control. It has been a force in
promoting the struggle against narcotics. The government has also set up special
antinarcotics units in some key regions.

15   Recognizing the common harm to mankind, China hopes to make a greater contribution to the world struggle against drugs. She is now strengthening cooperation
with the responsible organizations of the United Nations and taking the initiative in
developing bilateral and multilateral cooperation with countries along her borders.

READING

1. How long did it take Britain to drain China of its silver? How did Britain accomplish this? When China went on its antidrug campaign in 1949, how long did it
take to wipe out drug abuse?

2. What are the four ways noted in the article that narcotics are affecting the world
today?

THINKING

1. Ling Qing says, "Recognizing the common harm to mankind, China hopes to
make a greater contribution to the world struggle against drugs." Do you see other
countries recognizing the dangers of narcotics and making a significant effort to

do something about the problem? Which countries are or are not trying to solve the problem? How?

2. The article states that drug trafficking ranks second only to munitions trafficking in value. Does that statement frighten you? Do you think drug trafficking or munitions trafficking is more dangerous to society? Why?

PREWRITING

Make a list of all of the penalties you think may be appropriate for drug dealers. Then make a list of all of the ways you think could be used to eliminate drug abuse. How do they compare and contrast?

WRITING

1. Many people feel the solution to the drug problem in American society today is to stiffen the penalties for drug dealers. Write a proposal to the judge in your county who sentences the drug traffickers in your area. Tell him what you feel the penalties should be for drug dealing. Be specific.

Home-work

2. China was able to wipe out drug abuse in one year, but drug abuse gradually returned to her society. Write an argumentative essay stating how you feel drug abuse could be wiped out permanently in America. Be creative with your solution.

REVISING

The writing assignments for this section ask you to write an argument. To write an argument, you must have an arguable topic. For instance, arguing that child abuse or rape is good wouldn't make much sense because most of American society already disagrees with the statement. What is Ling Qing arguing in this essay? Write a direct statement of his argument. Then ask if it addresses a problem with no easy answer. Does it try to convince the reader of something or motivate the reader to act on the problem? Does it present a position that the reader can disagree with? If the statement does all of these things, it can be argued.

Now write a direct statement expressing the argument of your essay. Ask the same questions about your statement. Do you have a good argument? Make any necessary adjustments to your argument. Then go over your essay to see how you can improve it to more directly reflect your argument.

EDITING

The use of **strong verbs** makes your writing more exciting and powerful. Look at the following examples:

This first mighty act against drugs *sparked* a great patriotic movement of the Chinese people.

> . . . Britain *dumped* opium worth 3.4 million pounds . . . .
>
> . . . Lin *mobilized* the people . . . .
>
> . . . traffic in narcotics *spawns* illegal international organizations . . . .
>
> Money *smooths* the way . . . .

See how these action verbs enliven the writing, presenting a more precise description of what is happening in the sentence. Your writing should always be as specific as possible. Strong action verbs help your writing to be more concise.

A **linking verb** simply joins the ideas in your sentence. The most common linking verbs are forms of the verb *to be* (*is, am, are, was, were, been, will be, could be, would be*). Other linking verbs are *become, seem, appear, look, feel, sound, taste, smell,* and *turn* and *get* (when they mean *become*).

Examples:

> The situation *is* grim.
>
> The 19th-century opium trade with China *was* one of the sources . . . .
>
> Today the US and Western Europe *are* the main markets for narcotics.

Go through your writing assignment and identify the verb of each sentence. Is it an action verb? Can you change it to an action verb if it is a linking verb?

The Dynamics of Anti-Semitism

Cherie Brown

PREREADING

Jews are frequently referred to as Semites, so anti-Semitism means anti-Jew. What do you know about the Jewish people and Jewish traditions? Have you heard of people being against Jews? What were their reasons? Have you known any Jewish people? How were they like or different from anybody else you know?

DEFINING

oppression (¶1)   keeping down by cruel or unjust use of authority

manifests (¶1)   shows, demonstrates

scapegoating (¶1)   making one group bear the blame for the mistakes of others

synagogues (¶1)   buildings used by Jews as places of worship

antagonism (¶1)   active opposition

imminent (¶2)   about to happen

Holocaust (¶4)   the systematic execution of the Jews by Hitler

continuum (¶6)   something whose parts cannot be separated

deriving (¶7)   coming from

etched (¶8)   figuratively scratched or carved into

alliances (¶10)   connections of interests between persons

dynamic (¶11)   motivating force

vulnerability (¶11)   open to attack or criticism

collusive (¶11)   fraudulent, conspiring

accommodating (¶12)   allowing

consciousness raising (¶15)   making people aware

The Dynamics of Anti-Semitism
Cherie Brown

1   The oppression of Jews manifests itself in two ways. The first is more widely understood: specific acts of scapegoating Jews. We all know about the overt acts, the bombing and burning of synagogues, the acts of violence against Jews, the discrimination against Jews. But there is another way that we are oppressed that is more subtle, but nevertheless equally vicious. Jews occupy some highly visible positions in public life that make them appear to be economically or politically powerful, though in fact by and large we are not. We are in positions where, by the nature of the jobs, we exert daily control over the lives of more visibly oppressed groups. We are not the owners of the corporations, but we are the managers, the lawyers, the doctors, the teachers, the social workers who staff large corporate and governmental bureaucracies. And we are the shopkeepers of small- and medium-sized businesses. The particular jobs that Jews hold are ones that give us the appearance of power or control over more visibly oppressed groups—and they resent us instead of the people who hold the real power. Jews are sometimes the ones who stick out, and this provides a focus for antagonism that might otherwise be directed at the real oppressors. When groups who are hurting, particularly economically, look for someone to oppose, they often turn against Jews.

2   Jews really have an invisible "loose noose" around their necks: Jews have more economic and political mobility than many other oppressed groups, so it doesn't look like we are oppressed. But the invisibility of our oppression is central to keeping us in this place. Every Jewish person fears that when times get tight it is possible that Jews will become scapegoats again. So most Jews carry inside feelings of terror and insecurity, and fears of imminent betrayal.

3   We Jews often push ourselves to function on top of the layer of terror. When some groups get scared, they become paralyzed. But when Jews are scared, we build five new organizations. Fear propels us into constant new activity and busyness—this is our particular survival strategy. Unfortunately it's very difficult to maintain fresh, creative thinking and responses when there is still so much fear propelling our thinking.

Cherie Brown, "The Dynamics of Anti-Semitism," *Tikkun,* Vol. 6, No. 2, March/April 1991, pp. 22–28. Reprinted by permission of *Tikkun,* a bimonthly Jewish critique of politics, culture, and society based in Oakland, California. Subscriptions: $25/yr (six issues). Call (800) 545-9364.

Please note maps in appendix for references to places in this article.

4   This survival strategy differs from that which others adopt when facing internalized oppression and fear. I saw this once when working with two Dutch women, one a working-class Catholic raised on a farm, the other a Jewish survivor of the Holocaust. Both decided they wanted to learn how to dive. The Jewish woman immediately went to the diving board and dove off; the Catholic woman required two weeks at the pool before she was willing to go to the diving board. Then one day, long after the Catholic woman was secure enough to dive, the Jewish woman got to the edge of the board and froze in terror. She hadn't overcome her terror just by acting as though she weren't scared. It was only after the Catholic woman felt more secure that the Jewish woman could risk feeling her own fears.

5   This is what happens to Jews. Our fears are still there. They show up in insomnia, in asthma, in overeating, in a failure to take good care of ourselves, in a drivenness to constant activity—all rooted in a deep terror. And living with that fear—and the crippling impact it sometimes has on our lives—is part of the way that Jews are oppressed. The worst part of it for many Jews, particularly progressive Jews active in social change movements, is that there is so much denial of any real anti-Semitism that we end up believing these difficulties are just individual problems—we don't know to connect these difficulties to less visible forms of institutionalized anti-Semitism being directed at us.

6   These dynamics have a big impact on how Jews act in the political arena. Many Jews find themselves having to choose between two different ways to live. They either choose a life built primarily on the theme that, "I'm for everybody else, I'm a humanitarian"—and embedded in this form of self-presentation is a great deal of shame about being Jewish, which leads people to take on everybody else's struggles and *not* Jewish struggles. Or they choose a life of being visibly Jewish, proud of being Jewish, and living a life predominantly with Jews, though all too often isolated from deep relationships with other groups. Most Jews are on a continuum somewhere between these two poles. These choices have dramatic consequences for how Jews function in the public arena.

7   There are plenty of Jews active in the leadership of progressive movements, but they are there *as* Jews. As a result, the Jewish commitment to those struggles becomes invisible to other people in those movements. Internalized anti-Semitism often limits our ability to be effective in political work. I have yet to meet a Jewish person (even those who lead actively Jewish lives) who does not carry somewhere inside an internal recording of self-disgust, deriving from hundreds of years in which the world has said to us: "There's something so wrong with you that you don't deserve to exist," and now, "You don't deserve a homeland." Those messages *do* get internalized, even in those who are proudly Jewish. One way that this disgust gets manifested is in not taking care of ourselves and our bodies, because at some deep level we don't see ourselves as precious beings. And we don't always have the courage to take care of each other or of the Jewish people.

8   Every oppressed group internalizes the record of its oppression and turns against members of its own group, particularly those who in any way behave according to stereotype. Some Jews will turn against Jews because they aren't "good enough Jews"; others will turn against Jews who act "too pushy" or "too assertive."

Jews who more visibly show their fears tend to generate a lot more disgust or with-drawal from other Jews. I've listened to some Israelis, for example, who pride themselves on being strong Israelis who express contempt for Jews who look or act "like Holocaust survivors." It seems to be too painful for many of us to stay close to each other when we see the scars of the oppression etched in each other's behav-iors. We can be highly critical of one another, holding each other to the same per-fectionist standard that the world holds us to.

9   Rarely do Jews get praised by each other for the work that they do. We are good at pointing out the negative and forgetting to express the appreciations. In-stead, we abandon each other or viciously attack one another—particularly when a Jew or small group of Jews tries to do something new or courageous. Our fears about security are enormous—so we attack those who try new directions or those who take courageous stands for fear that they will endanger all of us. However, none of these responses are our fault; they stem from a long history of anti-Semitism. We need to get rid of all these manifestations of internalized anti-Semitism, but we also need to be gentle with each other—even when we are acting out the internal-ized oppression.

10   Complicating all this, making it all the harder for us to build alliances is this: It's difficult for many Jews to relax enough to allow deep closeness to develop. Jews have historically been kept separate from the world, and have become used to feel-ing isolated from others. Even though the initial experience of isolation may have been with non-Jews, this isolation also gets internalized and will keep us from building close, trusting bonds with each other. And this sense of isolation often af-fects family relationships and our ability to have genuine closeness. We love each other, but we don't trust each other. A fear of being abandoned always keeps even the closest relationships from having a deep sense of trust.

11   Some non-Jews have accused us of being pushy, manipulative, controlling. What they don't understand is that they are seeing our terror and our isolation, not our power. In social change movements and the antiwar movement to date, the whole nature of anti-Semitism and internalized anti-Semitism remains un-known and unchallenged. Anti-Semitism involves *two forces*. Most people under-stand one or the other, but rarely both. Jews will sometimes participate in the op-pression of another group (in Israel, it's the Palestinians) because we have been convinced by outside forces that it is our only path to safety. Then, when we partici-pate in this role of "surrogate oppressor," we get isolated, targeted, attacked, and betrayed. It is not the fault of Jews that this dynamic happens. Throughout history, ruling class interests have set up individual Jews over and over again to be visible oppressors. The only reason Jews have ever agreed to this role was the slim hope of survival—and the oppressors' offer to protect Jews. In this dynamic, the leaders representing the ruling class (Saddam Hussein, for example) are able to use Jews as a convenient scapegoat when they need one. Many leaders within the Jewish community will actively and correctly speak out about Jewish vulnerability and scapegoating but fail to understand and speak against the collusive role that Jews or Jewish leaders have been forced into playing, which contributes to this scape-goating. Many members and leaders of progressive social change movements will

actively and correctly identify the collusive role that some Jews (or the Israeli government) play but will fail to understand or speak against the very *real* vulnerability and lack of security for Jews. This isolation pushes Jews further toward the Right. The antiwar movement then sees this alignment with the Right and incorrectly blames Jews even more. And so the cycle continues. The very policies the antiwar movement is striving to achieve will not happen without an active and vigorous policy against anti-Semitism.

12   The Left likes simple forms of oppression—"good guys" and "bad guys"—so they miss anti-Semitism, which requires a more complex analysis. It is this double dynamic—real, very systematic vulnerability followed by an effort to overcome vulnerability by accommodating to oppressive forces, who are only too willing to let Jews become the more visible oppressors of others. One of the major ways that progressive movements could effectively respond to the Gulf conflict would be for them to make a major commitment to dealing with Anti-Semitism in all of its manifestations—because it is precisely this anti-Semitism that Saddam Hussein is seeking to exploit in the war.

13   Because of our internalized fears, Jews on the Left have had a difficult time requiring the peace movement to deal with anti-Semitism. Since the real dynamics of anti-Semitism are not understood, many Jews do not realize that combating anti-Semitism is not just good for Jews but absolutely necessary for the success of *every* social change movement. Anti-Semitism is not in the interests of Blacks, not in the interests of the labor movement, not in the interests of anyone who really wants to see a transformed world. The way anti-Semitism functions is that these groups come to believe that Jews are the impediment to their own progress—so that they never get to take on the real source of their oppression. Fighting anti-Semitism is really in the interests of all social change movements. None of these social change movements will succeed until they also deal with anti-Semitism.

14   There can also be enormous despair and discouragement and a fear that we will never have real allies in progressive movements. One way to break that cycle is to act from the assumption that there are allies out there waiting to be reached. They need the information about anti-Semitism just as much as we need them to have it. We need to heal enough of our fear so that when we are at peace events or other social change events we speak out about anti-Semitism. And we need to require that the issue of anti-Semitism be included in the central agendas of all progressive movements.

15   Jews need to have consciousness-raising sessions just as people did in the women's movement. We need to identify and heal the internalized messages that keep us scared and then functioning on top of fear (which leaves us open and vulnerable to being targeted). We also need to practice and coach each other to speak up against anti-Jewish policies and statements. We need to coach each other to reach out for allies with confident, powerful voices. And ultimately, we must expect that our allies in social-change movements will themselves speak out against anti-Semitism so that this does *not* fall entirely on Jews. We can do this by making one-to-one friendships in these movements and then by asking our friends to speak out.

16   The struggle against anti-Semitism in the Left and in the peace movement is a high priority—and should be seen as such by anyone who wishes to build an effective opposition to Bush and his policies.

READING

1. What are the two ways in which the oppression of Jews manifests itself?

2. What are Jews afraid of? How do the fears of Jews show up?

THINKING

1. Cheri Brown says, "I have yet to meet a Jewish person (even those who lead actively Jewish lives) who does not carry somewhere inside an internal recording of self-disgust, deriving from hundreds of years in which the world has said to us: 'There's something so wrong with you that you don't deserve to exist,' and now, 'You don't deserve a homeland.'" What do you think of this statement? Why would Jews think that other people do not believe that they deserve to exist? Do you think that these feelings may go back to how Hitler treated the Jews? Or do you think something else must be causing these feelings?

2. Brown feels that none of the extreme reactions Jews seem to have to so many circumstances are the fault of the Jews themselves but of the society that has oppressed them for so long. Where do you think the fault lies? Why?

PREWRITING

Freewrite about your idea of a perfect world. What would it be like? Record all the things you would want to eliminate and all the things you would like to add.

WRITING

1. Brown feels that combating anti-Semitism is important for all social change for "anyone who really wants to see a transformed world" (¶13). Write an essay expressing your vision of a "transformed world." Your classmates will be your audience. Indicate the most important changes you think need to be made for the world to be the best place for all people to live. Be sure to show how these changes can be made and who needs to be involved.

2. You have been having a discussion with your history professor over the meaning of the word *oppression,* so your professor has asked you to write a short essay that will clearly show what you mean when you use the term oppression. Be sure to include specific examples to illustrate your point.

REVISING

Writing exercise one requires you to define a "transformed world" before you can really write the essay, and exercise two requires you to define oppression. Read through "The Dynamics of Anti-Semitism" to see all Brown says about "a transformed world" and "oppression." Look these terms up in your dictionary.

Now look at the rough draft of your writing assignment. Do you feel that you have really captured the meaning of the terms you are writing about? Sometimes the meaning will go beyond a simple dictionary definition to a more elaborate or figurative meaning. Be as specific as you can. Always avoid saying, "According to the dictionary, this word means . . ." The use of examples and illustrations can also help to clarify the meaning of terms that you use. Read over the draft for your writing assignment and see what you can do to clarify the meaning of these and other important terms.

EDITING

The **colon** is used in writing to act as an introduction to information that follows. A colon can come before a list, a quote, an example, an explanation, or an appositive. Cherie Brown effectively uses a colon twice in her article. As with dashes and exclamation points, colons are most effective when they are used sparingly.

Examples:
The first is the most widely understood: specific acts of scapegoating Jews. [This is an example.]

Jews really have an invisible "loose noose" around their necks: Jews have more economic and political mobility than many other oppressed groups, so it doesn't look like we are oppressed. [This is an explanation.]

If you have a complete sentence following a colon, the capitalization of the first word of that sentence is optional.

Colons are also used to separate titles from subtitles, and they are used in parts of bibliographic referencing. Be sure to check with Modern Language Association (MLA) standards to use colons correctly in these circumstances.

Look back over your writing assignments to find anywhere that you could effectively use a colon. Try practicing using a colon for introducing a list, a quote, an example, an explanation, or an appositive that you have already used in your writing assignment.

Girl's Gang Friendship Is Fatal

George Ramos

PREREADING

Martha Navarette was in the wrong place at the wrong time and ended up murdered because of it. Do you worry about being safe where you go? Are you careful about whom you are seen in public with because you fear for your safety? Are you more afraid of public violence now than you have been in the past? What has caused this change in your feelings?

DEFINING

predominate (¶2)   are in control

inevitable (¶2)   unavoidable

affiliations (¶2)   associations with

alleged (¶4)   declared or asserted without proof

complied (¶4)   agreed to

tedious (¶9)   tiresome, boring

menial (¶12)   lowly, relating to service jobs

supremacy (¶14)   the condition of being in power

infectious (¶16)   influencing, catching

Girl's Gang Friendship Is Fatal

George Ramos

1   It started off innocently enough. Martha Navarette, 17, a bubbly Hollywood girl who worked hard on her basketball dribble and dreamed of going to college, borrowed an older cousin's car to buy ice cream on Sunset Boulevard. An obedient teen-ager, she promised to return promptly. Navarette got her ice cream cone, but minutes later, authorities said, she became the 100th victim this year of streetgang violence in greater Los Angeles, shot to death April 10 with two other Latino immigrant teen-agers in what police term a "coldblooded execution."

2   A Fairfax High School junior sent to Los Angeles nine years ago by Ecuadorean parents who wanted her to have an American education, Navarette was not a gang member. The two youths killed alongside her as they sat in her cousin's car were with a gang, according to investigators. Navarette knew them well enough, friends said, to give them their final ride to Hollywood Boulevard. In many city neighborhoods where gangs predominate, such acquaintances are an inevitable fact of life. Teen-agers who do their best to avoid becoming gang members often find themselves making friends among boys and girls who have gang affiliations.

3   "She knew of people who were in the gangs," said Douglas Rivera, 17, a fellow student at Fairfax. "Who doesn't in this part of town?" It is a fatal relationship that should be avoided at all costs, said Fairfax High Principal Mike O'Sullivan. "We have to effectively stop this idea that it's OK to be friends with gang members," O'Sullivan said. "In their own way, kids have to stop associating in any shape or form with gang members. They think they can live a double life—study hard in school and be friends with gang members. It just doesn't ever happen."

4   According to police, the events that led Navarette to her death started when she and an unidentified girlfriend were met on Sunset by three male acquaintances—all alleged gang members—after they stopped for ice cream. The three boys asked for a ride several blocks north to Hollywood Boulevard. Navarette complied, said police. At Hollywood Boulevard and Bronson Avenue, the carload of teen-agers stopped to allow one of the boys to make a phone call, investigators said. As they waited near the pay phone, a passerby believed to be on foot shouted a gang slogan at one of the three boys. One of them replied with a slogan. Enraged by the reply, the passerby, a 16-year-old member of a rival gang, chased after Navarette and the three boys, according to police. The four teen-agers piled into her Chevrolet El Camino, parked at a service station on Hollywood near Bronson. The gunman was right behind them. He shot each of them in the head.

5   Navarette was taken to Queen of Angels-Hollywood Presbyterian Medical Center, where she was pronounced dead. Two of the boys, Roberto Orozco, 17, and Carlos Flores, 15, died in the car. The fourth teen-ager, Alexander McLellan,

Please note maps in appendix for references to places in this article.

16, was taken to Cedars-Sinai Medical Center, where he is in critical condition with a bullet wound to the head. The friend who bought ice cream with Navarette was unhurt.

6   The suspect in the shootings, whose identity is apparently known by police, is a male juvenile, said Los Angeles Police Lt. Brad Merritt, a detective with the department's West Bureau CRASH anti-gang unit. Merritt declined to reveal the suspect's name because of his age. When the youth is apprehended, Merritt said, authorities will seek to try him as an adult for the triple homicide.

7   In the flats of Hollywood, working-class apartments and bungalows sandwiched between movie studios and television stations, residents who have long grown used to the city's numbing statistics of gang violence described Navarette's death as an unfair act of fate. "When the news came out that she died, they said it was a gang thing," said Rivera. "But she was no gang member. She didn't deserve that. For her, it was home to school and school to home. That's it. That was her." Added Fairfax girls co-basketball Coach Michelle Sheesley, who oversaw Navarette's season as a point guard on the girls' junior varsity team: "She was at the wrong place at the wrong time. Who knows why?"

8   According to Margarita Navarette, who lived with her husband and her cousin Martha in a well-kept bungalow near Melrose and Western avenues, the teen-ager wanted to make something of herself. "She was always studying," Margarita Navarette said. "She used to say, 'I'm going to study hard, go to college, get a job, and pay you back for all you've done for me.' And I told her she didn't have to pay me back. Just go to school and get good grades. That's all I ever asked for."

9   Greg Keeling, a Spanish teacher at Fairfax, said that the student, a native Spanish speaker, could have easily ignored much of his class's tedious homework. Instead, Keeling said, Navarette "worked hard, very hard." She planned to study computer science in college and was preparing application forms for entry to several Southland colleges, among them USC, UCLA, and UC Santa Barbara. Several days after her death, information forms for her upcoming Scholastic Aptitude Test (SAT) arrived at the family home.

10   Navarette seemed equally determined when she joined the junior varsity team as a sophomore. Only 5 foot-2 inches, she sat on the bench during most of her first year because she lacked control in dribbling. To improve, said Coach Sheesley, she "stayed after school to work." The hard work paid off. Last season, Navarette became starting point guard on the junior-varsity team. Although they suffered through a 2–20 record, Sheesley said that Navarette's determination and cheery smile kept the team together. "She pretty much carried the team," the coach said.

11   If there was one thing Navarette was warned not to participate in, it was the neighborhood's street gangs. Margarita Navarette told her cousin to stay away from them. "If they say 'Hi,' say 'Hi' back—and that's it," Margarita Navarette repeatedly told Martha. "'Don't run around with them.' And she didn't. She never gave me any trouble."

12   Yet, because of the close contacts that occur each day at school and at home among gang members and unaffiliated teen-agers, it was not surprising, friends

said, that Navarette agreed to give a ride to the neighborhood boys who were also gang members. The youths came, as Navarette did, from immigrant families who had settled in the Hollywood area, where housing is cheap and menial jobs as gardeners, dishwashers, and handymen are easily found.

13   Flores' family moved several times in the Hollywood area in the last two years since they arrived from war-torn El Salvador, according to former neighbors. Orozco's family also based themselves in Hollywood after moving there at some point in the last six years from the Mexican town of Sahugayo, a community of about 30,000 in the western state of Michoacan. Orozco dropped out of the 10th grade and was working as a dishwasher, according to friends. Flores' educational history is sketchy, but friends—who declined to allow their names to be published—said the Salvadoran spent more time on the streets than in class.

14   "[Flores] was always hanging with 'Lefty,'" said one teen-ager, dressed in the Raiders' black garb favored by some gang members in Hollywood. Lefty, Merritt said, was Orozco's street nickname. Orozco and Flores "had previous contacts with police officers," said Merritt. Anti-gang detectives said the two boys apparently were associated with a Latino gang that has been feuding over territory with several rival groups. Among these rivals, investigators said, is a Lennox-based gang that has been trying to move into Hollywood, East Hollywood, and Silver Lake. The suspicion among neighbors is that the fight for supremacy over these areas was the root cause of the killings.

15   Neighbors said that the two boys killed with Navarette may have been associated with gangs, but they did not deserve to become part of the city's ever-spiraling gang death toll. "Sure, those boys were gang members," said Luisa Martinez, walking to her modest home near Paramount Studios. "You could see them hanging around at night. But what violence . . . this is no way to live. That's no way to die. Even they did not deserve that."

16   Meanwhile, Margarita Navarette, the older cousin, was left to mourn the loss of the black-haired girl with the infectious smile. At a recent memorial service, she sobbed uncontrollably as she lingered over the casket. "My pretty little girl," the cousin lamented. "My pretty little girl. Why are you dead? Why?"

READING

1. How did Martha Navarette put herself in a situation where she could be murdered?

2. Where was Navarette from? Why was she in America?

THINKING

1. The principal of Navarette's high school says, "We have to effectively stop this idea that it's OK to be friends with gang members." But with the large numbers of gang members in Navarette's school, students say that knowing gang members is unavoidable. What would you do in this situation? Do you think talking to gang members would be OK? Why or why not?

2. The people of Navarette's neighborhood said the boys Navarette gave the ride to did not "deserve" to be killed. What do you think they meant by that? Does anyone "deserve to be killed? Did Navarette "deserve" to be killed? What do you think of the apparent philosophy of the gangs, which puts so little value on human life? What do you think about the fact that so many innocent bystanders are killed in acts of gang violence?

PREWRITING

Freewrite, exploring what you know about gangs and their activities in your community. Are gangs a significant problem where you live? If they are, are they active mostly in certain areas of town? Who are gang members? What kind of a person seems to join a gang? Why do you suppose that people get involved with gangs?

WRITING

1. Gangs cause problems all over America today. Many people become involved in gangs because they feel threatened. Many innocent bystanders are injured or killed by gang activity. Write an essay proposing a solution to the gang problem. How can we as Americans take back control from the gangs?

2. You are a student at the high school Navarette attended. You have been asked to deliver a school assembly speech that remembers Navarette and encourages students to not find themselves in situations similar to the one that got her killed. Keep your audience in mind as you compose your speech because there will be gang members present.

REVISING

Emotional appeals can be effective when you are trying to reach your audience in a manner that will encourage them to change their behavior. George Ramos creates a vivid image of Martha Navarette as a hard-working student with a desire to further her education in college. He also shows how she diligently worked and improved as an athlete and how she was naively friendly to students who were friendly to her. With an image like this, emotional feelings are stirred that make the reader empathize with the family and become angered about the gang situation and its arbitrary violence. The biggest appeal to emotion comes in the last paragraph, as Mr. Ramos quotes:

> "My pretty little girl," the cousin lamented. "My pretty little girl. Why are you dead? Why?"

Each reader can put himself or herself in the position of the cousin and share the grief and anger.

Look at your writing assignments. Have you used an emotional appeal? Can you add an emotional appeal or strengthen one you already have? Try to help the reader identify with what you are writing.

EDITING

Frequently writers will write what they hear and not realize that they are making an error. This happens especially with **used to** and **supposed to.** The writer doesn't hear the *ed* pronounced on the ends of these words, so the past tense suffix is left off.

Examples:

She *used to* say, "I'm going to study hard, go to college, get a job, and pay you back for all you've done for me."

She was *supposed to* come right back home.

Look through your writing assignments to see if you have used *used to* or *supposed to* correctly. Remember to watch out for this common error in your future writing.

Gangsta Girls

Allison Abner

PREREADING

What do you know about gangs? Do you have gangs in your community? Do you know anyone who is a gang member? Do you think gangs are a serious problem in American society? Why or why not? Why do you think someone becomes a member of a gang?

DEFINING

predominantly (¶2)   mostly, having greater quantity

immersed (¶3)   fully engaged, absorbed

maniacal (¶3)   suggestive of insanity

vulnerability (¶6)   likeliness to be easily persuaded

flirtatious (¶6)   playfully romantic

voluptuous (¶6)   suggesting of sensual pleasure

affluence (¶9)   having a great quantity of goods or wealth

incarcerated (¶9)   put into jail

bombarded (¶11)   attacked with

dysfunctional (¶12)   abnormal functioning

affirmation (¶12)   truthfulness, acceptance

proliferation (¶15)   rapid growth

internalize (¶17)   to make part of one's attitudes or beliefs

prevalent (¶18)   occurring widely

supersede (¶19)   to take the place of, replace

persona (¶22)   role one assumes in public

reenacting (¶23)   performing again

victimization (¶23)   being made a person who suffers harm

disillusioned (¶24)   to be free of false beliefs

capitalize (¶25)   to turn to one's advantage

prioritized (¶25)   put in order of importance

intervention (¶28)   interference to hinder or alter an action

curriculum (¶28)   course of study

conjunction (¶28)   the act of working together with

viable (¶31)   capable of living

Gangsta Girls

Allison Abner

1   Tracy embodies all the changes and contradictions of adolescence. Her six-foot frame is becoming more shapely, and she is shedding her tomboy mannerisms. Her hair is swept into a sophisticated French twist, but baby-doll ringlets frame her intense brown eyes and strong jaw. Peeking out from above her socks is a rose tattoo that used to have a boy's name but now reads "Anna," after her mother. Despite her changing body, Tracy (this name and all others have been changed) has a self-confidence that makes her seem older than 17.

2   Tracy lives in a middle-class neighborhood in a predominantly Black area that borders South Central Los Angeles. She lives with her mother, who holds a master's degree in childhood development; her stepfather, who is a civil servant in the public-school system; and her 24-year-old brother. Yet Tracy's transition from adolescence to adulthood has not been a smooth one, and her life is not that of a typical middle-class Black teenager. She speaks of leaving home as if she were marking time in prison. "I can't wait to get out of here," she says. "This doesn't feel like a home. I just come here to shower and sleep. We don't have meals together. Nothing. There's no family here."

3   When asked about happier times, Tracy recalls being 11 and going to stay with her grandmother, who lived a bus ride away. She says her grandmother gave her the love and attention that her parents didn't provide. She also found more freedom there. Her grandmother, who was very permissive, allowed her to run the streets, so she could "kick it" with the Athens Park Bloods, partying and drinking

Allison Abner, "Gangsta Girls," *Essence,* July 1994, vol. 25, no. 3, p. 644. Reprinted by permission.

Please note maps in appendix for references to places in this article.

malt liquor until dawn. After her grandmother died, she withdrew from her family and immersed herself in the rough-and-tumble life of a gang banger. Recalling her criminal past, Tracy expresses both deep sorrow and pride. Her maniacal laugh punctuates her description of how she and fellow gang members have risked and taken other people's lives to show their devotion to one another.

4   "It's like a family. If someone hurts one of our own, we do dirt. We've run in people's houses and smoked them. It's all part of the program," she laughs, but the laughter is followed by a distant stare and a retreat into thought. "I've been through a lot," she finally says quietly. "I cry every day."

5   Stormy, like Tracy, has also given up hope of ever having a close-knit family. She realized early that her mother didn't take any real interest in her. "My mom never shows me love. We always argue because it seems like everyone comes before me," she says. Her smooth brown face displays her pain as she tells of both her mother's many boyfriends and the four siblings whom she feels have pushed her into the background. When she was hospitalized last year for a gunshot wound, her mother came only once for a quick visit, three days after she was admitted.

6   Her amber eyes that are always filled with anger earned her the street name Stormy. Her strong, contradictory emotions—rage mixed with innocence—are what led her to a life of gang banging at age 14. When she joined the Kweens Wood Style Crips, the male gang members quickly responded to her vulnerability, flirtatious smile and voluptuous body. "It's no wonder I got into a gang. I always smiled and had fun. And they paid attention to me," she says.

7   Unlike Stormy, Jonelle is not fragile. She looks like a girl who can take care of herself. Her short hair is straightened and neatly combed, her slacks are crisply pleated and her blouse is pressed. Though she takes pride in her appearance and acts older than her years, her age, 16, peeks through in her round face and soft eyes, which earned her the street name Baby J.

8   When Baby J. talks about her family, she sounds wise yet seems removed from her past. She grew up in the projects, where her uncles, cousins and father were O.G.'s ("original gangsters"—founding or older members) of the Grape Street Watts Crips. "My father was a high roller [drug dealer], and he had ten thousand in his pocket every day," she recalls.

9   Despite his affluence, Baby J.'s father couldn't imagine a life beyond the projects, and that was where she and her family remained until he was arrested and incarcerated. "When he went to jail, we started going broke. I wanted to be Mr. Big Shot and support my family," she says.

10   At 10, Baby J., the eldest of three daughters of an imprisoned father and a crack-addicted mother, turned to selling drugs to keep her family together. When at 11 she joined the Grape Street Watts Crips, her determination and sense of responsibility earned her their respect. That same determination and sense of responsibility eventually pushed her out of the gang when she was 14. After an arrest and two years in a stable group home, Baby J. thinks of how her life has changed. "I like family, people who stick together. I feel like I have that here," she says now of her group home. "I never did need the gang, but I didn't know it until now."

Why Kids Join Gangs

11   Today the expectations for a better life that many young people held during the sixties and seventies have given way to a sense of despair. Many young African-Americans live in segregated neighborhoods, which are locked out of a technologically advancing world. Unemployment rates as well as dropout rates for Black and Latino youngsters are still unacceptably high. Black youngsters, like other young people in American society, are also bombarded with images of material wealth and the good life—fast cars and designer clothes—as a means to enhance self-esteem. They are shown the results of hard work but are not given the jobs that will enable them to reach their goals. They often feel that they are forgotten and unwanted by the general society. Dr. Terrence J. Roberts, Ph.D., a psychologist and the chairman of the psychology department at Antioch University in Marina del Rey, California, explains, "Most of these kids have no sense of building a future because their worth isn't reflected in mainstream society."

12   Many youngsters at risk also come from dysfunctional and abusive families, and they often look for affirmation and a sense of self-worth in the street. "Group affiliation is an important part of development because it gives us a sense of belonging," observes Roberts. Many kids in gang-infested areas have few socially acceptable outlets and thus turn to gang activities as a way to foster a sense of identity. Gangs fill the void that these young people feel. They may also offer them the chance to make money through criminal activity.

13   The influence of gangs is also increasing. In Los Angeles County alone, there are an estimated 46,000 African-American gang members (about 15,000 Bloods; 31,000 Crips), according to Sergeant Wes McBride, the operations sergeant for the Los Angeles County Sheriff's Department.

14   "When I started on the gang unit in the late seventies, there were 225 gangs. Now there are at least 1,100, and they're flourishing," he says.

15   Sharon Stegall, Los Angeles County deputy probation officer for the Metropolitan Specialized Gang Unit, states that gang proliferation is directly related to the lack of available jobs and community programs, as well as to the increase in drug and arms trafficking. "In neighborhoods where demands are high for drugs and guns, you will also find high rates of gang activity," says Stegall. "That's how they sustain themselves."

16   The conditions that create gangs exist in other cities as well. "Aside from the big cities like New York and Chicago, smaller cities like Denver, Phoenix, Des Moines, Shreveport, Oklahoma City, and Kansas City are seeing a remarkable growth in gang activity," says McBride. Initially the gangs spread when gang members left Los Angeles, usually taken away by parents desperate to get them out of the gang environment. These transplanted gang members, seen as "real" gang bangers, became leaders of new or existing gangs and established drug concessions with help from their "homies." These new gangs recruit the most vulnerable young people, those who are attracted to the glamorized gangster image.

17   Gangs are also recruiting more young women. In Los Angeles females comprise approximately 15 percent (about 6,000) of the gang population. As with their male counterparts, girls who join gangs usually suffer from alienation

and family abuse. "At least 90 percent of girls who join gangs have experienced severe emotional, sexual or physical abuse, usually by a caretaker," says Diane Griggs, a licensed clinical social worker at Inglewood's Didi Hirsch Community Mental Health Clinic. "Their low self-esteem and isolation keep them from trusting anyone. So they internalize the abuse and enter the gang to act out their rage and anger." Left to cope alone, these girls turn to the gangs for a support network.

Rites of Passage

18 Most girls become involved in gangs through their relationships with friends, boyfriends or family members who are members. Because gangs are so prevalent in some areas, many girls join to avoid harassment from gang members. Says Tracy, "About 75 percent of the people I know are in gangs, so you just choose the group of people you like hanging with the most."

19 Generally a girl's involvement is gradual, beginning with casual socializing until she expresses the desire to be "jumped in" or "courted in" (initiated). Before they are accepted, members must prove in a variety of ways both their loyalty and their desire to join. For Tracy it meant fighting a male gang member for three minutes, then drinking an excessive amount of liquor, smoking marijuana, and finally battling drunk with several female members. Once accepted, members are bound by loyal neighborhood-gang ties that supersede blood ties, even in the face of death.

20 This code of honor appeals to many girls who have come from abusive or neglectful families. Stormy remembers being comforted by the knowledge that her homeboys were always there for her. "They treated me like a little sister, and if I ever had any problems, they'd help me out. I'd never had that before," she says.

21 For many girls, gang membership is primarily a social activity. They spend most of their time skipping school, getting high, gossiping, listening to music, and flirting with male gang members. Girls anxious to make money, like Tracy and Baby J., may also use gang ties to hustle drugs.

22 But whatever their initial involvement, most girls quickly discover that their commitment to the gang will deepen the longer they stay in it. Hard-core members, who make up about 5 percent of all female gang members, adopt the defensive macho persona of their homeboys. To prove they can "handle theirs" as well as any male, they often participate in high-risk criminal activities, such as robberies, car jackings, burglaries and shootings. These girls often speak of earning the "respect" of their homies as an achievement that justifies their reckless conduct. Griggs believes, however, that this behavior is, in reality, suicidal. She believes that these girls feel that society does not protect them, so they tempt death, adopting the aggressive role of their abusers and taking it one step further. She recalls a teenaged client who said she had participated in drive-by shootings, hoping to catch a stray bullet. Many hard-core gang members harbor a death wish and believe they won't live to see their twentieth birthday.

23 Some girls, especially those who have been sexually abused, also engage in

high-risk sexual behavior. These girls, who are called toss-ups, often earn their reputations by sexually servicing male gang members. As Griggs states, "They are constantly searching for love and a connection while reenacting their victimization." Stegall has witnessed what happens to these toss-ups. "Some become pregnant. Others turn to drugs and support their habit by prostituting for their supplier— often a homeboy from the set," she says. Their considerable rage is always turned inside rather than outward.

Time to Change Their Lives

24   Eventually gang life takes its toll. "After a while," says Baby J. wearily, "I got tired of seeing my homies die and tired of having so many enemies [that] I was afraid to walk down the street." Stormy began to see her victims differently: "I started thinking about robbing and jumping people and how I'd feel if it was my mother or sister." Even Tracy, who admits she still hangs with her homies, realized, "I'm getting too old to be shooting and robbing." Disillusioned by the violence and senseless killings, eventually the hardest gang member may realize that all roads lead either to a jail cell or a casket.

25   After her fourth arrest for petty theft, Baby J. was placed in a group home. While there, she became determined to build her self-esteem. "I looked in the mirror every day," she recalls, "and told myself I didn't need the gang." But she wasn't able to capitalize on her efforts to improve until she was placed in a foster home. Her foster mother laid down strict rules that prohibited socializing in the streets and prioritized schoolwork and household responsibilities. She also put order into Baby J.'s life through weekly family meetings with the six other girls—her two daughters and four foster daughters—who lived with her. In the meetings they learned how to discuss family problems, resolve conflicts, and express feelings. For the first time Baby J. felt loved and respected by a caretaker, which allowed her to concentrate on her education and her day-care-center job. Since entering her foster mother's home, she has stayed out of trouble.

26   Roberts agrees that girls like Baby J. who are able to turn their lives around can only do so with the help of a trustworthy and loving adult. Explains Roberts, "If the parent, or any adult, connects with the child and shows her unconditional love, that girl will develop a sense of worth and a desire to change." Griggs believes that most girls know the gang does not provide the support kids are looking for. As Baby J. acknowledges, "Most homies will tell you in private they wish they could get out, and what they really want is just to be wanted, noticed, and loved by their parents." Given the choice, most kids will choose a trusting adult over the gang.

27   "You hear so much about boys in gangs," says Steve Wells, a deputy probation officer, "but girls have a harder time because there aren't any resources to help them." Recreational activities and educational and job-training programs that are designed to aid male gang members don't address female issues like pregnancy prevention or sexual abuse. Without these services, girls at risk will continue to fall back on the security of the gang.

Saving Girls At Risk

28   Most experts dealing with girls in gangs agree that early intervention is imperative. Deborah Prothrow-Stith, M.D., assistant dean of the Harvard School of Public Health and author of *Deadly Consequences: How Violence Is Destroying Our Teenage Population and a Plan to Begin Solving the Problem* (Harper Collins), believes that intervention must include examining cultural attitudes about violence. "We live in a society that celebrates violence," she states, "and has contributed to the current epidemic of youth violence." Recently she constructed a nonviolent curriculum for teens 13 to 17 that encourages options to violent behavior. "Everyone needs to learn how to handle their anger," she says. "And though the curriculum is a preventive measure, it has to work in conjunction with other activities, like counseling, to help kids deal with the trauma and violence they've experienced." Girls who are able to deal with their anger constructively are less likely to engage in high-risk behavior.

29   In response to the rise in violence among students, an increasing number of schools are developing mediation and peer-counseling programs. Michael Kesselman, the coordinator for such a program at North Miami Beach Senior High School in Dade County, Florida, is beginning to see the results of his efforts. "So far this year, students have overseen 130 mediations, as compared to 30 last year. At the same time our school has seen a dramatic drop in the number of suspensions for violent acts," says Kesselman.

30   As this generation of adolescents prepares to move into adulthood, those who learn to interact effectively and nonviolently will be the future role models. "Many girls have only seen women as victims," says Prothrow-Stith. "They don't know any women they view as powerful who aren't violent."

31   The cycle of violence will end when children feel they have access to empowering alternatives. Our community can only save girls at risk by giving them viable options and letting them know they belong to a world that has invested in their well-being.

READING

1. How many gang members are there in Los Angeles County? Are gangs just a Los Angeles problem, or do other places have gangs, too?

2. What are two of the possible solutions to gang participation that are discussed in the article?

THINKING

1. How do you feel about each of the girls written about in the article? Do you think they had alternative choices, or do you think their gang participation was inevitable? Why?

2. The article mentions that gang participation is related to a lack of jobs and community programs. How do you feel about this? Would more jobs help? Where would they come from?

PREWRITING

Write freely for ten minutes about gangs. Be sure to include anything you can think of relating to gangs, who is in them, and what they do. Think also about what could be done to solve the gang problem or help people who have become involved in gangs.

WRITING

1. Your community has a significant problem with gangs, and you want to do something that could really make a difference to the girls who are currently involved in gangs. Write a proposal that you will be able to share with a group of female gang members who are considering changing their lives. Tell them what you think they should do and how you or your community can help them.

2. Go to your library and find two articles related to gangs in your area. Write a synthesis of these two articles and "Gangsta Girls" to share with your classmates. To write a synthesis, you must first clearly define your purpose. Examine the three articles and see what they have in common or what argument they could work to support. Write a thesis statement, and then develop your argument being sure to use information from each of your sources.

REVISING

A synthesis is a discussion of a clearly defined thesis that incorporates information from several sources while allowing the author's voice to be clearly heard. The quality of the synthesis depends on the quality of the materials chosen for sources, the comprehension by the writer of those sources, and the writer's ability to discuss the materials in relation to the purpose of the thesis. To write a synthesis, first be sure to understand what you are trying to say. Make sure your thesis clearly states what you will attempt to prove with your synthesis. Carefully read each of your sources highlighting the facts that relate to your thesis and see how the materials relate to each other. Be sure to look up any terminology in your materials that you aren't familiar with. Outline your paper showing the relationships between your materials and your thesis in your outline, then write your paper utilizing materials from all of your sources. Remember, when writing a synthesis, you aren't simply restating what someone else has said. You are developing your own ideas and supporting them with facts you find in the materials you researched.

EDITING

One of the most common errors with pronoun use is putting the incorrect pronouns after the words **like, between, except,** and **but** (when **but** means **except** and is not being used as a coordinating conjunction to join two sentences together).

Examples:

> The disagreement was *between him* and *me.*
>
> Everyone was involved *except them* and *us.*
>
> Everyone supported the decision *but me.*

Read through your writing assignments to see if you have used any of these words. Be careful to always use the objective case of pronouns when they follow *like, between, but,* and *except,* even if it sounds wrong, because you may not be used to hearing these words correctly.

A Tragedy in the Making

Todd Shields

PREREADING

People starve to death all over the world every day. Write how you feel about hunger and starvation. Have you ever been really hungry? If so, what was it like? Are there people in your country who may be starving? Are there hungry people in your community? Have you ever done anything to help alleviate this situation? If so, what? Do you feel that it is your responsibility to help with this problem? How could you help?

DEFINING

Khartoum (¶1)   the capital of Sudan, Africa

hovels (¶1)   open sheds, poor shelters

scarified (¶3)   the skin decorated by making small cuts that heal into scars

plaited (¶3)   braided

envoys (¶3)   messengers

famine (¶3)   lack of food on a large scale, causing starvation

withered (¶4)   shrunken, dried up

rebuffed (¶5)   refused

faltering (¶6)   uncertain, unsteady

entailing (¶6)   including

pessimism (¶6) feeling of doom, negative attitude

beset (¶6) enclose, surround

expatriate (¶7) one who has withdrawn from his or her own country

swaths (¶10) broad sections

incessant (¶15) unstopping, unyielding

perversely (¶15) wrongly, incorrectly

inextricably (¶17) so complicated that it can't be solved

implicit (¶19) suggested, implied

aloof (¶19) separate

regime (¶19) political system, social order

blithe (¶21) bright, joyous

reciprocated (¶23) given after getting, given in return

rhetoric (¶23) written or spoken language

missteps (¶25) mistakes, goofs, foul-ups

impoundment (¶25) gathering, taking into legal custody

ostensible (¶25) apparent, seeming

daunting (¶29) intimidating, disheartening

squalor (¶31) the condition of being filthy or foul

A Tragedy in the Making
Todd Shields

1   Out on the fringes of Khartoum, on a dusty plain behind the capital's twin city of Omdurman, is a vast maze of mud huts and burlap hovels. The free-form slum, long a home to unfortunates from the countryside, grows weekly now, swelling with refugees from the drought. They arrive by the busload and by truck to find a community where work is rare, food is scarce, families are split, and children suffer.

2   Children like Rawha Salih, a frail one-year-old with a tattered green dress, a weak cry, and a blank middle-distance stare. Her belly is round and bloated, her hair thin and frizzy, her legs wasted and her skin tough and scaly. Around her is a feeding clinic where a score of mothers urge bread, lentils, and milk upon other babies who had been starving.

3   The women are handsome, with the fine chiseled features, scarified cheeks, and plaited hair of western Sudan. Like Rawha and her grandmother, many have recently arrived from the heart of dryness in the western provinces of Kordofan

Todd Shields, "A Tragedy in the Making," *Africa Report,* March/April 1991, pp 54–57. Copyright© 1991 by the African-American Institute. Reprinted by permission of *Africa Report.*

Please note maps in appendix for references to places in this article.

and Darfur. The migrants are expected to be the forerunners of a torrent of misery, envoys of a famine created by misrule and economic collapse.

4   For a second year running, drought has withered crops across wide areas of the western provinces, and in the normally fertile hills by the Red Sea in the country's east. The United Nations estimates the grain shortfall at 1.2 million metric tons, and says massive food aid is needed for more than 7 million people who are at risk of starvation. If Sudan consumes its own supplies at the customary rate, it would be left with no food at all from July through September this year.

5   In the face of the emergency, Sudan's military government has rebuffed Western efforts to launch a relief program. It refuses to acknowledge publicly that help will be needed, to enter into an agreement on how food aid would be used, or to ensure that relief organizations now in place will be allowed to operate. The result is uncertainty about whether food aid will be properly used or even welcome—an uncertainty that has led donor countries to delay shipments at a time when stocks should be building for the hard months ahead.

6   The faltering beginning afflicts what ideally would become a major relief program entailing early preparation, tightly choreographed shipping schedules, and the expenditure of $500 million or more. But with few significant steps taken so far, gloom and pessimism beset those responsible for mounting the campaign against starvation. "Certainly a tragedy is in the making here," said one senior Western diplomat, in a comment typical of relief experts in Khartoum. "The longer you wait the more serious it becomes, and the more likely it is large numbers are going to die . . . some loss of life is inevitable."

7   The Gulf crisis, in which Sudan has leaned toward Iraq, only complicates the picture. The expatriate staffs of several international aid organizations left Sudan in January in fear of terrorist attacks or anti-Western rioting. Similar concerns prompted the United States to evacuate its embassy in Khartoum, and led a top United Nations official to postpone a visit aimed at securing the government's cooperation. The moves promise to further delay relief efforts, even should warfare not block the Red Sea shipping lanes through which imported grain must pass.

8   Already, shortages within Sudan have sent food prices soaring, to roughly 10 times their level of one year earlier. Peasants desperate for grain have sold their flocks, pushing livestock prices to historic lows. Inflation, running at nearly 100 percent by official figures and almost double that by more comprehensive estimates, adds to the strain. A selective famine, targeting the poorest of the poor, appears to have begun.

9   Its victims are people like Rawha, the stick-thin child in the feeding clinic. Her father has stayed behind in Kordofan and now, along with her grandmother, she depends on the 25 to 30 Sudanese pounds that her mother earns in a day of house-cleaning. Twelve ounces of milk costs an unaffordable 10 pounds; a month's supply of grain would cost 600 pounds, if the family could buy in bulk on the mother's meager pay.

10   The story of hunger in the face of impossible food prices is repeated throughout the country. In the poorest districts of Khartoum, survey after survey shows mal-

nutrition rising to alarming levels. Across broad swaths of rural Sudan, malnutrition had by the beginning of the year surpassed levels that normally trigger emergency assistance. Yet some hard-hit areas had no relief program at all.

11   The government barred journalists from visiting the drought zones, but travellers' accounts suggested grim conditions. More than 27,000 people were encamped at the end of 1990 on the outskirts of the important provincial town of El Obeid, where water supplies are failing. The November harvest was said to have yielded watermelons the size of tennis balls in rural Kordofan, which one visitor described as "dry, without any pasture, any crops, or anything green."

12   Other travellers from the west described sheep and goat carcasses at roadsides, deserted villages, dried-up wells, and blowing sand that covers vehicle tracks within minutes. In one place, 15 villagers bled continuously from the mouth, victims of the vitamin deficiency known as scurvy. At another village, a district health officer reported nine hunger deaths over three months.

13   Conditions were no better, and perhaps worse, in the eastern hunger zone, where nearly one-third of all children surveyed needed extra feeding. In one town late last year, 27 children were severely malnourished—likely to die within a month unless they received emergency feeding.

14   The distress was foreseeable as long ago as July, when the rains began to fail. Yet the government spent the autumn denying there was a food shortage. A new year's eve address by the military ruler, Gen. Omar Hassan al-Beshir, illuminates the prevailing attitude.

15   With the diplomatic corps assembled before him at the Palace of the Republic on the banks of the Blue Nile, Beshir laid out his plans for the coming year. He mentioned "the incessant revolution for progress and achievement," and "the enemies, traitors, and plotters" who threaten the nation. He praised Arab unity and announced Islamic law. He perversely noted progress in agriculture. He said nothing about the looming famine.

16   Guided by such priorities, the government has yet to issue a formal appeal for help, or to agree that relief grain would be distributed by international nongovernmental organizations—a pledge Western donors would take as a guarantee that food would in fact go to the neediest. Without these steps, according to a wide range of relief and diplomatic sources, donors likely will remain reluctant to mount a full-scale effort. Said one diplomat, "We're not going to get put in a situation where the U.S. or the EEC just feeds the army or the people in the cities and lets the rural victims starve." Said another, "It's just not in the cards. No combination of donors is going to give them 1 million tons and say, 'Just give it to your people.' No way."

17   The regime's unwillingness to come to terms appears inextricably linked to its deep suspicion of the West. The officers, a mostly middle-aged group who in 1989 overthrew a fumbling but democratic parliamentary system, have since installed the basics of an Islamic state. Their proclaimed vision is one of solidarity with Arab countries, not the West. They came of age while watching their country steadily decline under Western-style political institutions, and under the patronage of Western economic powers.

18   The officers, who publicly reject much of what preceded their rule, now find it politically and even intellectually difficult to ask the West for help, according to official and private observers in Khartoum. The tendency is reinforced by the regime's campaign for self-sufficiency, promoted under the well-publicized slogan, "We Eat What We Grow, We Wear What We Make."

19   The pride implicit in the slogan adds another reason to stand aloof from international efforts. The regime's narrow base of support and brittle hold over public opinion leave it anxious to insist that all is well, which further complicates matters.

20   "Declaring there is a famine is a public admission of failure, and so it doesn't exist," said one Sudanese intellectual. A diplomat from a Third World country, who is in close contact with senior Sudanese officials, said they believe that "Western donors are more interested in humiliating this government and bringing it down than they are in doing anything else."

21   Within the government, the political and emotional overtones have created an almost blithe assessment of the problem. "It is not serious. It is not serious at all," Col. Mohamed el Amin Khalifa, a member of the ruling Revolutionary Command Council, said in an interview. He said Sudan, which is bankrupt, would commercially import the grain it needs.

22   Khalifa said there would be no appeal for aid. He spoke after Finance Minister Abd al-Rahim Hamdi, who carries a reputation for sophistication and rationality, quietly sent letters to embassies asking for help with grain imports. But by late January, Hamdi's semi-private appeal remained unsupported by an overt request from the soldiers in charge. It was followed by a pledge from Beshir, delivered at a rally outside Khartoum, to "stop the relief and do away with its organizations which pursue their dubious designs."

23   The mistrust evidenced by Beshir's remark is reciprocated by the Western donors, and is compounded by their dismay over a broad range of issues. These include continued economic mismanagement and broad human rights abuses—the regime has arrested and held without charge hundreds of actual or potential opponents. The controlled press is rich in anti-Western rhetoric, which widens the gulf, as do Sudan's pro-Iraq leanings in the Gulf crisis.

24   The government's obstruction of previous relief efforts aimed at the country's non-Muslim south increases official Western reluctance to grant it the benefit of the doubt, as does its current harassment of non-governmental relief organizations. The groups, mainly well-known charities like CARE and Oxfam, have suffered attacks in the press and interference in hiring local staff, seen their directors called in for intimidating interviews with security police, and had radios essential for rural work confiscated.

25   Government missteps, like its one-month impoundment last autumn of donor and private grain alike for the ostensible purpose of performing inventory, complete an atmosphere of distaste and weariness among Western donors.

26   "We really do suffer because it's Sudan," said one aid official responsible for detaching relief funds from his capital. "Donors are not that excited about helping out here."

27   The delay caused by the sour atmosphere threatens fatal consequences, if only because of the physical difficulties of operating in Sudan. All of the envisioned 1.2 million tons of grain would have to come through the country's sole commercial port, Port Sudan, on the Red Sea. To move that amount before the next harvest, a loaded long-haul truck would need to leave the docks every 11 minutes, day and night, for nine months.

28   It's unclear whether there are enough trucks in Sudan to fill such a schedule. Those that head inland would use a road on which all but seven of 112 bridges need repairing. The pavement ends about halfway across the country, where hundreds of smaller trucks must be used to reach the western provinces where the drought is concentrated. By the end of its journey, some of the grain will have been moved more than 1,000 miles inland, to parts of Sudan that are closer to the Atlantic coast than the Red Sea.

29   If all goes well, it will take weeks to move the grain about the country. Before that, several months are needed from the time a Western capital decides to order grain until the shipments reach dockside. The daunting logistics impose an unyielding schedule: Large amounts of food must appear early in the year if the needy are to be reached in time. Yet at most 100,000 tons—one-tenth of the envisioned need—was scheduled to arrive by the end of February. During the 1984-85 famine, which killed several hundred thousand people, March was the month of peak mortality in Darfur.

30   The sluggish pace is likely to remain so, while hunger increases among people who know little beyond their fields or their village. Pessimism grows, accompanied by a forlorn hope that all the crop and market assessments and dire predictions were somehow faulty. "We can all hope and pray that the figures are wrong," said Frederick Machmer Jr., who heads the U.S. Agency for International Development's operations in Sudan. "That's our only hope now."

31   Ajuma Kookoo, who left Kordofan with her daughter and alarmingly skinny grandchild in early January and settled in a hut behind Omdurman, expresses herself more directly. Standing in the dust and squalor of the slum that is her new home, she reviews prospects for those who stayed behind: "It is known that they will die."

READING

1. How many people are at risk of starvation in Africa this year?

2. Why won't Sudan allow Western aid? Who is starving?

THINKING

1. Sudan is bankrupt, yet it says it will import the grain it needs. How could they do this when they have refused Western aid? One Sudanese intellectual said, "Declaring there is a famine is a public admission of failure, and so it doesn't exist" (¶20). What do you think about this statement?

2. In Sudan the press is tightly controlled so that the information that the public receives is only what the government wants them to know. The press is anti-Western, and the people who can read are not informed about the masses of starving people in their country. The people in the cities have enough food to get by, while the poorest of the poor have none. Do you think that this is mere government inefficiency, or do you think maybe the government is trying to solve its population problem by passively eliminating part of its people?

PREWRITING

Freewrite on the problem of hunger and starvation. What do you know of these problems in your community, your nation, and the world? How do you think these problems can be solved?

WRITING

1. Many Americans routinely contribute money to help the people starving in Africa. Even though they are honestly trying to help, the Sudanese government is still letting many of its people starve. Using the information that you read in this article, write an essay explaining why you think the Sudanese government can allow this to happen.

2. The United States has problems with hunger and starvation today. We often receive no news of these problems or receive biased news indicating that the problem are being taken care of while we can see street people living out of garbage cans in every city. Write an essay indicating what you feel should be done about the hunger problem in the United States or in your city.

REVISING

Reread paragraphs four and five in "A Tragedy in the Making." Notice the variety in sentence structure. The first sentence starts with an introductory element and is a compound sentence joined by a coordinating conjunction. The second sentence is also a compound sentence. The third sentence is complex: a dependent clause followed by an independent clause. The fourth sentence starts with an introductory element followed by an independent clause. The next sentence is a list containing long elements. And the last sentence contains a dash that is followed by powerful information. Each of these items is discussed in the revising and editing sections of this book. See the index if you need to review any of the terms.

Now look at your own writing assignments. Have you used a variety of sentence structure? Frequently a writer will fall into the pattern of using the same sentence form over and over again, or a writer may choose to write only simple sentences to avoid the possibility of making errors. If you have not used a variety of structures, try revising some of your sentences to see how they can be varied.

EDITING

Restrictive elements—clauses, phrases, or appositives—in sentences are necessary because they limit the meaning of the words they refer to so they cannot be set off by commas.

Examples:

Peasants *desperate for grain* have sold their flocks, pushing livestock prices to historic lows. (¶8)

The pride *implicit in the slogan* adds another reason to stand aloof from international efforts. (¶19)

The mistrust *evidenced by Beshir's remark* is reciprocated by the Western donors . . . (¶23)

The restrictive phrases in these three examples are necessary to make the meaning of the sentences clear so they cannot be set off with commas. For instance, all peasants have not sold their flocks, only peasants desperate for grain. And all pride doesn't add another reason, only the pride implicit in the slogan.

Check your writing assignment to see if you have used any unnecessary commas around restrictive elements. Remember that a restrictive element can be a clause, a phrase, or an appositive.

Sex After the Fall

Merle Hoffman

PREREADING

What do you think about birth control? Who should or should not use it? Why? What do you think about abortion? Why do you feel this way? What forms of birth control do you know about? What do you think is the best form of birth control? Why do you think that? What do you think about using abortion as a means of birth control?

DEFINING

uncanny (¶1)   eerie, weird, unsettling

oppression (¶3)   arbitrary and cruel exercise of power

consumerism (¶3)   the movement seeking to protect and inform the consumer

contraindications (¶3)   reasons that make medical procedures inadvisable

autonomy (¶4)   independence

arbitrary (¶7)   determined by chance or impulse as opposed to reason

pensioned (¶8)   paid a sum of money regularly as a support

erratic (¶8)   lacking consistency or regularity

paternalistic (¶8)   treating people in a fatherly manner

subsidized (¶8)   paid for

poignancy (¶9)   feelings very distressing to the mind

intelligentsia (¶9)   the intellectuals of superior status

capitalism (¶12)   an economic system where things are privately or corporately owned

clandestine (¶12)   done in secret

insulated (¶13)   isolated, prevented from exposure to

feminist (¶13)   a person who believes in equality of the sexes

catapulted (¶13)   thrust or hurled

status quo (¶14)   the current state of affairs

pragmatically (¶14)   practically, factually

groundswell (¶15)   a sudden gathering of force

coercion (¶15)   the power or ability to force people to think or act in a certain way

illusory (¶17)   deceptive, having the nature of illusion

colossus (¶21)   huge statue

hovered (¶23)   lingered, waited close by

stricture (¶23)   criticism, censure

optimum (¶23)   most favorable condition

collectivism (¶23)   system of ownership and control by people collectively

envisioned (¶26)   imagined

fanciful (¶26)   unreal

replicate (¶28)   duplicate, copy

transcendent (¶28)   supreme, surpassing others

obscure (¶28)   to conceal or hide

patriarchy (¶29)   society governed by males

propaganda (¶30)   material distributed by people advocating a cause

transfixed (¶30)   motionless, amazed

profane (¶31)   contempt for something spiritual

delegation (¶31)   a group of persons elected or appointed to represent others

liaison (¶32)   someone who works between and with two or more persons or groups

elite (¶32)   superior social class

elicited (¶34)   brought out, brought forth

Sex After the Fall

Merle Hoffman

1   In some ways my personal and political ties with Russia seem to have an uncanny quality—almost like destiny.

2   The ties began with CHOICES, the women's medical center I founded in

Merle Hoffman, "Sex After the Fall," *On the Issues,* Spring 1993, vol. xxvi, pp. 24–29. Reprinted by permission.

Please note maps in appendix for references to places in this article.

1971, and around which I've built my life and work. In the 1980s, as the immigration policies of the Soviet Union eased, masses of Russian emigrees found their way to New York and many of the women found their way to CHOICES. Counselors at the clinic would tell me that a surprising number of these women had 10, 15, and 20 previous abortions; and so we learned that abortion was the major form of birth control in the Soviet Union. For these women, the "issue" of abortion posed no questions of morality, ethics, or women's rights versus fetal life. There was only the harsh reality that sex rarely came without anxiety and that the price one often paid for it was high and dangerous. Then one day there was a 35-year-old woman who came to me for her 36th abortion. She expressed relief and some pleasure at the supportive and positive aspects of the clinic as opposed to the brutal conditions she was familiar with, but seemed quite resigned to having continued abortions. Like so many other Russian women, she was violently opposed to using birth control because she was taught by her doctor that the Pill was far more dangerous than repeat abortions, and other forms of contraception were practically unavailable.

3   Thinking about her and the conditions of her life, I began to have dreams and fantasies of going to Russia to rescue women from this brutal system of sexual oppression. Several months ago my dreams came closer to reality when two Russian feminist publishers visited New York and familiarized themselves with my work. My philosophy of informed medical consumerism, Patient Power, and the need for personal and sexual styles to be part of an individual's birth control decision astonished them. In Russia you got whatever was being pushed at the moment. If they had a stock of old fashioned spiral IUDs, that's what was dispensed. If they had high-dose estrogen pills, that's what was prescribed—regardless of any individual contraindications or preferences!

4   The two feminist publishers had dreams also: Dreams of giving Russian women dignity, autonomy, and choice—and they viewed me as the vehicle to help make those dreams a reality.

5   Two weeks after they left New York for home they faxed me an official invitation to lead a team of physicians and counselors from CHOICES to Moscow for an educational exchange. We would be meeting with gynecologists from a state-subsidized teaching hospital to demonstrate state-of-the-art women's healthcare.

6   Taking little time to say yes, three months later I was on my way to Russia with nine of my staff, carrying visions of being a pioneer and of changing their world.

7   As the plane began its nine-and-a-half hour flight, I recalled a different time 10 years earlier when I first traveled to Russia. I was with a friend who was familiar with the culture; she begged me to take a suitcase full of contraceptives: pills, diaphragms, condoms—anything. My concerns about arbitrarily distributing hormonal medication and diaphragms which would not be fitted by physicians were laughed off. "They need anything and everything they can get." After learning that the two most popular forms of birth control were douching with lemon juice, and jumping off ice boxes if periods were late, I stuffed my bags full.

8   Now, here I was again—in Moscow. My hosts had arranged for us to stay in a pre-revolutionary mansion called Perendelkina that now functions as a government artist colony where pensioned writers and old artists retire. Perendelkina is in

a so-called "green zone" 20 minutes outside of central Moscow, and boasts the grave of Boris Pasternack. As I walked the carpeted halls, with fading old Persian rugs buckling under my feet, I could hear the muted sounds of typewriters. These writers seemed content and secure in their work, but, in general, very little works properly in Russia at this time. At Perendelkina, the phone system is primitive and erratic. For a complex of 100 rooms there is only one outside line which often crosses wires with a private home. Getting anything done is always a matter of extreme negotiation. My hosts told me that despite the fall of communism many people are not ready for a "market economy." Most Russians did not work hard under the old system because the paternalistic state took care of everything—housing, healthcare, and vacations were subsidized. Now they can't imagine why they have to work harder to get paid more. It seems that everyone wants to feel and use the only power they really have—the power to say no. Everything is a struggle; at least one to two hours a day are spent negotiating and navigating just to be able to get from one place to another—or trying to find a phone that works.

9   Our first lunch at Perendelkina combined politics and poignancy. Apologizing for the country's economic crisis, an attentive staff served us a meal of boiled eggs, bread, cheese, squash, and oatmeal. In the evening we were taken to an extraordinary banquet at the Artist Guild. The hall is a famous meeting place for intellectuals, artists and writers of the Russian intelligentsia. Oak-beamed walls and ornate glass chandeliers were the background to a pianist playing Chopin and Rachmaninoff with an occasional American favorite like "Feelings" thrown in.

10   I was aware as I looked at the table spread out with cavier, lox, sturgeon, and vodka that my hosts had gone to unusual expense and time to produce this. The dinner continued for hours with each one of us in turn rising to propose a toast, then drinking our vodka "to the end." One of my hosts rose and expressed her gratitude for my coming and for the chance to exchange ideas. She asserted that the country needs women to take it in hand and lead it out of crisis.

11   There was an easy affection, an ability to touch and to connect with each other's eyes and energies without the need for continual translation—and there was also a strange tension and excitement in the air. As I looked about me I saw that people had broken up into small groups and were discussing potential business deals—everybody was hustling!

12   There was a keen awareness that with the fall of communism people were able, indeed, desired, to show creativity and entrepreneurial spirit. One person rose to toast capitalism—and I found myself saying "Yes, capitalism, but capitalism with a conscience!" The next day brought meetings and interviews. I spoke with Dr. George Kavkassidze, who specializes in infertility, which has reached epidemic proportions in Russia. He was eager to assist with the creation of a women's health center where there could be pregnancy testing, counseling, and state-of-the-art abortion care. I learned that there are practically no pregnancy tests available in Russia; that by the time many women find that they are pregnant they are well within their second trimester. If they are to receive a state-sponsored abortion at no cost, they must have the approval of three physicians, including a psychiatrist. Because most women cannot, and will not, navigate this difficult bureaucracy, most

opt for "clandestine abortions," done in their homes by state gynecologists eager to earn extra money. The unsanitary and dangerous conditions result in many teenagers and young women becoming sterile.

13   Most of the women that I spoke with seemed to be insulated from feminist thought and the feminist movement as we know it in the United States. They continually referred to me as Miss or Mrs. Hoffman and one of my staff corrected them and wrote out "Ms." "But is she married or single?" I explained that yes, I am married but that it is not necessary that my marital status be public—and they loved it! It was as if I were catapulted back 20 years to the dawn of the women's movement, remembering the "clicks of consciousness," the constant explosion of insights.

14   An interesting thought then occurred to me. There is no word for "counseling" in the Russian system, because they don't perceive a need for it. Abortion is not only the status quo, but the only choice the majority of women have to control their fertility. There is no organized opposition on religious or moral grounds (although there is a growing right-to-life presence in Moscow), and women regard their multiple abortions pragmatically, as just a way of "getting cleaned out." Abortion is not a major moral crisis for Russian women—it's just life.

15   If I bring in the concepts of "choice" and "responsibility," the need for women to think deeply about birth control and abortion, the need even for counseling prior to abortion, will I be adding to an antiabortion groundswell? Will I inadvertently be introducing anxiety or guilt to an already overburdened and oppressed female population? After all, the slogan of many prochoice activists in the U.S., "Abortion on demand and without apology," is a reality in Russia. Russian women have abortions on demand—on request really—no apologies needed because there are no other choices. But because there are no other choices, abortion has little to do with freedom and privacy and much to do with oppression and coercion. As in most societies, women's health and women's lives are not a high priority for the Russian government.

16   The day of the Educational Symposium, I awoke with an intense feeling of excitement. This was the day I would make my presentation and challenge the assembled feminist physicians and journalists to create a truly revolutionary society—a society where women's lives really count for something.

17   At the symposium, I spoke of how reproductive freedom must be the bottom line of women's autonomy. If a woman cannot decide when, or whether, to bear children, the other choices in her life are diminished. The availability of legal and safe abortion is critical to her health and quality of life. But, it is not enough. Without full information about all reproductive and sexual issues, access to abortion is an illusory freedom.

18   I stressed what I know to be true in the most personal and political sense, that "there is no choice without knowledge. If we accept that the exercise of free will defines what it is to be moral and fully human, then women who lack the information to make choices will be destined to remain second-class citizens."

19   The speech was received extremely well. The audience was intense, like sponges soaking up every word. Most interesting, I found a piece of antiabortion

literature on a chair as I left the hall. It was exactly the same propaganda that the antichoicers thrust into the hands of patients every day at CHOICES—except that it has been translated into Russian and printed in Alaska. I had to laugh; in a strange way, it made me feel right at home. It also reinforced a truth I have always known: The war against women's freedom is global and has no boundaries.

20   Along with translated literature, T-shirts, and magazines, I had brought 7,000 condoms with me to distribute after the presentations. Suddenly, the well-dressed professional journalists, feminists, and physicians turned into a swarming mob. We were surrounded and pushed and shoved as a frenzy of hands reached out to grab the condoms. I was left breathless and amazed.

21   While condoms are the only birth control method produced and sold in Russia, they are not highly utilized. Most are substandard and break easily—and the strength of the "macho" myth prevents many men from even using them. I think of the enormous statue of Yuri Gagarin, the first man in space. It stands like a colossus overlooking the main thoroughfare in Moscow. How a society with the technology to conquer space cannot find its way to produce an adequate rubber speaks volumes about its priorities, and the primacy of politics over reason.

22   I was still recovering from the onslaught of grasping hands, when I found my way to the ladies' room. I was with my translator, who was part of my staff, and with whom, before leaving for Russia, I had practiced a few phrases like "Women of the World Unite." We were saying it together and laughing as an old lady came in to clean. Listening to us she asked, "Unite? What do they want to unite for? And if they unite, what will they do?" Looking at her and picturing my mother saying, "Are you playing Joan of Arc again?" I said, "Well, maybe we will make the world a little bit better place." "Okay," she said resignedly as she went off with her bucket and pail.

23   The next day my staff was scheduled to perform abortions and Norplant inserts at the state teaching hospital, Gynecological Hospital #53. It would be historic: the first time Norplant would be inserted into Russian women, and the first time abortions would be performed with state-of-the-art technology. We had brought equipment, machinery and drugs with us that had never been imported to Russia. The entire hospital was on full alert. There were approximately 25 people in the operating room where CHOICES physicians would be giving a demonstration. Students of anesthesia, gynecology residents, and the administrative staff of the hospital hovered around the operating room tables. The patients were brought in in their own nightgowns because of the shortages of paper and supplies. Fashions ranged from plain flannel to see-through red lingerie. The women's stoicism and seeming lack of modesty amazed me—even more so when I remembered that these are women who were taught to be so ashamed of their bodies that they were not permitted to mention the word menstruation in mixed company. It's a dangerous form of modesty that I've seen lead to medical and sexual problems. Of the small amount of birth control available, out-of-date spiral IUDs are the most commonly used (by 5 percent of the population). But because of the social stricture against openly acknowledging menstruation, women are too embarrassed to go to their gynecologists during their periods, the optimum time when IUDs should be

inserted. As a result they are often left infected and infertile. Yet, there in the operating room there was no observable modesty, and absolutely no concept of privacy or patient dignity. The collectivism of this society even extends to the medical sphere where it is not uncommon to see four or five abortions performed in the same room at the same time. The women did not notice the large audience as they obediently lifted their gowns above their waists. It is just the way life is here, and they deal with it: they place themselves on the table and follow orders.

24   I looked at their faces and into their eyes. What I saw there were the thousands of women before them whose hands I'd held. We are all sisters.

     The staff at the hospital was extraordinary—eager to learn—eager to please—eager to participate with me in a joint capitalist venture. The abortions cost 900 rubles, which equals $3.00—less than the cost of a McDonald's hamburger and about one week's average salary.

25   The next day brought a meeting at the Russian Family Planning Association; it was to produce an historic feminist act. Formed nine months earlier and existing on donations and government subsidies, the Association is the major voice in Russia calling for a reasoned and intelligent family planning program. The director, Inga Grebesheva, famous for being the "only woman deputy" of the Central Committee of the Communist Party, told me she became a feminist when, at party meetings, her colleagues began to refer to her as the "woman minister." She recognized that they had never thought of her in relation to her work or her title, but only to her gender.

26   Grebesheva, having produced one film on the horrifying state of abortion care, was raising funds which she hoped would educate people further on the Russian abortion system. She envisioned producing 12 hours of tape of individual women telling about their abortion experiences. It seems that having 15, 20, or even 30 abortions does not equal coming to terms with it. Most women are ashamed to talk about their abortions, and doctors, with their fanciful prescription for birth control, do not help them break the silence: They tell them if they worked harder, they would not have time to think about sex and, therefore, would not get pregnant.

27   My mind immediately flashed to all the soap box actions I had arranged in the American abortion wars—all the "My name is Joan or Ruth or Karen, and I've had an abortion"—feedback that led me to the knowledge of how important it is for women to own that experience.

28   When I suggested to Grebesheva that we replicate this in Red Square, she loved the idea but said, "Our Russian women do not yet have the courage for this." But the energy in that room was so strong and driving, I urged them to do something *now*. The result was a decision to draft an open letter to Boris Yeltsin outlining the grave conditions of women's healthcare and demanding economic funding for birth control and education. When I asked Grebesheva if she could have it done by the next day so that leading feminists at the Feminist Round Table where I would be speaking could sign it, she smiled "I've been writing it in my head for four years," she said. This was one of those transcendent connections, the times when you meet someone—a group of women—and you know that the different

languages and different realities cannot obscure the one reality—that we are all struggling with the same issues and the same problems.

29   The next afternoon brought over 30 feminists together to share information at a "Feminist Round Table." Writers, scientists, journalists, and representatives from governmental agencies engaged in lively dialogue. A self-described radical feminist made the distinction between women who were part of the "women's movement," and women who called themselves feminists. Women who were part of the women's movement believed in a philosophy of "women are people, too," whereas feminists wanted to change the patriarchy. I asked whether it was the difference between being a liberal and a radical, and she said it was much greater than that. Another raised her voice to say that it didn't matter what women called themselves, "all women are feminists and fighting for the same thing."

30   And still others said that they never thought of using the word sisterhood, that the concept was always one of "brotherhood." Women never considered themselves unequal or oppressed because they believed the propaganda fed to them by the communists—that men and women were truly equal. At that point, Grebesheva came into the room and, not taking time to remove her coat, proceeded to read the letter she had drafted to Yeltsin. I watched the faces—pleasure, pride, anger, anxiety. Some got up to sign, some left the room and some watched transfixed. A feminist movement begins?

31   The mixture of the spiritual and profane surrounded me. Lunch in a Moscow hotel had me sitting next to a young couple who held hands across the table, had their eyes closed tightly and mumbled under their breaths. This went on for about five minutes, and I realized that they had been praying. As the young man left the table, the woman turned to me and started a conversation. It seemed that they were missionaries; Evangelical Christians who had been in Moscow one year and had started their own church on October Street. "This is extremely fertile ground for gathering new souls," she told me as she searched her handbag for prayer cards. "Now that communism is dead, their spiritual hunger can be fed." In Moscow I saw advertisements for Billy Graham's Crusade and remembered the delegation of Bible students who shared my plane ride over. Souls are a new growing market, ripe for the picking.

32   Conversations in the hotel leapt into my memory. They continued to affirm that the personal is the political. The one with Maya, for instance, a Russian chemist who was my liaison, who stated, "You can build a clinic for the elite. We can treat women who are part of the government or married to high government officials." I explained that I would have no part of that—my clinic would offer the highest quality care to all women regardless of who they were. Fees would be based on an ability to pay, so that if there were any profit to be made it would not be made off the backs of the poor. Maya listened to me with amazement and said, "But that is not what we do here—you must be a Christian." I replied, "No, I'm a Jew and the Jews taught before Jesus (who was also a Jew) about equality and social justice." Maya informed me that she knew nothing of Judaism because it was so suppressed. She also told me she had been taught that "Capitalism is cruel."

33   Then, there was Svetlana, a dark-eyed Russian journalist, who was writing a newspaper piece on my visit. We had gotten into a discussion about Stalin's criminalization of abortion, when she put down her pen and said quietly, "You know, there was some good in what Stalin did. If he had not criminalized abortion, I would not be here." I responded that Stalin's motivation was to populate Russia with soldiers to counteract Hitler's rising militarism. Certainly, encouraging the birth of girl children was not part of the equation. Nevertheless, she still thought it was a good thing because she would not have been here.

34   I was being moved and challenged on all counts. So much of myself elicited through these extraordinary meetings—so much to give back.

35   Now, once again in New York, I think frequently of Moscow and recent reports of street demonstrations calling for the return of communism. I worry that the driving need for security may indeed stamp out the sense of risk, the desire for growth, and the seductive pull of freedom that this new era has ushered in. I think of the women I met, the energy, the drive, and the vision for a better life—of the new society that is being created: One where women can have a hand and a voice, one where they have the opportunity to create, to make a true revolution, to make their world a place where a woman's life really matters.

READING

1. What is the most common form of birth control in Russia? Why is it so widely used?

2. How do most Russian women view sexuality and reproduction? Why do they have this attitude?

THINKING

1. Were you surprised or shocked about the attitudes of women in Russia towards sex and birth control? How do their attitudes differ from how you feel? What do you think Russian women should do about their situation? Do you think they can make changes? Why or why not?

2. A Russian chemist said that she had been taught that "Capitalism is cruel" (¶32). She had been raised with Communism in Russia. Do you know the difference between capitalism and communism? If not, look up these terms and think about which one seems more logical to you. Which way would you rather live? Why?

PREWRITING

Make two lists. The first list should have the pros of the abortion issue, the second should have the cons. Make two more lists. One should have the reasons you like to live in America, and the other should have the reasons you would like to live in Russia.

WRITING

1. Most people have strong feelings about abortion, either for or against. Write an essay to share with your classmates in which you explain your feelings toward abortion. First, write a thesis statement where you clearly state your position. As you write, be objective. Use specific examples. Base your argument on facts.

2. Write an essay explaining why you like to live in America or why you would prefer to live in Russia. Be specific. Give detailed reasons with examples of why you want to live the way you're writing about.

REVISING

In "Sex After the Fall," Merle Hoffman uses many examples of how the women in Russia live. Which examples do you like best? Why? Do the examples she chooses make her writing easier to understand? Why or why not?

How many examples have you used in your writing exercise? Are they fully developed? Do you think that your writing for this assignment would be better if you used only one big example or do you think that this assignment requires several, smaller examples? Experiment with your assignment to see what works best for the effect you are trying to create.

EDITING

A **semicolon** can be used effectively to join two closely related independent clauses. This is a technique that sometimes works to correct a comma splice or a fused sentence.

Example:

"Everything is a struggle; at least one or two hours each day are spent negotiating and navigating just to be able to get from one place to the other. . . ."(¶8)

Notice how the ideas in the two independent clauses relate to each other. Go through your writing assignment to see if there are any simple sentences that you could join with a semicolon to make your writing clearer. Remember, as with all special techniques, don't use too many semicolons—even if you use them all correctly.

Color-Blind Parents vs. Color-Coded Rules

John J. Raasch

PREREADING

What do you think about adoption? Would you adopt a child who is of a different race from yours or who is a mixture of races? Why or why not? Do you know anyone who is adopted? How do they feel about being adopted? Do you think children should be placed for adoption in homes where the parents are of a different race than the child?

DEFINING

pseudonym (¶1)   a fictitious or phony name

amidst (¶1)   surrounded by

theology (¶1)   the study of the nature of God

transracial (¶2)   across two races, as a European couple adopting an African-American child

bicultural (¶3)   from two cultures

exclusion (¶3)   prevention from being included

altruistic (¶4)   unselfishly concerned for the welfare of others

transcend (¶4)   rise above

bigotry (¶4)   the attitude of one strongly partial to one's own group

devalue (¶9)   lessen the value of

exaggerated (¶9)   to enlarge or increase the value of

contrived (¶12)   invented artificially

Kunta Kinte (¶12)   main character in Alex Haley's novel *Roots*

misinterpreted (¶13)   interpreted incorrectly

Afrocentrism (¶16)   believing in the superiority of African-Americans

exclusivity (¶16)   excluding some, not sharing

underutilization (¶17)   not using adequately

disservice (¶17)   harmful action

languish (¶19)   exist in miserable conditions, remain neglected

disarray (¶19)   a state of confusion

dynamics (¶20)   the social forces that produce change

infertility (¶20)   inability to get pregnant

rhetoric (¶22)   use of language

respondents (¶34)   the people who respond

equate (¶35)   to consider as equal to

abound (¶37)   to be great in number

affiliated (¶40)   associated with

implementation (¶41)   to put into effect

prevailing (¶44)   the most common or frequent

dilemma (¶48)   a situation that requires a choice between options that are equally unfavorable

Color-Blind Parents vs. Color-Coded Rules

John J. Raasch

1   After the Nolans (a pseudonym) applied to adopt a special-needs child, the private New Jersey adoption agency approached them with a nine-month-old African-American baby girl.

Both Europeans, the Nolans had recently returned from the South Pacific. Their family had lived amidst a black culture there, and they thought their two young sons could accept an African-American sister. Working at that time on his Ph.D. in theology and having a personal interest in race relations, Dr. Nolan says he and his wife felt equipped to parent an African-American child.

2   That was 25 years ago, and though neither of the Nolans regrets the decision to adopt transracially, both wonder if transracial adoption really works. "The arrangement was hard on the whole family," Dr. Nolan recalls. African-American and European friends alike told them they didn't approve, strangers called them

John J. Raasch, "Color-Blind Parents vs. Color-Coded Rules," *Image,* October 1994, p. 341. Reprinted by permission.

Please note maps in appendix for references to places in this article.

"nigger lovers," and a woman from their church angrily accused Dr. Nolan of being "too liberal." From some people their family drew looks of curiosity; from others, "downright hate."

3   In an effort to create a bicultural environment, the Nolans chose integrated churches and schools, sought out Black friends, and had African-American art and literature in their home. Still, they couldn't protect their daughter, Esther, from exclusion by Europeans or from rejection by African-Americans when they found out she had White parents. She rebelled as a teenager and later became a single mother. With all the pressure on kids today, Dr. Nolan says, the racial difference "added one more burden." Esther moved to the inner city to find her roots, learned "black" English, then moved to a European community where she felt more comfortable. "She's still trying to work through it," says Dr. Nolan.

4   With their altruistic motives and idealistic worldview, the Nolans were not un-like many others who rode the first wave of transracial adoptions in this country. Previously a service to provide childless European couples with healthy newborn European infants, adoption began to open up during the civil-rights movement of the 1960s. Many European families pursued transracial adoption, hoping to tran-scend barriers of race by becoming integrated. Through their children they felt a kinship to the African-American community and sincerely believed that their ef-forts could move race relations forward. These families expected bigotry and rejec-tion from Europeans, but did not expect public outcry from the African-American community.

5   At the same time, another movement was taking place. African-American people were beginning to take pride in being African-American and wanted to control their own destinies. "For a people who have always taken pride in the care of their children, the transracial adoption movement was an attack on one of the few sources of pride in our history," says Sydney Duncan, Director of Homes for Black Children, in Detroit.

6   These two movements clashed in 1972, when the National Association of Black Social Workers (NABSW) issued a formal statement opposing transracial adoption, calling it a form of "cultural genocide," provoking a debate that has raged for more than two decades. Following the statement by the NABSW, transracial adoptions de-clined sharply, from over 2,500 in 1971 to under 1,000 the following year. In the years that followed, some agencies began to favor race-matching policies.

7   Many adoption workers agreed that African-American children would be best served by being placed with African-American families. Some feared that an African-American child could not be protected in this society without the help of a family of like race. They worried that, uprooted from his heritage, he would have everything uniquely African-American about him replaced by white cultural norms and values, and the black community would be the lesser for it. They were con-cerned about what he might think of himself if he believed his own kind didn't want him or didn't have the resources to take him in, or if his image of African-American people depended upon the media or limited and confusing contact with African-Americans. Exposure to African-American culture, they argued, is not the same as living it.

8   Other adoption workers questioned the value of allowing children to remain in foster care until a same-race family was located, if an eligible family of another race was available. They cited reports of children being uprooted and parents prevented from adopting due to race, even when bonded to a child.

9   Research has provided ammunition for both sides of the debate. Many studies indicate that transracial adoption does not have a measurable effect on a child's self-esteem or personal identity. One of those, a notable series of studies by Rita Simon and Howard Altstein, follows several transracial adoptees and their families over time. In contrast, the research of Ruth McRoy and others at the University of Texas at Austin, studying transracially versus same-race adopted children, has shown racial identity to be "more of a problem for the African-American children who were being reared by European families." In particular, African-American children tend to devalue or not acknowledge an African-American identity if their white parents de-emphasize racial identity and make no efforts to provide African-American role models. Such children have been found to have stereotyped impressions of African-Americans and exaggerated feelings of "differentness." Still other studies have found that the older a child is when adopted transracially, the deeper will be the effects of these problems.

10   Interviews with the children of those early transracial adoptions, now adults, have failed to resolve the debate. While many have reported confusion ranging from mild to extreme, some acknowledged that the arrangement was advantageous, exposing them to both European and African-American cultures.

11   David Watts was adopted at age two by a European family. Half African-American and half European, Watts admits that the "equipment" given to him by his white family allows him to move more easily in society "because I understand that side of it. But that doesn't help me personally." Now 27, with a master's degree in psychology, Watts says his struggles over his racial and personal identities have outweighed any advantages.

12   Watts remembers some of his parents' efforts to encourage his racial identity—like visiting African-American friends and going to an African-American church—as feeling contrived and "uncomfortable." When he was called "nigger" and "Kunta Kinte" in grade school, his parents told him the namecallers had the problem, not he. But talking with European parents after being called names by European classmates felt "isolating," he says, because he didn't feel they could relate. African-American parents, Watts feels, could have shared their own stories of being called names. Even if they said nothing, he feels it would have been a comfort to go home to someone who looked like him. Watts's experiences led him to conclude that white parents can't help black children deal with racism.

13   Further, Watts feels living in a European family can be dangerous to an African-American child if he learns to expect acceptance from the European community. "If I'm going to be identified as an African-American man by the police, I need to know what that means. If I get out of the car and walk toward [them], it could be misinterpreted as aggression due to misconceptions and assumptions about African-American men." Last year such an incident occurred and Watts knew how to handle it, knowledge he attributes to his recent involvement in New

York City's black community. Watts also discovered in that community a comfort level he hadn't known before. "People understood what I had gone through; there was a whole community of people who knew about oppression," he says.

14   Sandi Ililonga was legally freed for adoption at age 2½ and lived in 10 foster homes and two orphanages before she was adopted transracially at age 12½. Ililonga believes waiting in foster care for a racially matched family can do more damage to a child than transracial adoption. "Ethnic identity means absolutely nothing to a child who belongs to nobody," she says. Of African-American, European, and Indigenous-American descent, Ililonga describes herself as multiethnic. Seeing white children being adopted, she thought she was bad, or not cute enough. "If being Black meant no one would adopt me, I didn't want to be Black."

15   Even after being adopted, she wanted to be a European child, and didn't have a black identity. Her adoptive parents shared African-American culture with her nonetheless and introduced her to people in the civil-rights movement. She remembers her awkwardness at introducing her Black Panther boyfriend to her parents, but says her parents let her be who she had to be, which included being a "strong Black woman."

16   Ililonga feels qualified to talk about transracial adoption because, at 40, she is old enough to know "who I am, what I want, and where I fit." And she is vocal on the subject, likening race-matching policies to apartheid. "Afrocentrism is not cool with me. Exclusivity is not cool with me," she says. "My skin color doesn't give me special insight. We only know what we learn, and you don't have to match skin color to teach."

17   Everyone goes through a period of searching, Ililonga says, and our sense of self becomes clearer through experience. She sees transracial adoptees' issues as different, but not more difficult. The underutilization of transracial adoption, in her estimation, does waiting African-American children a disservice: "We shouldn't punish children for what the system is lacking." Ililonga questions whether she would have lived this long if she hadn't been adopted. "When I was adopted, I was committed to for the rest of my life. I had a chance to grow, blossom, and become the real me." For her, a *real* family is one where everyone looks different. "We are the American dream," she says.

18   Today, because there are nearly 500,000 children in foster care nationwide, the debate has taken on a new urgency. Supporters of transracial adoption blame race-matching policies for the backlog in foster care. They call such policies "unfortunate" and "unconstitutional," and they doubt there are enough African-American families to adopt all the African-American children who need homes.

19   Joe Kroll is President of the North American Council on Adoptable Children (NACAC), made up mostly of Whites who have adopted transracially and now support same-race placements. Kroll feels the media distorts the argument when they blame racial matching policies for *all* the children being in foster-care. "Most children languish in foster care because of the disarray in that system," he says, "not because workers are trying to place children with families of the same race." Moreover, while the foster care population went from 276,000 to 450,000 between 1986 and 1993, the number of children freed for adoption increased only from 30,000 to 35,000.

20   Leora Neal, of the Child Adoption Counseling and Referral Service in New York, adds that approximately half the children in foster care are European, but they are not the children European families want. "They want healthy babies under two years of age," she says. And they would rather adopt an infant of another race than an older, same-race child. This is another example of how transracial adoption dynamics have changed. European families adopting African-American children in the 1960s were part of the civil-rights movement, hoping racism would end if families became integrated. Now, according to Neal, European couples wish to adopt African-American children due to infertility.

21   The status of foster parents has also changed. Rarely considered in the past, foster parents are now given primary consideration as potential adopters. When a "bond" is thought to exist with the foster parents, courts are reluctant to move a child. If a child is not placed in a same-race home initially, this policy comes into direct conflict with race matching.

22   Zena Oglesby questions the attachment and bonding rhetoric used in support of giving foster parents first preference. Oglesby is the Director of the Institute for Black Parenting (IBP) in Los Angeles, a licensed adoption and foster family agency. "The research on bonding supports the idea that a child who *hasn't* attached or bonded to a caretaker is the one who needs to be left where he is. A child with healthy attachment can reattach," he says.

23   NACAC supports adoption by foster parents who have provided long-term care. They add, however, that the foster care system needs to be community-based, utilizing families and resources within the children's communities of origin.

24   Carol Coccia is a member of Michigan's National Coalition to End Racism in America's Child Care System, which supports transracial adoption. Coccia states that most transracial adoptions occur as foster parent adoptions, where an attachment already exists. She agrees that more African-American foster parents should be recruited, to avoid problems if the child is later freed for adoption.

25   Many states give consideration in the foster or adoptive placement of a child first to relatives, second to a family of the same racial/ethnic heritage as the child, and last to a family from the broader community. Those opposed to transracial adoption support such measures, but are concerned that language supporting race matching has softened in some states. Texas, for example, recently enacted a law requiring race to be given no greater weight than any other factor in adoptive placements.

26   On the flip side, Carol Coccia objects to certain states' vague and inaccurate policies. Nebraska's policy, she says, refers to "identity problems" that will result if a child is not placed with a same-race family. Coccia, citing Simon and Altstein's studies, holds that this assumption is not supported by research. Additionally, the Nebraska policy states that children should "preferably" not wait longer than six months for a same-race home.

27   Coccia and others opposed to race-matching policies criticize a bill currently before the U.S. Senate because it puts no limit on the time that children can be held for same-race placement. Co-sponsored by Senators Howard Metzenbaum and Carol Moseley-Braun, the Multi-Ethnic Placement Act of 1993 threatens with-

drawal of federal assistance to foster care or adoption agencies that "unduly delay or deny the placement of a child . . . solely because of the race, color, or national origin of the adoptive or foster parent or parents or the child."

28   Those who strongly favor same-race placements fear the withdrawal of federal funds could weaken minority agencies and hamper efforts to recruit ethnic families by making it easier for adoption workers to take whatever family is accessible.

29   Coccia believes stronger language prohibiting the delay of placements for racial matching purposes would actually step up recruitment efforts. She points to Michigan's 1985 Quinn decree, which set a 45-day limit on the time allotted to search for a same-race family. After it was enacted, says Coccia, recruitment efforts increased because workers knew an ethnically diverse pool of applicants was needed to make same-race placements quickly.

30   Leora Neal contends time limits are of no use unless agencies are required to document efforts to find African-American families. They currently are not. With such a requirement, Neal feels, transracial placements would be unnecessary. "Minority-run agencies have no problem finding Black parents for black children," she says. "White agencies just don't have—and in some cases don't want—access to the Black community. It is easier to place with White families."

31   Coccia argues that state licensing laws requiring agencies to document search efforts *are* in effect. She questions whether there are enough African-American families to adopt all the African-American children available. In Detroit, she notes, the population is 80% black, and they have never had enough black families.

32   Sandi Ililonga also doubts there are enough African-American families to adopt all the children who are considered African-American, which may include bi- or multiracial children like herself. She worries that standards are lowered or overlooked to allow more African-American families to adopt, placing African-American children at risk and sending the dangerous message that "these white children deserve this [level of care], but you're black, so you have to settle for this [lower level]."

33   Zena Oglesby says standards aren't lowered—and can't be—because they are set by the state. He asserts that the explanation for a shortage of African-American families is that minority families have been denied equal access to traditional agencies. He says the child welfare system is "racist by default" in that it was designed by European people at a time when only European people were adopting and hasn't changed to meet the needs of a new cultural mix. "It doesn't matter what color the workers are today because the problems are systemic." The shortage of African-American families, says Oglesby, is false.

34   Oglesby's view is supported by a finding of NACAC's 1990 national survey that 83% of respondents from child placement agencies said they were aware of institutional barriers that discourage families of color from adopting. Oglesby points also to *Transracial Adoptees and Their Families,* Simon and Altstein's book in which they discuss two recent National Urban League studies showing that out of 800 African-American families applying to adopt, only two families, or 0.25 percent, were approved—compared to a national average of 10 percent. Also cited in the book are findings of a study published in the *NASW* (National Association of Social Workers) *News* in April 1984 that show 40-50% of black families sampled would consider adoption.

35   Primary reasons for the shortage of approved African-American adoptive homes in spite of the willingness among African-Americans to adopt include (1) lack of recruitment in the African-American community, (2) suspicion of public agencies among many African-Americans, and (3) fees and financial concerns. Also cited are differences in mind-sets between African-Americans and Europeans. Some African-Americans equate paying an adoption fee with buying a child, finding it distasteful in light of the history of slavery. Also, childless European couples seek out adoption agencies, but most African-American families who adopt already have children, and hence more effort is needed to reach them. Furthermore, informal adoption is common in African-American culture, and agencies' formal processes can be cumbersome and seem unnecessary.

36   Agencies specializing in same-race placement of minority children have been successful in overcoming these obstacles. The NACAC survey found that such agencies placed 94 percent of their black children in same-race homes, while traditional private agencies did so only half the time. Moreover, the minority children placed through public and specializing agencies were often older or had special needs, and still they were placed with same-race families at higher rates than healthy infants placed by traditional agencies. Based on their research, NACAC recommends that agencies committed to same-race placement focus on (1) recruitment and retention of ethnic families, (2) simplifying the "home-study" process whereby families become approved to adopt, and (3) reducing or eliminating fees.

37   Successful African-American agencies abound. Operating in the way NACAC suggests, Oglesby's IBP has streamlined its home-study process and doesn't charge a fee. It utilizes the federal Adoption Assistance Program, through which ethnic children classified as having "special needs" are often eligible for financial assistance. The agency has over 100 African-American families being studied at any given time. Homes for Black Children, a similar agency, recently placed 132 African-American children in African-American homes in one year, more than the other 13 child welfare agencies in Detroit combined. The Chicago-based One Church, One Child, with offices in 37 states, has helped place over 40,000 African-American children in African-American homes nationwide in the past 13 years.

38   NACAC stresses the need for increased state funding of recruitment and retention programs, as well as ongoing support. Sydney Duncan, of Homes for Black Children, also calls for increased funding of black agencies. She says that solutions for Anglo-American children who need families would not be sought in the African-American community—yet most public funding for adoption services is invested in training white staff to serve black children, rather than investing in the African-American community and its agencies. "When the African-American community is appropriately permitted to be involved in the adoption needs of African-American children, the most significant barrier to their being adopted will be removed and the problem solved," says Duncan.

39   Everyone in the adoption community seems to agree on one point: African-American families are the best option for African-American children. To this end, new and creative ways of meeting the needs of ethnic children are being explored.

40   In an effort to make more appropriate first placements of children in foster care, Los Angeles County's Department of Children's Services implemented the Vacancy Control Office two years ago. This system gives social workers access to all ethnic homes available in the foster care system, as well as those affiliated with private foster family agencies.

41   In a similar effort, Orange County Adoptions in Southern California has implemented a new orientation program to help prospective foster and adoptive parents decide from the outset whether they wish to provide foster care, adopt, or combine the two. Workers can then match children with families earlier and more appropriately.

42   Even with such efforts, recruitment remains a vital need. Oglesby sees partnerships between traditional agencies and community-based organizations, such as the Urban League, as one creative solution. "You don't have to be Black to recruit in the Black community," he says.

43   Even African-American families that cannot be foster or adoptive parents can be involved. In Oregon, for instance, One Church, One Child started the Building Bridges program, which links African-American children to their community by putting African-American families in touch with European families that have adopted African-American children. In Maine the NAACP helped a small adoption agency link up with African-American families to provide a similar service. The child and both families can benefit from such an arrangement. African-American adults can serve African-American children who are stranded in the system through the Big Brothers and Big Sisters programs.

44   Even if same-race placements become the prevailing policy, exceptions will arise. It is reasonable to expect that transracial adoption will continue. For European families who have already adopted transracially, support is available from agencies such as NACAC. For European families considering transracial adoption, Carol Coccia's organization has a "parenting assessment guide" to help families decide. Dr. Nolan would advise such families that transracial adoption can only work "if done with love and caution." He would remind adoptive parents that they have to be committed, that they will never be anonymous again, that some people won't like them, and that it could cause trouble for the child.

45   Most agencies that support transracial adoption as an alternative to foster care recognize that European families adopting an African-American child need to be sensitive to the child's culture. Says Coccia, "We must ask: If we are making transracial placements, how can we make them well? This always means starting from the needs of a child. Maybe an African-American child has medical needs and an European family lives near the medical services that are needed. Maybe a child has Down's syndrome and won't ever be aware of her race, but she will be aware if the person she knows as her mother is taken away." The environment is also important, she says; living in Detroit would be different from living in a predominantly European rural town.

46   Transracial adoptee David Watts suggests that white families should be involved in the African-American community before considering adopting a African-American child. This way, their efforts to become involved in the African-

American community won't be a change for the family or seem contrived to the child.

47   Ultimately, the struggle has caused the greatest pain for the African-American children who have been adopted transracially. Says Sydney Duncan, "Any time adults argue about children, it has to threaten their security; if someone is arguing about the rightness of your home, that is the ultimate threat."

48   Duncan stresses that there is no danger in people seeking sincere and honest answers to the dilemma of African-American children in need of homes. Rather, a child is endangered "when policies that are intended to give direction to service are followed rigidly and without thought for [the child's] individual situation and circumstances."

49   Duncan says each person must answer the transracial adoption question for himself. "We can never solve conflict so long as we remain immersed in it. Our only solution is to rise above it."

50   Duncan hopes that "through understanding we can free ourselves of the struggles about the rightness of transracial adoption; that through understanding each other, and for the sake of the children who are caught in the middle, we can build a bridge that will allow us to transcend our differences, allow us to renew our dreams, and work together for the sake of the children."

READING

1. Are there enough African-American families to adopt all the African-American children eligible for adoption?

2. How many children are in foster care nationwide? Why are there so many?

THINKING

1. Think about what it would be like to have a foster child in your home. Would you like to have one? Why or why not? What kinds of challenges do you think you would need to face if you had a foster child? What kind of a child would you want?

2. What do you think about placing children in homes different from their ethnic origin? Did your attitude toward this change after you read "Color-Blind Parents vs. Color-Coded Rules"? Why or why not?

PREWRITING

Make a list of all of the things you think are required to make a good adoptive parent and a good adoptive family. Include as many things as you can possibly think about.

WRITING

1. Write a paper to share with your classmates arguing for or against same race placement for adoption. Be sure to clearly identify your argument in your thesis statement. Use facts and statistics from the article to back up your argument, but be sure the paper is your opinion as opposed to just restating what John J. Raasch said.

2. Imagine that you are a twelve-year-old child in need of an adoptive home. Write a letter to the social services agency handling your case describing the kind of parents you would like to be placed with. Be sure to explain your reasoning.

REVISING

One of the biggest problems students have with writing is allowing enough time to do a good job. With so many students having to work while they attend college, being organized is vital. At the beginning of each quarter or semester, you should get a copy of the syllabus or course outline for each class. Then get a calendar for the same time period and write all of your due dates for assignments on this calendar. Knowing all of your due dates will help you schedule enough time to work on each individual assignment. Be sure to write on your calendar the time you have assigned for each task. Then the biggest job is to stick to your calendar. It is better to schedule too much time for each assignment and have time left over than to run out of time. Be sure that you schedule your writing time far enough in advance of your due date that you don't have to rush to do your assignment at the last minute. Writing is always better when you can take your time to plan, write, and revise.

For this assignment, be sure to take the time to read over "Color-Blind Parents vs. Color-Coded Rules" before you start to write. Then take time to do your prewriting before you do your writing, and always allow time for revision and editing before you turn your assignment in.

EDITING

Every word of your writing is important. Sometimes writers will put a wrong word into their writing, assuming they know the meaning. This can be very embarrassing when a word is used incorrectly. To avoid this problem, always go over the rough draft of your writing assignments word by word to be sure that you know the meaning of each word and that the words are used correctly. Be very careful if you use a thesaurus to look up your words to make sure that the word you choose means what you really want it to.

PART THREE
Culture and Tradition

The Culture and Tradition section contains articles about ways heritage affects how people live. This picture shows a woman from the Philippines doing a dance called Binasuan at a community festival. The dance is done with glasses filled with a beverage called Tubâ and is traditionally performed to entertain workers when they return from the fields after a hard day's work. What traditions from your culture, your family, or your community are you most proud of or most interested in?

Photo by Gregory Day used by permission of the photographer and Verna F. Dulay.

Female Students
Scorn Advice

Ian Stewart

PREREADING

What are your goals upon graduation? Do you think that marriage is an essential part of your future success? Why or why not? How do you feel your career and marriage interrelate? Do you think that you should choose a mate based on your career choice?

DEFINING

chauvinistic (¶4)   prejudiced belief in the superiority of one's own gender
intimidated (¶12)   filled with fear

Female Students Scorn Advice
Ian Stewart

1   SENIOR Minister Lee Kuan Yew seemed to make a more favorable impression on male students than women in his audience when he gave an address at the National University of Singapore on the path to career and marriage success.

Ian Stewart, "Female Students Scorn Advice," 13–14 August 1994, p. 8. Reprinted by permission.

Please note maps in appendix for references to places in this article.

2   While men found his speech "inspiring," female undergraduates took issue with his suggestion that they should set about finding a husband quickly.

3   Most women interviewed in a survey published in Singapore said they would not heed Mr. Lee's advice to find a mate while at university.

4   Petrina Goh, 20, who is studying computer science, said Mr. Lee's views were chauvinistic. She said she was not at university to get a boyfriend.

5   She said: "Those two things are unrelated and he's wrong to say they are."

6   Her comment was echoed by an arts student, Vanda Kwok, 19, who said getting a degree was more important at present.

7   Ms. Kwok said she "did not like the part that men should marry women who have qualifications just to have intelligent kids."

8   The former prime minister, who has often indicated that he favors social engineering, told his audience that if he was an undergraduate male he would "want to marry an equal or somebody better" because she could help "carry the load."

9   He said choosing an intelligent woman was "crucial" when it came to producing children.

10   Mr. Lee said, however, that the average Singapore male did not want a wife who was smarter than him or earning more than him.

11   But the women interviewed said they would rather have a degree, even if it reduced their chances of getting married.

12   "If men do not see us as their equals and are going to be intimidated by our degree, then they are not worth marrying," Amanda Lee, 20, said.

13   Junior college students noted that he focused on how the young should go about attaining material things like cars and homes.

14   "He didn't really have much to say about other values," 18-year-old Sharon Loh remarked. "What if I want to go explore the Amazon? Does that mean I'm not successful?"

READING

1. What kind of woman does Mr. Lee suggest that a man marry? Why?

2. What did the women interviewed in the article say about getting a degree?

THINKING

1. What do you think about Mr. Lee's prescription for success? Do you think women should get advanced degrees? Why or why not? Do you think that women who get advanced degrees face special challenges? What kind of challenges do you think those would be?

2. Mr. Lee talks more about obtaining material items than on other values. What do you think is more important? What material items are you most anxious to obtain after you start your career? Why? In what order do you want to complete your education, start your career, get married, and obtain material possessions?

PREWRITING

Do two clustering exercises. In the center of one, write "Marriage." In the other write "Career." Choose to do the writing assignment that you are able to generate the largest cluster about.

WRITING

1. Write a paper to share with your classmates that explains why you think people should or shouldn't get married. Be sure to include the qualities you feel are important in a mate, and the qualities that make a good marriage.

2. In order to apply for a scholarship, you need to submit a paper that describes your future goals. Be sure to include what kind of education you are planning, and fully describe what you are looking forward to as a career.

REVISING

When we write, we know in our minds what we are trying to say, but we don't always fully express ourselves on paper. Sometimes we leave important details out because we assume our reader will understand or know what we are trying to convey. Exchange a rough draft of your paper with another student who is doing the same writing assignment. Read the paper and then answer these two questions.

What did you like best about the paper?
What did you want to know more about?

Share you answers with the other student, and then see how you can improve your own paper based on what the student tells you about your paper.

EDITING

When using the pronouns **who** and **whom**, choose the one that fits the pronoun's function in the sentence. If the pronoun is in the subject of the sentence, use the subjective form **who**. If the pronoun is in the predicate of the sentence, use the objective form **whom**.

Example:
Mr. Lee said, however, that the average Singapore male did not want a wife **who** was smarter than him or earning more than him (¶10).

In the above example, you could substitute **she** for **who** so you can tell that you have selected the correct pronoun. If you can substitute **him** or **her** for the pronoun, then you know you need to use **whom**.

Check through your writing assignment to be sure that you have used **who** and **whom** correctly.

One Man's Dream

Nancy Ballou

PREREADING

Allensworth was a town created by "One Man's Dream." It now is a deserted ghost town. Have you ever been to a ghost town? Write about how you think the community you live in now could become a ghost town. What could cause this to happen?

DEFINING

bondage (¶1)   slavery, involuntary servitude
envisioned (¶2)   imagined, saw as a possibility
premise (¶3)   a previous statement that serves as the base for an argument

One Man's Dream
Nancy Ballou

1   Born a slave in 1842, Allen Allensworth was punished frequently because he could read and write. He had been purchased to work as a jockey in Kentucky

Nancy Ballou, "One Man's Dream," *Westways,* May 1991, p. 26. Copyright 1991 Automobile Club of Southern California, reproduction by permission, courtesy of *Westways.*
Please note maps in appendix for references to places in this article.

esclavitud

when the Civil War broke out. Escaping bondage by joining the Union Army as a civilian nurse, he later became a Baptist minister and was commissioned as chaplain of the all-black Twenty-fourth U.S. Infantry. By the time he retired in 1906, he was the highest-ranking black officer in the U.S. Army.

2   Colonel Allensworth envisioned a community where black Americans could work, educate themselves and live in peace. His wife, Josephine Leavell, was a music teacher who shared his ambition. In 1908, after much traveling and research, Allensworth filed plans in southwestern Tulare County in California. His lifelong dream became reality—the town of Allensworth was created.

3   Founded on the premise of economic and political self-sufficiency, the town of Allensworth attracted farmers, craftsmen, and merchants. Land was fertile and costs reasonable. Families could raise turkeys, chicken, or cattle. Acres of alfalfa, grain, cotton, and sugar beets sprang up. Soon, a thriving hotel rented rooms for seventy-five cents a night and provided local entertainment with a player piano. The village boasted a brass band and a glee club. Children attended classes in the two-room schoolhouse through grade eleven.

se lardeaba

4   Delilah Beasley, noted black historian and the author of _The Negro Trail Blazers of California,_ praised the townspeople and said, "Allensworth is destined to become a great city."

5   Unfortunately, the realty company that sold the subdivided land to Allensworth had drastically underestimated the needed water supply. Diversion of water and deep-well pumping nearby lowered the region's water table. The city fought a long, costly court battle over water rights, but it lost some of its spirit when Colonel Allensworth was struck and killed by a motorcyclist in 1914. Within nine years, with the water virtually dried up, Allensworth became a ghost town.

6   In 1976 the state acquired the land. Allensworth was thus preserved as a tribute to California's only community that was founded, financed, and governed by black Americans.

7   Visitors to Colonel Allen Allensworth State Historic Park can view the seven restored buildings, including the schoolhouse and the colonel's home. An exhibit trailer shows a twenty-eight-minute video, _The Spirit of Allensworth._ Barbecues and picnic tables are available, as are fifteen campsites for overnight stays. Twice a year celebrations are held at the park. The Old Time Jubilee, which includes musical and dance performances and poetry readings, will be held on May 11 this year, and the rededication ceremonies will be held on October 12.

8   Allensworth is located on state Route 43, seven miles west of Route 99 and Earlimart, and eighteen miles north of Wasco.

READING

1. What occupations did Allen Allensworth have during his lifetime?

2. Where is Allensworth? Why is it no longer a community?

THINKING

1. Allensworth was "founded on the premise of economic and political self-sufficiency" (¶3). Does this sound like a good idea for communities today? Do you think it would work in today's society? Why or why not?

2. Between 1908 and 1914, Allensworth was a thriving community with great potential. After Allen Allensworth was killed, the town no longer had a leader, and it ceased to exist because of a lack of water. Do you think that individuals are so important to city government today? Why or why not?

PREWRITING

Create two different clusters. The first one should have "what I really want to accomplish in my lifetime" in the middle, and the second should have "my ideal town" in the middle. See which cluster generates the most ideas.

WRITING

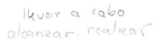
llevar a cabo
alcanzar, realizar

1. Allen Allensworth was able to accomplish all he did in his lifetime because he believed in himself. He was determined to do whatever he set his mind to. Write an essay about one thing in your life that you really want to accomplish, that you can accomplish through your own self-determination. Be specific and use examples.

2. Allensworth created his ideal town where people lived the way he had planned. Write a plan for your ideal town. Include where the finances would come from, where it would be located, who would live there, what would happen there, and anything else you can think of that you would really like to have in a town of your own.

REVISING

There is no ideal length for a writing assignment. Sometimes an instructor will assign a ten-page paper or a two-page paper, and you just have to fit your ideas into the space allowed. "One Man's Dream" is an article written for a magazine, and Nancy Ballou was probably told that she needed to write about 400–500 words to fit the space that she was allowed. Look over the article again. Do you think that she covered enough facts to make the article interesting, or did she leave you wanting more information?

When you organize your thoughts before you start writing, keep in mind the required length of your assignment so that you will know how detailed to make your ideas. If you have a short assignment, you can use a short outline, but if you try to write a long assignment with a short outline, or a short assignment with a long outline, you will run into much difficulty.

Before you start to write your assignment for this section, decide how long you want it to be when you are finished. Then organize your ideas so that they will fit into that amount of space.

EDITING

A **dictionary** is an important tool for writers to use. Many times writers just try to find correct spellings in a dictionary, but the dictionary serves a much larger purpose. First, be sure that you are using a good one. Look on the front to see if it is a college edition; if it is not, it may not have all of the words you need. Finding another dictionary when yours doesn't have the word you are looking for can be frustrating.

When you look up the word, you first see the proper spelling and how the word is divided into syllables. Following this the pronunciation will be listed. Sometimes this is difficult to follow, but all of the symbols to help you understand are usually listed in the front of your dictionary. Take time to find these symbols and see how they work, which is especially helpful if English is not your first language. Next, the grammatical function of the word is listed, so you can see if the word can be used as an adjective, a verb, a noun, or any other part of speech. Some words can act as many different parts of speech depending on how they are used in a sentence. This is one of the major things that is confusing about the English language. Next comes the etymology or where the word came from, followed by definitions, which may vary depending on how the word is used. Sometimes the dictionary will then include examples of how to use the word and maybe some synonyms and antonyms. Synonyms are words that have the same or nearly the same meanings; antonyms are words that have the opposite meaning.

Try looking through your dictionary and discover how it can help you improve your writing.

Missing Out

Michelle Tapia

PREREADING

"Missing Out" tells how Michelle Tapia would like to have been able to change the way she was raised in relation to her culture. Write about what you learned about your culture as you were growing up. Was your family proud of their heritage or not? Was your culture something you discussed or not? Did some members of your family seem to be more concerned about their cultural heritage than others? What did you like best about what you learned about your culture?

DEFINING

Hispana (¶1)   Spanish or Spanish-American woman, sometimes used for Mexican-American woman

tenaciously (¶1)   firmly

assimilate (¶2)   to become part of

encroached (¶3)   invaded, intruded on

Michelle Tapia, "Missing Out," *Intercambios*, Winter 1990, p. 17. Reprinted by permission of *Intercambios*. Please note maps in appendix for references to places in this article.

Missing Out

Michelle Tapia

1   I am a third generation Hispana. Like so many others, my grandparents came to the United States from Mexico in search of better opportunities and wealth. In their hearts and lifestyles, they brought with them the culture and traditions of Mexico. They settled in a predominantly Hispanic community, which helped them feel secure and reminded them of their homeland. The music, dance and attitudes of Mexico were tenaciously rooted in day-to-day living. Nevertheless, with each successive generation, these traditions changed.

2   For my parents, it was very important to assimilate into the American culture—after all, they were now Mexican-Americans. Home was where the traditions of their past survived. They celebrated Mexican holidays such as Dia de Los Muertos, the 16th of September or Cinco de Mayo—holidays not celebrated or acknowledged by American society at that time. There were always the traditional Mexican dishes—home was not home without beans, rice, and handmade tortillas. And most importantly, home was where my parents spoke Spanish.

3   But things changed as mainstream culture encroached on our traditions. Fearful that speaking Spanish would handicap us, my parents stopped speaking Spanish at home. When I was a child, my parents no longer spoke Spanish in our home. They felt it was important for their children to learn English in order to "survive" in America. Only in my grandparents' home did I hear Spanish. It was also at my grandparents' house that I experienced some of the traditions of my forefathers. My grandfather enjoyed singing the canciones (songs) of Mexico—especially the ballads. He would play the guitar for hours and sing those beautiful songs—playing *Cielito Lindo* especially for me because of the description of a beauty mark above the woman's lips which was similar to mine. Though I could not understand the meaning of the Spanish lyrics, the tone of his voice, his facial expressions and the rhythm of the music enabled me to understand what the song was all about. Those memories of my grandparents' home filled me with a yearning to discover the culture of Mexico and to keep it alive in my own family.

4   It wasn't until I was in high school that I began to seek out those links to my own heritage. My high school consisted predominantly of upper-middle class Caucasians. There were few Hispanic students in my class and, except for me, all of them were second generation. By getting to know them and their families, I began to experience some of the cultural traditions of my roots. I visited Mexico with them, learned Spanish from them, and became quite proud of my heritage.

5   Nevertheless, I also discovered how much I had lost through the "watering down" process the years had wrought. Sadly, I realized that my inability to communicate fluently in Spanish minimized full participation in the experiences of my culture. Unlike others who grew up close to their roots, I missed an element of myself that can't be recovered.

READING

1. Where was Michelle Tapia born? Where were her parents born? Where were her grandparents born?

2. What language was spoken in Tapia's home as she was growing up? What language did she learn in high school?

THINKING

1. Michelle Tapia is frustrated by the way her parents chose to raise her. Do you think her parents made the right decision in raising her the way they did? Do you feel that your parents did a good job of raising you to appreciate your cultural heritage?

2. After reading this article, does it make you want to know more about your cultural heritage? Do you think that it is important to know about your heritage? Will you teach your children about their heritage? Why or why not?

PREWRITING

Cluster putting the word "culture" at the center. See how many ideas you can come up with, and see how they develop.

WRITING

1. Write an essay about a tradition of your culture to share with your classmates. Be sure that you include as many specific details as possible so that your classmates can understand and appreciate this tradition.

2. Write a letter to your parents, guardians, or grandparents to express how you feel about your culture. Either thank them for all they taught you, or ask them to teach you now the things you missed.

REVISING

When you read "Missing Out," you learn about Michelle Tapia. What kind of a person do you think she is? Would you like to get to know her, or at least learn more about her? Do you think she has a positive or negative attitude about her parents and how she was raised? How does her writing show you her personality? The **tone** of writing is the dominant impression that it creates. The tone may be happy, angry, mean, or just friendly. What kind of tone does Tapia use in this essay? How does it show you Tapia's personality?

As you go over the draft of your writing assignment, decide what kind of tone you have used. Do you think that it is the most appropriate for this assignment? Why or why not? What kind of impression do you think your audience gets of you by reading your writing assignment? Is it the impression you wanted them to have?

How do you think you could change your writing to change that impression? Revise your writing assignment to create the tone and impression that you want your audience to receive.

EDITING

In writing this assignment, you may choose to use some words from a language other than English. **Foreign words** should be written in italics or underlined unless the word has become so familiar to the English language reader that it would not be noticed as foreign, such as pasta or taco. If you want to clarify the meaning of the word, you can either define it in the text of your writing or you can write a short definition enclosed in parentheses immediately following the word.

Example:

My grandfather enjoyed singing the canciones (songs) of Mexico—especially the ballads. (¶3)

Go back through your writing assignment and see if there is a place where you could add a word from another language. This would only be appropriate in the case of this assignment if your cultural background uses a language other than English, but you can always use this rule for other assignments when appropriate.

Malaysia Raps Rap

PREREADING

What kind of music do you listen to the most? Do you enjoy other kinds of music too? Why or why not? What kind of music do you think best expresses American society? Do you like rap? Why or why not?

DEFINING

industrialized (¶1)   a country or area developed in industry
deplores (¶2)   expresses strong disapproval
ostensibly (¶6)   apparently, appearing as such

Malaysia Raps Rap

1   The rap music of Malaysia is not inspired by the mean streets of Kuala Lumpur. One group, 4U2C, raps about the dangers of smoking and alcohol. Another, KRU, has concentrated on the plans of the prime minister, Mahathir Mo-

"Malaysia Raps Rap," *The Economist,* 18–24 June 1994, p. 39. Reprinted by permission.

Please note maps in appendix for references to places in this article.

hamad, to make Malaysia fully industrialized by 2020. "Dr M requests us to be united . . . To build Malaysia up to 2020 . . . Productivity and growth."

2   The government deplores the rise of rap at the expense of middle-of-the-road groups, such as the Alley Cats. Rap, says the information minister, Mohamed Rahmat, is "back-street music for American blacks who have nothing to do." Instead, he proposes Malaysian entertainment "to wean youths off western culture" and encourage discipline, hard work, and family values. The healthier alternatives are to include Broadway-style musicals with local themes, and touring musical roadshows which will stress Malaysia's identity and achievements. Concerts by western bands will not be banned entirely but guidelines will be issued in August to ensure that Malaysian values are not compromised.

3   Malaysia wants to have a western standard of development without the social problems that tend to go with it. Western culture is held responsible for most social ills. Rock music in particular has been blamed for drug addiction, promiscuity, alcoholism, abandoned babies, teenage runaways, and loafing. "Decay in the West started at Woodstock," says Mr Mohamed.

4   Drug addiction is increasing. Juvenile delinquency has been described as a "cancer that is spreading." As for loafing, a government survey claims there is more to it than wasting time: 70% of loafers have been found to smoke, 25% are believed to drink alcohol, nearly half watch pornographic films, and nearly a fifth indulge in casual sex.

5   As official concern about young people has increased, so have the moves against western music. Heavy metal is banned from the state-run radio along with groups known to have taken drugs and male musicians with long hair. Public concerts sponsored by a cigarette company brought big-name western groups to Malaysia. Such concerts have now been banned. "These concerts promote smoking, alcohol, free mixing of the sexes, free sex, and from there to AIDS," explained Mr Mohamed.

6   The film "Schindler's List" was banned in April ostensibly because it features violence and nudity. In May a government survey of western films found that 97% contained sex scenes and 91% had scenes of violence. The government now says it will strengthen censorship and cut down on foreign programs on television. By 2000 the information ministry wants 80% of what is shown on television to be locally produced.

7   Malaysian teenagers say they cannot see what the fuss is about. "We don't have the same problems as New York," says one musician. "We rap about things that mean something to us like falling in love, the environment, and our pride for our country. What's wrong with that?"

8   The music industry is optimistic that it will go on selling rap music. "We can still buy the albums, we can still hear the music at clubs," said one teenager. "We will probably go to the musical roadshows as well," said another. "There is little else to do and it's a good chance to hang out."

READING

1. Why is the prime minister of Malaysia concerned about rap music? What kind of music would he rather the country listen to? Why?

2. What do the teenagers of Malaysia say about the prime minister's attitude?

THINKING

1. Do you feel that the music you choose to listen to affects how you think? Why or why not? Do you think some kinds of music are dangerous to listen to? Why or why not? If you do feel some music is dangerous, what kind of music is that? Why do you feel that way?

2. Do you agree or disagree with the prime minister's concerns? Why do you feel this way? Do you think the United States would be better or worse if someone was controlling the kind of music we all are allowed to listen to? Why?

PREWRITING

Make a list of all of the issues you think are critically socially significant in American society today. See how long you can make your list.

WRITING

1. Write the words to a rap based on an issue that you feel is socially significant and important to people you know. Listen to some popular rap before you write your own so that you can get the sense of the timing and rhyming done in rap. Use lots of details and have fun with this assignment. Share your rap with your classmates.

2. Because of the prestige that American culture has, many small countries are trying to imitate anything American. A problem resulting from this is that small countries are losing their own sense of national culture. This may be inevitable with the global society that is resulting from television, news, movies, and satellite technology. Write a paper to share with your classmates that explains whether or not you feel the countries of the world will eventually all blend into one society instead of the many cultural groups we have now.

REVISING

The language that you choose to use when writing can be vague or specific. The more specific your word choice is, the clearer picture your audience can receive. Read through "Malaysia Raps Rap" to find specific examples. Where has the author chosen to use details that clearly illustrate what he means? Remember when you are choosing your words not to use vague descriptive words like **very, good, bad, pretty,** or **ugly,** because everybody has a different perception of what these words mean. If you use words like **blue, salty, scratchy,** or **deafening,** or if you use **specific names or numbers,** then your description will be more explicit so that everyone who reads it will have a similar interpretation.

Go through your rough draft to identify all of the descriptive words you have used. Work to make them as specific as possible.

EDITING

Conjunctive adverbs can be used to provide transitions within or between sentences. When you use a conjunctive adverb; however, you need to remember to have a comma on each side of it unless it comes at the beginning or end of a sentence, or if it is being used to join two independent clauses to make a compound sentence. The following is a list of conjunctive adverbs.

> **also, anyway, besides, certainly, consequently, finally, for example, furthermore, especially, however, incidentally, indeed, instead, likewise, meanwhile, moreover, namely, nevertheless, next, now, on the other hand, otherwise, particularly, similarly, still, then, therefore, undoubtedly**

Notice that some of these words may be used as other parts of speech; it depends on the role they play in the sentence. In the following examples, the words are used as conjunctive adverbs.

Example:
> "*Instead,* he proposes Malaysian entertainment 'to wean youths off western culture' and encourage discipline, hard work, and family values" (¶2).

This sentence shows how conjunctive adverbs can be used at the beginning of a sentence for a transition, but conjunctive adverbs can also be used in the middle of a sentence.

One of the key ways of distinguishing a conjunctive adverb from a coordinating conjunction is the conjunctive adverb's mobility. It can usually be placed in several different places in the sentence without changing the sentence's basic meaning, but a coordinating conjunction cannot move from the connecting point of the sentence.

Examples:
> The aggregate total of non-whites, *indeed,* overwhelms Caucasians, who comprise only around 27 percent of the population.
>
> Such an "outward" orientation, *on the other hand,* could affect the integrity of the work being done.

Conjunctive adverbs can also be used to combine two independent clauses into a compound sentence; in this case, they are preceded by a semicolon.

Examples:
> Raising animals was never worth much; *meanwhile,* the traditional sideline cannot complete with large-scale stockbreeding.
>
> He has the opinion that it simply requires an impartial and objective member of the community to arbitrate as necessary; *on the other hand,* problems have been known to arise.

Go over your writing to see if you have used any conjunctive adverbs. If you have, did you use them correctly? If you didn't, try adding a few.

Diving to Live

Kavitha Shetty

PREREADING

"Diving to Live" is an article about how people in India make a living diving in the ocean. Write about whether you would like to dive in the ocean every day to make a living. When you consider the modern industrialization occurring all over the world, can you think of an easier way to obtain what the divers are harvesting?

DEFINING

domain (¶1)   territory

sari-draped (¶1)   wearing a sari, a long silk or cotton garment worn wrapped around the body

12 km (¶2)   7.45 miles

4,000 kg (¶2)   8,818.4 pounds

120 km (¶3)   74.52 miles

74 mm (¶4)   2.91 inches

64 mm (¶4)   2.52 inches

trawling (¶5)   fishing with a special net

larva (¶5)   an insect's early stage of development

dally (¶6)   delay, linger, wait

foretaste (¶6)   vision of the future

286

Diving to Live

Kavitha Shetty

1   In the lung-bursting agony of their everyday existence, they find a bizarre sense of freedom. In the eerie blue swirling depths of the sea, with the jigsaw of corals around them and the occasional shark snorting at the rude interference into its domain, the sari-draped young women of Chinnapalem village and the well-built shell-collecting divers of Tuticorin look for a living.

2   Of the 600 people who live in the fishing hamlet of Chinnapalem 12 km from the coastal town of Rameswaram on the south-eastern coast of Tamil Nadu, there are about 200 women. Nearly 100 of them row half an hour to the Kurusadi Island every day in *vathais* (narrow wooden boats) and dive to depths of up to 15 feet looking for the seaweed *Marikkolunthu* which is used for making *agar* for food and pharmaceutical industries. Not for them the luxury and safety of oxygen cylinders and diving gear, just a crude version of goggles and the modesty and comfort of their saris. Together they scrape out about 4,000 kg of the seaweed after four hours at sea every day. It is sold at Rs 1.25 a kg to a local man who dries it and then sells it to an agent from Madurai at four times the price. "I've been diving for seaweed from the time I was nine. I would like to cook and stay at home with my baby like women in other villages. But I cannot afford that," says Selvam, 28, who leaves her six-month-old baby at home while at sea.

3   But the astonishing feat of these brave young women looks like a juvenile prank when compared to the death-defying 100-foot dives of the *chank* collectors (shells used for making bangles) of Tuticorin, 120 km away. Like the women of Chinnapalem they too wear goggles and carry a net bag to hold the *chank* and a circular aluminum plate tied to one foot which acts as a flipper to propel them.

4   For these men death is only a dive away, and on an average each of them dives 50-60 times a day. Apart from the constant danger of running out of breath, there is the lurking presence of fish like the sting ray, squid, and the shark which recently chewed off a chunk from a diver's bottom. The *chank* collection is a state monopoly and the divers are paid Rs 10 for a big shell (diameter 74 mm) and Rs 7 for the small ones (diameter 64 mm). The state government earns Rs 1 crore annually selling the shells to West Bengal where *chank* bangles are extremely popular.

5   Chinnapalem has been declared a marine biological park to preserve the seaweeds and, moreover, the new generation of girls, unlike their elder women who edged out men from the job, are not willing to risk their lives amid the waves. "My daughter says she will come out to watch us dive, but she will not gather seaweed," says 35-year-old Muniyayi. And the excessive trawling in the coastal region destroys the weeds and the *chanks* which are in the larva stage.

Kavitha Shetty, "Diving to Live," *India Today,* March 15, 1991, p. 74. Reprinted by permission of *India Today.*

Please note maps in appendix for references to places in this article.

6   For the divers who dally with death every moment such thoughts are not worrying. Not even the foretaste of an old age crippled by ruptured eardrums and limbs which refuse to propel them from the deep dark depths of the sea. "Sixty times everyday we hold our lives in our noses. If we worry about it each time, we will never survive a single dive," says 38-year-old Amaluddin.

7   Memories of the terrible beauty and power of the sea still haunt some old men like 70-year-old Umayannan who after half a century of diving, risks his life even now to collect *chanks*. For him like for many other divers of Tuticorin and Chinnapalem, the sea is life.

READING

1. What do the women divers harvest? What is it for? What do the men divers harvest? What is it for?

2. What kind of equipment do the divers use for diving?

THINKING

1. The younger generation of girls will watch the diving, but they refuse to do it themselves. Why do you suppose that after their mothers and grandmothers have been diving all of their lives the girls decide that they won't dive? What do you think the results of this decision will mean to their lives and the lives of their families?

2. A 70-year-old man is still diving in the dangerous waters because for him, "the sea is life" (¶7). What do you think is meant by this philosophy? Why do you think that he still dives at his age?

PREWRITING

List all of the unusual jobs you can think of. Then make another list noting why you think a person should or should not prepare for retirement.

WRITING

1. Write an essay identifying jobs in our society that are dangerous yet essential. Write what you think it would be like to work in such a profession. Be sure to include whether you think you could ever work in a profession like this.

2. Your good friend works at a job as a professional athlete, but that does not provide retirement benefits. Your friend tells you this is not a problem because your friend is young and healthy, and retirement is a long time away. Write to your friend either agreeing with his or her feelings or suggesting that planning for the future would be a good idea. State at least three reasons to support your argument.

REVISING

In "Diving to Live," Kavitha Shetty compares and contrasts men and women divers. Read back through the article and note how they are the same and how they are different. How does Shetty organize the content of the article? Do you think this is the most effective way Shetty could have written the article? Why or why not?

Either of the writing assignments for this article could be written using the compare and contrast rhetorical mode. Which of the assignments do you think would be more appropriate for this mode? Why? Try writing your assignment using comparing and contrasting. Which elements will you compare and contrast? Be sure to compare *and* contrast instead of just doing one or the other.

EDITING

Parentheses can be used to add information to a sentence or to define or clarify items in the sentence that might not easily be understood.

Examples;

Nearly 100 of them row half an hour to the Kurusadi Island every day in *vathais* (*narrow wooden boats*) and dive to depths of up to 15 feet. . . . (¶2)

But the astonishing feat of these brave young women looks like a juvenile prank when compared to the death-defying 100-foot dives of the *chank* collectors (*shells used for making bangles*) of Tuticorin, 120 km away. (¶3)

In both of these cases, the parentheses were used to provide a definition of a foreign term, but they also can just be used for clarification of an unfamiliar word or usage.

Go through your writing assignment to see if you can find anything that could be clarified by the use of parentheses.

The China Doll Syndrome

Linda Mah

PREREADING

How do you or did you choose the people you wanted to date? Did they have to be a certain age, height, and/or weight? Did they have to look a certain way? Did they have to live in a certain area, go to a certain school, and/or have a certain job? Where do you or did you meet the people you chose to date? How do you feel about dating and your experiences with it?

DEFINING

affinity (¶4)   natural attraction

benignly (¶5)   gently, mildly, without malice

demure (¶5)   modest, reserved

exotica (¶9)   curiously unusual, excitingly strange things

subservient (¶10)   being inferior

homogenous (¶12)   of the same or similar nature

intimidated (¶22)   made to be filled with fear

xenophobic (¶28)   a person who is fearful of that which is foreign

hermetically (¶29)   completely, unable to be penetrated by outside influence

The China Doll Syndrome

Linda Mah

1   My sister called him an "Asian Freak."

2   I've never used the term but I knew what she meant. He's the guy who comes up to you with an expectant look and starts speaking Japanese.

3   He's the guy who starts telling you how he spent time in Korea or Japan or Vietnam or somewhere else in the "Orient" and says . . . "you're really beautiful."

4   He's the guy who has no idea who or what you are but he's sure that your hair, your eyes, your skin tone means you are one of those Asian women for which he feels some mysterious affinity.

5   I've never had a real problem with an "Asian Freak." That may be because I have a tendency to smile benignly and walk away with a demure, "I'm sorry, I only speak English." or "Oh, that must have been interesting, but no, I've never been to the Philippines, I'm Chinese."

6   My sister's experience is quite different. She and some of her Asian female friends sometimes feel they're walking around with neon signs attached to their chests that blink on and off: "Asian Freaks, form line here."

7   That's the bad side of interracial dating and Asians—or at least Asian women.

8   That group of men who still find us strange, mysterious, exotic creatures.

9   There's a temptation to find that fascination flattering, but the truth is those who find Asian women nothing more than a bit of exotica will—at least in my case and my sister's case—always be held at arm's length. There's something disturbing about being treated as a mysterious idea and not a real human being with individual characteristics.

10   The strange thing in my story is that I've never once met an Asian man who held me in such high regard. That's not to say I don't think Asian men desire the subservient, China doll; I think many do.

11   I've just never met an Asian man who thought I fit that mold—at least not one who went so far as to ask me out.

12   To be fair, I've never lived in an area with a huge Asian population—San Francisco, Chicago, or New York—so maybe I just never met all those handsome, single Asian men. I grew up in a fairly homogeneous, small Midwestern town where all my friends and those of importance in my life—outside of my immediate family—were white.

13   But even when I was in college and had the chance to meet Chinese guys, none of them seemed very interested in me. I sometimes wondered if I gave off some invisible, unconscious signals that said, "Don't bother, I don't date Asian guys."

14   That couldn't be farther from the truth. I would have been more than willing to date a Chinese or other Asian man if I'd been asked. And, I suppose, I could have asked out a Chinese guy, but as I said, I never felt that I was the kind of woman they were looking for.

Linda Mah, "The China Doll Syndrome," *New People*, July–August, 1994, p. 13. Reprinted by permission of the author.

Please note maps in appendix for references to places in this article.

15   (Sometimes, I wonder if the problem was that most of the Asian guys I met were in Mandarin class, and I was so horrible at speaking Mandarin that they automatically dismissed me as inappropriate Chinese wife material.)

16   So there is the dating landscape for me.

17   On one hand, Asian Freaks and, on the other, Asian men who show absolutely no interest.

18   So who did I date before meeting my current man friend?

19   Anyone who seemed to have a genuine interest in me, or men whom I found genuinely interesting.

20   There are requirements, but they don't fall into the area of race or skin color. I've dated white men and black men, and I would have been open to dating a man of any race or culture if we seemed to have something in common.

21   The things I have always been more concerned with is being with someone who was nice. Someone who liked art, movies, food, music, traveling, adventure, education, family, having fun, and being partners.

22   I also wanted someone who was willing to celebrate my culture without being overwhelmed, intimidated, or strangely fascinated by it.

23   I have all of those things now with my current boyfriend. We share a sense of adventure and love of life. We can always manage to have a good time whether in the big city or home with our cats. We love to cook together, we love to eat together.

24   He's enthusiastic and supportive of my cultural and racial background. And I am of his.

25   But we have one difference.

26   He sometimes expresses disappointment that I am not with him because he is black. I think he would be much happier if I said I chose to be with him because he is black—not because of his skin color but because of that shared history and struggle which unifies the black American culture.

27   But in all honesty that is not what drew me to him. I celebrate who he is and being with him I have come to respect his race and culture even more, but I didn't choose to be with him because of that.

28   The statistics say that more and more Asians—men and women—are dating outside of their race. I don't find that surprising or shocking. I find it predictable human evolution. Asian cultures have been traditionally xenophobic and isolated, but as Asians spread across the world in study and business, interactions with other cultures had to multiply.

29   The result: expectations of mates and marriage have been challenged and changed. There are many, like my father, who cling to the notion that races should stay hermetically sealed. I feel sorry for them, I think they're in for a troubling future. There is a strength in knowing and celebrating your culture, but I don't think there is any strength to say it must be kept in the careful confines of dating or loving only one type of person.

30   The world is not as isolated as it once was.

31   The reality is choice and change that should be celebrated and respected, not feared.

READING

1. How does Linda Mah define "Asian Freaks"?

2. Who do the statistics show that Asian men and women date?

THINKING

1. Have you ever dated someone from a culture different than your own? Why or why not? Do you think people should date outside their culture? Why or why not?

2. What about a person appeals to you to make you want to get to know that person better? How do you choose your friends? What makes you not want to get to know a person?

PREWRITING

Make a list of all of the traits you think an ideal mate should have. See how long you can make your list. When you are finished, go back through the list and prioritize it. Put a number one by the most important trait and a number two by the next most important and so on until you have prioritized all the traits you decide are the most important. You can cross traits off your list at this point if you decide they aren't important after all.

WRITING

1. The high school you attended is publishing a "Survival Guide for High School Life," and your former English teacher has asked you to write an article for it called "How to Choose the Perfect Date." The teacher asked you this because you had a great reputation of being a fun person to date. Be sure to include qualities to look for and qualities to avoid.

2. You are away from home at college and you have fallen in love with someone from another culture. Write your parents to tell them about your relationship. Describe your new love anticipating how they will react.

REVISING

In the first four paragraphs of "The China Doll Syndrome," Linda Mah describes in detail the characteristics of what she calls an "Asian Freak." Notice her word choice. Do you feel that you have a clear picture of the type of man she is describing? What makes this description vivid and interesting?

In your writing you can improve description by adding specific details to your sentences. Look at the following sentence:

"My sister called him an 'Asian Freak'" (¶1).

After you read this sentence you know that the writer is referring to a man, but what about this man? Who is he? What is he doing? What does he represent? Now look at the following sentences with more details filled in:

> "He's the guy who comes up to you with an expectant look and starts speaking Japanese" (¶2).

> "He's the guy who starts telling you how he spent time in Korea or Japan or Vietnam or somewhere else in the "Orient" and says . . . 'you're really beautiful'" (¶3).

> "He's the guy who has no idea who or what you are but he's sure that your hair, your eyes, your skin tone means you are one of those Asian women for which he feels some mysterious affinity" (¶4).

See how much more vivid the description has become now. Mah has painted a picture of the man with enough detail to give you a definite impression of his characteristics.

Now go through your rough draft and try expanding some of your sentences with more detail. See what kind of descriptive words you can add to your writing to make it more vivid.

EDITING

Quotation marks can be used to set off slang expressions or words that may be offensive or used in a different way than they usually are.

Example:
"My sister called him an 'Asian Freak'" (¶1).

In this case the author wants to be sure that you know that these aren't words that the author typically uses.

When you quote something that you know is incorrect, such as a misspelled word, put **[sic]** after the word. **Sic** in **brackets** is used to show that the author realizes that something she has quoted is not as it should be.

Check your writing assignments to see if you need to add quotation marks or brackets used in this fashion.

A Khmer Renaissance

Susan Blaustein

PREREADING

"A Khmer Renaissance" tells how Cambodia is struggling to remember the arts it once had. Write about the arts of your culture or of the American culture. Remember the term *arts* covers many areas, including dance and theatre as well as visual art like painting. What are your favorite art forms? Why? What are your favorite works of art?

DEFINING

Pnompenh (¶1)   a city in Cambodia

Khmer (¶1)   Cambodian

vocations (¶2)   professions or occupations

feudal (¶2)   having to do with land held in fee

aristocratic (¶2)   having to do with a form of ruling government with titles or nobility

pillars (¶2)   supports

spry (¶4)   active, vigorous

collaborate (¶4)   work together on

irretrievably (¶4)   that which cannot be restored or recovered

exploitation (¶5)   making use of for one's own advantage or profit

socialist (¶5) a supporter of socialism, which is the system of sharing everything equally in a society

rhetoric (¶5) the art of using words effectively, written or spoken language

icons (¶6) images, figures, or pictures

replete (¶7) well-filled or supplied

regime (¶7) political system, social order

tout (¶9) praise highly

Stalinism (¶9) theories and practices of Joseph Stalin, Russian Premier 1879–1953

reeling (¶10) staggering from shock

A Khmer Renaissance
Susan Blaustein

1   In an old wooden rehearsal hall at the School of Fine Arts in Pnompenh, three elderly ballerinas strain to remember a tale from one of Cambodia's most beloved artistic traditions: the Khmer classical dance. Khmer ballet, like most dance, is passed on by example and word of mouth. By 1978, when the Vietnamese invasion put an end to the disastrous effort of Pol Pot and the Khmer Rouge to create an agrarian utopia, most of Cambodia's dancers were dead. Chea Samy, 70, is one ballerina who survived. "The classical dance is just like a mirror that reflects the society," she says. "It represents the Khmer soul." Today the future of that soul depends almost entirely on the memories of Chea Samy and a few frail practitioners. Only 10 female and seven male dancers survived "Pol Pot time," as the four years under Khmer Rouge tyranny are called. Proeung Chhieng, another survivor, who now directs the classical dance program at the government fine-arts school, says that of these 17 dancers, "some went mad and have lost their memories because of their suffering."

2   Artists, dancers, and musicians, whose vocations Pol Pot condemned as feudal or aristocratic, were among the thousands systematically jailed, tortured, and murdered between 1975 and 1979. The Khmer Rouge also destroyed most books, costumes, and musical instruments, making it impossible to reconstruct Khmer culture from documents or artifacts. The current government of Cambodia, installed by Vietnam, has made this reclaiming of Khmer culture one of the pillars of its rule. By rebuilding the most important Cambodian cultural institutions, senior officials hope to demonstrate that they are neither murderers like the Khmer Rouge nor Vietnamese puppets. By rebuilding their nation's artistic traditions, they hope to ally themselves with a rekindled sense of national pride that was so bruised by Pol Pot.

Susan Blaustein, "A Khmer Renaissance." Originally published in *Far Eastern Economic Review.* Reprinted here from *World Press Review,* February 1990, p. 73, with permission of World Press Review.

Please note maps in appendix for references to places in this article.

3   When Chea Samy returned to Pnompenh in March, 1979, after walking 100 miles from the rural "cooperative" where she had spent Pol Pot time washing dishes for 600 fellow inmates, she was asked to form a dance school and revive the ballet repertoire. She began by recruiting dancers from among the city's many orphans and searching for colleagues who were still alive. The School of Fine Arts reopened in 1980 with 100 students and two teachers and has since trained seven new teachers and an entire ballet company.

4   In a corner of the rehearsal hall, graceful young girls with delicately flexed fingers and feet are accompanied by three spry old musicians who sit cross-legged in front of wooden xylophones and a drum called a *sko*. The three gray-haired dance teachers explain how they go about remembering pieces of the ballets. Ein Thearv conjures up individual movements by chanting the words. The teachers often collaborate on the difficult passages. But most of the dance pieces are irretrievably lost. Of the more than 20 dances in the repertory, says Proeung Chhieng, the women have been able to reconstruct fully only three.

5   While the dancers scour their memories, the government has intensified efforts to persuade its critics that Cambodia has not fallen victim to a Vietnamese cultural invasion. In one extreme assertion of Khmer identity, the government is discouraging the use of French and Vietnamese. The few surviving professors of literature at Pnompenh University have been asked to put together a new dictionary that will replace words of foreign origin with Khmer words, many of which have to be invented. Fears of Vietnam's heavy hand are perhaps borne out by instances in which the government has called for the exploitation of age-old traditions to serve political ends. Chea Samy, for instance, has edited nine dance scripts for publication by the government, all of which are thick with socialist rhetoric.

6   Asked about "revised" and politicized cultural works, Culture Minister Chheng Phon explains that many are produced by students who have been encouraged "to adapt the tradition to modern times." Chheng Phon's ministry also encourages the mass production of central Khmer cultural icons in its effort to revive nationalism. Imposing oil reproductions of Cambodia's magnificent 12th-century Angkor Wat temple complex adorn the walls of almost every restaurant, factory, and government office. They are painted mostly by fine-arts graduates and students, all of whom are trained, in Chheng Phon's words, more as "reproductive artisans" than as "creative artists."

7   Indeed, there is little evidence of either experimental or critical art anywhere in Pnompenh. The only books printed in any quantity are long comics produced by the Ministry of Education. Most of these are elaborate morality tales replete with references to traditional culture and Buddhism, tips on health and hygiene, and unmistakable hat-tipping toward the current regime.

8   The artists claim that they do not mind being enlisted as instruments of propaganda for the government of Prime Minister Hun Sen. Free now to worship and to live with their families, subsidized, and encouraged to further their craft, they may calculate that the effort they have to devote to communicating the government's message is a relatively small price to pay.

9   Notwithstanding the discouraging signs of government interference in individuals' rights to self-expression, film maker Vandy Kaon is optimistic about the future of Khmer culture. He is particularly excited about the artistic potential he sees in comics and video, relatively low-cost media that so far have been used to tout the government's line. "We thought culture had been lost to Stalinism," he says. "But now we know Khmer culture will survive."

10   Asked why there are so few contemporary art works free of the government stamp, Vandy Kaon says that intellectuals and artists are still reeling from the Khmer Rouge period. "Soon they will begin to write, to create again," he says. By then perhaps Cambodia's government will feel secure enough to allow its artists simply to be themselves.

READING

1. What happened to all of the artists in Cambodia when the Khmer Rouge was in charge of the country?

2. What is the current state of the arts in Cambodia?

THINKING

1. Cambodia is having a hard time recovering much of its art because so many artists were killed. The classic Khmer ballet was always passed down by example, so how to do it wasn't recorded anywhere. Now a few very old ballerinas are trying to pass on this dance form to younger Cambodians so that future Cambodians will also be able to appreciate this art form and tradition. Can you think of any art forms or traditions in your culture, your family, or American society that have been passed down by example and word of mouth? Is this method effective? Why or why not?

2. Chea Samy, a famous ballerina, was forced to wash dishes for her fellow inmates. In many societies throughout history, talented and/or educated people were banished to farms to do manual labor as a form of making everyone in that governmental system equal. Theoretically, it sounds nice for all members of a society to be equal, but to force equality onto an existing society, the value of education and art is lost. What do you think is more important—to have an educated society with all members having the opportunity to be educated or to have an equal society? What is your reasoning?

PREWRITING

Freewrite on what you think is the value of art in society. Why do you feel this way?

WRITING

1. Chea Samy said, "The classical dance is just like a mirror that reflects the society" (¶1). What can you think of in your culture or in American society that you think "reflects the society"? Write an essay with your classmates as your audience explaining why you think this one thing reflects the society. Be sure to describe it in detail.

2. Your county is considering the establishment of a fine arts school even though their budget for all county operations is tight. Write an essay either supporting or condemning the proposed school. Be sure to state specific reasons for your argument.

REVISING

In "A Khmer Renaissance," Susan Blaustein shows how the government is encouraging artists to be artisans, to copy what former Cambodian artists did instead of create art work of their own. In America we strongly discourage copying. In writing, if someone copies the work of someone else, it is considered plagiarism, which is not allowed in college. Students may be expelled if they are caught plagiarizing. Look through the article to see how many times she mentions some form of copying someone else's work.

You should always be very careful to avoid plagiarizing in your writing. Plagiarism goes beyond directly copying to taking someone else's ideas and calling them your own. Frequently students will try to reword someone else's writing to say the same thing. This is called paraphrasing, and it is acceptable only if you give credit for the idea to the original author or source. Always check through your writing assignments to be sure that there is nothing that could possibly be interpreted as plagiarism.

EDITING

Subjects and verbs always need to agree, but sometimes this becomes confusing, especially when two or more subjects are combined by *or, either / or, nor, neither / nor,* and *not only / but also.* When any of these words are used, the subject closest to the verb determines whether the subject is singular or plural. If the subjects are singular, then the verb is singular.

Examples:

Not only artists *but also* dancers *are* being encouraged to recreate earlier works.

Either the teacher *or* the dancers *are* at the school.

Look through your writing assignment to see if you have written any sentences like these. Be sure that the subjects and verbs in all of your sentences agree.

Ancient Secrets

Pueng Vongs

PREREADING

Write how you feel about the practice of medicine in America today. Do you feel that doctors can and do take care of all medical problems, or do you think that faith healing or folk medicine has a place in our society today? Why or why not?

DEFINING

derived (¶1)   obtained from a source

pharmaceutical (¶2)   relating to pharmacies and pharmacists

biochemist (¶3)   a person who studies how chemical substances alter vital processes in living organisms

simultaneously (¶3)   happening at the same time

indigenous (¶3)   originating and growing in the same environment

undisclosed (¶5)   not exposed or uncovered

perpetrate (¶8)   commit, be responsible for

exponentially (¶9)   mathematical term indicating a great increase

300

Ancient Secrets

Pueng Vongs

1   Medical journals and newsletters are stacked chest-high in Sonserai Lee's cluttered three-room flat off New York City's Times Square. Lee flips through a textbook, pausing at an illustration of *xuan fu hua,* a plant found in northwestern China and used in traditional Chinese medicine to treat respiratory ailments. Chinese healers have harnessed plants for centuries to cure the sick, she says. Now many of the very same plants are beginning to offer the world clues to new drugs. Western doctors, for instance, use a drug derived from xuan fu hua to treat asthma and bronchitis. "There is a lack of interest in American society about traditional medicine," says Lee wistfully. "Asian cultures have far exceeded the West in the study and use of medicinal plants."

2   Lee believes that China's ancient secrets could become modern cures in the U.S., where a majority of drugs are chemically engineered and most of those used to treat cancer are highly toxic. During a three-and-a-half year tour of hospitals and pharmacies in Asia, Lee stumbled across an extensive database and volumes of journals on Chinese herbal medicine at the Beijing Traditional Medical School. Lee, 29, decided she wanted to provide greater access to existing research on traditional medicine for scientists and pharmaceutical companies.

3   The biochemist set to work compiling and marketing a database of medicinal plants she believes will lead to everything from cures for disease and drug addiction to new types of birth control. By using information from isolated and largely unknown journals and other databases around the world, Lee will pinpoint where each plant is grown and provide information on how it can be put to best use. Information for the database is being compiled simultaneously by a number of organizations, including Rutgers Medical University in New Jersey, Peru's Health Ministry, the Shanghai Medical University, and the Health Ministry of China. Medical students and doctors are being trained in the U.S., the Amazon region, and Asia to help indigenous populations use the database. In Peru, the effort is managed directly by indigenous peoples and the information is available in both Spanish and English.

4   Medicine runs in Lee's blood. Her parents and three siblings are all doctors. After moving to New York from Seoul in 1976, Lee studied biochemistry at Columbia University, where she also obtained a master's degree in molecular biology and is currently working towards her Ph.D. in the same field. But Lee decided to pursue clinical and research work rather than become a doctor. "Having grown up in the U.S. I can use my knowledge of traditional medicine to challenge the health care structure here," she says. "Besides, there are already too many doctors in my family."

Pueng Vongs, "Ancient Secrets," *Asia Inc.,* June 1994, vol. 3, no. 6, pp. 54–55. Reprinted with permission.

Please note maps in appendix for references to places in this article.

5   With the help of an undisclosed amount of money from a family fund, Lee launched the Knowledge Recovery Foundation in 1990. So far, fund-raising efforts and assorted grants from the United Nations, private institutions, corporations, and members have contributed more than $1 million to the foundation. Today the New York-based nonprofit organization operates on a $250,000 annual budget with assets of $3 million.

6   The database, which Lee hopes to complete later this year at a total cost of $1.5 million, is expected to raise some $10 million in sales revenue in its first year. Users will be charged an initial $100 subscription fee. Already Lee and her staff of six receive 100 requests a day for more information and have produced an interactive video-disk library of the database to display at conferences and museums. They are also marketing their research for television documentaries and home-video sales.

7   Lee plans to reinvest the proceeds to make the database available to people in developing countries around the world. "We want to make the information accessible not just to academics or the upper class," she says enthusiastically, "but to the public or individuals like those indigenous people who have a shortage of aid or support in medicine."

8   Lee is excited about the prospects. Database users, for example, will be able to research taxol, a drug made from the bark of the yew tree grown in America's northwest. Most recently the yew has attracted attention for its effectiveness in treating ovarian and breast cancer. An extract from the tree has been used in Asia for years to relieve arthritis and rheumatism. Lee also hopes the database will help perpetuate growth of the yew and other medicinal plants.

9   Pharmaceutical and natural product companies can put the database to good use. The World Health Organization estimates 80 percent of the world's population relies chiefly on traditional medicine. In Japan, where consumers spend over $2 billion annually on Chinese medicinal plants and herbal products, more than 180 plants are scientifically recognized for medicinal purposes. In Europe, Germany represents 70 percent of the world's natural medicine market. And, as European trade barriers are lifted and the continent integrates Germany's more relaxed regulatory approach to medicinal plant products, there is a potential for the market to increase exponentially from 60 million to some 330 million consumers.

10   What's more, says Lee, the database will help create many more products for a rapidly expanding natural products industry. Last year medicinal plants and herbs made up $1.3 billion in sales worldwide, the fastest-growing segment of a $4.4 billion natural products industry. "Discoveries are waiting to be made," says Dr. Dennis McKenna, who used a similar database with Shaman Pharmaceuticals in San Carlos, California. Shaman uses state-of-the-art technology on plants widely used by native cultures in Africa, Latin America, and Southeast Asia. It is among several pharmaceutical companies in the U.S., including Merck & Co. and Bristol-Meyers Squibb Co., devoting extensive research to medicinal plants.

11   In the U.S., just 10 percent of medicinal plants have been studied for medical use and only 1 percent have undergone any significant research, says Lee. Cur-

rently only one-fourth of all drugs in the U.S. are derived from medicinal plants. Even so, they represent $8 billion a year in prescription sales. America's National Institutes of Health and the National Cancer Institute continue to fund research and screen medicinal plants for potential drug use. And as U.S. President Bill Clinton reforms the healthcare system at home, says Lee, "alternative medicine must be addressed."

READING

1. What is Sonserai Lee working to compile? Why is she doing this?

2. How much of the world's population relies on traditional medicine? Why?

THINKING

1. What do you think about taking medications? Do you take a pain pill at the first hint of a headache, or do you refuse to take anything until you are really ill? Why do you feel the way you do about taking medications?

2. Lee came from a family of doctors. She was interested in medicine, but decided to take a different approach to her career. What do you think about her decision? What kind of a career are you considering? Can you think of different approaches you could take to that career?

PREWRITING

Freewrite about how you feel that medicine is practiced in America today. Do people have the freedom to obtain the kinds of medical care that they want or need? Why or why not? What nontraditional approaches to medicine do you know about?

WRITING

1. People have different beliefs in regard to the care of their bodies. Some go to a *curandera,* some go to massage therapists, some believe they can heal themselves through the power of positive thinking. Other people don't believe in bathing, eating meat, or taking blood transfusions. Write an essay where you explain how you take care of yourself physically. Be sure to use specific examples.

2. As a nursing major, you have been asked to write a report to share with the class on any one nontraditional approach to practicing medicine. This can be anything from your neighbor who sells herbs to make people feel better, to a health institute that people can go to in order to become purified by purging themselves, to the people who go to Mexico to get the drug Laetrile (a drug made out of apricot pits) for cancer. You may need to go to the library to find some facts about a different approach to medicine. Be sure to include why people feel that this approach works.

REVISING

When you quote material that you get from the library to help you with an assignment, documenting the material accurately according to the Modern Language Association (MLA) standards is important. This is explained in detail in the revision section following "No Pablo, No Story." That section tells how to do a Works Cited entry for a magazine article. For the writing assignment that you are doing for "Ancient Secrets," you may find information in a book, so it is important for you to know how to do an entry for this item, also.

Examples:

> **Flachmann, Kim and Michael Flachmann.** *The Prose Reader: Essays for Thinking, Reading, and Writing.* **2nd. ed. Englewood Cliffs, NJ: Prentice Hall, 1990.**

> **Flachmann, Kim and Michael Flachmann.** names of authors

Notice that the first name listed is in reverse order for the purpose of alphabetizing. The next author's name is in normal order.

> *The Prose Reader: Essays for Thinking, Reading, and Writing.* title and subtitle

Notice that the main title comes first, then a colon and the subtitle.

> **2nd. ed.** (book edition)
> **Englewood Cliffs, NJ:** (city of publication followed by a colon)
> **Prentice Hall,** (publisher followed by a comma)
> **1990.** (copyright date followed by a period)

Notice also where there are periods and commas. These are necessary to indicate the divisions in your documentation. Be sure to document any quotes that you use in your writing and include a Works Cited sheet at the end.

EDITING

Abbreviations should generally be avoided in academic writing, but they are allowed in the case of indicating personal and professional titles. A personal title would come before a name like *Ms., Mrs., Dr.,* or *Mr.* A professional title would come after a name like *M.D.* or *Ph.D.*

Example:

> "... where she also obtained a master's degree in molecular biology and is currently working toward her *Ph.D.*" (¶4)

In this case the **Ph.D.** stands for doctorate of philosophy. If you want to write a person's name and title and include the person's first name, you may abbreviate the title before the person's name.

Examples:

    Dr. Jane Smith   Prof. John Brown   Rev. Jesse Jackson

If, however, you are only using the person's surname, you should not abbreviate the title.

Examples:

    Doctor Smith   Professor Brown   Reverend Jackson

Check through your writing assignment to be sure that you have used personal and professional titles correctly.

When writing people's **names**, the first time the name is used the person's full name should be written in order to clearly identify him or her. After that, the person can be referred to just by his or her last name.

Examples:

> Then *Mark Ludwig*, a violinist in the Boston Symphony Orchestra, began bringing it to light—a task that still consumes him.

> Intrigued, *Ludwig* spent two years making inquiries and obtaining copies of the music by mail.

Notice how both of the references to the person's name do not have to come in the same paragraph, just in the same piece of writing. Check over your writing assignment to see if you have written proper names correctly.

The Legendary Bay's Historic Betrayal

Peter C. Newman

PREREADING

The Hudson Bay Company is famous for fur trading. Write how you feel about using animal pelts for coats. Are there any animals that you can think of that you wouldn't mind wearing a coat made of their fur? Do you wear leather shoes or carry a leather purse? What is the difference between wearing a fur coat and wearing leather shoes?

DEFINING

lamenting (¶1)   feeling sorrow, grieving

insatiable (¶4)   incapable of being satisfied

peering (¶4)   peeking, looking

myopically (¶4)   nearsightedly

minted (¶5)   made or created

dividends (¶5)   portions paid to stockholders of the year's surplus profit

domiciled (¶5)   established in residence

matrix (¶5)   that from which something originates

Inuit (¶5)   Eskimo from northernmost North America

ecosystem (¶9)   a system made up of all of the elements in an environment

ostentatiously (¶12)   boastfully

The Legendary Bay's Historic Betrayal

Peter C. Newman

1   When Barry Agnew, the Hudson's Bay Co.'s vice-president of sales and marketing, announced last month that the chain was closing its 20 fur departments, reactions were predictable. Animal rights activists, celebrating their victory, handed out pink roses to Bay shoppers. Trappers in the Northwest Territories lamented this latest threat to their already diminished standard of living, since selling pelts all too often is their only link to self-sufficiency.

2   My own reaction was much more mixed. These are tough days in the retail trade, and it's entirely understandable that the hard-pressed Bay, which managed to lose $72 million in the past decade, wants to use its floor space for more profitable merchandise. But I've spent most of 10 years researching and writing a history of the Company (the last volume in the trilogy, *Merchant Princes*), and the decision to cut its final link with the fur trade hit me hard.

3   John Buchan, the Scottish author who as Baron Tweedsmuir became governor general of Canada in 1935, summed it up best when he noted that "the Hudson's Bay is not an ordinary commercial company, but a kind of kingdom by itself." And so it was. The 1670 land grant by Charles II of England to his cousin Rupert (who had helped restore him to the throne) eventually extended to nearly one-twelfth of the earth's land surface. During the two centuries of its undisputed monopoly, "the Governor and Company of Adventurers of England Trading into Hudson Bay" founded the world's largest—and oldest—commercial empire. Its outposts stretched from the Arctic, across Western Canada and much of the northern United States, down to San Francisco and over to Hawaii.

4   The cause of all the activity was an attempt to satisfy the European market's insatiable demand for beaver pelts, used to make the hats that stayed in fashion for most of 200 years. Peering myopically from its mud-and-twig castle, the beaver led the Bay men ever westward. As each pond was fished out, the trade kept moving deeper into the new land. "By its defenselessness, no less than by its value, the beaver was responsible for unrolling the map of Canada," noted the modern Canadian explorer Eric Morse.

5   The Bay minted a fortune on the fur trade, often returning as much as 50 per cent in annual dividends. The profit, of course, went to the Company's proprietors, domiciled in London until 1970, when the Company moved its headquarters first to Winnipeg, and later to Toronto. But what gave the Company its significance were the tough Scotsmen with pursed lips who sat out their lives in the little outposts, trading with the Indians while claiming a continent. They were castaways in a tightfisted land, yet they achieved something truly magnificent: they endured. And out of their endurance was born the matrix for modern Canada—its geography, history, and character. In the 20th century, the Bay repeated its conquest of the

Peter C. Newman, "The Legendary Bay's Historic Betrayal," *Maclean's* 1991. Reprinted by permission of Maclean's and the author.

Please note maps in appendix for references to places in this article.

West by establishing a fur-trade monopoly over Canada's Arctic, this time dealing with Inuit who traded for sealskins.

6   In the context of that long history, the Bay's move out of the industry that gave it birth takes on added significance. By distancing itself from the fur trade, the Hudson's Bay Co. has inflicted real hurt on those who least deserve it, the people who live in that part of Canada the poet Al Purdy has called "north of summer."

7   Hunting and trapping in the North is not a blood sport nor a hobby. It's a way of life, and fur is the only cash crop. I remember Bertram Pokiak, an Inuit elder from Tuktoyaktuk, telling the 1974-1977 Berger royal commission on the proposed Mackenzie Valley natural-gas pipeline: "Just like you white men work for wages and you have money in the bank, well, my bank was here, all around with the fur. The North is my bank."

8   About 50,000 Canadian natives still depend on the fur trade as the only alternative (or supplement) to welfare. Their choice is dictated not by preference or because they don't love animals, but by climate and location. "It would be a little different," the Right Rev. John Sperry, Anglican bishop of the Arctic, has noted, "if those who work against trapping and hunting were themselves vegetarian, but they're not. So why should they pick on a comparatively small number of northern people who have lived merely from animals because they happen to be above where crops can be grown. They've no fruit trees and no wheat. It's a sad and sickening situation."

9   At a deeper level, to Inuit—and Indians—hunting is something of a spiritual experience. They see themselves as part of an interlocked, animate universe in which every animal is treated as a relative of man. Georges Erasmus, first chief of the Assembly of First Nations, recently talked about man being part of nature. "We were not put here from another universe," he said. "It is very possible to play a responsible, productive role—for all of human society to be part of a balanced ecosystem."

10   None of this sounds theoretical when you visit the small communities of the far Arctic, as I did during my Bay research. That famous photo showing Brigitte Bardot petting a white-haired seal pup with imploring eyes devastated not only the St. Lawrence harp-seal catches, but the ringed-seal trade of the North. Although they don't hunt baby seal and although they shoot adult animals instead of clubbing them, the Inuit became the unwilling victims of the fur protesters. Ringed-seal prices tumbled to $2 from $30 a pelt; the economic basis of the region collapsed.

11   The Inuit's material culture has traditionally hinged on the seal (or caribou) hunt, to furnish them with food, clothing, and shelter. But a central part of that life-giving equation required the sale of sealskins for cash, so that rifles, ammunition, traps, and outboard motors could be bought, not to mention food and clothing. Instead of the 40,000 sealskins that were exported out of the North only a decade ago, no more than 1,000 skins are now sold and demand is still declining.

12   The Hudson's Bay Co. was not responsible for any of this. On the contrary, in the past decade, its store managers kept handing out credit long past the time the pelts had real value. But by so ostentatiously shutting down its fur departments, the Company betrayed its history and the fur traders who made it great.

READING

1. What is meant by the article's title, "The Legendary Bay's Historic Betrayal"?

2. How many Canadians depend on the fur trade?

THINKING

1. The fur trappers in Canada live far enough north that trapping is about the only way they can support their families. Fur trapping has been a tradition for these people for many years. Their whole economic system has been destroyed because people now feel that it is inhumane to trap animals for their fur. Do you think that there is harm in trapping? Why or why not?

2. The Inuit and the Indians of Canada consider man to be a part of nature. Chief George Erasmus said, "It is very possible to play a responsible, productive role—for all of human society to be part of a balanced ecosystem" (¶9). What do you think Chief Erasmus meant by this statement? What do you see as humankind's role in relationship to animals?

PREWRITING

Since you've read this article, have your feelings changed about making coats out of animals' pelts? Make a list of all the reasons we should or should not use animal pelts for coats.

WRITING

1. Your favorite department store has decided to stop selling fur coats. Write to the management to either congratulate them or to express your disappointment. Be sure to clearly express the reasons for your feelings.

2. Your local pound is almost broke, but they have come up with a plan to make enough money to keep the pound open by making coats of dog and cat pelts from the animals that they have to euthanize (put to sleep). Write an essay either supporting or rejecting the pound's idea.

REVISING

When arguing on such an emotional issue as animal rights, people have a tendency to use faulty logic. "The Legendary Bay's Historic Betrayal" is written in an objective manner that encourages the reader to see the other side of the argument, one that is generally ignored. How does Newman express himself in an objective manner? Look through the article to find examples.

For your own writing assignments on animal rights issues, the most likely logical fallacies that you would fall into would be appeal to pity and appeal to ignorance. Appeal to pity occurs when the writer tries to get the audience to go along with him or her by making it feel pity for a situation. For instance, the writer could describe the look on the poor baby seal's face as someone clubbed it to death by beating it on the head. An appeal to ignorance in this case would be trying to convince the reader that all of the animals that are used for fur are cruelly and inhumanely tortured to death.

Go through the rough draft of your assignment to be sure that you have not used either of these logical fallacies in your writing.

EDITING

The **past tense** form of a verb is usually formed by adding *-d* or *-ed* to a verb stem.

Examples:

Present Tense	Past Tense
like	liked
hope	hoped
want	wanted
look	looked

Go through your writing assignment and identify all of the verbs. Then make sure that they are either past or present tense as appropriate.

Beijing's Children's Palaces: What Education Is All About

Tony Cranston

PREREADING

Write about what you think about the elementary education children get in the community where you live. Are they exposed to the arts? Do you think learning about the arts enriches their educations? Why or why not?

DEFINING

spontaneity (¶1)   the quality of happening without an apparent cause

disillusioned (¶2)   freed from illusion

extracurricular (¶4)   happening outside of or in addition to the regular course of study

plagued (¶6)   annoyed

improvisation (¶10)   inventing without preparation

idyllic (¶11)   simple, carefree

potpourri (¶15)   a combination of things that usually don't go together

Beijing's Children's Palaces: What Education Is All About

Tony Cranston

1   The aim of every teacher is to broaden horizons and encourage learning, to allow the natural spontaneity and creative talents of the youngsters in their charge to flow out, and to foster their feelings of self-worth.

2   As a teacher in the northeast of England, I became more and more disillusioned as I saw the essential creative spark, the sense of wonder, slowly fading from the faces of the students, to be gradually replaced by the gray uniformity of boredom and frustration so familiar to everyone in my country. Why? It's not the youngsters who are to blame—nor the teachers, nor the schools.

3   The unfortunate fact is that in a cost-effective economy, where schools are to be run as businesses dealing in short-term profits, education suffers. The order of the day is: "Basic education, with little left over to explore or create." Or: "What's anybody going to learn from music, painting, and all that nonsense?"

4   I finally gave up and created an extracurricular group dedicated to exploring the arts—theater, mime, music, and dance—including the skills of stagecraft, choreography, costumes, stage design, and film-making. It was a runaway success. . . .

5   But here I must stop a moment and say I am by no means a genius, just an ordinary teacher like any other. Luckily, being a great fan of *China Today* (or *China Reconstructs* as it was then), I had learned of the wonderful Children's Palaces in Beijing. These are child-oriented centers for the arts and performing arts, and for education and the sciences, which obtain 80 percent of their funding from the state. Time after time I had read of the remarkable achievements made by youngsters in these extraordinarily enriching environments.

6   It was the inspiration of these palaces that sparked our own successes. We are not yet in the same league of course, for we are still plagued by lack of funds, but my dream is to build a Children's Palace in England so that children here can have the same opportunities. Hopefully, Children's Palaces will catch on in the rest of Britain and other countries, too.

7   *China Today* invited me to Beijing on a 28-day fact-finding tour in August 1993. They arranged for me to visit, talk to, and learn from the teachers and youngsters at both the Children's Palaces and the China National Children's Activity Center at Guanyuan. I was sponsored by Northern Arts in Britain, by the British Council in Beijing, and by friends who were familiar with my work.

8   Formerly part of the imperial palace and park, the exquisite setting for the Beijing Children's Palace in Jingshan Park (just north of the Forbidden City) extends over 50,000 square meters and consists of a park, beautiful courtyards, pavilions, terraces, and buildings. Here about 8,000 youngsters a year, aged between

Tony Cranston, "Beijing's Children's Palaces: What Education is All About," China Today, February 1995, vol. XLIV, no. 2, pp. 19–20.

Please not maps in appendix for references to places in this article.

four and 17, come to over 280 classes. Forty-five programs are available in art and sculpture—traditional and modern, Western and Chinese. There are also courses in music, dance, theater, martial arts, sports, languages, media, environment, radio, film, and more. Young people learn from dedicated teachers and from many special guest artists. A number of former students from the palaces' 40-year history, who have gone on to fame and fortune in theater, sports, the media and so on, gladly return to pass on their skills, enthusiasm and encouragement. Many students have continued to teach elsewhere and have now set up their own teaching networks.

9   As an English visitor, I, of course, had to see an English-language class. This gave me my first opportunity to observe teaching methods and provided a chance for the students, who were of a wide age-range, to practice their speaking and listening skills in English. One by one they introduced themselves, asked questions, and read me stories. I was told by their teacher to correct any faults—only to find that the students were able to recognize their own slight mistakes and correct them without help. I was impressed by their ability with English grammar and pronunciation—and very appreciative of the work their teacher had obviously put into this class.

Homework and Role-Play

10   A group of primary-level children were having a lesson in storytelling and improvisation, instructed by a teacher who was well known across China as a storyteller and actor. He would give the children a title, such as "A Day in the Park," and in twos and threes they had to work out a sketch with improvised props. Each group then performed the scene in front of the class. There was no shyness here as the kids went to work with confidence, using voice, gestures, classroom furniture, and a great deal of imagination. Afterwards the teacher commented and made suggestions for improvement.

11   In the afternoon I visited classes in dance and exercise for four- and five-year-olds, then watched dance rehearsals in the warm sun and idyllic setting of one of the palace courtyards. What an experience!

12   On the other side of Beijing is the China National Children's Activity Center (CNCAC). These modern buildings, set in 80,000 square meters of flowers, trees, and fountains, are an out-of-school center for further education. Its 4,000 or more flowers and trees blossom and bear fruit all year round, reflecting the hopes of parents and teachers for their children.

13   Tourists mingle with parents in the park, while children take part in classes. Later the parents can watch the kids playing or roller skating, or soak up the sun while eating ice cream bought from one of the vendors. The center has become an experimental development center for children's education. The fact that it draws thousands upon thousands of kids is not surprising: imagine playing on the dodg'ems or having an ice cream on a lush green lawn with all your friends, then running off to have a music or dance lesson, then coming back in the park to practice your English or check out the science exhibits in the marvelous Laser World. . . . And all this time your mum and dad are right there with you.

Partnership

14   Parents are encouraged to take an active role in the development of their children's education. In a class for keyboards accomplished four-year-olds play happily along with their teachers. Parents can actively take part in the lesson and see their children's progress for themselves.

Painting

15   Dance, music, computers, and science all blend together in a potpourri of available classes at the center. However, the pre-primary and grade-one-level art class is particularly noteworthy.

16   Teacher Zhao Xuechun's students are wonderful. Their artistic achievements are incomparable: Nine-year-old Wang Wei's copy of Michelangelo's *The Creation of Adam* is magnificent, and has already been displayed in Sweden and Canada. The paintings of five-year-old Zhou Yiezhuang are so technically accomplished and original that a film was made of little Zhou creating these works. I decided then and there that they should also be exhibited in England.

Performances/Exchanges

17   The children at both centers perform on a regular basis and sometimes go abroad to put on shows. Return visits by performers from other countries further encourage the development of new ideas and better understanding of other people and their cultures.

18   Academic achievement is not forgotten at the Children's Palaces; on the contrary, in the environment they provide, it positively thrives. The method of blending creative arts with traditional teaching methods works perfectly.

19   Unfortunately, when money becomes the root of education, there are limits to what teachers can do and what parents would like them to do. The Western system seems to hinder rather than help, and while we argue about school curriculums and systems, children's education, and with it their entire future, suffers. Perhaps Western educators should look more closely at this Chinese model.

20   Meanwhile I am still working on creating a Children's Palace in my own country, where any child can enter, free of charge, to broaden his or her horizons by exploring the arts and by simply having fun.

READING

1. Where does Tony Cranston teach? How does where he teaches differ from Beijing's Children's Palaces?

2. What is the CNCAC? Where is it located? What happens there?

THINKING

1. When you were in elementary school, did you learn anything about art, music, drama, or dance? How did learning either studying or not getting to study in these areas affect your education? Are you interested in any of these areas now? Why or why not?

2. In our present economy the tendency is to try to run schools as businesses. Do you think this is a good idea? Why or why not? What do schools have in common with businesses?

PREWRITING

Brainstorm a list of all of the activities you liked to participate in when you were growing up. Think of more formal things like dance lessons or organized sports or less formal things like fishing or building a treehouse in your backyard. See how many items you can generate on your list.

WRITING

1. You have the opportunity to propose a program for the elementary schools in your community that would take place in the afternoon hours after regular classes are over. The program would be free to the students enrolled. Write a proposal for what you think should be included in this kind of program. Be creative. Think about what you would have enjoyed doing or learning about after regular school hours when you were a child. You have an unlimited budget for your proposal.

2. Write an essay to share with your classmates about how an activity from your childhood has had a long-term affect on your life. Think of the things you enjoyed doing most such as dance lessons, being on the swim team, participating in Girl Scouts, playing soccer, doing youth theatre, or learning to cook at your mother's side. Use specific examples.

REVISING

Tony Cranston went to China especially to experience what it was like so he could write about it. He certainly couldn't have written this article if he hadn't had this experience. The more we know about something, the easier it is to write about. Your description of something undoubtedly will be more vivid and interesting if it is something you have actually seen or experienced. Many of the writing assignments in this book are based on actual experiences that you have had so that you can have the opportunity to write about what you know and are most comfortable with. Look through "Beijing's Children's Palaces." Notice the way Cranston describes what is happening and what he sees. Compare that with how a similar incident may have occurred in America. What would be the same? What would be different?

Read through your draft of your writing assignment. Have you written clear descriptions based on things you have actually seen and experienced? How can you improve this draft to make it more accurate or more vivid? Try adding specific details and examples.

EDITING

Some words are singular even though they end in s. In order for your subjects to agree with your verbs, recognizing these words, such as **news, mathematics, physics, politics,** or **measles** is important.

Example:

The **news** is about education in China.

Mathematics is the only course I have left to take.

Check through your writing assignment to be sure all of your subjects agree with their verbs.

Eating Big Bird

Joan Klatchko

PREREADING

Write about the kinds of food you like to eat. Do you like to try different things? Why or why not? What is the most exotic thing you have ever eaten? What kinds of foods do you really like? What kinds do you really not like at all? Why?

DEFINING

emu (¶1)   a large, flightless bird resembling an ostrich

paddock (¶1)   a fenced area chiefly used for grazing

60 kilograms (¶6)   about 132 pounds

wary (¶7)   on guard, watchful

hierarchical (¶7)   categorized according to status

assiduously (¶8)   diligently, persistently

stealthily (¶8)   acting quietly cautious, secretly

quirky (¶9)   unpredictable

peevishness (¶10)   ill-temperedness, discontentedness

penetrative (¶11)   abe to be penetrated

Aborigines (¶11)   a tribe in Australia

bushman (¶11)   person who travels the outback of Australia

lucrative (¶12)   producing wealth

hindered (¶15)   obstructed, in the way of

palate (¶15)   the sense of taste

capsicums (¶16)   a variety of tropical American pepper plants

splay (¶17)   with the emu, to spread the legs so wide that they can't stand

parched (¶17)   extremely dry

Eating Big Bird

Joan Klatchko

1   The first time Luci Teo met an emu, it almost ran her off her property: "I went outside and a big emu chased me around a bush about 50 times," the Singaporean recalls with a laugh. "I was so scared that the next time I went out to the paddock I took an umbrella. When the emus came over I clicked open the umbrella—'poof'—and they all ran away."

2   Teo hardly knew what a farm was, much less an emu, when she visited Australia in 1991. She and her businessman husband were simply looking for property so they could spend time with their daughter, a student in Perth. "I saw the emu farm for sale, only three hours out of Perth, and snapped it up," says Teo, in her mid-40s. "I was going to evict the emus and turn the place into a resort for Asian tourists."

3   Those plans changed after some quick market research by her husband and his partner. "They were so optimistic about the marketing potential of emu products in Asia that I immediately went out and bought 48 good breeders at [$180] a bird. I now have a pen of babies." The couple formed a partnership with a friend. A year later, Teo is commercially raising the big ostrich-like birds, once considered crop-destroying pests.

4   Although the country's first trial exports of emu meat were only in December 1991, there are already about 200 emu farms in Australia. That suggests that a multimillion-dollar industry is hatching. Many farmers stock emus alongside traditional produce. Now that the gourmet meat, oil, skin, and feathers of the bird are being exported to Hong Kong, Indonesia, Japan, and Taiwan, emu farmers like Teo are confident that Asians will soon be big customers.

5   "Friends told us we were crazy," she says gleefully. "'There's nothing out there,' they said. But I like the quiet life. And it's a challenge to build a business from scratch." Emu farming is such a new industry that even the manager of her farm, which is called the Banksia Country Emu World, knew nothing about the birds. "Neighbors teach me," she says. "Everybody here learns from one another. This is such a young industry."

6   Emus can be dangerous and are not particularly easy to work with. "Full

Joan Klatchko, "Eating Big Bird," *Asia, Inc.,* June 1994, Vol. 3, No. 6, pp. 82–84. Reprinted by permission.

Please note maps in appendix for references to places in this article.

grown they're over 6 feet [183 centimeters] tall and weigh more than 60 kilo-grams," says Graeme Ison, manager of Cyprus Emu Farm, half an hour outside Perth. "Yet their brain is tiny. With most animals you can anticipate what they're going to do, but not with an emu."

7   Wary workers, on guard against the emus' unpredictable behavior, carry sticks in the paddocks. The emus leap up and kick forward in the direction of a person's throat. Their hierarchical system: Biggest is best. The tallest birds domi-nate and instinctively attack anything smaller—a dog might last 30 seconds in an emu pen. They will also attack farmhands who fall. Says Ison: "Emus tend to get es-pecially aggressive when you load them onto a truck on the way to the slaughter-house." Maybe they're not so stupid after all.

8   Females dominate the males, even much larger ones. After the female emu lays her clutch of about a dozen eggs, the male guards them assiduously, sitting on them until they hatch and even raising the chicks. But in the confines of a farm, other emus will kill the babies, so farmhands must swiftly and stealthily "steal" the eggs and immediately place them in incubators.

9   Emus have other quirky habits. Explains Ison: "The father bird, who takes care of the young, rolls the eggs up to a certain date." So Cyprus developed special incubators. "The rack in these new incubators rolls the eggs just like the father does," he says. "Originally we used chicken incubators, just like everyone else. With emu farming it's learn as you go."

10   Putting up with peevishness means profit. Virtually every bit of the emu is marketable. Only the beak is thrown away. The skin, much finer than ostrich hide, is used as fashion leather for dresses and jackets. Several high-quality skins are needed to make a jacket that can fetch up to $1,400 retail. Skin from the legs, which looks remarkably reptilian, is made into wallets, purses and belts. Chinese, with their love of chicken feet, are the target market for emu feet. Feathers are used as souvenirs. The thick-shelled, pale blue eggs are sent to Aboriginal carvers, who turn them into works of art that sell for up to $140 each. Those who want to impress guests with an emu omelette have to pay about $20 per egg—though the volume of one emu egg is equal to 10 chicken eggs.

11   Emu oil retails at about $35 per liter. Japan, France, and the U.S. are experi-menting with it as a cosmetics base. There is also big potential in the pharmaceuti-cal industry; its anti-inflammatory and penetrative properties make it a boon for people with arthritis. Emu oil penetrates better than any other oil in the world: It must be kept in glass containers, not plastic, or it goes right through the bottle. Rub some onto the back of your hand with a bit of garlic, and within 30 seconds you will taste the garlic. Aborigines and old bushmen wrap emu fat around painful joints.

12   Each full-grown bird provides about 10 kg of low-fat, low-cholesterol gourmet meat (the neck, about 2 kg, is used for soup stock or smoked). Teo, who taught cooking in Singapore, sees that country as an especially lucrative market. "In Singapore there's a vigorous campaign for healthy eating," she says. "Emu meat is very lean and is best stir-fried. It takes only a few minutes to cook.

It's not gamy and tastes like good beef steak, but without the strong flavor. Actually, the more you chew the tastier it gets. I think it will have great appeal in Singapore."

13   The high cost of breeding and feeding emus has put the meat firmly in the gourmet range. Incubator temperature must be a constant 35 degrees Celsius for the 50-odd incubation days. Humidity control is another crucial and expensive factor (the father bird regularly douses himself with water so the moisture will soften the tough shell, allowing the chicks to break out of the egg). "Our electricity bills are so astronomical," says Ison, "that it costs about [$30] just to hatch one bird. Then there are strict regulations governing pen sizes, veterinary care, fencing, and record-keeping. It all adds up to an expensive product."

14   Until they start to earn income, farmers are required to maintain a minimum flock of 40 breeding pairs with a credit availability of $1,775 per pair to ensure that the birds are properly fed and housed. But captive emus, fed on an expensive high-protein mix, grow quickly. The birds are ready for market in 50 to 70 weeks, when they weigh 33 to 40 kg, much heavier than their counterparts in the wild.

15   Yet the delicacy's cost (in Australia fresh emu meat retails for about $20 per kg, while smoked emu costs $39 per kg in Hong Kong) hasn't hindered a steady increase in Asian sales. Henry Theil of T.C. Food Services has been importing emu meat into Hong Kong for two-and-a-half years. "We started off importing a few hundred kilos per year and now we're up to a couple of tons a year," he says. Many factors are steadily boosting sales: the novelty value, the adventurous palates of Chinese in general and Cantonese in particular, and the "health" factor. Theil says the price of kangaroo meat dropped dramatically in recent years, probably due to the increasing number of kangaroo farms, and the growth of emu farms may have the same effect on that product. ""It's a delicious meat, especially smoked," he says. "Many restaurants make a steak tartare with smoked emu. Wonderful."

16   Finding emu on a menu takes some looking. Watch for Australian food promotions. The Jakarta Hilton Hotel offers emu every Sunday, and Japan imports "substantial amounts," according to Western Australia's Department of Commerce and Trade. Qantas Airways serves emu meat to first-class passengers on its Australia-Japan route. Cathay Pacific served emu in its first-class buffet selection during an Australian food promotion last year. "It was very well received," says Ludwig Debatin, Cathay's catering manager in Hong Kong. "It was on the menu as smoked saddle [tail section] of emu and was served as a salad. We cut the meat in fine strips, marinated them, then served it with macadamia nut oil dressing with red capsicums, leeks, and carrots on a bed of romaine and red lettuce, with muntharie berries. We got very positive feedback."

17   On her farm, Teo speaks enthusiastically about restrictive feeding for babies (if they get too heavy their legs can't support their body weight and they splay) and other emu matters. Absent-mindedly shooing away flies, she surveys the parched landscape baking in the 40-degree heat. "You know," she says proudly, "I think I'm the only Asian emu farmer in the world." But maybe not for long.

READING

1. Why do people raise emus? What is the bird used for?

2. Why does it cost so much to raise emus?

THINKING

1. If you moved to Australia, do you think you would have bought the farm and raised the emus or sold the emus to make the farm into a tourist resort? Why would you make that decision?

2. Do you think the market for emu meat will continue to grow? Why or why not? Would you eat it? Do you think it would be a good investment?

PREWRITING

Read the two following writing assignments below. Choose the one that sounds most interesting to you to write about, and then freewrite about that subject for ten minutes. What kinds of ideas did you come up with? Did you think of enough information to write your essay? Be sure to organize your thoughts before you start to write.

WRITING

1. You have decided to enter a cooking contest where the person who can come up with the best tasting, most attractive recipe for the most exotic food will win the grand prize. Write a process analysis essay identifying and describing your outlandish dish. Be sure to include enough details so that your reader will be able to picture what it looks like and imagine how it smells and tastes.

2. The emu farm was a big investment for Teo, but she feels it was worth the risk. Write an argumentative essay for your classmates about why you think something would be a good investment. Choose something you are interested in such as a business, a piece of property, a work of art, or a car. Write a clear thesis, and then justify the points of your argument.

REVISING

Several different **rhetorical modes** have been discussed in the revising sections of this book: *definition, description, example, narration, cause and effect, process, division and classification, comparison and contrast,* and *argument.* A rhetorical mode is a way of organizing your ideas. Although the revising sections have so far asked you to just look at one of these modes at a time, these modes are usually used in combination. Read through "Eating Big Bird" to see how many rhetorical modes you can identify. Check the index if you need to review the modes.

Which rhetorical mode or modes do you think would be most appropriate for your current writing assignment. Why? Try experimenting with different modes to see if you like their effects better.

EDITING

Certain **collective subjects** require a singular verb if they are thought of as a unit and a plural verb if they are thought of as several individuals: *audience, team, group, family, committee, jury, army, navy, mob, all, organization, number,* and more.

Examples:

The *number* of home-grown museums *is* increasing.

A *number* of neighbors *are* getting together to open one museum.

Check through your writing to see if you have used any collective subjects. If you have, have you used the proper verbs?

Multiculturalism: Building Bridges or Burning Them?

Sharon Bernstein

PREREADING

Write about what you think multiculturalism means. Have you heard of the term before? Do you think people or different cultures can blend together as friends and in families, or do you think they should remain separate? Why do you feel the way you do?

DEFINING

fusing (¶1)   mixing together as if to melt

byword (¶1)   often used word

multiculturalism (¶3)   the act of relating to or joining of several cultures

interconnected (¶6)   to be connected with each other

inclusive (¶6)   comprehensive, including everything within certain limits

chauvinism (¶8)   prejudiced belief in one's own race

spearheaded (¶12)   was the leader of a movement

festooned (¶15)   decorated with strings or garlands hanging in loops or curves between two points

assimilation (¶18)   the process whereby a minority group adopts the customs of the prevailing culture

bolster (¶18)   support, prop up

curricula (¶27)   a group of related courses

poignantly (¶38)   touchingly, movingly

Multiculturalism: Building Bridges or Burning Them?

Sharon Bernstein

1   Multiculturalism—the notion that ethnic and cultural groups in the United States should preserve their identities instead of fusing them in a melting pot—has become a byword in education in Los Angeles and other cities.

2   But now, educators at the elementary, secondary, and university levels are re-thinking that idea—and worrying that past efforts to teach multiculturalism may have widened the ethnic divisions they were meant to close.

3   Fearing that the current approach—which relies largely on ethnic studies courses and the recognition of special holidays and heroes—may have unintentionally isolated students from each other, teachers and academics are gingerly beginning to question the way multiculturalism has been taught.

4   "I think many people, especially in the post-Rodney King era, are beginning to realize that we can't just study ourselves as separate groups," said Ronald Takaki, ethnic studies professor at UC Berkeley. "We've gone beyond the need to recover identity and roots, and now we're realizing that our paths as members of different groups are crisscrossing each other."

5   Not that these educators have abandoned multiculturalism as a concept. Nor do they suggest schools are solely to blame for ethnic tensions in society and on campus. But, in growing numbers, they are struggling to better define multiculturalism's goals and ways to teach it.

6   At present, many courses either focus entirely on one ethnic population or teach a standard history and throw a few ethnic names into the mix. The new approach would teach events as they had happened—as interconnected and inclusive history that changed lives in every ethnic group, and was also changed by all of those groups.

7   The discussion is so new that it has barely begun to show up in the pages of education journals. But it is gaining speed among teachers, administrators, and university professors, many who were surprised to discover that others are voicing the same concerns.

8   Even students, searching for reasons why violence erupted recently at North Hollywood High School and other campuses in the Los Angeles Unified School District, suggested that some youngsters have misunderstood lessons about ethnic pride, developing ethnic chauvinism instead.

Sharon Bernstein, "Multiculturalism: Building Bridges or Burning Them?" *Los Angeles Times,* 30 November 1992, p. A1. Reprinted by permission of the author.

Please note maps in appendix for references to places in this article.

9   "They teach you that you have to identify with your own group," said Karina Escalante, a senior at Cleveland High School in Reseda, where African-American and Latino students clashed last year.

10   She said students receive conflicting messages that teach them pride in their ethnic identities but not how those identities can and should mesh with others in society. "They tell you to keep with your own. Then they tell you to go out and mix. They should have a program that says: 'Yes, you should identify yourself but then you have to go out and mix.'"

11   Educators in the Los Angeles district say they are particularly troubled and point to the violence that broke out in October between African-American and Latino students at North Hollywood and Hamilton high schools.

12   Esther Taira, the resource teacher who in 1986 spearheaded the development of a multicultural curriculum for the district's high schools, said she would design her course very differently today.

13   "We do have ethnic-specific courses, but they do not create the bridges we need," said Taira, whose course is an elective offered only in some schools. "Even when we do talk about more than one group, we tend to focus on similarities, and that ignores the problems in the streets. It is the differences that are the issues."

14   Among youngsters, feelings of isolation can start early.

15   In Christine Toleson's fifth-grade and Marcia Klein's sixth-grade classes at Pacoima Elementary School, where the walls are festooned with posters in English and Spanish, students said they felt happy and proud when the school celebrated holidays or held "appreciation days" for their ethnic group. Most students said they remembered discussing their heritage in class.

16   But very few students raised their hands when asked whether they remembered discussing the culture of a different ethnic group.

17   "On Martin Luther King Day, they were celebrating black people," said Gerardo Nunez, a Latino fifth-grader. "I went over there. Other people were not my color. I felt all alone."

18   Originally, the term multiculturalism was used by minority activists in the mid-1980s who rejected assimilation. They believed that students should be taught about their ethnic and cultural backgrounds, which would bolster their pride and preserve their cultural identities.

19   Within that movement, two competing theories developed. One, called particularism, emphasized separate ethnic studies courses, such as Chicano studies or black studies. The other, pluralism, recommended that information about each group be woven into traditional courses.

20   By far, the particularists have dominated, bringing to campuses not only special ethnic studies courses but clubs, dormitories, and celebrations that have ethnic themes.

21   For example, a typical class in a multicultural program would be "a course that an African-American student can take which gives him a sense of identity," said Deborah Dash Moore, director of the American Culture program at Vassar College in Poughkeepsie, N.Y., and an organizer of a recent conference on ways to teach American studies. "It gives him a cultural connection with others, respect for

his past, and a sense of knowing where he fits within a larger society of which he can be proud."

22   The new movement finds particularists and pluralists moving toward a middle ground, where instead of treating each ethnic group separately, elements from all their histories are woven into discussions of particular topics.

23   "I'm in the movement toward bringing them together," said Los Angeles Board of Education member Warren Furutani, an advocate of ethnic studies who was formerly the program coordinator at UCLA's Asian American Studies Center. "Because it means people can understand their own experience, but bring it together with other people's experiences."

24   Raising questions about multiculturalism has been difficult for educators, in part because the movement has come under intense criticism from conservatives such as Dinesh D'Souza, of the American Enterprise Institute, whose book, *Illiberal Education: The Politics of Race and Sex on Campus,* reached *The New York Times* bestseller list.

25   "Many people are very defensive, and have been put on the defensive by attacks by conservatives," Vassar's Moore said. "They feel that there is no room for them to be self-reflective, self-critical, that if they do some critical thinking they are playing into the hands of people who really want to destroy the entire enterprise."

26   In the Los Angeles public schools, teachers at all levels are encouraged to talk about the different cultures represented by their students. Most schools conduct festivals or hold special assemblies or parties to celebrate such holidays as the birthday of Martin Luther King Jr. or Cinco de Mayo, which marks the day Mexico defeated French forces in the Battle of Puebla.

27   In addition, the district has developed for high schools elective ethnic studies classes—including African-American studies, Mexican-American studies, and courses about Asian and Jewish concerns. From kindergarten on up, the reading and history curricular include stories and information about diverse cultures.

28   Cultural Awareness, the class developed by Taira, explores similarities between ethnic groups and discusses the contributions of a number of cultures.

29   But Taira said if she were designing that course today, she would take pains to interweave the lives and experiences of members of different ethnic groups. Sharing her concerns, Takaki, the UC Berkeley professor, said he wished he had made his 1989 book *Strangers from a Different Shore*—which chronicles Asian immigration to the United States—more inclusive.

30   In schools and at universities, they and others said, even courses that spotlight several ethnic groups tend to treat each group separately. A course might highlight African-Americans one week, Korean-Americans the next, and so on.

31   And, experts said, most students tend to take only the classes that relate to the group to which they belong. In Los Angeles, administrators said, many schools offer only those courses that relate to the majority of their student populations.

32   In such a climate, even the celebration of ethnic holidays has caused problems, with one group believing that another got more attention or boycotting another group's festivities, said Casey Browne, who heads the peer counseling program at North Hollywood High.

33   "To some extent I think we bring on racial tensions when we celebrate one holiday over another," Browne said. "Some schools do a better job on certain holidays than they do on others, and then the other kids feel left out."

34   Such problems have developed, said Bernadine Lyles, the school district's multicultural education unit adviser, because "the climate was not prepared" for students to want to celebrate the cultures of others.

35   She noted that a framework for multicultural education adopted by the school board last spring emphasizes "activities that would bring groups together, rather than those activities that might look like separation."

36   In the new course that Taira is developing, lessons are organized around historical themes instead of ethnicity.

37   If the subject is American agriculture, Taira said, the teacher might discuss how farming and ranching affected the lives of black African slaves, Chinese and Mexican immigrants, and poor whites who worked as sharecroppers—all within broader contexts such as family farms or the plantation economy of the South.

38   "There has been a drawing back from the notion that we just have to add more African-Americans, or add more Latinos, as well as the notion that we have to focus on victims," Moore said. "People are in a complex relationship with each other. They may be victims in one set of relationships and served in others."

39   Students sum up the situation most poignantly—and appear to offer the most hope.

40   After last month's racial brawl at North Hollywood High, senior Pele Keith called out to a group of African-American and Latino students who were arguing about the events of that troubled day.

41   "They say brown pride, but look, I'm just as brown as she is," Pele, an African-American, said, placing her arm alongside the arm of a Latino friend, Patti Martinez.

42   "Look at that," Patti sang out in reply, "the same color."

READING

1. Why have educators started rethinking the idea of multiculturalism?

2. What kinds of classes do students take when offered classes about different cultures?

THINKING

1. How do you feel about multiculturalism? Have your ideas about other cultures changed as you studied about them in school, or have you had the opportunity to study about other cultures? Do you think students should study about cultures other than their own? Why or why not?

2. In an effort to teach about cultural differences, some ethnic groups have discov-

ered an ethnic pride and have drawn closer together as opposed to being assimilated into other cultures. What do you think about this?

PREWRITING

Write freely about how you think the issues of different cultures would be handled in schools all the way from kindergarten through college. Write for at least ten minutes to see how many ideas you can generate on the subject.

WRITING

1. Cultural traditions change or are forgotten as smaller cultural groups assimilate into larger ones. Write an essay to share with your classmates about a special tradition or belief in your culture or family. You might want to interview an older family member or friend about the way things were done in the past in relation to the tradition or belief you are writing about. Be sure to explain what you are describing in a clear way so that readers who are not familiar with what you are describing will be able to fully understand.

2. Write an essay to be published in your school newspaper that will argue how you think the issue of multiculturalism should be dealt with at your school. Do you think that different classes should focus on separate ethnicities, or do you think classes should consider all ethnicities related to the subjects being studied in every class? Be sure to give valid reasons for your argument.

REVISING

In "Multiculturalism: Building Bridges or Burning Them?" Sharon Bernstein talks to many different people to get their opinions about what she was writing about. Interviewing other people to see what their thoughts are on your topic can be a valuable tool for adding examples and dimension to your writing. Talk to several people about your writing assignment and see if you can add some of their quotes to strengthen your paper.

EDITING

Sentences should be consistent in **person. Person** can refer to the person speaking or the person being spoken to in your writing.

Example:
> If *a person* learns about another culture, *they* will be more understanding.

This example is incorrect because *a person* refers to one individual and *they* refers to more than one. A correct example of this sentence would be:

> If *people* learn about another culture, *they* will be more understanding.

or:

 If *a person* learns about another culture, *he or she* will be more understanding.

Notice in these sentences how *learn* and *learns* are used to agree with *a person* or *people*. Go back through your paper to check to see if your sentences show agreement in person.

The Torturous Realities of Female Genital Mutilation

Beth Corbin

PREREADING

Have you ever heard of female circumcision? What do you think about it? Did you know that it is practiced in areas throughout the world, even in the United States? How does this compare with other forms of mutilation that you've heard of? Do you think of tattoos or body piercing as mutilation? Why or why not?

DEFINING

mutilation (¶2)   disfigurement, making imperfect by cutting off parts

excisor (¶2)   instrument used for cutting or person who performs the cutting

septic (¶4)   causing infection

pulverized (¶4)   crushed

retention (¶6)   involuntary holding in

accumulation (¶7)   gathering up of, collection of

keloid (¶7)   red, raised, fibrous scar tissue

obliterated (¶10)   completely removed

inertia (¶10)   resistance to motion, inability to move

intrauterine (¶10)   inside the uterus (womb)

excruciating (¶16)   severe pain or torture

deprivation (¶18)   denial of

docile (¶20)   yielding to supervision

subservient (¶21)   being inferior

consummated (¶22)   to complete a marriage by the first act of sexual intercourse

categorically (¶23)   without exception

The Torturous Realities of Female Genital Mutilation

Beth Corbin

1   *"There is no other single practice that has such a dramatic negative effect on health in the broader sense."—Dr. Mark Belsey, World Health Organization.*

2   The health risks and complications of female genital mutilation depend on the gravity of the mutilation, the conditions under which the procedure was performed, how much the child struggled, and the skill and eyesight of the excisor. There are no health reasons why a young girl must suffer the torture of female genital mutilation. In reality, the risk to her health can be quite deadly.

3   There are three generally acknowledged degrees of mutilation, all of which are typically performed without anesthetic: 1) **Sunna**—which consists of the removal of the clitorial prepuce or hood of the clitoris and the tip of the clitoris. 2) **Excision**—which is the removal of the entire clitoris, usually together with the adjacent parts of the labia minora, and sometimes portions of the labia majora. Some excisors make additional cuts to enlarge the opening of the vagina which is believed to make childbirth easier. (The opposite is true.) 3) **Infibulation**—the most drastic and mutilating form, which consists of removal of the clitoris, the labia minora, and much of the labia majora. The remaining sides of the vulva are stitched together to close up the vagina, except for a small opening, usually preserved by the insertion of slivers of wood or matchsticks. The small opening is left for the passage of urine and menstrual blood.

4   The procedure is often performed on the ground, under septic conditions, with the same knife or tool used on the other girls. In some areas excisors throw dirt, ashes, or pulverized animal feces on the wound to stop the bleeding. Excision is often a coming-of-age ritual, performed on girls 12 to 14 years old. Infibulation is traditionally practiced on girls 6 to 8 years old, however, the procedure is being performed—stripped of all ritual—on younger children (including infants as young as 3 months old), as parents fear the older girls, once aware of what is involved, will rebel. In many ethnic groups, girls who are not mutilated are considered unfit for marriage.

5   Infibulation is performed to guarantee the virginity of the young woman and

Beth Corbin, "The Torturous Realities of Female Genital Mutilation," *National NOW Times*, June 1994, p. 5+. Reprinted with permission.

Please note maps in appendix for references to places in this article.

to make her "marriageable." Men almost always refuse to marry a woman who has not been excised, and since marriage is the only means of survival for many women in most of Africa, the practice continues. The groom, or a female relative, will often inspect the women before marriage to insure that she has been excised. The smaller the opening, the higher the brideprice.

Immediate Risks

6   Immediate complications include: death from hemorrhaging or from shock due to blood loss and pain; septicemia (blood poisoning); infections of the wound, including tetanus, which can be fatal; retention of urine following the procedure due to blockage or because of pain when urinating; (depending on the eyesight of the excisor) injury to adjacent tissue or organs, including the rectum, bladder, urethra and the vaginal walls; failure of the wound to heal and the spreading of infection.

Long-term Complications

7   Urinary problems due to chronic infection, which may also lead to sterility if the infection travels to the reproductive organs; difficulty in passing urine, and menstrual blood; sometimes a large foreign body forms on the interior of the vagina as a result of the accumulation of mucous secretions; Keloid scar formation on the vulva wound can become so enlarged that it makes walking difficult.

8   Other complications include dysmenorrhoea (extremely painful menstruation) since menstrual blood cannot escape freely. Menstrual blood, trapped in a young girl's body, can sometimes back-up, causing unbearable abdominal pains and swelling. The London-based Minority Rights Group reported that a 16-year-old girl brought to a Djibouti hospital complained of extreme abdominal pain. When her scarred vulva was opened more than three liters of blackish, foul-smelling blood was released.

Sexuality and Childbirth

9   The sexual life of a woman is forever changed when she is mutilated. As documented by Drs. Masters and Johnson, a woman's sexual satisfaction is achieved by stimulation of the clitoris. Women who have been mutilated do not experience orgasm. Not only is the pleasure of sex removed from the women, but intercourse is actually quite painful in most cases.

10   Infibulation makes sexual intercourse impossible until the woman's scar tissue is cut to allow penetration. Unassisted childbirth is also impossible. If there is no one to cut the infibulation, both the woman and baby die.

11   Complications during childbirth are unavoidable for infibulated women. The tough, obliterated vulva has lost its elasticity and, if not re-opened in time, may fatally hold up the second stage of labor. The head of the baby may be pushed through the perineum, which tears more easily than the infibulated scar, causing a high incidence of perineal tears. This results in unnecessary blood loss, and the

pain produced may result in uterine inertia. A long and obstructed labor can lead to intrauterine fetal death, or brain damage to the baby.

12   Custom demands that the woman be reinfibulated after each delivery. This may be done as many as 12 times or more.

HIV/AIDS Transmission

13   While there has not been extensive research on the transmission of HIV/AIDS among women who have been excised, the evidence that bleeding or open wounds increases the likelihood of infection has led to concern among health officials. The practice of female genital mutilation involves blood-letting and the use of one instrument in multiple operations carries a high risk of transmission of any infection, including HIV/AIDS.

14   *Warrior Marks*, the novel which accompanies the film (by the same name) released by Alice Walker and Pratibha Parmar, quotes Dr. Henriette Kouyate as saying: "The [excisor] has her own blade, she cuts and passes from one child to the next with the same blade, soiled with blood, her hands also soiled with blood. So, obviously, if she's a carrier of AIDS and cuts herself, she can transmit it. If one of the excised children is a carrier of AIDS, she can transmit it. More and more you see HIV-positive children born of HIV-positive parents."

15   It is estimated that by the end of the decade more than 3.5 million women in Africa alone will be living with AIDS.

Psychological Impact

16   Medical literature reports on the physical damage of bleeding and infection when the genitalia of young women are mutilated, but little attention is paid to the psychological scars.

17   Family members whom girls have loved and had trusted subject them to the excruciating pain of mutilation and its immediate aftermath. Once the procedure itself is complete, the young girl's legs are tied together, usually for a period of two weeks or more, while her wound heals. The girl's diet is restricted in order to prevent frequent bowel movements and she is given only a few sips of water at a time.

18   Physically and psychologically, female genital mutilation can only be compared to "the excision of part or all of the penile shaft," says Fran P. Hosken of Women's International Network.

19   "The permanent deprivation of one of her most powerful instincts, while at the same time forcing her to satisfy the sexual needs of her husband, would appear to leave psychological scars that have, for the most part, been ignored," said Hosken. "Suicides by young women, unable to cope with the ordeal of intercourse and childbirth, have been reported in Upper Volta."

20   The questions Hosken would like answered include: "How would a man like to have the most sensitive part of his 'member' cut off? Would this not interfere with his sexuality? Would this not change his personality? How many men would consider the removal of the tip of the penis an insignificant operation that should

be done routinely to their male children, much as they have it done to their female children?"

The Role of Men

21   One reason given for female genital mutilation is to curb a woman's sexual desire, making her docile and subservient to men. In some of the ethnic groups, where men are permitted to have several wives, it is said that since it is physically impossible for him to satisfy them all, it helps if they are not too demanding.

22   Without the procedure it is said that women would not be able to control their sexuality and would therefore be a threat to men. Activists fighting to end the practice would counter that men's sexuality is much more threatening worldwide than women's. The purpose of female genital mutilation is clear and is often carried out at the expense of women's health and sometimes their lives.

23   In what may be the cruelest irony of all, the torture that is inflicted on women—to insure their virginity for marriage, and to "enhance" sexual pleasure for their husbands—may actually have quite the opposite effect. It sometimes takes weeks for the marriage to be consummated as the husband attempts to open the infibulated woman's scar using either his fingers, a razor, or a knife. If a razor or knife is used, the husband—according to some tradition—must have prolonged and repeated intercourse with his wife for eight days to prevent the scar from closing again. During this time period the woman remains motionless, lying down, to keep the wound open.

24   It is questionable how men get any satisfaction from these practices. A survey by Dr. A.A. Shandall of 300 Sudanese men (in Sudan, men can have more than one wife, and have total control over if and when women are mutilated), found that 266 stated categorically they preferred to have sex with nonexcised women. The men said they enjoyed sex with these women because they seemed to share more the desire and the pleasure of sex. Shandall further reported that in Sudan some husbands resort to anal intercourse with infibulated wives when penetration of the vagina is impossible.

25   Questions remain as to what kind of man could enjoy having sex with his wife when it causes her so much pain, or when she is incapable of experiencing any sexual pleasure. What pleasure is derived from placing half the population at risk for early death and health complications?

READING

1. What are the three basic types of female genital mutilation?

2. What are the long term complications associated with female genital mutilation?

THINKING

1. Do you think that you could ever insist that your daughter submit to genital mutilation? Why or why not? Do you think you would approve of it if the culture you

were living in did it all the time? How much influence do you think a person's culture has on the decisions that person makes?

2. The World Health Organization is opposed to female genital mutilation because of the risks involved. Do you think organizations outside a culture should have any say in whether cultures should be allowed to do what they want if they all consent? What about if they can't consent as in the case of the babies and young girls who are mutilated?

PREWRITING

Freewrite for ten minutes about what you think about the practice of female genital mutilation. Had you ever heard of it before? What was your reaction to this article?

WRITING

1. Your good friend is an exchange student in Africa, and she is considering being infibulated because she has fallen in love with a man from a culture where infibulation is expected of a woman before she is considered marriageable. Write her a letter giving her advice about what you think she ought to do and why.

2. Write a definition essay where you explain to your classmates a practice from your culture or your family that you feel is different from the way most people do things. Be sure to clearly describe what it is and what its purpose is.

REVISING

Revision is so much easier when you write with a word processor. Saving each draft of a paper you write makes it easy to go back and choose the best parts of what you have written and combine them into the best essay. Use the cut and paste feature to move sentences or paragraphs to where they will be most effective. If you have a style search feature, this can be useful, but remember that you need to decide what really works best for what you are trying to express. Refer to the section at the beginning of this book on how to use word processors to write. When used effectively, they can really enhance your writing abilities.

EDITING

When including a **list of items** in an essay, sometimes it is helpful to number them in order to divide them into categories. Look at paragraph three of "The Torturous Realities of Female Genital Mutilation." Notice how the three degrees of mutilation first have a number, then a parenthesis, and then the explanation.

Look through your writing assignment and see if there is a list of things that could be divided out. If you have no list in this assignment, keep this technique in mind for future assignments.

Diversity Down Under

Franklyn Ajaye

Franklyn Ajaye had an experience different than he anticipated when he traveled to Australia. Before you read about his adventure, write how you feel about traveling to new places. Have you ever gone someplace that turned out to be much different than you anticipated? In what ways was it different? Do you like to travel? Why or why not?

DEFINING

gig (¶3)   an engagement to perform

eschew (¶6)   avoid, stay away from

reclusive (¶6)   being secluded and solitary

foray (¶13)   a raid in an attempt to provide food or other spoils

irony (¶18)   humor that comes from words being used that are the opposite of what they are intended for

constrained (¶19)   forced, restricted

intermediary (¶20)   go-between

notorious (¶20)   widely and unfavorably known

volatile (¶20)   likely to explode

infamous (¶22)   having a bad reputation

escalation (¶23)   speeding up

indigenous (¶25)   native, original

nomadic (¶25)   having no permanent home

squalor (¶25)   the condition of being filthy or foul

languish (¶25)   to become weak and dull

dismantled (¶26)   taken apart

netherworld (¶27)   the world of the dead or the punishment of hell

ambivalence (¶28)   feeling opposite emotions at the same time

incongruity (¶30)   a lack of harmony or appropriateness

polarization (¶30)   the having or showing of two contrary qualities

maelstrom (¶33)   dangerously agitated state of emotions

expatriate (¶34)   a person living away from his or her native land

Diversity Down Under

Franklyn Ajaye

1   I was working in Atlanta in 1985 when I received a call from my agent.

2   "How would you like to work in Sydney, Australia, for two months?" he asked. "They want to bring some American comedians down."

3   I wasn't confident I could entertain a foreign audience, but I needed an adventure to take my mind off of things—the rise of high-energy comedy, which doesn't suit my laid-back style; the breakup of my live-in relationship—so I took the gig. But when I told friends about my impending trip, their comments were often the same: "I hear they don't like black people over there."

4   "So," I always replied, "they don't like black people over here."

5   It wasn't a flip answer. I had worked the South without incident and, being a tennis buff, had read *Arthur Ashe: Portrait in Motion,* in which Ashe talks about his many trips to Australia and his warm feelings for the Australian people and their culture. So in late October I took off for Sydney, along with two other American comedians, Steve Bluestein and Bill Kirchenbauer.

6   The flight "down under" took 20 hours, but it was four days before I could stop falling asleep at 6 in the evening and waking up at 2 a.m.—just in time for *Bonanza* reruns. There wasn't much else that was familiar. But that forced me to eschew my normally reclusive ways and explore Sydney and the Australian way of life.

7   On my first walk from my hotel, the Southern Cross, past Hyde Park and through downtown Sydney, I noticed that white Australians readily made eye contact with me instead of offering the averted or suspicious glances common in

Franklyn Ajaye, "Diversity Down Under," *Emerge,* April 1991, pp. 52–54. Reprinted by permission of *Emerge.*

Please note maps in appendix for references to places in this article.

American cities. Many would smile and nod as they passed. At the corner of Pitt and George streets I stopped and turned slowly, soaking up not only my surroundings but also the fact that I was on the other side of the world.

8   "Excuse me, sir, but you seem to be lost," a woman's voice interrupted. I turned to see a white, fiftyish couple beside me. "May we be of some assistance?" the woman asked.

9   "No, I'm fine," I said. "Thank you."

10   They smiled and continued on their way. I was startled but also curious. Was I on the other side of the world or in another universe altogether?

11   A few weeks later I was walking through Dalinghurst, a section of Sydney populated by artists and gays, when I saw a sign that read "Hog Heaven." I looked at the menu on display in the window and saw American barbecue dishes, so I entered.

12   "G'day, mate," a man greeted me. He was dressed in a T-shirt, shorts, no socks, and wearing blue boat shoes—not at all uncommon in Sydney. His name was Danny Poole, and he was an African American from New York, which *was* unusual in Australia. Danny found me a table and took my order, then brought out a bottle of wine, sat down, and told me about his experiences.

13   In 1980 he had come over for a brief modeling job. When the job was completed, he decided to look around Sydney a bit before returning to the United States. Then he fell in love with an Australian, married her, and having been impressed by the society's racial tolerance, decided to stay. The one thing he missed though, was barbecue and sweet potatoes, so he opened up Hog Heaven—his first foray into business. It was so successful that he was now actively scouting for a second location.

14   I asked Danny whether his race had made it difficult for him to obtain financing for either restaurant.

15   "No," he said, "I never felt my color had any effect on the money people. If it was a good idea and they felt I could handle it, it was a go."

16   "Why do you think that is?" I inquired.

17   "I don't really know," he answered, "but it seems that Australians don't assume that black people are stupid. Plus, over here I'm considered American."

18   Over the course of my stay in Sydney I found both of Danny's observations to be accurate. Due to their geographic location, Australians understand what it's like to be an outsider. But to me it was a great irony—coming half-way around the world to be treated like an American. In the States I always felt detached; I considered myself in the society but not of it. There were too many contradictions. How could I be proud of my country when my country wasn't proud of me? The first time I ever felt like an American was before the 1983 NBA All-Star Game, when Marvin Gaye sang the national anthem.

19   Realizing, however, that I had no negative stereotypes to overcome in the mind of the average Australian was tremendously liberating. But where I felt liberated, the two comedians I had come over with felt constrained. As white males coming from a society that catered to them, they had to make great adjustments to the new culture.

20   One month into the engagement one of them asked me to be his intermediary. Notorious for his volatile temperament and lack of tact, he was having difficulty with the Australians.

21   "Hey," I told him, "this is their country. Over here you ask, you don't demand." It was a tough concept for him to grasp.

22   So where did the perception of Australia as a milder South Africa originate? It is an image not entirely without justification. First there was the White Australia immigration policy, which was enacted in 1901 (before that, unofficial restrictions were exercised) and in effect until 1966. The idea was to make it difficult for people of non-European lineage to emigrate to Australia. However, it was not aimed at blacks, as is assumed by many foreigners, but rather at Asians (specifically the Chinese), due in part to the proximity of Asia to Australia. In fact, after the policy was first proposed, a member of the Australian parliament made the infamous utterance "Two Wongs don't make a white." Even during the time the policy was on the books, however, blacks from the British Commonwealth emigrated to Australia without much trouble.

23   Since this policy was abolished, Australia has aggressively pursued a policy aimed at building a multicultural society. The reason was the country's realization—between the fall of Singapore to the Japanese in World War II and the escalation of the war in Vietnam—that it was part of the Pacific Rim, not Europe, and was vulnerable, being so far from its allies. Australia also realized it was economically weak and needed more citizens in order to broaden its economy.

24   In the streets and neighborhoods of Sydney there is now as much ethnic diversity as in any urban center in America. Missing, though, are people of African descent. In fact, I was the first African American that many Australians had ever encountered. Some assumed I was from the island of Fiji, since many Fijians look like African Americans with large Afros. They would greet me with the words *boola boola,* which I assumed was Australian for *nigger* until Danny told me it was the Fijian term for *hello.*

25   A second, and more fundamental, reason for Australia's reputation for racial intolerance is its treatment of the Aborigines, the indigenous people of the continent. The plight of the Aborigine can best be compared to that of the Native American. Mystical, nomadic, peace loving, with a deep reverence for and understanding of nature, the Aborigines—or Koories, as those in Melbourne prefer to be called—were not allowed to vote or even recognized as citizens until 1967. Reduced from a population of over 300,000 (and perhaps as much as a million) in 1788 to just 160,000 today, many Aborigines live in squalor on rural reserves, with homes that are nothing more than corrugated-tin shacks or worse. A significant portion live in cities. But there, too, they languish at the bottom of the socioeconomic ladder.

26   There have been three phases in white Australia's relations with the Aborigines. The first was called Decimation, an unofficial—and brutal—policy of the early 1900s under which Aborigines were legally hunted like animals on the island of Tasmania. The second, instituted around 1937, was known as Assimilation, but under this policy only mixed-race people were welcomed into mainstream society.

Full-blooded Aborigines were sent to the reserves. In addition modern homes were built (which the Aborigines dismantled), special schools were set up, and fair-skinned Aboriginal children were taken from their parents and placed in white Australian homes. The policy was resisted strongly by the Aborigines, and results were, at best, poor.

27 Australia now practices an approach known as Self-Determination, which is based on the premise that things should be done by Aborigines instead of to and for them. That does not, however, imply a hands-off approach. Twenty years ago the government spent less than $10 million a year on Aboriginal affairs. In 1990 it spent $915 million. Today there are affirmative action programs providing free education from preschool through college for anyone of Aboriginal descent. A program of the Department of Employment, Education and Training offers interest-free $10,000 loans for new Aboriginal businesses to help the people get out of migrant work and generate their own employment opportunities. But even with these incentives the destiny of the Aborigines seems bleak. With virtually no interest in assimilating into Australian culture and a younger generation equally disinterested in the ways of the past, Aborigines live in a netherworld, suspended between a new culture they justifiably resent and an old culture they no longer understand.

28 The situation of the Aborigines was a stark reminder that I was in no paradise, but I must confess that when Danny told me Australia's racial ambivalence did not extend to those of African descent, I felt a sense of relief. For once it was not I who was trapped in the void between a society's ideals and its practices. I awoke each morning knowing that having a good day or a bad day would not hinge on my race or on some slight, real or imagined.

29 I often hung out with Danny and a black West Indian named Richie, but not out of necessity. I interacted and socialized with people from a wider range of cultures and races during those few weeks in Sydney than I had in 36 years in the U.S.

30 On Boxing Day, an Australian holiday that falls the day after Christmas, I went to a park with a woman of Samoan descent, whom I had been dating, and two white South African friends of hers who had defected. As we talked and passed around a bottle of wine, I was struck by the incongruity of this foursome and thought about the deepening racial polarization I had left behind in America.

31 In Sydney I never gave a thought to race, except when I called friends in the U.S. and listened to their laments. They were always surprised that I didn't have any horror stories to tell—except one concerning the exporting of negative black images.

32 On Australian television there were few American shows aside from police/detective programs, with their disproportionate number of blacks in criminal roles. For most Australians this is their only perspective on African Americans and life in the U.S. This is true for consumers of American media around the world. After a constant diet of these images, is it any wonder that the Japanese make some of the statements they do regarding African Americans? Robert Townsend once told me that when he was in France promoting his movie *Hollywood Shuffle*, he had to explain that African American actors did not seek to play all

these black pimps and dope dealers, as the French had assumed, but that these were the main roles open to them.

33   My time in Sydney forced me to go to the core of my being and to define blackness apart from the narrow definitions put forth in America. I realized that my life and my essence were within me and should be constant regardless of my surroundings. I traded the pursuit of ethnic truth for the pursuit of universal truth in my comedy material and began to question how important race should be in one's consciousness. Unfortunately, in the unsettled American racial maelstrom, where diversity is tolerated but not accepted, race is fundamental.

34   I've been pondering what African American expatriate Vonetta Fields, a gospel singer in Melbourne, told me about her adjustments to Australian society: "I had to let go of racial defensiveness. I realized that over here I was just a person. It's worth the drop in income to get that feeling. A lot of black people never get to feel that."

READING

1. What is the name of the native tribe in Australia? How are these people treated?

2. Who got along better in Australia—Ajaye or his white companions from the United States? Why?

THINKING

1. Many people told Ajaye that he was going to have hard a time in Australia because they don't like black people there. How did what he discovered differ from what he anticipated? Why do you think they treat black people the way they do in Australia? Why do people treat black people the way they do in America?

2. Australia is now making a big effort to develop a multicultural society after spending years trying to keep Asians out and mistreating their own aborigines. Why do you suppose they are making this effort now? What advantages are there to living in a multicultural society?

PREWRITING

Freewrite about whether or not you think minorities should be more equitably represented on television or in the movies. Then make a list of all the attributes about yourself that you have no control over.

WRITING

1. Ajaye felt that any negative images of blacks in Australia came from the negative way blacks are portrayed on American television that is imported to Australia. Most races in America, except blacks and whites, are very underrepresented on television and in the movies. Write an essay indicating why you think the acting roles in movies should or should not be more equitably distributed among members of many cultures.

2. Ajaye said, "I awoke each morning knowing that having a good day or bad day would not hinge on my race or on some slight, real or imagined" (¶28). Frequently our days can be ruined by incidents or facts beyond our control. Write an essay for your classmates describing an event that happened to you because of something about you that you have no control over, such as your race, sex, age, or family background. Tell how this event affected you.

REVISING

Franklyn Ajaye wrote "Diversity Down Under" from a first-person point of view. He related his experiences as they happened to him so it was appropriate for him to use the personal pronoun *I* frequently. Look through the article to see how many times *I* was used. Both of the writing assignments in this section can be written using the first-person point of view. In both writing assignments you need to keep your intended audience in mind. The style of the first assignment should be a little more formal, while the second assignment can be more casual.

Go through the draft of your writing assignment and see if you have written it in the first-person point of view. If you haven't, try modifying your assignment to put it in first person. Then look at the style of your essay. Is it formal or casual? Is it appropriate for the assignment?

EDITING

The following **indefinite pronouns** are almost always considered singular when they are subjects of sentences: each, either, someone, somebody, neither, anyone, everyone, everybody, anybody, one, every, no one. The verb must agree.

Examples:

Everybody he met in Australia *gave* him a warm welcome.

Neither of his friends *was* as happy as he was.

Although these sentences were written in past tense, the same indefinite pronouns would be used with present tense.

Everybody he meets in Australia *gives* him a warm welcome.

Neither of his friends *is* as happy as he is.

Check over your writing assignment to be sure that all of your subjects and verbs agree.

An Indian Father's Plea: Don't Label My Son "A Slow Learner"

Robert Lake

PREREADING

Did you ever get labeled when you were in school? Labeling can include anything from being called a "slow learner" to being called "fatty." Did you ever give a label to another child? Do you think labels are damaging? Why or why not?

DEFINING

essence (¶3)   most important part

artificiality (¶3)   trickery, deception

intuitive (¶4)   gained by sensing, as knowledge

faculties (¶4)   abilities

regalia (¶7)   magnificent clothing

painstakingly (¶11)   very carefully

tentative (¶13)   uncertain, hesitant

psychic (¶13)   mental

adamant (¶14)   stubbornly unyielding

artifacts (¶17)   tools or weapons produced by people

unique (¶18)   singular

An Indian Father's Plea: Don't Label My Son "A Slow Learner"

Robert Lake

Dear Teacher,

1   I would like to introduce you to my son, Wind-Wolf. He is probably what you would consider a typical Indian kid. He was born and raised on the reservation. He has black hair, dark brown eyes, and an olive complexion. And like so many Indian children his age, he is shy and quiet in the classroom. He is five years old, in kindergarten, and I can't understand why you have already labelled him a "slow learner."

2   At the age of five, he has already been through quite an education compared with his peers in Western society. As his first introduction into this world, he was bonded to his mother and to the Mother Earth in a traditional native childbirth ceremony. And he has been continuously cared for by his mother, father, sisters, cousins, aunts, uncles, grandparents, and extended tribal family since this ceremony.

3   From his mother's warm and loving arms, Wind-Wolf was placed in a secure and specially designed Indian baby basket. His father and the medicine elders conducted another ceremony with him that served to bond him with the essence of his genetic father, the Great Spirit, the Grandfather Sun, and the Grandmother Moon. This was all done to introduce him properly into the new and natural world, not the world of artificiality, and to protect his sensitive and delicate soul. It is our people's way of showing the newborn respect, ensuring that he starts his life on the path of spirituality. The traditional Indian baby basket became his "turtle shell" and served as the first seat for his classroom. He was strapped in for safety, protected from injury by the willow roots and hazel wood construction. The basket was made by a tribal elder who had gathered her materials with prayer and in a ceremonial way. It is the same kind of basket that our people have used for thousands of years. It is specially designed to provide the child with the kind of knowledge and experience he will need to survive in his culture and environment.

4   Wind-Wolf was strapped in snugly with a deliberate restriction upon his arms and legs. Although you in Western society may argue that such a method serves to hinder motor-skill development and abstract reasoning, we believe it forces the child to first develop his intuitive faculties, rational intellect, symbolic thinking, and five senses.

5   Wind-Wolf was with his mother constantly, closely bonded physically, as she carried him on her back or held him in front while breast-feeding. She carried him everywhere she went, and every night he slept with both parents. Because of this,

Robert Lake, "An Indian Father's Plea: Don't Label My Son 'A Slow Learner,'" *Twin Light Trail*, no. 8, pp. 16–17. Reprinted by permission.

Please note maps in appendix for references to places in this article.

Wind-Wolf's educational setting was not only a "secure" environment, but it was also very colorful, complicated, sensitive, and diverse.

6   He has been with his mother at the ocean at daybreak when she made her prayers and gathered fresh seaweed from the rocks. He has sat with his uncles in a rowboat on the river while they fished with gil nets, and he was watched and listened to elders as they told creation stories and animal legends and sang songs around the campfires.

7   He has attended the sacred and ancient White Deerskin Dance of his people and is well-acquainted with the cultures and languages of other tribes. He has been with his mother when she gathered herbs for healing and watched his tribal aunts and grandmothers gather and prepare traditional foods such as acorn, smoked salmon, eel, and deer meat. He has played with abalone shells, pine nuts, iris grass string, and leather while watching the women make beaded jewelery and traditional native regalia. He has had many opportunities to watch his father, uncles, and ceremonial leaders use different kinds of colorful feathers and sing different kinds of songs while preparing for the sacred dances and rituals.

8   As he grew older, Wind-Wolf began to crawl out of his baby basket, develop his motor skills, and explore the world around him. When frightened or sleepy, he could always return to the basket, as a turtle withdraws in his shell. Such an inward journey allows one to reflect in privacy on what he has learned and to carry the new knowledge deeply into the unconscious and the soul. Shapes, sizes, colors, texture, sound, smell, feeling, taste, and the learning process are therefore functionally integrated—the physical and spiritual matter and energy, conscious and unconscious, individual and social.

9   This kind of learning goes beyond the basics of distinguishing the difference between rough and smooth, square and round, hard and soft, black and white, similarities and extremes.

10   For example, Wind-Wolf was with his mother in South Dakota while she danced for seven days straight in the hot sun, fasting and piercing herself in the sacred Sun Dance Ceremony of a distant tribe. He has been doctored in a number of different healing ceremonies by medicine men and women from diverse places ranging from Alaska and Arizona to New York and California. He has been in more than 20 different sacred sweat lodge rituals—used by native tribes to purify mind, body, and soul—since he was three years old, and he has already been exposed to many different religions of his racial brothers: Protestant, Catholic, Asian Buddhist, and Tibetan Lamaist.

11   It takes a long time to absorb and reflect on these kinds of experiences, so maybe that is why you think my Indian child is a slow learner. His aunts and grandmothers taught him to count and know his numbers while they sorted out the complex materials used to make the abstract designs in the native baskets. He listened to his mother count each and every bead and sort out numerically according to color while she painstakingly made complex beaded belts and necklaces. He learned his basic numbers by helping his father count and sort the rocks to be used in the sweat lodge—7 rocks for a medicine sweat, say, or 13 for the summer solstice ceremony (the rocks are later heated and doused with water to create purifying steam).

12   And he was taught to learn mathematics by counting the sticks we use in our traditional Native hand game. So I realize he may be slow in grasping the methods and tools that you are now using in your classroom, ones quite familiar to his white peers, but I hope you will be patient with him. It takes time to adjust to a new cultural system and learn new things. He is not culturally "disadvantaged," but he is culturally different. If you ask him how many months there are in a year, he will probably tell you 13. He will respond this way because he has been taught by our traditional people that there are 13 full moons in a year according to the native tribal calendar and that there are really 13 planets in our solar system and 13 tail feathers in a perfectly balanced eagle, the most powerful kind of bird to use in ceremony and healing. But he also knows that some eagles may have 12 tail feathers or 7, that they do not all have the same number. He knows that the flicker has exactly 10 tail feathers, they are red and black, representing the directions of east and west, life and death; and that this bird is considered a "fire" bird, a power used in native doctoring and healing. He can probably count more than 40 different kinds of birds, tell you and his peers what kind of bird each is and where it lives, the seasons in which it appears, and how it is used in a sacred ceremony. He may have trouble writing his name on a piece of paper, but he knows how to say it and many other things in different Indian languages. He is not fluent yet because he is only 5 years old and required by law to attend your educational system, learn your language, your values, your way of thinking, and your methods of teaching and learning.

13   So you see, all these influences together make him somewhat shy and quiet—and perhaps "slow" according to your standards. But Wind-Wolf was not prepared for his first tentative foray into your world; neither were you appreciative of his culture. On the first day of class, you had difficulty with his name. You wanted to call him Wind, insisting that somehow Wolf must be his middle name. The students in the class laughed at him, causing further embarrassment. While you are trying to teach him your new methods, helping him learn new tools for self-discovery and adapt to his new learning environment, he may be looking out the window as if day-dreaming. Why? Because he has been taught to watch and study the changes in nature. It is hard for him to make the appropriate psychic switch from the right to the left hemisphere of the brain when he sees the leaves turning bright colors and the geese heading south, and the squirrels scurrying around for nuts to get ready for a harsh winter. In his heart, in his young mind, and almost by instinct, he knows that this is the time of year he is supposed to be with his people gathering and preparing fish, deer meat, and native plants and herbs, and learning his assigned tasks in this role. He is caught between two worlds, torn by different cultural systems.

14   Yesterday, for the third time in 2 weeks, he came home crying and said he wanted to have his hair cut. He said he doesn't have any friends at school because they make fun of his long hair. I tried to explain to him that in our culture, long hair is a sign of masculinity and balance and is a source of power. But he remained adamant in his position.

15   To make matters worse, he recently encountered his first harsh case of racism. Wind-Wolf had managed to adopt at least one good school friend. On the way home from school one day he asked his new pal if he wanted to come home and play until supper. That was OK with Wind-Wolf's mother, who was walking with them. When they all got to the little friend's house, the two boys ran inside to ask permission while Wind-Wolf's mother waited. But the other boy's mother lashed out: "It is OK if you have to play with him at school, but we don't allow these kind of people in our house!" When my wife asked why not, the other boy's mother answered, "Because you are Indians and we are white, and I don't want my kids growing up with your kind of people."

16   So now my young Indian child does not want to go to school anymore (even though we cut his hair). He feels that he does not belong. He is the only Indian child in your class, and he is well aware of the fact. Instead of being proud of his race, heritage, and culture, he feels ashamed. When he watches television, he asks why the white people hate us so much and why they take everything away from us. He asks why the other kids in school are not taught about the power, beauty, and essence of nature or provided with an opportunity to experience the world around them first hand. He says he hates living in the city and that he misses his Indian cousins and friends. He asks why one white girl at school who is a friend always tells him "I like you Wind-Wolf, because you are a good Indian."

17   Now he refuses to sing his native songs, play with his Indian artifacts, learn his language, or participate in his sacred ceremonies. When I ask him to go to an urban powwow or help me with a sacred sweat lodge ritual, he says no because that is "weird" and he doesn't want his friends in school to think that he doesn't believe in God.

18   So dear teacher, I want to introduce you to my son Wind-Wolf, who is not really a "typical" kid after all. He stems from a long line of hereditary chiefs, medicine men and women, and ceremonial leaders whose accomplishments and unique forms of knowledge are still studied and recorded in contemporary books. He has seven different tribal systems flowing through his veins; he is even part white. I want my child to succeed in school and in life. I don't want him to be a drop-out or juvenile delinquent or to end up on drugs and alcohol because he is made to feel inferior or because of discrimination. I want him to be proud of his rich heritage and culture, and I would like him to develop the necessary abilities to adapt to and succeed in both cultures. But I need your help.

19   What you say and what you do in the classroom, what you teach and how you teach it, and what you say and what you don't say will have a significant effect on the potential failure or success of my child. Please remember that this is the primary year of his education and development. All I ask is that you work with me, not against me, to help educate my child in the best way.

20   My son Wind-Wolf is not an empty glass coming into your class to be filled. He is a full basket coming into a different environment and society with something special to share. Please let him share his knowledge, heritage, and culture with you and his peers.

READING

1. What kinds of rituals has Wind-Wolf participated in?
2. How did Wind-Wolf react to going to school?

THINKING

1. Have you ever been treated a certain way because of something about you that you couldn't control? Did it cause you embarrassment? How did you feel? Have you ever teased someone about something personal like a hairstyle, clothing, weight, or culture? Have you ever called someone a derogatory name? Have you ever been called a derogatory name? If you have, how did it make you feel, or how do you think it would make you feel if you haven't?

2. What do you know about the Native American culture? Did you learn new things about it by reading this article? Did you learn about other cultures as you read the other articles in this book? After having read most of this book, have your ideas changed about people who are different from you?

PREWRITING

Write two lists. On the first list include all the teachers you have had that you remember well for whether how well they treated you or how poorly they treated you. On the second list, write all the experiences that you have had that you can think of that had a significant effect on your life, whether positive or negative. Use the information you generate from these lists to help you decide which writing assignment to choose.

WRITING

1. Write a letter to one of your instructors, either current or past, explaining to this person how you think you should have been or should be treated differently in class than this person treats or treated you. Be sure to explain what about this instructor's manner or methods was or is a problem. Be specific. Use examples.

2. Robert Lake describes in vivid detail the experiences his very young son had. Write an essay to share with your classmates that describes in detail an experience you have had that changed your life. It can be an experience you had as a child or when you were older. Be sure to include the significance of the event and how it affected you.

REVISING

The ultimate goal of writing is communication. Sometimes we know what we're writing about so well that we leave out important details and information that would make our writing more clear. We just assume that our reader shares our same wealth of background information, and this is never true. Having a classmate or friend read your paper and then tell you what he or she thinks it said can be revealing. Try having more than one person read your paper, and then revise your paper keeping in mind the items you thought were there but your reader didn't see or understand. Remember to not get defensive when someone comments on your writing. Listen with an open mind to see what you can learn from what a reader tells you. So many times we cannot improve because we are too busy defending what we have already done. The process of having someone read what you write and explain what he or she understood can help you to enhance your assignment as well as improve your writing skills as you discover how to better explain and communicate what you are trying to say.

EDITING

A verb can have either an **active** or **passive voice.** The verb's voice tells whether the subject of the sentence is performing an action—which is the **active** voice—or being acted upon—which is the **passive** voice. See if you can identify the voice of the verbs in the following sentences:

Examples:
"From his mother's warm and loving arms, Wind-Wolf was placed in a secure and specially designed Indian baby basket." (¶3)

"He feels that he does not belong." (¶16)

In the first sentence the verb is **passive** because *was placed* shows what happened to Wind-Wolf. In the second sentence the verb is **active** because it shows what he *feels.*

Although the passive voice can be useful as in the example above, generally writing is more interesting when the active voice is used, because it gives more emphasis on the performer of the verb's action. Go back through your writing assignment and see if you have used active or passive verbs. See if you need to change your passive verbs to active verbs to make your writing more vivid.

Nigger, Please

Alison B. Hamilton

PREREADING

What was your reaction when you read the title of this article? What are your personal feelings about this word? Have you ever been called a derogatory name? If so, how did you feel when this happened? Have you ever called someone else a derogatory name? Why or why not?

DEFINING

slur (¶1) slander, belittling

bigotry (¶1) intolerance

etymology (¶3) the origin and development of a word

provocatively (¶5) deliberately inciting anger

toponyms (¶5) names of places

postulates (¶5) claims that

clique (¶6) small, exclusive group of friends

supplanting (¶7) taking the place of

disparagement (¶8) belittling

expounded (¶10) explained in detail

denoting (¶10) indicating

connotes (¶11) implies

linguistic (¶12) relating to language

inverse (¶12)   reversed in order

taboo (¶13)   socially banned

epithet (¶13)   abusive word

protagonist (¶15)   main character

stereotype (¶15)   oversimplified image

quandary (¶16)   state of uncertainty

integral (¶16)   essential

encompassing (¶16)   including

communal (¶17)   relating to a community

denominators (¶17)   common traits

cohesion (¶17)   ability to stick together

evokes (¶17)   suggests

fluctuated (¶19)   varied irregularly

exponent (¶19)   advocate, supporter

demystify (¶20)   to make less mysterious

naïveté (¶20)   innocence

barrage (¶21)   an artificial obstruction

desensitization (¶21)   to make less sensitive

derivative (¶21)   adapted from others

persistent (¶22)   refusing to give up

ingrained (¶22)   deep-seated, fixed deeply

potency (¶22)   capacity for strength

eradicated (¶22)   to get rid of by tearing up by the roots

evolution (¶22)   gradual process of change

nomadic (¶23)   people who roam with no fixed residence

bandied (¶24)   discussed in a casual manner

ambiguity (¶24)   uncertainty as to interpretation

volatility (¶24)   inconsistency

Nigger, Please
Alison B. Hamilton

1   *Nigger* is, perhaps, the most meaning-"full" word in the English language. *Merriam Webster's Collegiate Dictionary (Tenth Ed.)* (1993) defines *nigger* as: "[alter. of earlier *neger,* fr. MF *negre,* fr. Sp or Pg *negro,* fr. *negro* black, fr. L. *niger*] (1700) 1 : a

Alison B. Hamilton, "Nigger, Please," *Image Magazine,* October 1994, p. 16+. Reprinted by permission.

Please note maps in appendix for references to places in this article.

black person—usu. taken to be offensive 2 : a member of any dark-skinned race—usu. taken to be offensive 3 : a member of a socially disadvantaged class of persons <it's time for somebody to lead all of America's ~s . . . all the people who feel left out of the political process—Ron Dellums> . . . ." *Webster's* notes that *nigger* is now considered "perhaps the most offensive and inflammatory racial slur in English. Its use by and among blacks is not always intended or taken as offensive, but, except in sense 3, it is otherwise a word expressive of racial hatred and bigotry."

2   *The Random House Unabridged Dictionary of the English Language* (1987) defines *nigger* similarly, but dates its origin to 1640–50. However, *neger* is found earlier in Northern England in 1587, and *negre* in Middle French (early 1600s)

3   While the exact etymology of *nigger* remains unclear, both *neger* and *negre* come from *negro*, Spanish and Portuguese for the color black, which comes from the Latin *niger,* also meaning the color black. The classical Latin designations for African people were *Afer* and *Maurus* (Moor), not *niger,* although the Greek writer of *Acts of the Apostles* refers in chapter 13, verse 1, to "Simeon called Niger."

4   But where does *niger* come from? Does it connect to the River Niger or Nigeria? One source, the National Textbook Company's *Dictionary of Word Origins* (1991), states the Niger "river comes from the native *gher n-gherea,* river among rivers."

5   Recent scholarship by Martin Bernal (*Black Athena*, Rutgers University Press, 1991), however, provocatively suggests that the source of *niger* is the "beautiful blackness" of the Nigretai or Nigretes, nomadic tribes in Libya before 800 BCE. Their name, Bernal states, "came from the Semitic root √(n)gr (water to flow into sand) which was the origin of the toponymns Gar, Ger, Nagar and Niger, notably the River Niger, which unaccountably flowed east away from the Atlantic, apparently into the desert." In an interview, Bernal agreed that *gher-n-gherea* could be the source of *niger,* but he also pointed out that the root (n)gr, meaning "spring forth," "flow," "oasis," "river in the desert," could be found all over North Africa and southwest Asia. Bernal postulates that "the people of the Niger region—the people 'of the oasis'—were named after the place, rather than the place being named after the people." Thus, the Latin *niger* may indeed be connected to the Niger River *and* to the later *negro.*

6   *Partridge's Concise Dictionary of Slang and Unconventional English* (1989) makes note of two alternative 20th-century meanings of *nigger:* a member of a clique, originating in 1925 in Manchester, England; and a blackboard used to "kill" unwanted reflections from powerful lights, originating in 1930 in America.

7   The word *negro* fell out of use as a harmless adjective and slowly but steadily became a negative, degrading designation for Africans, supplanting Moor. Its first use in relation to African people traces back to approximately 1443, when Portuguese explorers went down the coast of Africa, past the Senegal River to Guinea, where they began trafficking African people as slaves. By 1555 (shortly after the first slaves were brought to London), *negro* was adopted by the English as their term for Africans and other people of color.

8   *Negros* had been traveling to the Western hemisphere since at least the early 1500s, when African slaves accompanied Cortes, Balboa, and other explorers and

traders. By 1619, when Africans were brought to North America to stay, *negro* was a firmly established designation for African people who had been enslaved. As in England and France, pronunciation variations likely contributed to spelling variations in America. Estate inventories in the 1650s listed "neager maides." The preamble of a 1652 act of the Warwick and Providence colonies states that it is "a common course practised amongst Englishmen to buy negers." Several writers, such as Geneva Smitherman, author of *Talkin and Testifyin* (Houghton Mifflin, 1977), concur that *nigger* in Colonial America was not distinguished in meaning from the words *negro* and *slave*. The 1933 *Oxford English Dictionary* defined *nigger* as *negro* but, by this time, *nigger* was shifting meaning into a distinct racial disparagement.

9   Clearly, the use of *negro* and *nigger* has centuries-old roots in oppression and indignity. Yet early black leaders such as W.E.B. Du Bois and Marcus Garvey campaigned for the use of *Negro*. In 1930, after persistent pressure from Garvey and others, the white press agreed to capitalize *negro* in reference to African Americans.

10   In the late 1950s, Richard B. Moore, author and founder of the Frederick Douglass Book Center in Harlem, formed the Committee to Present the Truth About the Name "Negro." The committee developed a resolution to adopt the terms *African* and *Afro-American,* and they petitioned the press to drop the usage of *Negro*. Moore published his book, *The Name "Negro": Its Origin and Evil Use,* in 1960. (It was republished in 1992 by Black Classic Press.) *Negro, black, nigger,* and *negress* were all unacceptable, Moore expounded, because they were put upon the Africans by the Europeans as labels denoting savagery, immorality, and distinct inferiority. According to Moore, *black,* too, was a label eventually reserved by Europeans for designating Africans. While the Black Power movement, beginning with Stokely Carmichael in 1966, successfully rallied for *Black* as the preferred term of identity, some would argue that the designation of *Black* still represents a European-based (negative) construct.

· · ·

11   Labels convey instant meanings. In modern usage, *nigger* connotes a variety of identities and relationships, depending on its use and its user. The meaning of a word at any given time is shaped by the interaction in which it is used. Names are propaganda devices of interaction; they categorize, influence emotions and behaviors, and they affect and shape realities. To Michael Hecht, Mary Jane Collier, and Sidney Ribeau, authors of *African American Communication* (Sage Publications, 1993), labels have two functions: "to denote similarities and differences, and to provide expectations and guide behaviors." Acceptable labels and names in one interaction may not be appropriate in another. Naming can also be name-calling. Richard Moore wrote: "The important thing about a name is the impression which it makes in the minds of others and the reactions which it invokes through the association of ideas."

12   Several linguistic studies have demonstrated that names have an impact on stereotypes. In a 1982 survey of 273 students of varied ethnic backgrounds, *Negro* was described with more positive characteristics than *Black,* except by black students, who perceived the inverse to be true. Less than one percent of the sample

listed the same characteristics for *Black* and *Negro*. In a 1985 study of 119 white college students, *African-American* was perceived as more positive than *Negro*, which was more positive than *Black*. *Blacks* were more likely to be thought of as "lazy, loud, and rude" than *African-Americans*.

13   In the context of Euro-Afro interaction, *nigger* is almost invariably taboo or at least problematic if a white person says it. Examples of censored interracial use of the word can be found throughout the 20th century: Paramount Picture's *The Nigger* was widely prohibited after its release in 1915. Many politicians and other public figures have been harshly criticized and/or forced to resign for using the epithet. A 1992 incident at George Washington University, caused by the student association president referring to a black student as "that nigger," led to an all-campus meeting on race relations. Kyle Farmbry, a former student association president, expressed the consensus of many participants: "If we so badly want others to stop calling us certain names, shouldn't we stop using them ourselves?"

14   In 1993 some parents and teachers at a Virginia school moved to ban the book *Jump Ship to Freedom*, by James Lincoln Collier and Christopher Collier, from the school library for its use of *nigger*. The primary character, Daniel, a slave in Connecticut, is referred to and refers to himself as a "nigger." The authors went so far as to provide an explanation of the use of the term: "We had to consider very carefully our use of the word *nigger*. This term is offensive to modern readers, and we certainly do not intend to be insulting. But it was commonly used in America right into the twentieth century, and it would have been a distortion of history to avoid its use entirely. In addition to historical accuracy, it was important to use the word to show how Daniel learned self-respect and developed self-confidence."

15   Opponents of the book argued that children might not get to the end, where the protagonist becomes a hero. They might only start the book, and come to internalize the stereotype of a "nigger." The book was ultimately left on the library shelves, with "guidelines to be developed" for its use in the classroom.

• • •

16   To understand how *nigger* works in African-American culture, it is important to look at the roots of African-American English. In *The Souls of Black Folks,* Du Bois discussed the double consciousness of African-Americans, wherein they are always being seen and judged through Whites' eyes. Carl, a 34-year-old employee representative at the Beverly Hills/Hollywood NAACP, sums up this quandary: "We're always having to redefine our identity for the other man. There has to be some description, some word, to validate us, and none of them are descriptions we chose for ourselves." African-Americans during the slavery era had to create a culture of survival within an environment of extreme oppression, and early "Black English" naturally reflected the tension. Language played and still plays an integral role in shaping that culture, encompassing African dialects and English terms of oppression. For example, the reversal process in Black English originates in African dialects: The word *bad* meaning "good" has its origins in the Mandingo language.

17   "Europeans" words have often taken on two levels of meaning—European and African-American—depending on the context. They become coded by their

users. Words with double meanings, such as *bad, boy, brother,* or *nigger,* are coded according to in-group/out-group distinctions, and the most subtle of shifts can indicate who is in, and who is out. In-group terms—terms with "secret" meanings—indicate familiarity, brotherhood, togetherness. Stated Joey, a 27-year-old advertising executive in New York City: "In a communal situation, a word like *nigger* becomes exclusive language. It embodies a familial code. For lack of other tangible common denominators, words exclusive to Blacks give us our cohesion." Corrie, a 40-year-old Los Angeles anesthesiologist, agreed: "When *nigger* is used in a positive or endearing way among African-Americans, it immediately evokes a sense of community. We try to find our ties, our commonality, and *nigger* reminds us of the suffering that binds us." Marc, a 26-year-old public relations executive, said, "It all depends on the tone. A black person probably wouldn't take offense at *nigger* because, well, you're one too."

18   As Marc notes, tone of voice often tells the listener the intent of the communication. Thus, for example, *nigger* can be "just as harsh among Blacks," according to Carl. Malcolm X, in the epilogue of his autobiography, said, referring to the Black Muslims, "We had the *best* organization the Black man's ever had—*niggers* ruined it!" Alex Haley noted that it was "the only time I ever heard him use, for his race, one word." "In some situations, even within our community, *nigger* signifies everything negative and dehumanizing that the white man wanted it to mean," Corrie said.

19   For the past 30 years, use of the word *nigger* has fluctuated in popular culture. Entertainers such as Dick Gregory and Richard Pryor were some of the first African-Americans to bring it into the public ear in the late '60s and early '70s. However, popular use seemed to decline in the '80s, perhaps because Pryor, the major exponent of the word, returned from Africa and declared that he would no longer use it. Comedian Paul Mooney, who wrote much of Pryor's pre-Africa material, has stood up to reenergize the debate with such routines as "Nigger Vampire" and "Nigger History Lesson" from his album *Race* (Stepsun Music Entertainment Inc., 1993).

20   Rappers, too, have joined in the controversy. In a recent *New York Times* article, several rappers asserted that they use *nigger* frequently in order to demystify it. *Nigger* can be heard virtually everywhere—on the air and in the streets. "Rappers bring out what's bad and make it popular. Nothing is sacred with them, and people love them. Rap has been the number-one selling music for the last two years. The problem is that a lot of [rappers] don't acknowledge who sweated for their success—the 'niggers' working in the fields, over 200 years ago," Terence, a 32-year-old photographer in New York City, pointed out. Author Ribeau sees value in some rap, but he too pointed out that many rappers have no historical perspective: "To demystify a word like *nigger* is a naïveté. Just by saying it a lot, you don't demystify it. *Nazi* maintains its horror."

21   *Nigger* is still a sensitive word, if only because attention is invariably drawn to its use. But pop-culture protagonists may have been successful with their barrage: constant exposure to the word has led to desensitization toward its troubled foundation. As Marc said, "It's not accepted, but people are getting used to hearing it."

Other ethnic groups, such as Puerto Ricans, have adopted *nigger* as a term of familiarity. And it seems that even white children have embraced *nigger* as an endearment. Joey relates, "I was standing on a platform, waiting for the train in Westchester County (New York)—a rich, white area. Some white prep school boys were waiting too. I was listening to their conversation, and every other word was *nigga* this, *nigga* that. I was surprised, but I wasn't offended. It's very trendy for kids to be using it; they're into rap, and they hear *nigga* as often as *brother* or *bitch* or any other word. I can't really blame them." Some white kids in Southern California have taken to using a derivative, *wigger.*

22   While many argue that the persistent use of derogatory terms, in whatever meanings, indicates deeply ingrained prejudice and oppression, others prefer to think that terms can change in potency and meaning. Richard Moore felt certain that negative terms like *Negro* could be eradicated, but seemingly few in the 1990s believe that *nigger* can, or should be. Sandra Evers-Manly, president of the Beverly Hills/Hollywood NAACP, said, "We can't get rid of *nigger* any more than we can get rid of racism. But we need to deal with it head-on. When I am called a nigger, I use reverse psychology or I get into heated debates." Sidney Ribeau adds, "We have to be looking at its evolution and at what it means in social contexts where race and class distinguish groups. We need to have people tell their stories. By erasing a word, you don't erase a history. If *nigger* could be banned, it still wouldn't get rid of the attitudes that it symbolizes. We need to create an environment for dialogue about the word's purposes and problems."

23   Is our use of and reaction to *nigger* based upon knowledge, perception, or belief? Is the word's power affected by local sensitization, or by media desensitization? Is the word's meaning from the mouths of African-Americans acceptable—but not from Europeans'? Does it make a difference if we accept its root as the name of the nomadic Nigretes?

24   As the word is bandied between classes, races, and generations, one thing becomes clear: *Nigger* exemplifies the ongoing ambiguity and volatility of a race in history and in America.

25   *Nigger.*

26   What does it mean to you?

READING

1. What was Richard Pryor's role in how the word *nigger* was used in the 1960's through the 1980's?

2. What was the controversy about the book *Jump Ship to Freedom?*

THINKING

1. Do you think the word *nigger* should be used at all? If so, in what context? The book *Huckleberry Finn* by Mark Twain uses the word in what the character Jim is called. The word is used in the historical context, and it was accepted at the time. Do you think that this book should be read in schools? Why or why not?

2. What is the worst word you can think of? Why does this word have such a strong effect on you? What other words bother you? Why do they bother you?

PREWRITING

Make a list of all the derogatory words you can think of. How did it make you feel to write this list? Remember, words mean things. What may seem like a casual passing comment to one person can have a devastating effect on another person. See how many words you can come up with, and think about the effects each of these words would have when directed to an individual.

WRITING

1. The book *Huckleberry Finn* has long been used as a required reading text in your local high school. Opposition has been raised because of the use of the word *nigger*. Write an essay to present to the school board sharing your views on whether or not the book should be used. Be sure to develop your reasoning.

2. Someone who you thought was your friend has used a derogatory word directed at you. Your feelings are hurt, but you would like to try to maintain your friendship with this person. Write a letter to your friend where you explain how it made you feel to be called this name, and explain how you feel about the use of such name calling in general. Be sure to use specific examples.

REVISING

Since this is close to the end of the book, go back through the articles in the book and note how they work together. What have you learned by reading these articles? What have you learned by using this book? How will you apply what you have learned to the rest of your life?

Go through the rough draft of this writing assignment to see if you can note how the articles that you have read from this book influence your writing.

EDITING

A common **comma error** to watch for is putting a comma before or after a coordinating conjunction when this conjunction is only used to join two parts in a compound construction, not a compound sentence.

Examples:
> *Nigger* exemplifies the ongoing ambiguity and volatility of race in history, and in America. (¶24)

The comma between *history* and *and* is placed incorrectly because *and* is just used to join two elements in the sentence. The sentence is correct as follows:

> "*Nigger* exemplifies the ongoing ambiguity and volatility of race in history and in America." (¶24)

Example:
> We need to create an environment for dialogue about the world's purposes and, problems. (¶22)

Confusion may occur in this sentence, but if you look at the content of the sentence, you can tell that the *and* is simply used to join the parallel element *purposes* and *problems*. See how different the correct sentence looks:

> "We need to create an environment for dialogue about the world's purposes and problems." (¶22)

Go through your writing assignment to be sure that you haven't included any unnecessary commas before coordinating conjunctions, especially before *and* and *or*.

Bridewealth as a Human Rights Issue

Merab Kiremire

PREREADING

What do you think the requirements should be for people to get married? Do you think that the man should ask the woman's father for her hand? Do you think the couple should go through counseling or classes? Does your culture or family have any special traditions relating to becoming engaged or getting married? Do you think that either the man's family or the woman's family should have to provide any kind of dowry or payment in order for the marriage to take place?

DEFINING

prestigious (¶1)   having high respect

surveillance (¶1)   close observation

token (¶2)   indication, sign

subservient (¶5)   being inferior

immemorial (¶6)   reaching beyond the limits of memory

patrilineal (¶8)   relating to ancestral descent on the father's side of the family

matrilineal (¶8)   relating to ancestral descent on the mother's side of the family

depicted (¶9)   represented, described

inevitably (¶9)   impossible to avoid

relinquished (¶9)   let go, surrendered

lineage (¶10)   ancestry

barrenness (¶12)   inability to have children

polygamy (¶12)   having multiple spouses

apportionment (¶13)   the act of dividing up

barter (¶13)   to trade goods or services

affluence (¶14)   wealth

perpetuate (¶14)   to cause to continue

subordination (¶14)   the putting down of, making inferior

abolition (¶14)   the act of doing away with

facilitate (¶14)   to make easy or easier

exploit (¶14)   take the greatest possible advantage

Bridewealth as a Human Rights Issue
Merab Kiremire

1   In many African social traditions and cultures, the payment of bridewealth is the practice of exchange of goods or wealth value for a bride. In the old days, families usually took brides from neighboring families of friends or relatives. It was not unusual for a new couple to be first or second cousins. In most cases, it did not matter who the bride or groom was, rather, what was important was the family status—was it a wealthy, prestigious or respectable family? A number of things constituted family status, ranging from family size (the number of wives the head of the family had and the number of males in that family), family wealth such as land, cattle and other assets, to the family head's position in the society around him (chieftainship, respectable elder, village advisor, or his age—wisdom was assumed to come with age). Thus, a socially respectable family-head represented, at least in part, some of these values. Therefore, a family's decision on which family they would take or offer a bride to, depended, to some extent, on these values, rather than on the couple involved. Such values, represented to the "giving family," not only assumed "security" for their daughter, but were also assumed to guarantee or at least enhance and boost their own social status. There were often statements such as *"she will open up a new gate for the family."* Another aspect was the value of the bride herself. If she was pretty, elegant, hard-working, well-bred, good-mannered, up-right, and "pure" (a virgin), she was worth more than otherwise. Consequently, as young girls grew up, one of the crucial roles of the female family elders was to ensure the promotion of these virtues as they were key elements that boosted a bride's value during the negotiation process between the two families. As a result, young girls were treasured and well protected because in real terms, they repre-

Merab Kiremire "Bridewealth as a Human Rights Issue," *African Woman,* London's Women's Center, December 1993–May 1994, Issue 8, pp. 13–16. Repriinted with permission.

Please note maps in appendix for references to places in this article.

sented potential wealth and prestige to their families. In some Hamitic tribes of North and Eastern Africa, a young girl was placed under perpetual surveillance from the time of her "maturity" (first menstruation) to the time she got married in order to guarantee "purity."

What Is Actually Exchanged?

2   The negotiation process was the determination of a bride's real worth. The male representatives of the two families concerned actually negotiated until they reached an acceptable agreement. The bride-wealth could be in the form of cattle, jewelery, pottery, home-made beer, or cash. The groom's family, if rich and prestigious, might want to show off and give very attractive offers, if they believed what they were acquiring was worth it. The negotiation process could be a very tough one if the bride's family believed both their family status and daughter were worth much more than what the groom's family was offering. Thus, the price varied from tribe to tribe, clan to clan, and family to family. Many people advance different reasons for bridewealth payment. Some say it is a token given to the bride's family as a sign of appreciation for a daughter so well brought up. Others say it symbolizes the strength of the bond between the two families. Yet others say it signifies the groom's ability to cater and provide for his future wife and family. But if that is the case, why the negotiation? Among some ethnic groups in Somalia, Ethiopia, Uganda (the Bahima), Kenya (the Masai), Tanzania (the Masai), Rwanda (the Batusi), Burundi (the Batusi), Zambia (the Tonga), the negotiation process is tough. Among the Bahima of western Uganda, a healthy looking young man of proven strength and stature was chosen and given a spear, and standing before the groom's family animal herd as they grazed, threw the spear with all his might into the midst of the herd. The point where the spear landed determined the part of the herd that constituted the bridewealth to be exchanged for the bride. We must therefore deduce that there was much more than "a token of appreciation," a "symbol," or an exchange of "gifts" since there was a demand involved rather than an offer of such tokens or gifts. What seems to have been at stake must surely be an exchange of goods for services.

The Real Value of a Potential Bride

3   ***Beauty***: this was important to the marrying family, a pretty girl was likely to produce pretty children. If they were girl children, their beauty was a plus during the negotiation process when they reached marriageable age. Handsome boys must surely boost their family status and prestige.

4   ***Physical strength***: a strong, healthy, hard-working girl represented potential good labor, including her offspring. Among the Bakiga of western Uganda, men still sit on top of hills and watch women tilling the fields in the valleys to determine the most hard-working young girls to marry either for themselves or for their sons.

5   ***Good breeding and manners***: a well-brought up girl with good manners was likely to make an obedient and subservient wife to both her husband and in-laws. She was likely to present fewer problems to her future family, and perhaps pass on such "good behavior" to her children, particularly her daughters.

6 ***Purity (a virgin)***: an "upright" bride has been, from time immemorial, every man's treasured dream—perhaps it was this that made a man feel totally fulfilled and greatly self-assured than the proof that he could adequately support his family or otherwise. It must have provided for him the opportunity to experience total monopoly and absolute possession of someone.

7 ***Wealth***: a bride from a wealthy family was a fairly good asset as she was likely to bring with her a lot of bridal gifts. That wealth automatically passed on to her new "owner" in totality. On the other hand, a bride accompanied by a lot of goods was good news to the groom's female relatives, as they were freely entitled to a generous share of their new in-law's possessions. It provided them with an opportunity for new clothing and handy household goods. After all, it was from the bridewealth paid for them that males in the family were able to pay for their wives.

8 ***Reproduction***: more than any of the above values, a new bride represented the continuation of her future husband's family, clan, and tribe through her reproduction. Of particular interest to note in this respect are the practices in, for instance, patrilineal inheritance where the children belong to the father and the family inheritance is through the male children. It was in these setups that the negotiation processes were lengthy and the bridewealth high. On the other hand, in matrilineal inheritance, where the children belong to the mother and her brothers, and inheritance is through the maternal male children, the negotiations were usually brief and the bridewealth far less. Among the Bemba of Zambia, where a potential bridegroom was required to live with his bride's family and provide labor for her exchange, the position of women in the family was stronger and more secure. Intensive premarriage counseling sessions and lessons ensured that the bride was fully prepared in every way, from sexual responsiveness and manners to the mastering of family chores and performances in order not to disappoint her in-laws.

The Bride in Her New Home

9 After the wedding and the arrival in her new home, a bride was given a new name by her new family. Her new name was not necessarily her husband's name, unlike in the west. Usually such a name depicted the value of the young bride in terms of her beauty, stature, physical strength, or expectations. It could for instance, mean beautiful, "brown" (light-skinned), delicate, soft, "productive." The name must, in effect, have been quite instrumental in concluding the "transfer." The bride now completely belonged to her new family—everything she represented: her ability to reproduce and labor. She was totally owned by her husband and his family. She could not question her husband's actions, his goings and comings, plans and decisions—she had no right to. The transfer was of a further significance since the bride has been paid for and given away to her new owners, she had inevitably relinquished any right to the property of her family of birth. Thus, we see that in such traditions and customs, inheritance is carried from male family members only and not female members. The impact of this transfer is devastating because it is through this act that women lost their economic empowerment and true worth. And what were the terms of "exchange" or "purchase"?

10   According to expectations, the bride must provide:

- sexual services to her husband
- produce children for him and his clan for lineage continuity
- provide the much needed labor force in the home

11   What then happened if the young bride failed to fulfill all or part of these duties and requirements? According to practices of many tribes and clans, her husband had a right to discipline his wife and institute such punishments for her as he felt befitting. The punishments ranged from a thorough beating, a minor face slap, a bottom caning, or denial of a night's sleep, to a denial of meals for a certain period of time. If, on the other hand, her so-called mistakes or errors were deemed too serious and her continued presence undesirable, her husband and his family would take her back to her people and retrieve part of, or the entire bridewealth, depending on what her contribution had been so far. Reasons for her failure might vary, ranging from lack of sexual satisfaction by her husband, due, for example, to sickness or heavy burdens, to barrenness, lack of sufficient labor output in terms of agricultural produce, and accusations of poor entertainment of visitors. In some unique cases, in tribes where wives, for instance, were communally shared between male members of the family (fathers, brothers, uncles, cousins), the crime might be a woman's refusal to be shared. Should the family reach an agreement that the woman be returned to her original family, her marriage would be terminated, her marriage names withdrawn, and if she had any children in her marriage home, she would leave them behind. She had no claim on any of her contributions to her marriage home; an act equivalent, in normal trade terms, to the return of inappropriate or unsuitable goods and services.

12   Sometimes if a woman found herself unable to fulfill some of her obligations, and was unprepared to face the impending consequences, she would approach her own family for assistance. For instance, if she was barren, found it difficult to fulfill her sexual duties due to household chores, or unable to produce sufficient agricultural output, she would arrange for her family to provide a younger woman for her husband, who could be a sister, a cousin or any other close relative. Thus, in some societies, we frequently find sisters or relatives also being co-wives. The children born of supplementary wives and the services so rendered, belonged, first to the husband who has paid for them, and second to the older wife. It would have to be much later in her marital life, after she was a mother of grown up sons, that she herself would be recognized. The alternative to such an arrangement by a barren, sick, or overburdened woman to make up for her "inadequacies," was that her husband could himself marry a second wife (if he felt that his "inadequate" wife was still worth keeping). In time, once the honeymoon was over and the younger bride settled down to the duties and responsibilities of reproduction and provision of labor, the vicious circle repeated itself, and inevitably, she too would go and seek for additional help or face an added rival brought upon her by circumstances. Such was the manner in which many African societies fostered polygamy.

13   What consequences did these practices have on women, and what was their status in their new homes? In a business transaction, the exercise of exchange of

goods and services for a cost is fairly straightforward. In effect, it entails the transfer of "control and ownership" and subsequently the transfer and handover of power over the "goods." We see a great deal of similarities in the traditional marriage and family structures where power goes down from the "boss" to the "subordinate"—in this case, the boss being the "purchaser," the husband, and the "subordinate" the "purchased," the wife. The duties of a wife in such a situation included such chores as washing her husband's feet and his clothes, making his bed, and serving him his meals while kneeling down on the floor. She had no right to sit and share a meal with him. She just served his meal, retreated to the back room to eat with her children and return to her husband only to clear the dishes away. Furthermore, the husband's meal was in most cases quite different from that of the wife and children. He was offered the best portions of the family meal. In some instances, he was the only one who could eat meat, chicken, eggs, fresh milk, and fish. The reason given for this was that if his wife ate some of these "nutritious foods" (like in central and western Uganda), ill luck would befall the family. Such special foods were served only to the husband, who would then call his male children according to their seniority for their respective portions. If the head of the house had a son above ten years of age, they shared the same eating space and special meals. Besides her husband, the woman was answerable to her mother-in-law for control, supervision, and instructions. It must be noted further that depriving the woman of control over her own life also meant that she could not make any decisions concerning any issues affecting her life. She could not, for instance, determine the size of her family, or choose the type of marriage she could have, whether she wanted a polygamous or monogamous marriage. If as a young girl she dreamed of marrying into family X, she might end up marrying into family Y, and if her dream was to have a husband all to herself to love and to cherish, she might find she had to share him with two, three, four, or five other women. If she found her marriage depressing and unpractical, she could not get out of it unless her male relations (father, uncles, and brothers) were willing to return the bridewealth and accept her back. In any case, she could not risk the loss of her children as she would have to leave them behind if she decided to leave. They belonged to the person who had paid for her reproductive efforts. Consequently, it was and continues to be the practice that women tolerated unhappiness and misery for the sake of their children. Her personal happiness was of no importance. She had to accept and adjust to her situation as a young marriageable woman, new bride, mother, and even as an elderly woman. Her life was always determined for her by somebody else, somewhere else. This meant a lifetime of misery in a majority of cases as illustrated by many a traditional wedding song by women that portrayed marriage as a hard, difficult, and torturous experience. If she produced ten bags of grain, it was someone else's prerogative to determine its apportionment, be it for home consumption, barter, or sale for cash. The wife might never see such cash or get to use it. Perhaps the most distressing deprivation these women were subjected to was participation in determining their daughters' future and true worth. It must have been extremely depressing to sit in back rooms while discussions were going on about their girl-children and their futures, which would probably never be improvements on their mothers' lives. Should a wife be widowed any time during her married life, she would be inherited by any appointed male member of her husband's family along with the children and the rest of his property. Her husband's successor could be a much older or younger man than herself. Whether he was already married or not was not important. She could be inherited by a male child of her husband, even her own son, though in the case of the latter, she did not have to perform sexual services.

Traditional Customs and Practices in a Contemporary Context

14   How do these traditional and cultural values relate to women today? Our societies have and continue to go through tremendous changes. The influences of modern, complicated money economies and their impacts are enormous. While a majority of the male members of our modern societies crave for modernization, their desire to cling to those old practices and beliefs that greatly cater to their continued "special place in the home" is greatly disappointing. Thus, whereas several aspects of an African woman's status in society are changing, sometimes positively, we find that the practice of payment of bridewealth has and continues to receive greater attention and value. In urban areas, the traditional marriage, which is potentially polygamous, has been modified and can now be registered at the local courts to legalize it. Bridewealth, which used to be paid in the form of family wealth, is now increasingly paid in cash. In some regions in north, east, west and southern Africa, the bridewealth paid is very high. With poor economic conditions in some of these regions, bridewealth has become so commercialized that even economic trends such as inflation and currency preferences (local or convertible) are taken into consideration when determining the bridewealth bill. Further considerations include the added value of the "investments" parents have made in their daughters, such as education, affluence, travel, exposure to other cultures, and so on. A pretty young woman with a university degree, a good job, well traveled, and exposed to international influences, is bargained for with higher value than an "ordinary" one. Some studies have shown that some fathers prefer their daughters to marry men who are rich enough to pay them large sums of money to enable them to purchase expensive consumer goods such as cars, farm machinery, and so on. We still continue to witness those practices and tendencies that perpetuate the subordination of women such as traditional pre-marriage counseling sessions that portray women as providers of sexual pleasures, rather than sexual partners, and emphasize wife-obedience and humble manners, hereby guaranteeing inequality and subservience. The payment of bridewealth is clearly a violation of women's human rights, and as such, deserves the immediate attention of the international community and all human rights observers to call for its immediate abolition to facilitate a process of real and positive change in the lives of African women. Then and only then will African women have a choice, be able to freely exploit their potential and rightly enjoy the sweat of their contribution. The abolition of bridewealth payment will go a long way in bringing about true liberation of African women.

READING

1. What are the consequences if a woman finds that she is not able to fulfill her obligations as a bride?

2. What are the six items that the new bride must bring into the marriage?

THINKING

1. Would you like to live in a culture where the groom is expected to pay for the bride? Why or why not? Do you think that there is some value in this system? Why or why not?

2. In the system described in the article, the women lose control over their own lives. What do you think about this? Do you think that any individual should have control over another individual? Think of some examples that you know of where a person has control over another person. Why does this situation exist?

PREWRITING

Do two clustering exercises, one for each of the writing assignments below. In the first one, put "the perfect mate" in the center of your cluster. In the second one, put "bridewealth" in the center. See how many ideas you can relate to each of the topics.

WRITING

1. Write a statement for your mate or potential mate in which you describe what you feel would be the perfect relationship and what you see as your roles for the rest of your lives together. Be sure to describe what responsibilities to the relationship you each have.

2. Write an essay to share with your classmates to defend or attack the idea of cultures using the tradition of bridewealth. Take into consideration in your writing what has happened in other cultures as their traditions have been condemned, eliminated, or assimilated into another culture. Be sure to clearly state your argument, then use specific examples and details to back it up.

REVISING

In "Bridewealth as a Human Rights Issue," Merab Kiremire uses the technique of drawing attention to specific examples in the list by putting what is called a **bullet** in front of each example.

Example:

> According to expectations, the bride must provide:

- sexual services to her husband
- children for him and his clan for lineage continuity
- the much needed labor force in the home

In your writing assignment, try putting some of the ideas in a list that can be written with bullets.

EDITING

Many different editing techniques have been covered throughout this book. Most people have only a few, specific writing problems that need to be corrected, but they may make mistakes with these problems frequently, which hurts the quality of their writing. Identify the problems that most frequently occur when you write. Keep track of these problems so that whenever you have a writing assignment for any class, you will remember to check for these problems on your rough draft before you turn your assignment in. Remember that to write is to communicate, and to take pride in your work is to take pride in yourself.

America's Little Italies: Past, Present, and Future

Jerome Krase

PREREADING

"America's Little Italies" is about the concentrated settlements of Italian people in different areas in America. In most cities and towns in America there are areas where people live together because they belong to the same culture. Write about the areas that you know of in your community. Are the areas large or small? Who lives there? What is different about these areas from the rest of your community? What is the same?

DEFINING

persistence (¶2)   endurance, continuous being

myriad (¶2)   large quantity, enormous number

extraction (¶4)   descent, lineage, coming from a certain family

serendipitous (¶5)   caused by apparently accidental fortunate discoveries

simultaneously (¶5)   at the same time

conversely (¶5)   on the contrary, opposite of

benign (¶7)   without harm

theoretical (¶7)   supposed, according to the theory

apparatus (¶7)   set of standards for measuring or testing

depicting (¶8)   showing

comprehensive (¶8)   all-inclusive, containing everything involved

stereotypical (¶8)   having no individuality

cohorts (¶9)   people in the same group

cameos (¶10)   small pictures

i.e. (¶10)   that is

festas **(¶10)**   celebrations, feasts

candid (¶12)   spontaneous, sincere, honest

Apulia (¶13)   in Italy, the region that appears to be the heel of the boot as you look at the country on a map

Mola di Bari (¶13)   a city in Apulia; *mola* means grindstone

assimilation (¶16)   the bringing together of different cultures

acculturation (¶16)   the transfer of one culture to another

dispersal (¶16)   distribution

homogenation (¶16)   making unified

replicate (¶17)   copy

perseverance (¶18)   refusal to give up, continuing

obliterated (¶18)   wiped out

intriguing (¶21)   exciting, fascinating

sojourners (¶22)   temporary residents, travelers

topographically (¶22)   depicted accurately according to a detailed description of a location

aesthetic (¶23)   with good taste, sensitive to art and beauty

facilitation (¶24)   the act of making easier or less difficult

millennia (¶25)   periods of a thousand years

default (¶26)   neglect, failure to take part

Pompeian-like ruins (¶27)   the city of Pompei was covered with volcanic flow

nonsensical (¶28)   not making any sense

anomalies (¶30)   irregularities, peculiarities

vestiges (¶31)   traces, signs, evidence

rabble (¶32)   a mob or disorderly crowd

epitomize (¶33)   summarize

exasperating (¶34)   irritating, enraging

America's Little Italies: Past, Present, and Future
Jerome Krase

1   Almost everyone—writers, scientists, and lay people—seem to be concerned with "stereotypes." Few people, however, actually understand what they are and the

Jerome Krase, "America's Little Italies: Past, Present, and Future," *Italian Journal*, Vol. IV, No. 5, 1990, pp. 24–29. Reprinted by permission of *Italian Journal*.

Please note maps in appendix for references to places in this article.

role they play in making social life possible in a complex world. Even fewer are able to explain how particular stereotypes come into being and are utilized by people to evaluate the world around them. Most dictionaries provide two definitions of the word "stereotype." The first, relating to the printing process, is "a one-piece printing plate cast in type mold (matrix taken of a printing surface) as a page of set type." The second, used in social psychology, is "an unvarying form or pattern; specifically a fixed or conventional notion or conception of a person, group, idea, etc., held by a number of people, and allowing for no individuality, critical judgment, etc."

2   In the area of ethnic studies, including Italian American studies, it seems that many of those who are engaged in research and writing about any particular group attempt to destroy old negative stereotypes and create new positive ones. These "professional ethnics" are especially good at creating superhuman myths of their favorite groups. "Super Italians," for example, all claim to have descended from Leonardo Da Vinci and argue that the Mafia is merely a Hollywood creation. Despite arguments against their use, stereotypes are inevitable. Some group stereotypes are more or less accurate. Some group stereotypes are more or less inaccurate. Generalizing about human beings creates stereotypes. The best explanation for the persistence of stereotypes is that they are useful. When people live in a complex social environment, they find it necessary to categorize events, people, and objects in order to effectively deal with the myriad of life occurrences that they experience. Without generalization the social world makes no sense.

3   Stereotypes, as all other social facts, have consequences, and these consequences can be positive, neutral, or negative both for those who employ the images and those who are their object. In this essay I will not be discussing traditional approaches to the study of ethnic stereotyping but will try to develop a different and perhaps more interesting way of investigating this common-sense aspect of everyday modern social life.

4   Specifically, I will focus upon the Italian American neighborhood as a "stereotypical" phenomenon. Even more to this point, I am interested in discovering, describing, and analyzing what there is of visual similarities in the neighborhood communities in which people who are of Italian extraction live. When people think of the Italian American community, a relatively common image comes to mind: The Urban Little Italy; colorful, lively, compact, as well as sensuous, sinister, and hostile to outsiders. Is this image accurate? If so, why? What is the role of history and culture in creating this image and its reality? What are the implications of this image for the past, present, and future of the community?

5   The origins of my research interests are both conventional and serendipitous. For almost twenty years I have been an activist social scientist who has simultaneously studied urban community life while involved in the search for solutions to practical community problems. My first modest contribution to the field was the demonstration of how the way people think of themselves (their self concept) affects the places in which they live, and conversely, how the way people define their neighborhoods has an effect on their own self-conceptions. This, in turn, led to a second-order problem of how people on the outside, especially those people with

political and economic power, view particular people and neighborhoods. Along these lines the final question is: what are the impacts of these perceptions on people and their communities?

6   Practically speaking, on the negative side, when people think little of themselves, they devalue the places they inhabit and this can result in the neighborhood being destroyed from within. At the second level, when outsiders define the same people and their locales as negative, the community can be attacked from without. Throughout history Italian American communities have been highly valued by those who live within them but have been negatively viewed by those outside them.

7   For the most part, my earliest research focused upon inner city non-white minority neighborhoods. Communities which were treated with "benign neglect" during the 1960s and 1970s. It is obvious, however, that my theoretical apparatus could be easily adapted to the study of local communities anywhere, anytime, and inhabited by anyone. There are many analogies that can be made between the fate of "Little Italies" and non-white ghettos in American society. The major differences can be traced to the relatively better ability of Italians to defend themselves both symbolically and territorially. One must note that Little Italies as long ago as the 1890s and as recently as the 1950s have been seen as "slums" and "criminal breeding grounds" by many social commentators.

8   The serendipitous side of my eleven-year study of Italian neighborhoods began as I attempted to collect photographs depicting Italian American community life in order to create a comprehensive archive of the "Italians of Brooklyn, Past and Present." As is still typical in Italian American Studies, the project faced many financial and academic difficulties. Without institutional support for either my time or expenses, I asked students in an extra course I taught for no compensation to provide photographic materials as part of their family histories. I also engaged several other students in Independent Study courses to go out and take pictures of "Italian Neighborhoods" in Brooklyn. Both projects awakened my interest in stereotypical phenomena: their origins, causes, and effects.

9   As I surveyed dozens of family histories and related documents, I noticed striking similarities, not so much in the individual details of each story but in the general form of presentation. For example, each student's insistence and emphasis on the "uniqueness" of their heritage was generalizable. Stereotypically speaking, these Italian American students saw themselves as "different" from their cohorts. They also seemed to be responding to a general, negative stereotype of their counterparts. They seemed to be saying, "I am not like THEM." They tended to counterpose their own family history to that found in standard texts.

10   From a visual perspective, what they presented as a display of their families' lives were almost interchangeable. Pictures of family members and stages of development included some funeral cards with cameos of the deceased. It is not so much that they all looked alike, but that they saw life alike, i.e., as a series of family events: baptism, communion, confirmation, birthdays, graduations, weddings, deaths, holidays, *festas*, home, and job and a great deal of candid eating around a table. The generational difference of their visions was most influenced by advances in camera technology; from early posed portraits to more spontaneous

glimpses of everyday life. The questions then arise as to why ethnics see themselves and their lives in similar ways? How do others see them? How do these views agree, or disagree, with each other? How do these images affect lives and life chances?

11   The second chance awakening occurred as I began to mount exhibits of the students' and my own work. My Independent Studies documentary photographers especially surprised me in their choice of subject matter. I had instructed them to go out and take pictures of Italian neighborhoods in Brooklyn. They were students who were well aware of ethnic stereotyping and its negative consequences. They were in fact quite proud of their own Italian heritage and sensitive to anti-Italian bias. Several had on occasion complained of discrimination and the way that outsiders portrayed Italians in the media.

12   What they presented to me as the fruits of their labor in the field was a large collection of candid and a few "posed" photographs that could have easily been the result of an assignment to create a stereotypical view of Italian neighborhoods. Most of the same elements were there; pizza parlors, wash hanging out to dry, men sitting in social clubs or hanging on corners, weddings, food shopping, etc. What I assume had happened was that the students had interpreted the assignment "show me an Italian neighborhood," to mean "show me a neighborhood that looks Italian." They did not take an objective photographic survey. They focused on what in the neighborhood looked Italian and what someone looking at their photographs would recognize as Italian-like.

13   The third surprise happened as I was visiting an Italian American community organization store front office to talk about some city funded social service programs. The group had recently mounted a photographic exhibition of the works of members. The framed prints were not of American locales but of places in Italy. Most of the pictures were more or less typical travel poster visions of Italy. One photo in particular fascinated me. It was of a triangular corner in a small Italian town. The image was quite ordinary in aspect but it intrigued me because my initial reaction to it was one of vague familiarity. I had seen it before, but where? I enquired as to the location of the scene and was told it was in a town in Apulia called Mola di Bari. I had at the time never been to Mola. I had traveled twice to Italy before the exhibit and once since. I had also surveyed many Italian and Italian American communities. Then it struck me that the scene repeated one that I had viewed in the Italian North End of Boston. The scale of the architecture was similar as were the stone streets, both a few centuries old.

14   I would not have been surprised by this observation if I had thought more deeply about it. There ought to be a connection between Italian Americans and Italy, and Italian American neighborhoods and neighborhoods in Italy. Discovering what the connections are, how they are expressed in visual appearances and analyzing their form and function became the goal of my subsequent research.

15   If there are regularities in the structure and functioning of Italian communities and connections between communities in Italy and the United States, we should ask what they are and why they exist. How does Italian culture influence the form and operation of the physical and social environments in which people live?

How does history create and modify the Italian culture of community? What happens when this culture is transported to America? How does the experience of Italians in America modify this culture? Can these questions be posed and answered through the employment of visual data such as photographs? I doubt that I will ever be able to answer, or even address, all of these questions adequately in this or any other form. I am, however, brave or foolish enough to make an attempt.

16 The shape of American ethnic communities is assumed to be the resulting combination, through the processes of assimilation and acculturation, of immigrant and American cultural values. Milton Gordon (1964), among others, has noted that cultural assimilation (acculturation) takes place more rapidly than structural assimilation (assimilation). That is, groups take on American culture at a faster rate than they blend into the new society. Part of structural assimilation is the random dispersal (for example, geographic and occupational distributions) of the new group in the host society. There are many factors which work against this ultimate dispersal or homogenization.

17 It can be assumed that immigrants attempt more or less successfully to replicate their home environment in the new location. In the extreme, one might suggest that they also may choose to locate in environments which most closely resemble their native ones and which make possible the preservation of central cultural values. The process of creating an ethnic ghetto has elements of what Louis Wirth in his work *The Ghetto*, called "voluntary and involuntary segregation." Of course ethnic groups in the United States have relative degrees of power to select their own environments, to maintain them or to modify situations to suit cultural tastes. One must also take into account the degree of difference between the immigrant's society and the dominant American social and cultural systems.

18 Not only do immigrant communities have relative abilities to select, maintain, and modify local environments to suit cultural tastes, they also differ in their ability and willingness to defend their neighborhood after it is established. The perseverance of urban Italian American communities is well documented. This local persistence is repeatedly demonstrated in Italy, for example, the communities almost obliterated by earthquakes around Avellino in 1981 were rebuilt on the same sites despite warnings of potential repetition by national authorities. Incredibly, except for the Po River basins, there is almost no place in Italy not prone to seismic disturbance of disaster proportion.

19 Most Italian communities count their age in centuries rather than decades. During such long periods of continuous habitation, the attachment of culture to specific pieces of territory and spatial arrangements has ample time to develop. Fustel de Coulange in *The Ancient City*, referred to these attachments as "sacred," and used the ritual founding of Rome by Romulus and Remus as an example of the importance of the "home" territory to ancient and primitive tribes. For contemporary Italians, the home continues to be sacred. One might suggest that the traditional Italian culture survives only to the extent that the local community survives and is maintained.

20 The Italian community in America is assumed to contain and display many elements of household, kinship, and local association which they hold in common

with their counterparts who remain in Italy. Much of the research on Italian Americans since the turn of the century has focused on the processes of assimilation and acculturation whereby Italians become more American and less Italian in their ways. Almost all of the literature emphasizes the relatively slow rate of change among Italian Americans as opposed to other groups. This is especially characteristic of those Italian Americans found in urban, working class neighborhoods which have resisted change due to cultural habits, discrimination, and voluntary segregation.

21   Despite the interest shown in the literature on the relationship between Italian American and Italian values, and the communities which represent and support those values, there has been little direct comparison of Italian communities in the United States and Italy. Carla Bianco's study of *The Two Rosettes* is a major exception to the rule. Her work is intriguing in that she notes not only common cultural elements but significant differences as well. For example, she notes that because American Rosettans emigrated in an earlier period of Italian history and then were cut off from Italian influences, they have preserved some of the traditions lost in the town of origin. Although both Rosettos were built on the top of a hill, Bianca noted that American Rosettans did not employ Italian architectural styles when they built their houses. I would predict, however, that a trained, or even a merely sensitive eye would find ample evidence of spatial expressions of cultural connections in Rosetto, Pennsylvania. In a related vein Donna R. Gabaccia in *From Sicily to Elizabeth Street*, noted the similarity between the home environments of immigrants and the neighborhoods in which they settled on New York's Lower East Side between 1880 and 1930.

22   Of course, most Italians did not have the opportunity, or interest as sojourners, to replicate topographically and architecturally their home towns. They came and stayed where economic opportunities presented themselves. For the most part these opportunities were in highly congested urban areas. Interestingly, dense environments were not unusual for Italian immigrants who left small, but highly populated villages and towns scattered throughout the countryside or who left behind congested neighborhood villages in large Italian cities. Italy remains today one of the most densely populated nations in the world, especially when one considers the ratio of population to residential spaces. This space, as well as arable land area, has always been limited on the Italian peninsula. Italy has a tradition of residential density.

23   An extremely important, although often overlooked, aspect of neighborhood community life is visual. We should be able to "see" culture. For example, the tradition of sex segregation in some Islamic and Mediterranean groups results in a particular arrangement of residential structures whereby interior spaces are provided for their activities out of view of nonfamily members. The cultural value of modesty therefore has a physical result. Women are not generally seen in public places, unless there for specific purposes, such as shopping, and seldom alone. Whereas for men, casual lounging in public areas is common. Even more easily seen are values which reflect social structure, such as age, sex, occupation, class, and caste are aesthetic values of color, design, and form. Ideally, the local community is an aesthetic

expression of the local culture. Most simply, the colors that people use to paint their houses are cultural expressions. With these ideas in mind, we should expect that Italian communities will have a certain "look" and that there should be some similarity in the appearance of Italian communities in Italy and the United States.

24   Based on hundreds of direct observations and thousands of photographs of Italian communities in Italy and the United States, I can outline some of the elements of the "Italian Culture of Community." These elements express themselves in physical arrangement, uses, and meanings of spaces and visual appearances. They are as follows:

1. The Italian community is small-scale and based around the facilitation of family and personal relations.
2. The community has a high tolerance, if not a preference, for high human and physical density.
3. The community exhibits the supremacy of private over public values in regard to space and activities.
4. The culture emphasizes individuality rather than conformity.
5. Italian residential communities tolerate mixed commercial and industrial uses within their boundaries.
6. Age and sex segregation for spaces and activities is a general feature of Italian communities.
7. Italian communities show attachment to traditional architectural aesthetics as exhibited, where possible, in design and construction, as well as colors and materials.
8. The Italian community places extreme value on the defense of individual and group territory.

25   In Italy, two millennia of natural, economic, and political disasters have found local communities to be virtually immovable. It, therefore, is not surprising that in the United States Italians have generally been the last to leave from changing inner city neighborhoods. This fierce attachment to the sacred soil, or pavement, has had many implications, both positive and negative.

26   Between 1930 and 1960, Italian Americans, through default, in many instances became *The* inner city white ethnics, living side by side with minorities in deteriorating central cities. When the Federal and local governments finally recognized the problems of poor non-whites in American cities, Italian Americans and other working class groups came to symbolize their oppressors. For example, busing for integration and neighborhood desegregation efforts at first focused on the few white communities left in large American cities. Residents of Italian American neighborhoods in the 1970s quickly became part of the increasingly vocal and socially conservative "Silent Majority."

27   In the 1980s there are new threats to what is left of the traditional American Little Italies while at the same time Italian American communities in the near suburbs and small towns come to realize that they are not immune to "progress" and change "American Style." Ironically, the greatest danger for urban Italian Ameri-

can neighborhoods comes in the form of Yuppies (Young Urban Professionals), co-ops, and condos. The history and resulting local culture of the Italian community made it possible for them to survive in places no one else wanted for so long, and yet this strength makes them most vulnerable in modern urban real estate markets. It could be concluded that urban Little Italies may exist only as "Ethnic Disneylands" in the future or perhaps as Pompeian-like ruins. Tour guides already speak in reverent tones of the Italian village-like life that once decorated the Little Italies, Sicilies, and Calabrias of Manhattan, Boston, Chicago, and San Francisco.

28   In recent years, there has been much talk, both informed and nonsensical, about a so-called new phenomenon in American cities—"Gentrification." Very simply, gentrification means the influx of higher status people into a particular area of a city. To some urban experts, particularly conservative economists, it is a blessing. To others, especially liberal social critics, it is a curse. Not long ago, the 1960s to be precise, the outflow of the gentry from the inner cities was seen as a major catastrophe by all except suburban developers. A leading civil rights proponent, Eleanor Holmes Norton, herself Black and, at the time Commissioner for Human Rights in New York City, openly expressed the fear that the city might become, in so many words—"too Black."

29   Today liberal social critics bemoan the movement of middle and upper-middle income people back to the central city because it causes "displacement." Displacement is a term for the forcing out of less advantaged residents from a neighborhood as rents and housing prices rise to meet the demand of the invading gentry. These same observers had earlier complained about the movement out of the city of the middle class in the 1950s and 1960s as part of the "white flight" phenomenon. People then moved out of the city because they were racists and now they are moving back because they are racists, or so it seems. Undoubtedly the perception of the middle class about the "livability" of the inner city has undergone significant change over three decades.

30   Throughout both these tidal movements of urban population, some concentrations of white ethnic neighborhoods remained relatively unmoved. One of these anomalies was the Italian American neighborhood.

31   It is not that Italian Americans did not participate in the exodus of whites from the central cities; they did in large numbers move and create new neighborhoods in urban fringe or suburban areas. They also expanded older Italian American communities already outside the central cities. However, significant or peculiar remnants stayed behind. It is these vestiges of Little Italies which, after surviving urban renewal, housing projects and minority group expansion, became threatened by the new gentry invaders.

32   There is a simple theory to explain the rise and fall of our cities' cores and the Italian American anomaly. The United States is a young nation by old world standards, and as an urban nation it is a comparative infant. American society is also probably the most anti-urban in the western world. One must note that our founding fathers especially feared the growth of cities and the rabble who would assemble there. Cities here have risen and fallen in single generations and some already rising again.

33   In American society and culture the most important values are economic, or materialistic, and as in all societies our cities epitomize our civilization. In Italian society and culture the critical values are blood ties and the connection of family to a particular place. It is not that Italy and Italians are unmaterialistic, far from it, but in comparison to Americans, they have always been far less successful at economics and politics than others. Although many like to think of Italy as Roman conquerors and Florentine sculptors, the "real" Italy for centuries has been millions of families struggling to survive in hostile environments ruled by materially and politically successful foreigners.

34   The defense of the Italian family has for ages been fought from within the walls of its home—the house, village, or neighborhood. The home is a fortress which can cut off the outside world with the closing of a gate, a door, or a window. Italian neighborhoods have survived thousands of years perched on mountain tops, on the sides of sheer cliffs, tucked in by dangerous coves, crammed into exasperating cities, fighting against rising floods and tides, lava-spewing volcanoes, and land-splitting earthquakes.

35   It is little wonder that Italians are the last to go from the constantly changing scene of American cities.

READING

1. According to Jerome Krase, why are stereotypes used? What are their consequences?

2. What were the similarities and differences that Krase noted between the Italian communities in the United States and Italy?

THINKING

1. Krase argues that the ways people think of themselves affect the way they live, and that neighborhoods are defined by people's self-concepts. Do you think this is true? When you look around your neighborhood, how do you think your neighbors feel about themselves? Why? When people from outside of your neighborhood look at the area in which you live, what do you think the outsiders think about you and your neighbors? Have you ever judged someone by where they lived? Why or why not?

2. As recently as 1981, the community of Avellino was destroyed by an earthquake and rebuilt on the same spot. Even though San Francisco still has major earthquakes, people continue to build and live there. Why do you think that people stay in areas that present such grave danger?

PREWRITING

Freewrite about why you think people of a common culture need to spend time together or why you think they should try to spend more time with people of various cultures. Then list the qualities of an ideal home.

WRITING

1. Paragraph 17 of "America's Little Italies" refers to "voluntary and involuntary segregation." On your campus, the dining room shows voluntary segregation every day by people from different cultures choosing to sit together to eat. Write an article for your campus newspaper either supporting the students' right to segregate themselves or encouraging the students to voluntarily integrate the dining room.

2. In paragraph 34, Krase says, "The home is a fortress which can cut off the outside world with the closing of a gate, a door, or a window." Write a description of your home or your ideal home to share with your classmates. Not only describe what it looks like, but tell what it means to you.

REVISING

The style you choose for your essay should remain consistent throughout. For writing assignments in some university departments, you will be asked to follow very specific formulas or formats. For instance, in some science classes you need to first write very specifically what you intend to prove, then write step by step how you prove your hypothesis. In history classes, you may be told to never use first person when you are writing. For instance, you would never use the personal pronoun *I*. In business or management classes, you may be told to follow a format with an introduction saying "In this report I will . . ." followed by the body of the report and the conclusion, which says, "In this report I have. . . ." In general academic writing or writing for your English classes, you need to follow a direct writing approach where, after you have organized your thoughts, you state them in a direct manner, being as specific as possible while still keeping your writing interesting. In "America's Little Italies," Krase chooses to shift his style in paragraph three to a style that doesn't really fit with the rest of the essay:

> Stereotypes, as all other social facts, have consequences, and these consequences can be positive, neutral, or negative both for those who employ the images and those who are their object. In this essay I will not be discussing traditional approaches to the study of ethnic stereotyping but will try to develop a different and perhaps more interesting way of investigating this common-sense aspect of everyday modern life. (¶3)

How does it make you feel when suddenly you realize that Krase is speaking directly to you when he says, "In this essay I will not. . . ." Do you find this effective, or as a reader would you prefer that the whole article remain in the same style? Read through the rest of the article to see if you can discover any other examples of shifts in style.

Look at the rough draft you have done for your writing assignments. Have you maintained the same style and approach to your writing throughout the assignment? Are you happy with the style you have chosen? Make any necessary changes before you submit your final draft.

EDITING

When writing the **titles** of items that are long or that contain smaller elements, those titles should be underlined or italicized. This applies to titles of items like books, newspapers, magazines, plays, record albums, or television series. Titles of shorter items, such as chapter titles, article titles, poems, songs, or television shows, should be enclosed in quotation marks.

Examples:
"America's Little Italies: Past, Present, and Future"
The Ghetto
The Ancient City

The option of underlining or using italics depends on whether you are writing on a word processor that can do italics. They both indicate the same thing.

Check your writing to see if you have used quotation marks and underlining or italics correctly.

Map Appendix

RUSSIA

U.S.

Greenland
(Den.)

CANADA

*Hudson
Bay*

UNITED STATES

*ATLANTIC
OCEAN*

U.S.

MARSHALL
IS.

*PACIFIC
OCEAN*

MEXICO

ECUADOR

BRAZIL

NAURU

K I R I B A T I

PERU

BOLIVIA

PARAGUAY

TUVALU

VANUATU

W. SAMOA

FIJI

TONGA

CHILE

URUGUAY

NEW
ZEALAND

ARGENTINA

BAHAMAS

CUBA

GUATEMALA

BELIZE

JAMAICA

HAITI

DOM.
REP.

ST. KITTS and
NEVIS

ANTIGUA and
BARBUDA

Puerto Rico
(U.S.)

Guadeloupe (Fr.)

HONDURAS

DOMINICA

Martinique (Fr.)

ST. LUCIA

EL
SALVADOR

NICARAGUA

ST. VINCENT and
the GRENADINES

BARBADOS

COSTA
RICA

PANAMA

GRENADA

TRINIDAD &
TOBAGO

VENEZUELA

French
Guiana

GUYANA

COLOMBIA

SURINAME

ICELAND

NORWAY
SWEDEN
FINLAND

RUSSIA

KAZAKHSTAN

MONGOLIA

UZBEKISTAN
KYRGYZSTAN
TURKMEN.
TAJIKISTAN

CHINA

N. KOREA
S. KOREA
JAPAN

IRAN
AFGHAN.
BAHRAIN
QATAR

NEPAL
BHUTAN

PACIFIC
OCEAN

W. Sahara
(Mor.)
CAPE
VERDE
MAURITANIA

ALGERIA
LIBYA
EGYPT

SAUDI
ARABIA
UNITED
ARAB
EMIRATES
OMAN

INDIA

MYANMAR
(BURMA)
LAOS

TAIWAN

HONG
KONG

PHILIPPINES

SENEGAL
GAMBIA
GUINEA
BISSAU
SIERRA
LEONE
LIBERIA
IVORY
COAST

MALI
NIGER

BURKINA
NIGERIA
BENIN

SUDAN

ERITREA
YEMEN
DJIBOUTI

BANGL.

THAILAND
CAMB.
VIETNAM

BRUNEI

FED. STATES of
MICRONESIA

PALAU

TOGO
GHANA
CAM.
GABON
CONGO
SAO TOME & PRINCIPE
EQ. GUINEA

CEN. AFR.
REF.
ETHIOPIA

RWANDA
UGANDA

SOMALIA

SRI
LANKA

MALDIVES

MALAYSIA

SINGAPORE

PAPUA
NEW
GUINEA

ZAIRE
BURUNDI
TANZANIA
KENYA

SEYCHELLES

INDONESIA

ATLANTIC
OCEAN

ANGOLA
MALAWI
ZAMBIA
ZIMB.
MOZAMBIQUE
NAMIBIA
BOTS.
SWAZILAND
SOUTH
AFRICA
LESOTHO

COMOROS

MADAGASCAR

MAURITIUS

INDIAN
OCEAN

AUSTRALIA

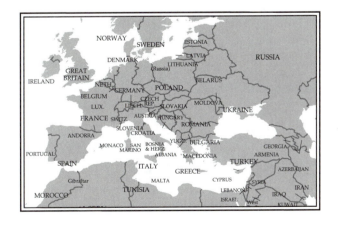

NORWAY
SWEDEN
ESTONIA
LATVIA
DENMARK
LITHUANIA
(Russia)

RUSSIA

IRELAND
GREAT
BRITAIN
NETH.
BELGIUM
LUX.

GERMANY
POLAND
CZECH
REP.
LIECH.
SLOVAKIA
AUSTRIA
HUNGARY
SLOVENIA
CROATIA

BELARUS

MOLDOVA
UKRAINE

FRANCE
SWITZ.

ROMANIA

ANDORRA

PORTUGAL

SPAIN

MONACO
SAN
MARINO
ITALY

BOSNIA
& HERZ.
YUGO.
BULGARIA
ALBANIA
MACEDONIA

GREECE

GEORGIA
ARMENIA
TURKEY

AZERBAIJAN

Gibraltar
MALTA
CYPRUS

IRAN

MOROCCO
TUNISIA

LEBANON
ISRAEL
West

SYRIA
IRAQ
KUWAIT

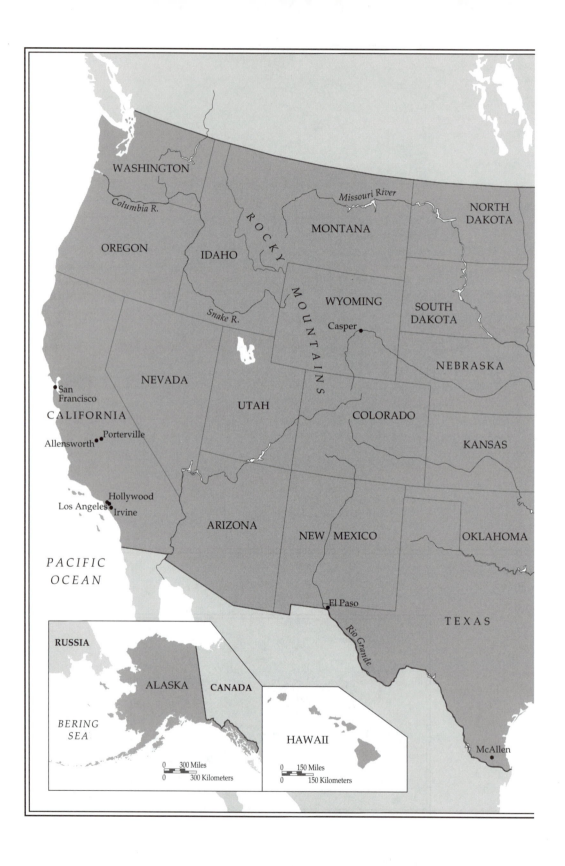

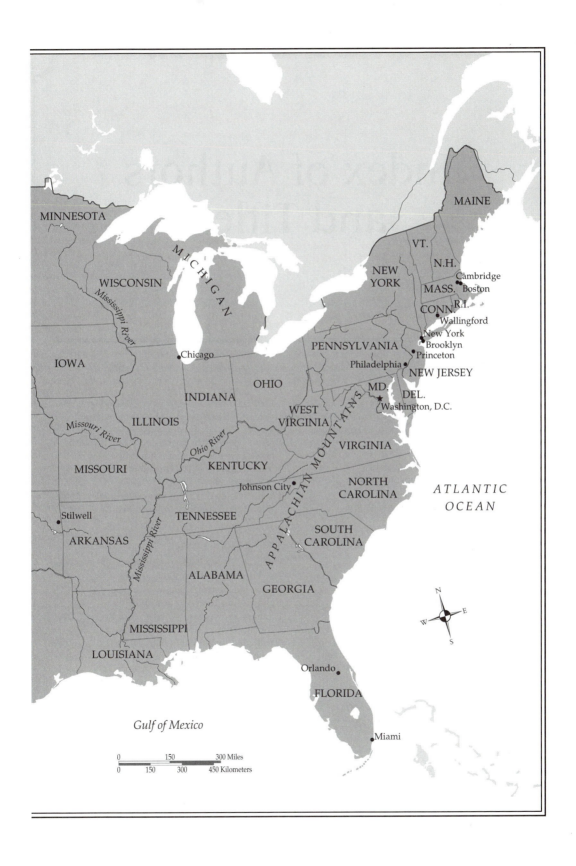

Index of Authors
and Titles

Index of Editing Strategies

Index of Revision Strategies